CH00641146

Reminiscing with
LEGENDS

Reminiscing with
LEGENDS

Hearts' exhilarating journey to Scottish Cup glory in 1998

By Anthony Brown
Foreword from Gilles Rousset

First published in Great Britain in
October 2020 by Ten Caats Publishing

A CIP catalogue record for this book
is available from the British Library

ISBN 978-1-8382233-0-4 (Paperback)
ISBN 978-1-8382233-1-1 (Hardback)

Pictures copyright of The Scotsman and Edinburgh Evening News
unless otherwise stated, and used with their kind permission

Designed, edited and typeset by Scott Coull

Printed and bound in Great Britain by
J Thomson Colour Printers Limited, Glasgow

Contents

Foreword

By Gilles Rousset

An absolute privilege. That is the best way I can describe what it meant to me to be part of Heart of Midlothian Football Club when Jim Jefferies and Billy Brown were in charge in the mid-to-late 1990s. It was a magical period in my life, and I know my wonderful team-mates from that era, who helped bring the Scottish Cup back to Gorgie for the first time in 42 years, all feel the same way.

It wasn't just about the success we had in beating Rangers in the final on 16th May 1998, it was the whole experience: the journey we went on as a group, the camaraderie and unity we enjoyed, and the memories we made while playing for this special club.

Working under two great men in Jim and Billy. The unique thrill of walking out of the Tynecastle tunnel and being driven on by the passion of that amazing crowd every second week. Being part of a close-knit dressing-room, surrounded by fantastic players from different backgrounds who all had the same winning mentality. Spending time socialising with lovely people in Bar Roma. Feeling the love of the fantastic Hearts supporters, home and away or at supporters' club functions on a Saturday evening. Learning more about the club from boyhood Jambos like Gary Locke and Gary Mackay. Competing in cup finals. Living in beautiful Edinburgh. Beating the Hibees. The madness of Magaluf (never again!). Winning at Ibrox. The crazy celebrations against Celtic. Partying in Newcastle (and making the front pages of the newspapers!). Challenging for the title. Making friends for life. And, the icing on the cake, winning the Scottish Cup.

All of these things helped create an experience that I never imagined would be possible when I first left France as a 32-year-old in October 1995 to sign for this club I had barely heard of. We all arrived at Hearts at various stages in the team's journey, and at different stages in our own careers, and we all stayed at

Tynecastle for different durations. But when our time as Hearts players came to an end, all of us involved in that incredible 1997/98 season knew we had been part of something special, something career-defining, and – for many of us – something life-defining. That was the year in which everything Jim and Billy had been working towards came to an amazing climax and all of us – players, management and supporters – got to celebrate one of the greatest days of our lives.

Although it was a mostly positive time to be at Hearts, we shouldn't forget that we had some dark days along the way. I arrived when the team were bottom of the league, we had two cup final defeats against Rangers (how could I forget the first one?) and we had some other terrible results along the way that earned us criticism and tested our character. All good teams have to be strong enough to deal with adversity, though, and I think we proved over a period of time that we could do that. We took our hits along the way but we kept coming back for more because we had a brilliant collective spirit about us and we knew we were a bloody good team who were improving all the time. We could sense our moment was coming.

Let's face it, this book would probably never have been written if we hadn't held on to beat Rangers on that famous day in May 1998. As well as we performed over the course of that season, and even in the two years before that, it was winning that elusive trophy which earned us hero status among the Jambo people, to the extent that our achievement is still talked about more than 20 years on and will hopefully be savoured for another 20 years and more. What an amazing feeling it is to know that you went into a club and achieved something that the people who hold it dearest – the supporters – still celebrate after all this time.

Because of that, and everything we went through to get to that point, there is a special feeling between everyone who was part of that team. I have been really busy as a coach since I left Hearts in 2001 so I can't get to Tynecastle as often as I would like, but whenever anything is organised by the club for the 1998 team, I jump straight on the plane because I love it. I love being in their company. We were all back together in 2018 for the 20th anniversary of the Scottish Cup win and it was a very, very special evening. Obviously it was especially emotional because our great friend and colleague Stefano Salvatori wasn't there alongside us, which was so sad for all of us. It was wonderful to see all the boys, though, and we all clicked with each other instantly. It felt like we had never been apart. We have all changed a lot in appearance since we were players, but we still – and I'm sure we always will – have the same connection.

All the guys loved the reunion and we promised each other we would try and meet up more often, which we really need to do. In the meantime, however, it is absolutely fantastic that Anthony Brown has given us this chance to reflect and reminisce together about what we achieved at Hearts in a way that allows the magnificent supporters to read in great depth all about our respective journeys and get a real insight into what it was like to be part of that special dressing-room and be at the heart of such an amazing and historic episode in this proud club's history.

By winning the 1998 Scottish Cup, we created something really special; we created a family. I genuinely feel like these guys are part of my family. We are all from different countries, different cities, different cultures, different mentalities and different families, but that team that won the Scottish Cup, we are all brothers. Sometimes it is really tough to put words on feelings but I just love those guys, all of them. I really do love them because we all did something special together. That is for life... that is for life. And this is our story.

Legends Return

*"I looked in my mirror and saw
a pair of legs hanging off the roof"*

Alan "Scooby" Scott was clearly in an agitated state as he tried to steer his be-sieged Park's of Hamilton coach off Gorgie Road and on to McLeod Street. "Lockey, for fuck's sake, let me get round this corner," he shouted. His front windscreen was blurred by relentless streams of champagne and beer; there was a thin line of luminous police officers on foot struggling against the surge of the crowds; a band of intoxicated young footballers in fawn suits and sunglasses were dancing on his roof; and well-oiled Hearts captain Gary Locke was thrusting the Scottish Cup trophy up against his front window, impeding his view of the left wing mir-ror and acting as a lightning rod for more unbridled chaos on the outside of the bus. In short, the driver was under the cosh. "There's somebody collapsed there, that's what I wanted to avoid!" lamented "Scooby" as he manoeuvred his vehicle of freshly-anointed Gorgie legends past the Tynecastle Arms at walking pace.

It was the balmy evening of Saturday 16th May 1998 and all the rules had gone out the window in this jubilant little pocket of west Edinburgh. "Scooby" had driven the Hearts team to away matches since 1985 and grown to love the club as a result. The 46-year-old from Bannockburn was on nickname terms with all the players and was as euphoric as anybody of a Hearts persuasion about what had happened earlier that day in Glasgow's east end. The thrill and pride of driving the team's Scottish Cup-winning heroes back along the M8, however, soon gave way to tension and trepidation as he spent the final half-mile of the journey home to Tynecastle fretting about the possibility of any of the merry-making thousands coming to harm either in front of, underneath or on top of his bus. "When we got along to the railway bridge near McDonald's, that's when it really started getting serious because the police motorbikes left us and the horses came in front of us," recalls "Scooby". "When Hearts won the cup in 2006, it was a lot different because they had barriers out along Gorgie Road but in 98 they didn't so I was driving along worrying about everybody piling in front of the bus and at the side of the bus. There was beer and everything getting thrown at the windscreen. I could hardly see a thing and there were people running out in front of the bus so I was worried about running over somebody.

"What made it even worse was when we got about half-way along Gorgie Road I looked in my mirror and saw a pair of legs hanging off the roof. I turned to Jimmy Johnston, the security guy, and said 'Jesus Christ, the players are on the roof'. It wouldn't have been easy for them to get up there, but they had obviously managed to push the skylight open. I couldn't see to the back of the bus because everybody was standing up in the first couple of rows so it wasn't until I saw the legs dangling from the bus that I knew they were up there. If I had my way, they would certainly not have been on that roof! My biggest worry initially was that my air conditioning was going full pelt and all the fans for the air conditioning were on the roof so I was thinking if one of the players falls and puts their fingers in the mesh, they'll end up getting them chopped off. I had to turn everything off that I could to stop that happening. So not only am I worrying about that, I'm worrying about all the supporters round about the bus and I'm worrying about the possibility of the players, who had been drinking heavily all the way from Celtic Park, falling off the top of the bus.

"By the time we eventually got to the top of McLeod Street, I knew I was going to have to turn left and cut the corner and at that particular point, I was absolutely petrified that I was going to run somebody over. I could only see so much out of my mirrors, the crowds were pushing against the side of the bus and as we turned the corner, I actually hit the brake because I thought somebody had fallen under the bus. Jimmy was telling me to keep going and I'm thinking 'I know I need to keep going but I need to make sure I don't cause anybody a serious injury'. As the driver of the bus, it was scary."

As the end neared on the most remarkable journey of his life, "Scooby" was enduring a comparable level of pressure to that which the likes of Paul Ritchie, David Weir and Gilles Rousset had been subjected by Rangers at Celtic Park a little over three hours earlier. Not that the triumphant Hearts players were in any state to be worrying about what their trusty bus driver was going through as he negotiated his way anxiously but expertly along a canal of maroon-and-white giddiness back to Tynecastle. "A couple of boys might try and claim credit for it but I was the first one to go up on the roof," boasts Hearts winger Neil McCann. "I battered the sunroof out and Scooby was going fucking mental. 'Get fucking doon!' I got up and before I knew it, I don't know how many of the other boys were up there with me. I remember being on the roof of the bus and the fans were spraying champagne at us. If we'd fallen off, we'd have been crowd-surfed. I'm sure Jose Quitongo lost one of his wee slip-on shoes. We were up there not giving a shit. It was madness!"

This was Heart of Midlothian in all their glory, savouring the release of 36 years' worth of trophyless frustration, banishing ghouls of 1986 and celebrating the exploits of one of the most revered teams in the club's entire history.

The Change

*"If we'd stuck with what we had
we'd have probably lost our jobs"*

Three years previously, on 13th May 1995, the end-of-season celebrations in Gorgie were of a far more subdued nature. In what was a nerve-shredding finale to their 1994/95 campaign, a 2-0 win over second-placed Motherwell – achieved by a Brian Hamilton goal early in the second half and a late John Robertson penalty – at a work-in-progress Tynecastle proved just enough to spare Tommy McLean's Hearts from the ignominy of finishing second-bottom of the ten-team Premier Division.

As they climbed from eighth place up to sixth with their last-day victory, leaving Roy Aitken's ninth-placed Aberdeen side to head into a play-off with First Division runners-up Dunfermline Athletic, there was momentary delight among the Hearts support born out of relief at fending off the threat of relegation. When the post-match joy subsided and the dust settled on the Edinburgh side's grim campaign, however, it was clear to most that the win over Alex McLeish's high-flying Motherwell had merely papered over the cracks. McLean – McLeish's predecessor at Fir Park – was the first new manager brought into Tynecastle since catering magnate Chris Robinson and law specialist Leslie Deans completed their takeover of the club from long-serving owner Wallace Mercer at the end of a testing 1993/94 campaign in which Hearts had battled relegation under rookie boss Sandy Clark. The appointment of the more experienced McLean as Clark's replacement didn't go to plan, however, as the former Motherwell manager riled players and supporters in equal measure with the way he went about his business and failed to deliver the desired results. For McLean's part, he felt he wasn't given the resources he was promised as Hearts battled to keep their finances under control while also modernising their stadium. After a couple of months of close-season uncertainty at Tynecastle, the unpopular manager was eventually relieved of his duties on Friday

21st July 1995, but only after a wrangle with the board over payment of the remaining two years of his contract. "Tommy was tactically astute but it was very obvious to all and sundry that it wasn't gelling," says Deans, who was chief executive at the time. "There wasn't a rapport and there was friction between him and the board so we decided to go our separate ways."

In the wake of a second consecutive season battling relegation, and with the first manager hired by the new ownership regime being deemed an unmitigated disaster by supporters, all seemed pretty forlorn at Tynecastle for much of summer 1995. In addition to the three years of mediocrity the team had displayed through Joe Jordan's last season (1992/93) and then under Clark and McLean, Hearts seemed burdened by the lingering psychological effects of May 1986, when they famously blew the league title away to Dundee and then capitulated against Aberdeen in the Scottish Cup final a week later. The fact they lost six consecutive semi-finals – five in the Scottish Cup and one in the League Cup – in the space of just nine years between 1986 and 1995 did nothing to banish the notion that Hearts were a club weighed down by the pressure of being without silverware since the League Cup triumph under the legendary Tommy Walker in 1962.

At the point of McLean's departure – just a matter of months after a humiliating Scottish Cup semi-final defeat by First Division Airdrieonians at Hampden in April 1995 – Hearts hadn't enjoyed any tangible success for a whopping 33 years. During this lengthy trophy drought, all of their main rivals had won something of note. City rivals Hibs had secured two League Cups. Dundee United had won a league title and three domestic cups while also reaching a European Cup semi-final and a UEFA Cup final. Aberdeen had won three league titles, nine domestic cups, a European Cup Winners' Cup and a European Super Cup. Furthermore, Kilmarnock had won a league title, while Dunfermline Athletic, St Mirren, Motherwell, Partick Thistle and Raith Rovers had all won a major trophy within a remarkable and increasingly embarrassing period of Jambo famine which didn't reflect well on a club traditionally viewed as one of the country's biggest.

With supporters growing disillusioned and crowds often falling below 9000 on a matchday, the pressure was on Robinson and Deans to find a way to engage and energise the fanbase at a time when the process of improving a previously dilapidated Tynecastle was well under way. Mercer had overseen the building of the Wheatfield Stand in his last season at the helm, and the School End (or Roseburn Stand, as it is now better known) was built in the closing months of the 1994/95 season, in readiness for the beginning of the following campaign. This meant Hearts would have a new manager and a new stand for the start of the 1995/96 season; but, crucially, who would the manager be? And would he be equipped to a deliver a Hearts team that would bring supporters flocking back to the new-look Tynecastle?

Lifelong Hearts fans Robinson and Deans had been introduced by a mutual friend, Fraser Jackson, shortly before their takeover of the club, and their alliance – which came about because neither man had the clout to buy out Mercer on their own – was never a particularly harmonious one. Indeed, by the time their dual ownership came to an acrimonious ending in 1999, they had developed a mutual contempt for each other. "The relationship between Chris Robinson and I was not a particularly good one," says Deans. "In fact, I would not ever wish to go into business with Chris again."

Thankfully for all Hearts supporters, the pair were able to find some common ground when it came to picking McLean's successor. As they assessed potential candidates, one name jumped off the page: Jim Jefferies, the burgeoning Falkirk manager and former Hearts captain. Within a week of McLean's departure, Hearts were homing in on their one clear target. "There were other names mentioned and considered, such as Jimmy Nicholl at Raith Rovers, because we weren't absolutely certain that Jim Jefferies would come," says Deans. "It would be presumptuous in the extreme to just assume Jim would come because he was still contracted to Falkirk. But was Jim always our favourite? Yes, he was."

A boyhood Hearts supporter who had gone on to make 310 appearances during nine years as a defender for the first team between 1972 and 1981, the 44-year-old Jefferies, assisted by his childhood friend and trusty lieutenant Billy Brown, was on an upward curve in management following two productive years at Berwick Rangers in the late 1980s and then an exhilarating five-year reign at Falkirk which encompassed two promotions and a Challenge Cup triumph. It culminated with the Bairns finishing fifth in the Premier Division in 1994/95, a comfortable five points above McLean's grim Hearts side.

After what became a dramatic mid-summer pursuit, in which Falkirk tried everything they could to hold on to him and Hearts steadfastly refused to give up the fight, Jefferies was eventually installed as the new manager of the Tynecastle side at the start of August. "George Fulston (the Falkirk chairman) put me under a lot of pressure," recalls Jefferies. "He was only trying to do what was best for his club, so I certainly wouldn't criticise him, but he was saying things that emotionally were just too much to consider. It wasn't a nice time for me."

Upon recalling the state of the Hearts squad at that point in time, it is easy to understand why Jefferies – head frazzled amid an agonising few days of negotiation and career-defining decision-making – may have been temporarily stricken by doubt about returning to Tynecastle. Henry Smith, Craig Nelson, Stephen Frail, Gary Locke, Dave McPherson, Colin Miller, Willie Jamieson, Craig Levein, Neil Berry, Fraser Wishart, Brian Hamilton, Gary Mackay, Jim Bett, Scott Leitch, John Millar, George Wright, David Hagen, Colin Cramb, John Robertson, John Colquhoun, Kevin Thomas, Allan Johnston.

Those were the 22 players with first-team experience in situ at Hearts when Jefferies first took the reins. On the face of it a decent squad of experienced, reputable professionals, perhaps; but, ultimately, this was a bloated and ageing pool, with most of the standout names having seen their best days. Of the 22 players, 11 had entered their 30s. Incredibly, six of them – Smith, Berry, Levein, Mackay, Robertson and Colquhoun – remained from the side which squandered their chance of the league and cup double nine years previously. Of the 11 players who were under 30, and relatively untarnished by the tribulations of the previous decade, it summed up the predicament Hearts were in that two of the better ones – Thomas and Frail – were sidelined by serious knee injuries that neither would ever properly recover from. Although youngsters like Locke and Johnston represented a couple of welcome beacons of hope, it was instantly and abundantly clear to the new management team that a period of substantial transition was required in order to banish the staleness and elevate the team to a level whereby they might one day be able to challenge a formidable Rangers side who – having won each of the previous seven Premier Division titles – had just shelled out £4.3 million to buy English superstar Paul Gascoigne from Italian side Lazio. Reflecting on the extensive squad rejuvenation mission he had to embark upon, particularly in his first season at the helm, Jefferies regularly refers to the process as "the change". "I think the reason Hearts were so keen to get me is that they knew I'd go in there and change what needed to be changed," he says, clearly of the belief that if he had stuck predominantly with the players left behind by McLean – several of whom had become club icons – he would simply have gone the same way as his immediate predecessors and been sacked before too long. "The change had to happen. One of the reasons Hearts weren't taking 'no' for an answer from me was, when I had my interview, they said 'look, you're a Hearts man, you come along and watch us when Falkirk aren't playing, why are we struggling?' I said 'I think you have to face facts: you've had a lot of great players who deserve all the credit they get for what they've done for this club over the years, but they can't go on forever. Over the last ten years, you've had four or five good managers but it's not worked out, yet most of the same players have all been here right through that period'.

"That was meant as no disrespect to the players, who had been fantastic for the club and deserved to be put on pedestals. But if the club's not doing well, something has to change. I said 'if I'm to take the job, that's something that will happen, I will change it'. It would probably have been a lot more difficult for the previous managers to do what I was planning to do. I'm sure they would have wanted to do the same as me but would have been wary of the backlash because the players were slightly younger and were still held in such high esteem by the supporters. But after two years in which they had been battling relegation, I think the supporters were probably at a stage which made it ideal for me to go in and start the change. There were certainly no guarantees it was going to work, but I knew it had to be changed."

In the prime of his managerial life, Jefferies – who had proved himself an adept squad-builder at both Berwick and Falkirk – was clearly eager to make his mark at the club of his heart. His willingness and ability to make bold but necessary squad alterations would be vindicated in the most emphatic fashion imaginable on Saturday 16th May 1998 – just under three years into the job – when a team featuring only one of the 22 first-team players he inherited defeated Rangers 2-1 in the Scottish Cup final to secure Hearts' first trophy in 36 years. McPherson, the veteran defender, was the solitary player to survive the entirety of Jefferies' first three seasons and start the 1998 final. Robertson, who would become the club's record league goal-scorer under Jefferies, was the only other member of the original 22 to make the matchday squad, while Locke would have been involved if not for injury. Thomas was still officially on the books but well out of the picture and heading for the exit door.

In less than three years at the helm, the ruthless Jefferies effectively culled 19 of the 22 first-team players who were at the club when he arrived and built a vibrant and bullish new team capable of delivering when history beckoned them forward. Although "the change" was expertly executed by the management team in a little over two years, it was a gradual process, with players being phased out at various junctures. "We had to be fair and look at everyone who could do us a turn," said Jefferies. "Hearts had no money to change it instantly so we had to box clever. We made a couple of short-term signings initially to get the impetus of the change going."

The earliest arrivals of the Jefferies reign were anything but box-office. Alan Lawrence, a 33-year-old Airdrieonians striker, was recruited just in time to make his debut in the Premier Division opener at home to Motherwell, a match which ended 1-1. For context, it is worth recalling the team that took to the pitch for Jefferies' first league match in charge: Smith, Locke, Wishart, McPherson, Levein, Colquhoun, Hamilton, Mackay, Johnston, Hagen, Lawrence. The subs were Nelson, Berry and Leitch on a day when Hagen scored an equaliser to cancel out Dougie Arnott's opener for McLeish's visitors. A few days later, 28-year-old defender David Winnie, a Scottish Cup winner with St Mirren in 1987, joined from Aberdeen and made his debut in a 2-1 League Cup victory at home to Dunfermline Athletic. That tie would prove to be the last-ever competitive match of Levein's career as the classy 30-year-old Scotland centre-back was carried off with a serious knee injury from which he would never recover. Midfielder Bett, who had been one of McLean's better signings, became the first player to leave Hearts since Jefferies' arrival as he moved to Dundee United in late August.

After continuing their reasonably promising start to the season with a 4-1 home win over Falkirk in the second league game, the new-manager bounce – which had also incorporated a rousing 5-1 pre-season friendly victory over Manchester City a few days after a 1-0 defeat by Kevin Keegan's much-vaunted Newcastle United – soon started to fizzle out. Hearts suffered their first loss of the campaign when they went down 2-0 away to Partick Thistle, and this was immediately followed by a barmy Coca-Cola Cup quarter-final at Dens Park in which they were eliminated on penalties by Dundee following a 4-4 draw. The hosts, featuring teenager Jim Hamilton and 21-year-old Neil McCann in their attack, had got their third goal of the match after a terrible sliced clearance by Smith across the face of his own goal and into the path of the grateful Paul Tosh. The veteran goalkeeper, just six months shy of his 40th birthday, sealed what was a turbulent evening for himself when he chose to take a penalty in the shootout and clipped it wide of the post and towards the huge, expectant Hearts support on the terrace behind the goal. For those present, it was one of those infamous 'did that really happen?' moments. Cruelly, this proved to be the last of the popular Smith's 598 competitive appearances for Hearts, meaning he effectively bowed out at Dens Park, where he had been part of the team that had endured that disastrous final-day collapse almost a decade previously. "Henry had been second choice (behind Nelson) when we came in and we'd effectively had to bring him out of retirement," reflects Jefferies. The manager clearly didn't fancy the hitherto unconvincing Nelson, but pitched him in for the following league match at home to Celtic. In a further notable change, Paul Ritchie, a 20-year-old left-sided defender who had been in the youth system for several years but had failed to make the step up, was handed his debut at left-back. For the second game running, Hearts conceded four goals, this time without even scoring themselves as Burns' side eased to a 4-0 win.

Ritchie, following a chastening start to life in Hearts' first team, immediately dropped out of the side as the steady but unspectacular Canadian left-back Colin Miller and midfielder George Wright were handed rare starts under Jefferies for the next game away to Hibs. Hearts, who had been so dominant in the Edinburgh derby for much of the previous decade before losing their proud 22-game unbeaten run under McLean in 1994, ended up needing a 92nd-minute equaliser from Robertson to salvage a 2-2 draw. The following match – a 2-1 midweek defeat at home to Aberdeen – proved to be the last for 25-year-old Wright, a player who had come through the ranks at the club and been part of the first-team set-up through-out the early 1990s but was unable to make himself a mainstay.

Jefferies, frantically trying to generate some response from his struggling team, changed the goalkeeper once more as homegrown 21-year-old Gary O'Connor replaced Nelson between the sticks for a trip to Kilmarnock. Hearts lost 3-1 and had now gone six games without a win in all competitions. A 5-1 defeat at home to Coventry City in Levein's testimonial match – attended by less than 3000 people – did little to ease the early-October gloom in Gorgie. A little over two months into his reign, Jefferies could already sense his back against the wall. "If we'd stuck with what we had we'd have been in trouble and probably lost our jobs," he reflects. He dipped into the transfer market once more to bring in 30-year-old left-back Neil Pointon, formerly of Everton, Manchester City and Oldham Athletic, and 25-year-old midfielder Stephen Fulton from Falkirk. Hagen and Wright moved to Brockville in return, with Jefferies unable to believe his luck that his former club, by now managed by John Lambie, had allowed him to be reunited with Fulton, the mercurial former Celtic playmaker who had revived himself at Brockville following an unfulfilling year in England with Bolton Wanderers and Peterborough United. "When I got the Hearts job, Stevie was one of the first players I had my eye on signing," he reflects. "I felt there were a couple of players I could afford to let go to get him, but I didn't think I had any chance of getting him when I made my approach. I was delighted we managed to get him because he was such a gifted footballer."

Both Fulton and Pointon made their debuts as Hearts ended their grim winless streak with a 4-2 victory at home to a Raith Rovers side featuring a 22-year-old Colin Cameron and gearing up for their glamour UEFA Cup tie against Bayern Munich at Easter Road just a few days later. This win was something of a false dawn for Jefferies, however. Hearts' first encounter with Gascoigne went disastrously as the English superstar curled a sublime first-minute opener beyond O'Connor in a comfortable 4-1 victory for Rangers at Ibrox. It wouldn't be Hearts' biggest defeat at the hands of Walter Smith's side that season. Nor would it be the last time Gascoigne scored against the Tynecastle side.

Having used three different goalkeepers (Smith, Nelson and O'Connor) in the opening nine league matches of his reign, and failed in a bid to land St Johnstone's

Andy Rhodes, Jefferies craved a safe pair of hands to solve what was one of several problem positions. The manager's prayers were answered when Mike Morris, a Lancashire-based agent who had facilitated Pointon's move to Edinburgh a couple of weeks previously, got in touch to tell him he might be able to bring him a highly-regarded 6ft 5ins keeper who had gone to the European Championships in Sweden with France a little more than three years earlier. Gilles Rousset duly flew into Scotland, trained with Hearts for a couple of days and was deemed ready to play as a trialist in a critical bottom-of-the-table showdown at Falkirk that weekend. The 32-year-old's impressive debut was the only bright spot of a wretched return to Brockville for Jefferies as Falkirk won 2-0 through goals from David Weir and Maurice Johnston to leave Hearts at the foot of the table ten games into the campaign. The Tynecastle side were staring at the prospect of a third consecutive relegation battle, and Jefferies knew that if his dysfunctional team continued in this vein, he would be in danger of losing his dream job and his reputation as one of the country's most upwardly-mobile managers.

"It all came to a head when we lost at Falkirk," he reflects. "After that game we decided we had to ramp up the change. I told the players that, after starting the first couple of games okay, they had slipped back into old ways and that it had to change. I said to myself that if I try and make the changes and it doesn't work and I get the sack, at least I'll know I've tried to change it."

In what was a challenging start to his Hearts reign, one of the easiest decisions Jefferies had to make was to offer a contract to Rousset. Not only had the giant Frenchman arrived in Edinburgh boasting a CV which included service with Lyon, Marseille and the French national team, he had backed it up by proving at Brockville that, even in his veteran years and without having played since the previous season, he was still a perfectly capable goalkeeper. "When we got word in that Gilles was available and looked at his track record, you're thinking 'this is too good to be true'," explains Jefferies. "We brought him over, got on well with him right away and he looked the part. It was a last-minute decision to put him in against Falkirk. We lost but he had a great game that day and we thought 'right, we've got to get this change going'."

The signing of Rousset came during a busy week for Jefferies as he tried all he could to spark some form of upturn for the following match at home to Partick Thistle. By the time that game came round, he had managed to add three further new faces to his squad: 33-year-old former Juventus and Torino centre-back Pasquale Bruno, 29-year-old Swedish striker Hans Eskilsson and 33-year-old midfielder Paul Smith, a boyhood Hearts fan who had spent his peak years with Dunfermline and had previously enjoyed one season working under Jefferies at Falkirk. Bruno and Smith went straight into the starting line-up for the visit of the Jags, while Eskilsson started on the bench. Another notable change that day was that Locke, aged just 20, had been asked to take over the captaincy from McPherson. "That was a big call because there were a lot of experienced players still at the club, but I felt giving Gary the captaincy gave us a freshness," says Jefferies. "He was a Hearts fanatic, popular with everybody, and had great tenacity, will and desire about him. I think even the more experienced players thought 'actually, that's a good shout'. It was a big task for Gary to go in there and be captain to a lot of experienced players who had been at the club a long time, but he took to it great and that was the start of the change."

In a further freshening up of the team, young Ritchie was restored to the starting line-up for the visit of a Jags side featuring former Hearts pair Nicky Walker and Wayne Foster. New-look Hearts eased to a convincing 3-0 win, with the charismatic Bruno – known as "O'Animale" (The Animal) in his homeland due to his aggressive on-field approach – endearing himself to the home support instantly. This routine victory, sealed with a scrappy goal by fuzzy-haired substitute Eskilsson, was to prove a clear turning point for Jefferies and Hearts as they embarked on a four-game run in which they took ten points from a possible 12. Following back-to-back defeats away to Celtic and at home to Rangers, Hearts rediscovered their poise by taking four points from consecutive December away games against Raith Rovers and Aberdeen. The 2-1 win at Pittodrie, featuring a debut for homegrown defender Allan McManus, was particularly exhilarating as it involved a dramatic late turnaround, with goals in the last nine minutes from Johnston and Colquhoun cancelling out Dean Windass's early opener. Having spent Halloween rock-bottom of the Premier Division, Hearts were able to enjoy their Christmas dinner in the knowledge that they were up to sixth, eight points clear of last place and within four points of the fourth-placed Dons. "It all started to improve very quickly for us," recalls Fulton. "Me and Neil Pointon used to have a laugh with the gaffer because he used to say it changed for the better when Gilles and Pasquale Bruno came in, but they came in a couple of weeks after me and Neil! What was he trying to say, that me and Neil were tarred with the same brush as the boys who'd been there before?" he jokes.

A 2-1 defeat away to Hibs on New Year's Day – 48 hours after the Easter Road side had lost 7-0 to Rangers – represented a frustrating start to 1996, especially since Eskilsson had missed a golden chance to double Hearts' lead following Pointon's early opener. It would prove to be only a blip, however, as Hearts started to motor in the early months of the year. They won nine of their next 12 matches in all competitions, including the famous 3-0 triumph away to Rangers when 22-year-old Johnston scored a stunning hat-trick. With Locke and Johnston revitalised by Jefferies following a demoralising previous season for both under McLean, and Ritchie and McManus having swiftly become regular fixtures in defence, this quartet of Gorgie youth products made up more than a third of a rapidly-improving Hearts team. "When I first came in, I was told there wasn't a lot behind the scenes in terms of boys in the youth team," recalls Jefferies. "But I sat back and looked at that and thought 'well, they've won the Youth Cup and the Reserve League (in 1993) – how does anybody know they're not good enough if they've not been given a chance?'. When I put in Locke, Johnston, McManus and Ritchie and mixed them with a sprinkling of foreigners, we hardly looked back, to be honest. We just grew and got better and better. I'm sure Sandy Clark, who had them in the reserves before he became first-team manager, would have been delighted if he had been allowed to stay on and get the benefit of these boys."

After a freak 5-2 loss at home to Partick Thistle in late March, Jefferies was able to banish some Brockville demons as Ritchie and Locke scored in a 2-0 victory away to Falkirk, five months after that grim defeat at the same venue. On the last day of March, the manager pulled off what would be one of the most significant signings of his reign as he captured the aforementioned Cameron from Raith Rovers in a deal that saw the Kirkcaldy club receive £250,000 plus John Millar. While Jefferies was delighted at landing the diminutive box-to-box midfielder, he was disappointed at not being able to sign the Stark's Park side's other burgeoning young talent in addition. "I remember Jim was in the huff with me when he wanted to sign Colin Cameron and Stevie Crawford from Raith Rovers and I told him he could only have one of them," says Deans. "But he plumped for Colin and it turned out to be one of our best signings."

Cameron was cup-tied so unable to feature in what was another landmark win for Hearts at the start of April as they beat Aberdeen 2-1 in a nervy Scottish Cup semi-final at Hampden. This victory, achieved in their iconic Argentina-style away kit, secured the club a first appearance in a final for a decade and sent excitement levels soaring among supporters. The feelgood factor continued as Hearts went through their last five league games unbeaten – a run which included a 2-0 home win over cup final opponents Rangers in Cameron's debut – to finish fourth in the table, level on points with third-placed Aberdeen. "It wasn't a brilliant season but it was definitely better than the previous two," reflects Locke. "The gaffer brought in a brand of football that you associate with Hearts in terms of getting on the front foot and getting in about teams so it was a decent season. I think if you asked any boys that played for Hearts in that era, finishing third or fourth was acceptable but if you finished below that we had failed. Finishing in the top four and having a decent cup run was the sign of a reasonable season; we were making progress."

The final league game of the season – a 1-1 draw away to Motherwell in which Cameron scored his second goal in four appearances – featured a debut off the bench for 17-year-old left-back Gary Naysmith. This meant that, as the 1995/96 campaign was coming to a close, six of the impending legends of 1998 had played for Hearts' first team – five more than at the start of the season.

Sizing Up Rangers

*"The Coca-Cola Cup run showed we
were capable of matching any team"*

Paul Gascoigne versus Jim Jefferies. Two of the most highly-regarded men in Scottish football in 1995/96 had the chance to cap their first seasons at Rangers and Hearts, respectively, with Scottish Cup glory. Gascoigne had scooped all the player of the year awards going as the Ibrox side won an eighth consecutive Premier Division title; Jefferies, meanwhile, had begun the process of breathing new life into Hearts as he elevated them from last place in late October to fourth place by the end of the campaign. This surge up the table incorporated back-to-back league victories over Rangers in the second half of the season, fuelling belief within the Hearts squad that they could defeat the Ibrox side in what would be their first Scottish Cup final appearance in a decade. Ultimately, however, Jefferies' team were still a work in progress, while Rangers were in their pomp, led by the formidable duo of Gascoigne and Brian Laudrup and buoyed by finishing four points clear of a Celtic side who had lost only one league game all season under Tommy Burns.

The difference in quality shone through on 18th May 1996 as the Tynecastle side were obliterated 5-1 in the Hampden sunshine. "I think we were probably at our peak at that time," says Rangers assistant manager Archie Knox. "Everything we touched seemed to go in that day." A devastating early knee injury to 20-year-old captain Gary Locke and a wretched, goal-costing error by goalkeeper Gilles Rousset, in which he somehow allowed a routine cross from the right from Laudrup to squirm through his legs and into the net, exacerbated a dire day for Hearts as the irrepressible Dane – in arguably his finest game for Rangers – scored twice and Gordon Durie hit a hat-trick. John Colquhoun netted Hearts' solitary goal a minute before the champions struck their fourth in a match that would become renowned in Scottish football circles as "the Laudrup final". "Let's be honest, even if Gilles hadn't let that goal in, we wouldn't have beaten them that day," Stephen

Fulton reflects. "Rangers were just a better team than us then. Gilles was devastated after that, probably even more devastated than the rest of us because he'd have been sitting there focusing on his own mistake. The big man never made many mistakes; it's just one of those bloody things that it happened in a cup final when the whole country was watching."

The Hearts team that started that day featured four players who would also start the Scottish Cup final against the same opponents two years later: Rousset, Dave McPherson, Paul Ritchie and Fulton. Six Rangers players, meanwhile, would survive from the 1996 final to start the rematch in 1998: Andy Goram, Richard Gough, Stuart McCall, Ian Ferguson, Laudrup and Durie.

Jefferies, viewing the big picture, was in no mood for recriminations despite the meek nature of Hearts' defeat. "I said to the players after the 96 final, 'listen, Hearts had to win on the last day to avoid relegation last season. If you'd said to me we'd finish fourth and make it to a Scottish Cup final, even losing by that score, I'd have bitten your hand off'. I said to them 'you've done the club proud. You're all down today because we've not performed and not done the right things, but the best way to get it out your system is to learn from it and get back to a final as quickly as possible and do it differently next time'. Nobody needed to feel down. It was a really good season for us, the change was starting to happen, we were improving as a club and the fans were coming back to us and enjoying the style of football."

By the start of the 1996/97 league campaign, "the change" had been ratcheted up further as Hearts cast aside several players and added some quality new recruits over the summer. Craig Nelson and Brian Hamilton headed to Falkirk in a player swap that brought 26-year-old defender David Weir to Tynecastle, while long-serving 33-year-old Neil Berry also joined the Bairns but wasn't deemed part of the deal for Weir. The signing of highly-rated Dundee winger Neil McCann, who had just turned 22, for a nominal fee represented another significant coup for Hearts, while Jeremy Goss, the well-regarded 31-year-old Welsh international midfielder, joined from Norwich City, and 29-year-old striker Darren Beckford, a former team-mate of Neil Pointon's, arrived from Oldham Athletic. Egil Ostenstad, the burgeoning Viking FK striker, was also close to moving to Tynecastle before Graeme Souness's Southampton eventually came in with a better offer for the Norwegian internationalist, but Jefferies could be content with his eye-catching summer transfer activity. The main disappointment for the manager – a huge fan of quality wide players – was that he had lost Allan Johnston under freedom of contract to French side Rennes, denying him the mouthwatering scenario of having Johnston on one flank and McCann on the other.

Fifteen of the 22 first-team players he inherited a year previously had left Tynecastle or kicked their last competitive ball for the club by the start of Jefferies' second season. Alan Lawrence, Paul Smith, David Winnie and Hans Eskilsson – remembered more for his wretched miss in the New Year derby at Easter Road than the two goals he scored, both against Partick Thistle – also moved on in the summer of 1996, with the manager adamant that these players, who had joined in his early months in charge, had played their part in getting Hearts moving in the right direction. "I've got great respect for people like Alan Lawrence and Paul Smith who came in short term and did us a turn," he says. "They enjoyed their time at Hearts and they were part and parcel of getting the change going. We had to wait until the opportunity came to get better with the likes of Cameron, McCann and Weir. And because of the success we had in the first season, the board backed us in terms of bringing these players in."

For Cameron, the sight of other highly-regarded Scottish players like Weir and McCann following him in choosing to move to Tynecastle to further their careers served as vindication that he had made the right decision himself a few months previously. "I had played against Neil when he was at Dundee and I was at Raith Rovers and I knew he was an exciting player; he was rapid and he could score a goal," recalls Cameron. "I felt, personally, with him on the wing I would get more opportunities to score because I was the type of player who liked to get into the box and get on the end of things. When he and big Davie arrived, it made me realise I'd definitely made the right decision to join Hearts because Jim had backed up exactly what he'd said to me when he was trying to get me to sign. He had explained what he was trying to do and he backed it up with the signings he made."

Fulton was equally impressed with the way Hearts were shaping up in his second season at the club. "When I first joined, Hearts had about a dozen boys from through the west but maybe six months down the line you're lucky if there was half of that remaining," Fulton says, outlining how quickly the change in personnel was being undertaken. "The first couple of years, there was a big turnover of players but you could feel the team getting progressively better. You only had to look at the players we were bringing in to see that: Davie Weir, Neil McCann, wee Mickey (Cameron). Once all these guys came in, you could see they were a step up from what we had before. It was just a gradual progression."

Despite the excitement surrounding the new arrivals, Hearts didn't exactly hit the ground running in the 1996/97 season. Encouragement could be found in a spirited away-goals European Cup Winners' Cup exit against Red Star Belgrade following a 1-1 aggregate draw in August, but the league form in the early months – although slightly better than a year previously – was patchy and unconvincing. Any optimism from an opening-day 3-2 victory at home to Kilmarnock – in which Ritchie scored a double and his fellow centre-back Weir got his first goal for the club – was lost amid a 4-0 thrashing away to Aberdeen in match two. Similarly, a home win against Dundee United in early September was followed by back-to-back away defeats against Dunfermline Athletic and Rangers. The match at East End Park was most notable from a Hearts perspective for being the night that 28-year-old former AC Milan, Fiorentina and Atalanta midfielder Stefano Salvatori made his debut as a substitute. The Italian would have been entitled to wonder if he had made the wrong decision in moving to Scotland when, in his first start for the club four days later, four of his team-mates – Pasquale Bruno, Weir, Pointon and Ritchie – were sent off in a 3-0 defeat at Ibrox. In what was the only meeting of the two sides in the period between their two cup final showdowns in 1996, the scoreline could have been far worse for Hearts if Rangers – for whom Durie,

Gascoigne and Ally McCoist scored – hadn't taken their foot off the gas during the farcical closing 23 minutes when it was eleven men against seven.

The main source of solace for Hearts in the early months of Jefferies' second season came from the fact they were still in the Coca-Cola Cup by virtue of narrow victories at home to Stenhousemuir (on penalties) and away to St Johnstone (after extra-time). Just three days after their infamous visit to Rangers, however, their cup run was widely expected to be halted as they prepared to face in-form Celtic in a home quarter-final with four of their key players suspended. Jefferies had some notable problems to solve, particularly in the decimated defensive area of his team. He responded by recruiting Andy Thorn, a rugged former Wimbledon centre-back, on a short-term deal and pitching him straight into the heart of a defence which also featured 17-year-old left-back Gary Naysmith, who was given his first start four months after making his debut as a substitute away to Motherwell. In addition, Kevin Thomas, who it transpired had lost his explosiveness as a result of the knee injury he had sustained some 18 months previously, was handed a rare start under Jefferies. The end result was a remarkable 1-0 win for Hearts after extra-time in which Salvatori was sent off, Thorn was heroic, Naysmith was man of the match and John Robertson scored the winner. Hearts, despite struggling in the league, were heading to their second successive semi-final under Jefferies.

In between the Coca-Cola Cup quarter-final and semi-final, Hearts went unbeaten through their four league games, drawing three times and winning 3-1 away to Hibs. This period also included the arrival of striker Stephane Paille, a former Sochaux team-mate of Rousset's who had earned eight caps for France and been named as the player of the year in his homeland in 1988, just before the likes of Jean-Pierre Papin, Laurent Blanc and David Ginola landed this prestigious accolade. The move to Hearts served as an opportunity for the 31-year-old to get his career back on track after he had been found guilty of cannabis use and given a two-month ban from playing a year previously. "Stephane was a very good friend of mine and when Jim asked me about him I said 'yes, he is a fantastic player'," recalls Rousset. "He'd had some troubles back home, and I explained everything to Jim. But he was a fantastic player and a very nice guy so I told Jim to get him in for a trial and have a look for himself. When Stephane came, I said to him 'Steph, this is your last chance, don't blow it. Make sure you are on top of your game because I've told Jim the truth about your good and your bad aspects. Don't let me down because I've asked Jim to take you on trial'."

Paille made a swift impact on supporters, scoring his first goal and being named man of the match in his third appearance for the club as Hearts defeated Dundee 3-1 in the semi-final at Easter Road in October, exacting an element of revenge for the penalty shootout defeat at Dens Park in the same tournament the previous year. Jim Hamilton, incidentally, scored Dundee's consolation goal. It would be his last for the Tayside club.

The four league games between the semi-final and the final brought a defeat away to Dundee United, back-to-back 2-0 wins over Dunfermline and Motherwell, and a grim 0-0 draw at home to Hibs most memorable for the fact that Rangers striker McCoist, in jovial mood after a few pre-match drinks on Rose Street, dressed up as Hearts mascot Hearty Harry for the half-time entertainment. With the Old Firm derby having taken place two days earlier, Rangers were idle so McCoist, who was also a News of the World columnist at the time, took the opportunity to head through to Tynecastle. "We were in at half-time, up in the lounge, and the Hearts mascot Hearty Harry is getting changed next to me," McCoist recalled on Talksport radio in 2019. "I've had a little bit of a nice lunch, and I've looked at him, and he's looked at me. He shook his head, and I've nodded my head, and I've went 'yes'. I put the outfit on and I was out on the Tynecastle pitch for the most bizarre ten minutes of my life, dancing in front of the supporters and all that stuff."

Unfortunately for Hearts, the Scotland striker was back to his day job the following weekend. This involved leading the Rangers attack in the Coca-Cola Cup final against Hearts in what represented a rematch of the Scottish Cup final just six months previously. Unbeknown at the time, it would also count as the second in a remarkable series of three cup finals between the teams in the space of two years and a notable landmark on Hearts' route to glory. Staged at Celtic Park as Hampden was being redeveloped, the Coca-Cola Cup final brought another defeat but this time Hearts were able to leave a national final with a genuine sense of pride and hope mixed in with the regret that they had been unable to make their stirring performance count. As the snow fell on Glasgow's east end, the game was in doubt beforehand. "It was a horrible night, but we were such a confident team, even at that stage, and we were desperate for the game to go ahead," says McCann. "I remember Jim coming into the dressing-room and saying stuff like 'I'm not sure Rangers want it to go ahead' and he was asking us if we wanted it to go ahead. We were like 'yeah, we want to play, of course we want to play'. It was all mind games from the gaffer. He was just geeing us up."

For all their pre-match bullishness, it looked like another cup final capitulation was on the cards for Hearts when McCoist scored twice in the opening 27 minutes to put Rangers in control. Jefferies' side – inspired by a sensational display from McCann – summoned their resolve, however, and hauled themselves back into the match, with Fulton pulling one back a minute before the interval. Rangers were rattled and McCoist and Gascoigne ended up in a ferocious argument with each other as the teams went up the tunnel at half-time after the striker had failed to read a pass from the English midfielder in the closing seconds of the first half. It led to a stressed Gascoigne famously downing a shot of whisky to calm himself down. "We're in the dressing-room and the two of us are still at it, so Walter Smith comes in and says 'right, everybody shut up and calm down'," said McCoist, recounting the tale on Talksport in April 2020. "Eventually when it calmed down Gazza got up, went out of the dressing-room and straight into the director's room – in his gear by the way – and had a whisky. He threw it down his neck, came back into the dressing-room, sat down, Walter did his team talk, and then he walked out for the second half."

The fraught mood in the Rangers camp wasn't helped when Robertson equalised for Hearts in the 59th minute. At that point, with the wind in their sails, the Tynecastle side looked likely winners. The booze-fuelled Gascoigne had other ideas. Having hitherto endured a frustrating afternoon, the Englishman suddenly turned on the style when it mattered most and scored two sublime goals in the space of three minutes to swing the game back in Rangers' favour. "We did well to get 2-0 ahead but then all of a sudden Hearts found a bit of freshness and got back into the match," says Knox. "When it went 2-2 we were struggling to get our game going again. But when you've got someone like Paul Gascoigne in your team, you know you've got someone who can turn a game round. He had that aura about him to be able to do that."

Hearts were shellshocked by Gascoigne's sensational double whammy but refused to throw in the towel and pulled another goal back through Weir with two minutes left to make it 4-3. For all the improvement they had shown compared to their previous final, ultimately it was another case of heartbreak for the likes of Robertson and Gary Mackay and the club's long-suffering supporters. "We produced a great performance that day and after getting back to 2-2, it felt like there was only going to be one winner but Gascoigne was unstoppable," Jefferies says. "The positive for us was it was 4-3, it wasn't a 5-1 like the previous one. We were a lot closer to them."

Amid the anguish, there was a feeling among the Hearts squad that something special might be brewing under Jefferies and Brown. "We knew at the beginning of that (1996/97) season that we were still very much a work in progress," Cameron reflects. "It takes time to get players to gel and understand each other but the Coca-Cola Cup run showed that in one-off games we were capable of matching any team. We beat Celtic on our way to the final and then the final – which was probably one of the best there's ever been for the neutral – was settled by a few minutes of magic from Gazza. We just fell a wee bit short that day but we felt that we could still get improvement out of each other and that things could happen for us."

At that point, little did anybody know that six of the players who started the Coca-Cola Cup final for Hearts in November 1996 – Rousset, Weir, Ritchie, Fulton, Cameron and McCann – would get the chance to use their experiences from this near-miss to make amends against the same opponents at the same stadium just 18 months down the line. Salvatori, incidentally, missed the 4-3 defeat with a hernia issue, while McPherson was absent after being forced off with a minor knee injury in the derby the previous weekend. The veteran defender was replaced in the team by Bruno who, by that point, had begun losing his status as a regular starter. Just four players who started for Rangers in the Coca-Cola Cup final would also start the 1998 Scottish Cup final: Goram, Gough, Joachim Bjorklund and Laudrup.

"We should have won the Coca-Cola Cup final," says Rousset. "We had the feeling after that game that we were getting closer and we were much more competitive than in the previous final."

McCann pinpoints this as a significant occasion on the journey of an evolving team. "I remember coming back on the bus that night and we were playing Hearts songs," says the winger. "It wasn't just music, it was Hearts songs we were playing. I sat on that bus thinking 'we're on the edge of getting something really special going'. I think there was a great belief there that we were getting close to doing something. I really thought that was a defining moment for the team."

There was no immediate bounce from the gallant Coca-Cola Cup final performance, however, as Hearts went on a five-game winless run in the league. This culminated in a 4-1 home defeat by Rangers in which 33-year-old Colquhoun, on as a substitute, made his last competitive appearance for the club and 21-year-old Grant Murray, a boyhood Jambo from Mayfield, also came off the bench to make his debut. Hearts were seventh in the ten-team Premier Division at Christmas, a scenario that certainly wasn't in the plan for Jefferies at the midway point of a season in which he had clearly made some exciting signings in his quest to build on the fourth-place finish and general promise of the previous campaign. Amid the disappointment of the pre-Christmas results, there was a beacon of positivity when Hearts signed the aforementioned Hamilton from Dundee for £200,000. The highly-regarded 20-year-old striker's arrival meant Jefferies had managed to snare Cameron, Weir, McCann and Hamilton – four of Scotland's most burgeoning talents – within the space of ten months and for well below £1 million combined.

Hamilton had a swift impact at Hearts, with the match in which he made his second start – a 3-2 win at Dunfermline on Boxing Day – kicking off a much-needed run of four consecutive victories which elevated the Edinburgh side to fourth in the table. He scored his first goal in the following match – a 4-1 home win over Motherwell – and then added a double in a 4-0 New Year's Day win away to Hibs as well as a match-winning goal against Raith Rovers at Stark's Park. Within a month of signing, Hamilton had netted five times in seven appearances. His arrival in Gorgie paved the way for fellow striker Beckford, whose scoring contribution at Hearts totalled two goals in the Coca-Cola Cup run, to join Preston North End a few weeks later.

Hearts – although generally perceived to be making progress – continued to be inconsistent in the latter part of the campaign, picking up enough points to remain in fourth place but unable to generate the required momentum to put any pressure on a Dundee United side who were motoring towards third and UEFA Cup qualification under a certain Tommy McLean. There was a clear sense of irony in this given that McLean was galvanising United in a manner he had so badly failed to do at Hearts just two seasons previously. Indeed, it was United – featuring their much-vaunted Scandinavian contingent of Lars Zetterlund, Kjell Olofsson and Erik Pedersen – who eliminated Hearts from the Scottish Cup in a fourth-round replay at Tannadice in February. This was a particularly frustrating setback for Jefferies' side in light of the fact they had reached the final in their two previous tilts at the national knockout competitions. The 1-0 defeat at Tannadice also represented the penultimate appearance in maroon for 33-year-old Mackay, who ended his remarkable unbroken 17-year association with the club in March by joining Airdrieonians after Jefferies deemed that he was no longer going to be a prominent member of the team. "Jim had said to me late in 1996 that he would offer me another year and that I could maybe do a bit of coaching with the younger players but my first-team game time would be limited," recalls Mackay. "As a player, you always want to play so I had to think seriously about it and discuss the situation with my wife. A wee while after that, Jim told me that Alex MacDonald wanted to take me to Airdrie and that they were going to pay a nominal fee for me. But I felt that, after the service I'd given to the club, I should have got the money instead of Hearts. It took my ex-wife to talk to Jim about it and for Leslie Deans to tell Chris Robinson that I should get the nominal fee because of my loyalty for it to be resolved, and I eventually left in March 1997.

"The dream for me would have been to stay on and coach at the club when I finished playing but that never happened and there was a bit of resentment from me, towards Jim in particular. Hearts was all I'd known in my professional life, so I was focused on my own disappointment and feeling like I was being hard done by. Gradually, though, as time passes you realise it isn't all about yourself. When you look back on it with hindsight, letting me go proved to be the right decision from Hearts' perspective. I wasn't the only one Jim moved on. It was nothing to do with me as an individual. He just wanted to better the football club and he had to make changes to freshen things up.

"With hindsight, Jim was only showing the same type of ruthlessness that had served Hearts well when Sandy Jardine and Alex MacDonald were trying to revive the club in the 80s. Jim and Billy had proved their worth as a management team at both Berwick and Falkirk and they knew that they had to freshen things up and get in the right types of players who would be able to handle cup final situations and games like that. I didn't like it because I was shown the door as part of that but I had to respect what they were doing. When you're the one having to leave the club, it's not nice at the time, but when I look back now it was 100 per cent the right decision for the football club. I'm absolutely fine with Jim now."

Bruno, who had turned 34, had also been phased out of the team in the second half of the season as his body started to feel the effects of a long career and it came as no surprise when the popular Italian departed the club at the end of the season. Incidentally, Bruno pulled off the quite remarkable feat of spending the entirety of his 19-month stint at Hearts living in one of Edinburgh's most prestigious hotels at the club's expense. "Pasquale used to call the Caledonian his house," laughs Jefferies. "Chris Robinson, quite rightly, said to me, 'listen, can you have a chat with Pasquale about the bills that are coming in from the Caledonian?' because he was eating there regularly and the a la carte obviously wasn't cheap, even back then. I had a chat with him and he was great. He said 'no problem gaffer, I understand, I will go across and eat in Bar Roma instead'. I told Chris what was happening and he was happy with that but it turned out the bills were bigger because he started taking his friends with him. We had to put a stop to that! Pasquale was fantastic for us though."

Another experienced foreign player kicked what would prove to be his last ball for the club in April after it emerged a month later that, following a defeat away to Kilmarnock, Paille had tested positive for Dinintel, a stimulant drug often used as an appetite suppressant. The Frenchman claimed it was "a genuine mistake" and that he had been taking the tablets to control a weight problem. The reprieve he was hoping for at a club with which he had developed an affinity never came. Although Jefferies had been looking forward to the prospect of seeing Paille take his game to new heights after a rigorous pre-season, Hearts felt they were left with no option but to sack the Frenchman when he was hit with a four-month ban by the Scottish Football Association. "Steph was great when he was at Hearts, honestly he was great," says Rousset of his old friend, who passed away aged 52 in June 2017. "He was very happy in Edinburgh and was quite unfortunate to fail a drugs test because of tablets he was taking. He was not very clever on that situation but he was unfortunate. It was a stupid story and he was quite unlucky." There would be a revolving door for French strikers called Stephane at Hearts at the end of the 96/97 campaign.

A little over a month after Mackay's departure, another of the 1986 squad officially left the club in poignant circumstances. On the Tuesday before the final league game of the 1996/97 season, a press conference was called at which a tearful Craig Levein, accompanied by his wife Carol, announced that he was retiring, aged just 32, after being unable to recover from the knee injury he had sustained against Dunfermline in Jefferies' third competitive game in charge, almost two years previously. "Although I didn't play with him, Craig was always round about the place in my first season," recalls Weir. "He was coming to the end of his playing career but he still had an influence and he was good. I liked him, he was very honest. I was basically brought in to replace him if I'm being honest and that can sometimes be difficult, but I never felt that was a problem. He was good with me, he helped me in terms of my football. He was complimentary about how I was as a player and he helped me just in general day to day."

With the old guard diminishing in influence under Jefferies, the manager's second season was generally a time for the new arrivals to start making their presence felt, as evidenced by the fact Cameron, Weir and McCann – who scored a derby winner at Tynecastle in March – were the three outfield players who appeared most regularly in the 1996/97 campaign. Weir's impact in his first season at Tynecastle was highlighted when he was one of the four nominees for the Scottish PFA player of the year award, alongside illustrious company in Laudrup and Celtic pair Jorge Cadete and Paolo Di Canio, with the Italian the eventual winner. While this exciting new wave of early-to-mid-20s talent were getting their feet under the table at Tynecastle, however, Robertson – for now, at least – remained the king of Hearts. The season climaxed in rousing fashion, with the 32-year-old striker scoring a double in a 3-1 home win over Rangers to break Jimmy Wardhaugh's all-time league scoring record for the club. Robertson finished the campaign as Hearts' top scorer with 19 goals – eight more than Cameron, the team's second-top scorer.

That final-day victory over Rangers, who were in party mode after securing their record-equalling ninth title in succession in their previous match away to Dundee United, meant that, over the course of Jefferies' first two seasons at Hearts, the Tynecastle side had won three and drawn one of their ten meetings with Walter Smith's team. This was a decent record considering the vast disparity in resources between the clubs and the fact that, from 1995 to 1997, Rangers were widely deemed to be in their most formidable phase of the 90s: a decade in which they dominated Scottish football, thrived in Europe and could legitimately claim to have been one of the strongest sides in the whole of Britain.

Although the last day of Hearts' season was most memorable for Robertson's record-setting exploits, the victory over the champions was also notable for being the occasion in which French striker Stephane Adam first got the chance to take the acclaim of the Tynecastle crowd. The 27-year-old, whose contract at Metz was expiring, had agreed earlier that week to move to Hearts for the following season and was paraded on the pitch at half-time. For all the excitement that surrounded the new recruit, nobody would have foreseen at that point that a little over a year down the line there would be such a remarkable role reversal, with Adam making a historic goal-scoring contribution in an end-of-season match against Rangers and Robertson coming in from the periphery to take the acclaim of the support.

Title Bid

*"I've never seen Tynecastle rock like that
– the place went absolutely mental!"*

At the conclusion of a fulfilling three-year stint with Crewe Alexandra in which he had been a team-mate of players such as Neil Lennon and Danny Murphy, a 22-year-old Robbie Savage was looking for a new club in order to progress his career to the next level. The four genuine options put on the table by George Urquhart, the agent of the burgeoning blond midfielder, were Leicester City, Crystal Palace, Malmo and Heart of Midlothian. The fact the former Manchester United youngster and Urquhart – a Scot who had played for St Mirren briefly in the late 1960s – felt compelled to embark on a four-hour drive from north-west England to Edinburgh to speak to Jim Jefferies in the first week of July 1997 served as an indicator of the eye-catching progress that had been made by Hearts in the manager's first two years in charge. Just a over a month previously, Savage had made his first start for Wales in a friendly at Rugby Park against a Scotland side for whom Hearts defender David Weir was making his international debut.

The Welshman later confirmed in his autobiography – published in 2011 – that "as soon as I talked to Jim Jefferies, I wanted to sign for Hearts". Unfortunately for the Tynecastle club, Savage had agreed to speak to his other suitors before making a decision, and the lure of joining Martin O'Neill at English Premiership side Leicester ultimately proved too strong to resist. "I knew he would be a terrific signing for us if we could get him," recalls Jefferies. "He came up to Pinkie (the school playing fields in Musselburgh where Hearts trained) with his agent and we had a chat about what he was looking for in his life. He was really keen to consider us. He didn't train with us because he arrived just after we'd finished training but he met the boys and he liked the set-up. It would've been a real feather in our cap if we'd been able to get him because he's an inspirational character and his enthusiasm for the game was great. You wouldn't say he was the most technically-gifted player ever but he certainly had enough skill to have shone in our team. It was disappointing that we couldn't get him but he phoned us up and was very apologetic about it. He said it was touch and go between Leicester and us. He wasn't the big celebrity figure he is now but he was certainly a good player and it would've been a coup if we were able to get him. That's how well we were going at that time though; good players knew we were on the up and were keen to consider joining us."

As disappointing as it was that he chose to join Leicester instead, the failure to land Savage – who went on to become an established Premier League player and a passionate football pundit – was never going to blow Hearts off course. Under Jefferies, this was a club with the wind in their sails. Having reached a cup final and finished fourth in both of his first two seasons as Hearts manager, while also carrying out the significant change in personnel he promised, the challenge for Jefferies in year three was to take it to the next level and ensure his impressive rebuild would bring some genuine success to Tynecastle. Could he lift Hearts into the top three for the first time since Joe Jordan led them to second place in the Premier Division in 1991/92? After finishing 28 and then 23 points adrift of second-placed Celtic in his first two seasons at Hearts, could he give the two Glasgow sides any kind of challenge to think about as Celtic, who were under the charge of Dutchman Wim Jansen, prepared to try and stop Rangers clinching an historic tenth title in a row? And after finishing runners-up in each of his previous two seasons, could he go a step further in the knockout competitions and finally bring a trophy back to Gorgie for the first time since Tommy Walker presided over League Cup glory in 1962?

Although the signing of Savage would have added some extra sheen, Jefferies was clearly pretty satisfied with the make-up of his squad as there would be only two new arrivals in the summer of 1997; this was in stark contrast to the frenzied 21st-century transfer windows at Hearts which have often involved in excess of ten players being recruited. With Stephane Adam having already agreed to join from Metz just before the final match of the previous season, the only other new face to check in at Tynecastle for the start of the 1997/98 campaign was Thomas Flögel, a 26-year-old Austrian internationalist who had hitherto spent his entire career with Austria Vienna. The highly-regarded midfielder had been on trial with Dundee United before Hearts got wind of his availability via Brian Whittaker, a former defender at Tynecastle who went on to play under Jefferies at Falkirk in the early 90s. Tragically, Whittaker, who was working as an agent at the time, lost his life in a car crash just two months after helping facilitate Flögel's transfer to Hearts.

With the esteemed trio of John Colquhoun, Gary Mackay and Craig Levein – all former team-mates of Whittaker's – having departed the club within a busy spell of ins and outs the previous season, only five of the 22 first-team players Jefferies initially inherited now remained at Hearts: Dave McPherson, Gary Locke, Kevin Thomas, Stephen Frail and John Robertson, who had just signed a new one-year contract amid reported interest from French clubs Guingamp, Le Havre and Sochaux. By the end of July 1997, the squad was made up almost exclusively of players signed, promoted or valued by Jefferies. Within two years of taking the job, the manager had assembled a group that would have permitted him, if he wished, to send out a starting XI of Gilles Rousset, McPherson, Weir, Paul Ritchie, Gary Naysmith, Flögel, Stefano Salvatori, Stephen Fulton, Colin Cameron, Neil McCann and Adam. Incidentally, this was an XI that would never once start together in a league match. "I was impressed with the Hearts squad straight away," recalls Flögel. "There were so many good players. I remember thinking McCann was fast as fuck; you didn't want to be against him in the sprint training."

After a typically gruelling, character-building pre-season under Jefferies and Billy Brown – including friendlies away to Blyth Spartans, Hull City, Berwick Rangers and Grimsby Town as well as a 3-2 home win over Rangers in a testimonial match for McPherson in which former Scotland rugby internationalist Gavin Hastings made a cameo appearance for Hearts – the competitive action began with a formidable-looking trip to Ibrox in the league. On a sunny early-August Monday evening in Govan, Hearts – sporting their new white away kit freshly produced by Olympic Sportswear – hoped to deliver an early-season statement of intent in front of a live Sky Sports audience. Rousset, Frail, Weir, Ritchie, Neil Pointon, Flögel, Grant Murray, Salvatori, Fulton, McCann and Jim Hamilton were the eleven men sent out to kick off what would prove to be one of the most exhilarating campaigns in Hearts' entire history. It got off to something of a false start, however, as Rangers eased to a 3-1 win, with their lethal new Italian striker Marco Negri scoring a double shortly before half-time and Alec Cleland adding a late third just before substitute Cameron pulled one back for Hearts with a lovely finish from inside the box. With Celtic having lost away to Hibs the previous day, this was Walter Smith's side asserting themselves as hot favourites to go on and win a tenth league title in a row.

For Hearts, it had been a chastening night, particularly for Flögel whose competitive debut ended with him being substituted at half-time. Adam, meanwhile, came on for the last 17 minutes and set up Cameron's goal with an excellent cross. Despite their baptism of fire in Glasgow, the presence of the two new arrivals from overseas had added to Fulton's optimism for the campaign ahead. "I knew straight away we had a good team that season," Fulton insists. "I know we lost at Ibrox on the opening day but I remember still feeling good about the team. After that game, we started winning pretty much every week."

Hearts subsequently enjoyed a three-game winning burst, with Coca-Cola Cup victories away to Livingston and Raith Rovers either side of an emphatic 4-1 triumph at home to Aberdeen in which goals from Robertson, Fulton, Cameron and substitute Flögel cancelled out Mike Newell's early opener for the visitors. "From the friendly games and even after losing the first game at Rangers, you could feel there was quality in the team," says Adam. "We built up a good spirit in pre-season, with the mix of the players who were there already and the new players, and I could feel early on that we had a team that could challenge at the top. After the Rangers game, we were 1-0 down against Aberdeen and we came straight back into the game and beat them convincingly. From that point, you could feel the confidence and the quality was there. You could feel something good was going to happen."

In addition to Hearts' magnificent performance against the Dons, that match was also notable for being the first played in front of the newly-built Gorgie Stand, albeit with no supporters in it on this occasion. There were few people inside Tynecastle that day more satisfied than Leslie Deans, who – as part of an agreement from the start of their dual reign as Hearts' majority shareholders in 1994 – had earlier that year taken over as chairman from Chris Robinson, who in turn became chief executive. "I take a lot of pleasure from the fact that in my time as chairman I was able to oversee and complete the total refurbishment of Tynecastle to give us four stands – the three new ones and the existing main stand which was replaced in 2017 under Ann Budge," says Deans, who along with Robinson had picked up the baton after the Wheatfield Stand was constructed during Wallace Mercer's tenure. "I look back on that with a great degree of pride and the club was able to move forward as a result. The alternative would have been a significantly reduced capacity which wouldn't have made things viable because at that time things were beginning to happen on the pitch."

Indeed they were. Sadly the same couldn't be said for Jeremy Goss, whose underwhelming spell in Gorgie came to an end a little over a year after his much-hyped arrival from Norwich City. The veteran Welsh internationalist – an unused sub in the win over Aberdeen – departed by mutual consent after being unable to command regular game time under Jefferies, managing only eight starts and 15 appearances in total. "A case of wrong move, wrong time, wrong club," was Goss's rueful verdict of his time at Hearts, as delivered in his autobiography in 2014.

After the euphoria of dismantling Aberdeen, Hearts suffered a setback in their next league match when they lost 2-1 away to Dunfermline Athletic. Cameron viewed that poor display at East End Park as a turning point for a team he knew was capable of far better than a return of just three points from their opening three league games. "That was a bit of a kick up the backside for us," the midfielder recalls.

Hearts' next test was away to a table-topping Hibs side managed by Hamilton and McCann's old Dundee boss Jim Duffy, and featuring Weir's former Falkirk colleague John Hughes, Cameron's old Raith Rovers team-mates Tony Rougier and Stevie Crawford, as well as Jean-Marc Adjovi-Boco, an old adversary of Adam and Rousset's from their time in France. McCann flicked in the only goal of the game with a deft finish with the outside of his left foot before gleefully cupping his ears to the home supporters. That 1-0 derby victory, on the weekend of Princess Diana's death in Paris, would be the first of five league wins in a row for Jefferies' team. "Hibs had started well and had already beaten Celtic but we went across there and did a number on them," recalls McCann. "The feeling of winning that game was brilliant. We'd had a couple of defeats at the start of that season but you could tell there was a bit of a spark about us and that it was only a matter of time before it took off. That game at Easter Road was a bit of a catalyst for us and after that you could feel us going through the gears."

Hearts' next fixture took them back to Dunfermline – scene of their recent league defeat – for a midweek Coca-Cola Cup quarter-final tie. This time the performance was far better and the Edinburgh side could consider themselves hugely unfortunate as former Hearts winger Allan Moore scored the only goal of the tie in extra-time to take the Pars into the semi-finals. It was a hammer blow for a Hearts side who had reached the final of the competition the previous year and had genuine aspirations of winning a trophy. "That was the night when I realised we were a really good team," says Rousset. "I remember it well, we were fantastic; we played really, really well and were very unfortunate to lose. And after that game, I could tell by the reaction of the guys that we had a very good team because they were fucking unhappy; you know, really, really upset by the elimination. After that we bounced back very well and had a fantastic season."

A couple of headed goals from Hamilton gave Hearts a well-deserved 2-1 win at St Johnstone in the next league game before a victory by the same scoreline at home to a Dundee United side who had finished third the previous season. In what was the first match with spectators in the new Gorgie Stand, Hearts' opener was an own goal from United defender Steven Pressley, a man who would be wearing maroon a year later. With Kjell Olofsson equalising right on half-time for the visitors, Robertson – who by this stage was having to get accustomed to the role of substitute – emerged from the bench to score the winner and send Hearts to the top of the league for the first time.

While belief levels were already starting to soar in the dressing-room, perhaps the first real indication to those outside Tynecastle that something special was beginning to unfold for Jefferies' team came on the last weekend of September when they travelled through to Kilmarnock and romped to a 3-0 win in which all the goals – scored by Weir, Hamilton and Adam – came in the first half. Remarkably, Hearts performed an even more impressive demolition job away from home the following weekend as they raced into a three-goal lead after just 20 minutes on their way to beating Motherwell 4-1. Cameron, Adam, McCann and Hamilton were the men on target on a day when 4000 jubilant Jambos bounded out of Fir Park singing "we shall not be moved", a chant traditionally reserved in football for supporters of buoyant, table-topping sides. "Honestly, there were times in that season when we would absolutely blitz teams, just blow them off the pitch with our sheer ferocity and pace," recalls McCann. "That game at Motherwell, 3-0 up after 20 minutes, you're just thinking 'hang on a minute, we're a good side'."

Throughout this five-game winning run that had taken Hearts top of the league going into the October international break, 23-year-old Allan McManus – primarily a centre-back – was holding down the right-back position. This meant Locke, who had endured an injury-disrupted summer, had to bide his time on the substitutes' bench while his colleagues took the Premier Division by storm. "The gaffer moved me out to right-back for defensive duties but by that stage I was just absolutely delighted to be on the pitch in that team," says McManus. "Looking back, to play the amount of games I did within that talented squad is something I can be proud of. Lockey at that time was a fantastic right-back destined for bigger and better things so when he got himself fully fit he was always likely to get back in."

With the likes of McCann, Hamilton, Cameron and Adam causing havoc for opposing defences, Hearts bolstered their attack further when they paid £90,000 to sign Angolan winger Jose Quitongo from Hamilton Accies. "It was a big step up for me," says Quitongo. "Hearts are a big club and they had started the season really well. They had a very strong team. I was just like 'wow'. I was so excited to be joining them and the boys made me feel very comfortable straight away."

Quitongo completed his move to Tynecastle on the eve of a benefit match for Craig Levein against Hibs. With an attendance of just 2711 at his testimonial match against Coventry City two years earlier, it was a reflection of the feel-good factor now gripping the club that just over 8000 turned up to honour the retired centre-back second time around. In a friendly staged a day after Scotland had defeated Latvia at Celtic Park to secure their place at the upcoming World Cup in France, the Hearts team featured popular former players Levein, Mackay, Colquhoun, Pasquale Bruno and Scott Crabbe, while Hibs' team included Monaco midfielder John Collins – fresh from his exploits with the national team 24 hours earlier – and TV personality John Leslie. The Easter Road side won the match 1-0 through a goal from 19-year-old Andrew Newman.

Hearts had bigger fish to fry, however. In their next league game, the leaders were hosting a Celtic side who sat three points beneath them in third place, albeit with a game in hand. Having won six of their seven league matches since losing at Rangers on the opening night, Hearts were determined to show they meant business by adding one of the Glasgow sides to their growing list of scalps. "If you have any aspirations of winning the league you've got to beat Rangers and Celtic, and after winning five in a row we were obviously confident going into that one," recalls Cameron. Hearts fell flat, however, and goals in the first 21 minutes from Marc Rieper and Henrik Larsson – in the Swede's first season in Scotland – were enough to secure Celtic a deserved 2-1 win. With the defeat causing them to drop from first place to third, having played a game more than both Rangers and Celtic, Hearts' bubble was widely deemed to have burst. In an era when the Old Firm were generally monopolising the top two places in the league, most people outwith the Tynecastle club believed they had seen the last of Jefferies' team at the top. "Although we were disappointed to lose, we weren't too downbeat because we had been on a good run and we felt if we kept going, we could get on another run," says Cameron.

And sure enough, Hearts dusted themselves down and set about embarking on a fresh six-game winning streak. They rounded off their October schedule with a 3-1 midweek victory at home to Dunfermline in which Locke made his first start of the season and McCann, Adam and Fulton were the men on target. "There were goals coming from all angles," says McCann.

Underlining the level of goal threat in the Hearts squad, Jefferies changed two of his strikers for the early-November trip to Aberdeen and still came away with an emphatic 4-1 victory. Adam missed out through suspension while Hamilton dropped to the bench after failing to score in his two previous matches. Robertson came in for his first start since the victory at Hibs two months previously and the veteran was partnered in attack by Flögel, who was given his first start since the opening-night defeat at Ibrox. On a grim, wintry afternoon in the Granite City, the Austrian marked his surprise return to the team with a double as Hearts scored all four of their goals in the second half to cancel out Dean Windass's first-half opener. McCann and Robertson, with a deflection off Gary Smith, got the other two. As well as being the second time in the opening 11 league games of the season that Hearts had come from behind to beat Aberdeen 4-1, the match at Pittodrie represented the fourth occasion they had dismantled an opponent by a three-goal margin. It was particularly memorable for Quitongo as he made his debut as a late substitute. "I remember that match well," says Quitongo, erupting into a fit of giggles. "Everybody was supposed to wear a tracksuit but the boys told me 'Jose, we wear a suit to Aberdeen'. I turned up wearing a suit and they were all in a tracksuit! The boys were all laughing, man."

Within weeks of his arrival, the charismatic Quitongo was in with the bricks at Hearts, adding to dressing-room camaraderie off the pitch and influencing football matches on it. The little Angolan showman marked his home debut by scoring the second goal in a 2-0 home win over Hibs after replacing Robertson, who had opened the scoring early on. Tynecastle was in raptures once more the following weekend when a last-minute penalty from Cameron secured a 2-1 win over St Johnstone after Flögel's opener had been cancelled out by George O'Boyle. And there was yet more drama in Gorgie in the next match when rampant Hearts beat Kilmarnock 5-3 courtesy of an Adam hat-trick and goals from McCann and substitute Quitongo. "I know Killie kept coming back at us but we just blew them away with our attacking power," says McCann. There was an air of invincibility building around this swashbuckling Hearts side. "It wasn't just the fact we were winning, it was the way we were winning," says Fulton. "We were running over the top of teams. When you're winning games like we were, you don't think you're going to lose games."

Incredibly, with everyone having played 14 games, Hearts were four points clear of second-placed Rangers at the top of the table, five points clear of Celtic, and a whopping 14 points ahead of fourth-placed Dundee United as they headed to Newcastle for their Christmas party at the end of November. They had no game that weekend due to the fact United, their scheduled opponents, had made it to the Coca-Cola Cup final, where they would lose 3-0 to Celtic at Ibrox. After that one-sided final, Murdo MacLeod, Celtic's assistant manager, endorsed Hearts as legitimate rivals to his own team and Rangers in the battle for the championship. "Make no mistake, Hearts will be tough to stop," he said. "They are up there on merit and nobody should underestimate their title credentials."

At the very moment those words of praise were leaving the lips of MacLeod, Hearts' players were merry-making in England's north east, intoxicated by the dual combination of alcohol and table-topping joie de vivre. The positive effect of this close-knit squad's latest social gathering was temporarily dashed, however, when they returned to Edinburgh to find they had become front-page news in the Daily Record, accused of having behaved in a "loud and obnoxious" manner by another diner at Newcastle restaurant Sabatini's. Inappropriate songs, the smashing of glasses and plates, and dancing on tables were among the antics the woman pinpointed as having ruined her night. The Hearts players were furious at what they were reading. Jefferies called the restaurant to check it out for himself and found that staff had no issue with the way his squad had behaved. The Hearts

manager said the story was "ridiculous" and had been "blown out of all propor-
tion" as he accused the Glasgow-based newspaper of "trying to do this every year".
A few days later, in his weekly column in the Edinburgh Evening News, Locke
revealed that the players had held a meeting and after "getting the same treatment
over the last three years by the newspaper in question", they had "unanimously
decided that no-one will be speaking to any reporters from that newspaper".

"That report caused us a lot of problems and it wasn't true," recalls Pointon, the
chief organiser of the party. "We didn't do anything wrong. We had our own private room in the restaurant so we didn't bother anybody else. A woman had told
the paper we'd ruined her birthday but that was nonsense; she came in and had
her photograph taken with the players and we bought her a bottle of champagne,
so I don't see how we ruined her night. It happened at a time when any sort of story
about footballers on a night out was becoming big news. We were doing well, we
were at the top of the league, which probably added to it all from the newspaper's
perspective. But it really stuck in my throat because any time we went out, we tried
to do things sensibly, and still somebody found a way of coming up with a stupid
report."

Occasional nights out were key to this Hearts squad generating a level of togetherness few of the players involved ever experienced at other times in their
career. "It was the best bunch of boys I ever played with in terms of having a laugh
and socialising and things like that," says Fulton, whose sentiment was echoed by
others. With such a strong bond in the group, and a genuine belief in their ability
to sustain a title challenge, Hearts weren't about to let the fallout from their trip
to Newcastle knock them off course. On their return to action on the first weekend of December, goals from Cameron and Flögel secured a 2-0 home win over
Motherwell. "It was really impressive that we managed to get in the newspaper,"
laughs Flögel. "We had a really nice night out in Newcastle – and probably had a
bit too much to drink for our own good. The gaffer wasn't happy about it and said
we had to make up for it in the next game. Thankfully we beat Motherwell and
everything was forgotten about. When you're successful you can afford to go out
and have a beer now and again."

Hearts – having now won 11 of their last 12 league matches – ended the weekend
a point ahead of Rangers, who had played a game more, and a remarkable seven
clear of third-placed Celtic. "We started the season pretty well and just managed to
get the momentum going," recalls Hamilton. "Celtic and Rangers were struggling
a little bit in games, while we kept winning against the teams that we probably
didn't beat the year before in a consistent manner. We were just coming out the
stalls really quick and sometimes having the game wrapped up after half an hour."

While the threat of defending champions Rangers in particular was still taken
seriously, there was now a genuine belief at Hearts that they could win their
first league title since 1960. "At that point, we were thinking 'we're in with a right
chance here'," says Cameron. "Okay, we'd lost to Rangers and Celtic, but the only
other defeat we had up to that point was away to Dunfermline."

Hearts missed a chance to re-establish a four-point lead when – in their game in
hand over Rangers – they were held to a 0-0 midweek draw away to Dundee United

on a night most notable for the fact such a large travelling support descended on Tannadice that around 400 Jambos were locked out. This led to calls for all of Hearts' matches to be made all-ticket.

Jefferies' team were two points clear as they prepared for a critical, mettle-testing mid-December double-header against the Old Firm, with Celtic away followed by a home game against Rangers. "We had shown we could beat everyone else in the league but we knew if we were serious about winning the league, we had to do something in our games against the Old Firm," says Cameron.

Unfortunately, Hearts got the worst possible outcome of zero points from these two fixtures as they lost 1-0 at Celtic Park after a late goal from Craig Burley before crashing to a 5-2 defeat at home to ten-man Rangers. That demoralising afternoon – Gordon Durie scored a hat-trick for the visitors, who had Rino Gattuso sent off with almost a quarter of the match remaining – would go down as the last one in which Robertson scored a competitive goal for the club at Tynecastle. Hearts spent Christmas Day in third place, two points behind Rangers and one below Celtic. While they would have taken this scenario at the start of the season, there was a feeling in the Hearts camp that things could and should have been that bit better. "We didn't have a great December," rues Cameron. "When we lost those games against Celtic and Rangers, you start thinking 'have we really got a chance because whenever we come up against the Old Firm, we're not able to get victories'. That was four games against them with no points. Even if we'd got one victory out of those four games, I think that would have had a massive effect on us with regard to our chances."

Two days after Christmas, Hearts travelled to Dunfermline and got themselves back on track with a 3-1 victory. Hamilton, who had been the subject of interest from St Johnstone in early December during a period when he spent eight successive games on the bench, returned to the starting line-up and opened the scoring. There was also an own goal from Pars goalkeeper Ian Westwater and a long-range strike from Salvatori which would prove to be the Italian's only goal for the club. He celebrated by running gleefully towards Jefferies in the dugout. Hearts' supporters were admonished afterwards by Robinson after a champagne bottle and coins were thrown on to the East End Park pitch.

Up to second place after Celtic had lost away to St Johnstone, Hearts were buoyed further ahead of the New Year's Day derby at home to bottom-of-the-table Hibs when it was revealed that Jefferies – whose stock level was sky high – had signed a new five-year contract, tying him to the club until the end of 2002. It looked like a perfect start to 1998 was on the cards when Fulton scored twice in the opening ten minutes to put Hearts 2-0 up. Jefferies sensed a chance to avenge the 7-0 defeat he had endured as a Hearts player against Hibs exactly 25 years previously. "We were 2-0 up and started like a train, firing on all cylinders," recalls the manager. "Colin Cameron had a header hit the bar at 2-0. If that had gone in, we'd have gone on to win comfortably. Even Jim Duffy said that afterwards. We should have been out of sight, but Hibs got a goal out of nothing and got back into the game."

Second-half goals from Andy Walker and Pat McGinlay gave Hibs a 2-2 draw their second-half play probably merited and Hearts were left to lament the squandering of a golden chance to have returned to the top of the table, with third-placed Celtic going on to defeat leaders Rangers the following evening. With 11 days until their next fixture – a Monday-night trip to St Johnstone – Hearts flew to Portugal for a five-day warm-weather training camp at the luxury Club Barringtons complex in Vale de Lobo. In his Evening News column, Locke explained that Hearts were put through something resembling a "mini pre-season" at their Algarve base as they sought to banish any lingering negativity from a festive period in which they had won only one of their previous five games.

Jefferies had selection issues to ponder for the trip to Perth, with regular starters Pointon, Salvatori and Locke all suspended. In their place came Frail, who hadn't started since the 5-3 win over Kilmarnock; McPherson, making his first start of the season following injury issues; and Naysmith, who had featured only once previously in the season due to a combination of injury and diminished form. The 19-year-old left-back marked his return to the side by scoring a spectacular volley from the edge of the box and delivering a man-of-the-match performance in a 3-2 victory. Hamilton netted the other two goals. Hearts looked on course for back-to-back victories for the first time since November when they led 2-1 at Kilmarnock through a McCann strike and a Gus MacPherson own goal, but the hosts equalised with 14 minutes left. This 2-2 draw counted as a disappointment considering they had won so convincingly at Rugby Park earlier in the season. "Although we didn't lose any games between December and April, we were a bit hit and miss; there were too many draws in that period," says Cameron.

That match in Ayrshire saw Frail – a late substitute – make his last appearance for the club before he headed south to join Tranmere Rovers for £100,000. The former Dundee right-back, who could also operate in central midfield, had been touted for a Scotland call-up prior to sustaining a serious knee injury in March 1995, but he proved unable to get back to peak form and fitness in the three years thereafter. The departure of Frail – who would get a brief chance to manage Hearts under Vladimir Romanov some ten years later – was a rare piece of transfer activity in or out of Tynecastle in the 1997/98 campaign. Jefferies, who had a core group of around eight players who would usually start when fit, was pretty content with his squad. He ran the rule over various trialists, including Austrian defender Gunter Zeller, former Manchester United defender William Prunier and Belgian midfielder Axel Smeets, but ultimately deemed that they weren't ready to come in and make an instant contribution to a side operating on a different level to most – if not all – other teams in Scotland. The signing of Twente Enschede's former Motherwell left-back Rab McKinnon on a pre-contract for the start of the 1998/99 campaign showed that Jefferies, although in the thick of a three-way title race, wasn't taking his eye off the ball with regard to the sustained improvement of his team in the longer term.

After a 2-0 win at home to Dundee United at the end of January in which Cameron scored a double, Hearts were locked together with Rangers and Celtic on the 48-point mark; the three teams separated at the top of the table only by goal difference. When Rangers were held to a surprise 1-1 draw at home to Dunfermline on the first Saturday of February, Hearts and Celtic had the incentive of knowing that a victory in their eagerly-awaited showdown at Tynecastle the following day would take them two points clear of the Ibrox side at the summit. It looked like Celtic would be the team to do just that as they led through Jackie McNamara's first-half goal. However, substitute Quitongo forced in a scrappy 93rd-minute equaliser, sparking one of the wildest crowd celebrations ever witnessed inside Tynecastle and ensuring the three teams remained tied at the top for another week. "Oh man, I still get abuse from all my Celtic-supporting pals to this day for that goal," laughs Quitongo. "I've never seen Tynecastle rock like that; the place went mental, absolutely mental!"

With Hearts claiming their first point of the season against one of the Glasgow clubs, McCann believes that wintry Sunday of Gorgie bedlam was the day when many people truly started to believe the Tynecastle side might just have the bottle and resilience required to become the first non-Old Firm side to win the league since Aberdeen claimed back-to-back titles under the great Alex Ferguson in 1984 and 1985. "What an incredible atmosphere that was," exclaims McCann. "I actually had a swipe at it before wee Jose put it in the net, but if you watch the footage back when Jose scores, the camera is actually shaking. That was very, very real; Tynecastle was rocking. I remember Jim Jefferies and Murdo MacLeod were going at it at full-time. I think Murdo was annoyed about the amount of time the officials had added on because the full-time whistle went just after we scored. Celtic were furious but I believe the Hearts fans at that point were thinking 'we're gonna win the league' because that was a huge result for us."

That remarkable match against Celtic also marked the first attended in more than 30 years by Alfie Conn, one of Hearts' greatest-ever players who had never previously set foot in Tynecastle since being made to feel unwelcome by the club when his request to buy tickets for a match in the 1960s was declined. With just three months of the campaign remaining, Jefferies' players knew they had given themselves a real chance of writing their own names into club folklore alongside luminaries like Conn, who had been key to the club's success in the mid-1950s.

Next stop on this stirring Jambo adventure was Motherwell on Saturday 21st February, and it threw up the most dramatic match of the campaign for the huge travelling support. With Jefferies staying at home to nurse a back problem, assistant Brown took charge of the team. It looked like being a disastrous day for Hearts as goals from Owen Coyle and Willie Falconer put the hosts 2-0 up within 37 minutes. Staring down a barrel, the visitors suddenly "turned on the gas and blew them away", as McCann puts it. Hamilton pulled one back just before the break and once the big striker equalised just before the hour mark, there was only going to be one winner: goals from Fulton and Adam in the closing 25 minutes secured a stunning 4-2 victory to keep Hearts level at the top, alongside Celtic and Rangers on the 52-point mark. "That's one of the games from that season that really sticks in my head," says Hamilton. "We were 2-0 down less than 40 minutes into the game thinking 'oh no, what's happening here?' The boys actually talked about this later, if we went in 2-0 down, we could imagine Jim being on the phone from his house screaming his head off. Thankfully I managed to score just before half-time to make it 2-1 and that calmed us down a wee bit, and in the second half we were brilliant."

It was the second game in succession Hearts had come from behind to pick up a significant result. "That was a big game for me because it showed everyone we had a bit of resilience and fight about us, which we all knew anyway from training with each other," says McCann.

With Hearts enjoying the rare thrill of being in a title race in late February, they allowed Robertson – who hadn't started a league game since the New Year derby – to join First Division leaders Dundee on a month's loan with a view to honing his match sharpness and returning to Tynecastle for the run-in. The form of Hamilton and Adam in particular in the central attacking positions had made it difficult for the veteran to get the regular game-time he had been used to throughout his career. On the same Wednesday night that the legendary Hearts striker made his debut in a 2-1 win away to Partick Thistle which enhanced Dundee's second-tier title prospects, his parent club were doing likewise by taking Aberdeen apart for a third time at a packed-out Tynecastle. The 3-1 win, achieved by goals from Hamilton, the burgeoning Naysmith and McCann, took Hearts two points ahead of Rangers – who had drawn at Kilmarnock the previous night – and kept them level with Celtic. At this point, Hearts, with 59 goals from 26 league games, were the joint-highest scorers in the whole of Britain alongside Notts County, and even then the English Third Division leaders had the benefit of having played eight games more than Jefferies' scintillating side.

With the stakes growing higher with each passing game, Hearts faced another serious test of their credentials on the last day of February as they returned to Ibrox, scene of their opening-night 3-1 defeat. "Beat Rangers and you can take the title" was the headline on former Hearts player Eamonn Bannon's weekly column in the Evening News on the eve of the biggest game of their season yet. The capital's local paper made the unprecedented move of paying for Evening News advertising boards to adorn the periphery of the Ibrox pitch in order to help the Hearts players feel more at home inside a stadium where their players and supporters had so often been induced with trepidation as soon as the traditional pre-match tune of Simply The Best started reverberating. "I never felt we had any inferiority complex in terms of playing against Celtic and Rangers," says defender Weir. "Rangers were probably still the better team in terms of having the better players. If I'm being honest, they were probably still the benchmark; the ones you had to beat because they had been winning the league regularly. But we were a confident team and we thought on our day we could go to Ibrox or Celtic Park – or obviously at Tynecastle as well – and were capable of beating Rangers or Celtic."

On a snowy day in Govan, when an orange ball was required for the first half, Hearts came agonisingly close to achieving this feat. After McCann's opener was cancelled out by Jorg Albertz's deflected strike before the break, Hearts looked on course for a momentous victory when Hamilton netted from close range in the 76th minute and celebrated in front of the delirious Hearts fans housed in the bottom tier of the Broomloan Stand. In a match which saw both Rangers defender Richard Gough and his Hearts counterpart Murray sent off in the second half, the visitors' dreams of what would have been a hugely significant win in the context of the title race were dashed in the most gut-wrenching fashion imaginable when Albertz fired home a second deflected strike of the afternoon deep into stoppage time. "I remember sitting in the dressing-room absolutely devastated after that and the gaffer said 'that shows how far you've come that you're disappointed leaving Ibrox with a point'," recalls McCann.

There was at least some solace in the following days for Hamilton and Naysmith when they landed February's Bell's player of the month and young player of the month awards respectively. The next league game – the day after former Newcastle United and Blackburn Rovers midfielder Lee Makel joined in a £75,000 transfer from Huddersfield Town – brought a frustrating 1-1 draw at home to Kilmarnock, with Hearts showing signs, perhaps for the first time since the turn of the year, of feeling the strain of the title race. After a match in which McPherson's goal was cancelled out by John Henry in the first half, Killie midfielder Gary Holt expressed surprise at how quickly the home support had turned on their title-chasing players as they clung on for a barely-deserved point largely thanks to Rousset's heroics between the sticks. Hearts had gone into the match without the injured Adam and Cameron – who had started to feel the effects of a pelvic problem – and their woes were compounded when captain Locke was stretchered off with a serious-looking knee injury, leading to Makel being pitched in for his debut off the bench earlier than planned. Ominously, Hearts – having generally avoided injuries to key men in the first half of the season – were starting to find more of their main men entering the treatment room as the season drew closer to its conclusion. The impact of the two dropped points against Kilmarnock was softened slightly by the fact Rangers and Celtic – who were also feeling the pressure of one of Scotland's most significant and competitive post-war title races – both slipped up that mid-March weekend.

Two points behind leaders Celtic and three ahead of third-placed Rangers, Hearts headed to Tannadice with the backing of 5000 supporters. Twelve years after many of them had seen the team's previous genuine title challenge come to a heartbreaking end across the road at Dens Park, this time they were able to depart Tannadice Street with their dreams of glory still intact after an early goal from Hamilton – his 15th of the season – secured a 1-0 win over Dundee United and kept them within two points of Celtic ahead of the following weekend's top-of-the-table showdown at Parkhead. If Hearts were to win in Glasgow's east end on the final weekend of March they would be top of the league with just six games to play. Excitement levels were high all week in the capital as an army of 2000 Jambos prepared to make their way along the M8, with chairman Deans expressing disappointment that the club had been unable to source more tickets. In the build-up, Salvatori described the match as "similar to a cup final" in magnitude. Although Hearts were unable to pull off the game-changing victory they craved in Glasgow, they could be hugely satisfied with a strong display which secured a 0-0 draw and kept them within two points of top spot with half a dozen matches to go.

Of their six remaining fixtures, four were at Tynecastle. In addition, five of them were against sides who languished more than 20 points beneath them in the table. Even their home match against title rivals Rangers looked significantly less daunting in light of the fact Hearts had drawn their previous three matches against the Old Firm and the Ibrox side, who had just sold Paul Gascoigne to Middlesbrough, were in a strange and debilitating predicament of knowing several big names were due to be following manager Smith out the exit door at the end of the campaign. Given the pressure on both Rangers and Celtic – respectively obsessed with achieving and stopping ten in a row – there appeared to be a clear opportunity for Heart of Midlothian to banish the ghouls of 1986 and become champions of Scotland for the first time in 38 years.

All they had to do was hold their nerve and make the most of a fixture list that was as favourable as they could realistically have hoped for at such a critical phase of the season. In the second week of April, Hearts had a midweek game at home to a Motherwell side they had already beaten three times followed by a weekend trip across the city to face a Hibs team adrift at the foot of the table and staring down the barrel of relegation. With Rangers and Celtic due to meet in the final Old Firm game of the season the Sunday after the Edinburgh derby, there was every chance that if – as expected – Hearts had won both of those games, they would have been top of the league. Gallingly for the Edinburgh side, they botched their opportunity. On a nervy night in the Gorgie rain, Hearts looked like eking out a hard-fought win over Motherwell when McCann struck on the hour. However, the hosts – missing the hitherto ever-present and on-form Ritchie from their defence for the first time through injury – looked ill at ease in the last half-hour and as they dropped deeper and deeper, Tommy Coyne equalised for the luminous yellow-kitted visitors with 11 minutes left after Adam had given away possession cheaply on the half-way line. "That was the week that cost us," insists assistant manager Brown. "It was a really rainy night, we were sitting in the directors' box early on before the Motherwell game and the referee came and said 'I'll put it off if you want'. But we thought 'well, if we win tonight and we go to Easter Road and win on Saturday, we'll probably go clear at the top'. Unfortunately Motherwell scored late on and then we went to Easter Road and got beat 2-1. I think we were a better team than Rangers and Celtic but the five points we dropped in those two games, for me, cost us the league."

Having fallen four points adrift of Celtic after the Motherwell lapse, the Hibs match effectively counted as a last chance for Hearts to haul themselves back into contention. As mid-April sleet fell from the Leith sky, Robertson, back from his short loan stint at Dundee, came off the bench and gave the Tynecastle side a glimmer of hope of reviving their fading title bid when he fired in a 71st-minute free-kick to cancel out Barry Lavety's opener. It proved to be the little hitman's last-ever competitive goal for his beloved Hearts but ultimately it wasn't enough to keep them in the title hunt as Kevin Harper – instrumental in Hibs' New Year fightback in Gorgie – scored a shock winner for Alex McLeish's First Division-bound side with ten minutes left. It was Hearts' first defeat in any competition since the weekend before Christmas and, after Rangers won the Old Firm derby 2-0 at Ibrox the following day, it left them four points behind both of the Glasgow sides with just four games to play. "That Hibs game was the one that cost us," says Ritchie. "I think if we'd won that weekend at Easter Road we could still have had the chance to win the league. That was the one that knocked the wheels off the league run we were on."

With the wind well and truly removed from Hearts' sails, a 1-1 draw with

St Johnstone at Tynecastle – their third consecutive home game which ended with that scoreline – followed by a meek 3-0 home defeat by Rangers officially killed off any lingering hopes of Hearts winning the title, leaving the Old Firm to fight it out in the last couple of games. "I felt like we were the equal of the Old Firm that season although that argument is undermined by the fact we couldn't beat them in the league," says Fulton. "I genuinely felt we could have gone toe-to-toe with them right to the end. It was just in the closing weeks we let ourselves down against the likes of Kilmarnock, Motherwell and Hibs."

In their penultimate league fixture, with the pressure of fighting for the title having dissipated, Hearts drew 2-2 against Aberdeen at Pittodrie through goals from McCann and McPherson, who scored three times from defence across his last eight league appearances of the season. At the end of a match which meant little to them in the grand scheme of things, Hearts' travelling support were roused by news from Edinburgh that city rivals Hibs had officially been relegated following a 2-1 home defeat by Dundee United. On a more poignant note, that early-May Saturday was also the day Justin Fashanu, who had played for Hearts in the 1993/94 season, tragically took his own life.

After six league games in a row without a win, Hearts ended their stirring Premier Division campaign on a high note as they defeated Dunfermline 2-0 at sun-kissed Tynecastle. Adam and teenager Derek Holmes scored the goals on an emotional afternoon which saw McManus, Pointon and, most significantly, Robertson make their final appearances for the club. The victory – followed by a well-deserved lap of honour in front of their proud and appreciative supporters – meant third-placed Hearts finished seven points behind champions Celtic and just five adrift of a Rangers side who were left to lick their wounds after ending up without the league title for the first time in a decade. This gallant effort from Hearts was in stark contrast to three years previously when they had required a last-day victory over Motherwell to fend off the threat of relegation, but regret remains a prominent emotion among the players when reflecting on what might have been. "I definitely think to this day we kind of blew it a little bit in the league nearer the end, against the likes of Kilmarnock, Motherwell and St Johnstone at home," rues Hamilton.

A similar feeling prevails among Hearts' French contingent. "We felt we could win the league and I think we should have won it, to be honest," says Adam. "We finished seven points behind Celtic, which hadn't happened for quite a long time before or after that. We challenged as far as April and then we had a few injuries and dropped a few points that just killed us. Up to April, we were right up there, just two or three points behind them, so, yes, we definitely felt we could have won it."

Rousset pinpoints an inability to defeat the Old Firm in any of their head-to-heads as the key factor in why Hearts didn't get the title their magnificent football arguably deserved. "In terms of names, we weren't equal to Rangers and Celtic, but in terms of the football we played that year we were equal to them," he says. "We were a very attack-minded team; but that's why we lost so many times to Celtic and Rangers that season, because we were attacking all the time. They were much more experienced and more clever than us and they let us come on to them and then hit us on the break. I'm not saying we should have won the league, but I think we certainly could have won it. We dropped too many points towards the end but the biggest problem was that we didn't beat Celtic or Rangers. We lost three games against Rangers and drew one; we drew twice against Celtic and lost twice. We finished only seven points behind Celtic, so the difference was our direct matches against them. It was great because we competed nearly until the end but we were disappointed because we could have won it. It was a sign that we were vastly improved though."

Captain Locke rues Hearts' lack of squad depth in comparison to their moneyed Glasgow rivals. "The disappointing thing for me is that we were maybe just one or two signings short of winning the league," he says. "It's always difficult to challenge Rangers and Celtic over a season because of the strength in depth they always have and I think we were just a bit short in numbers towards the end when wee Mickey (Cameron) was struggling with his stomach, I was injured and others had a few wee niggles. We had boys with wee niggling injuries that were having to play whereas if we had a wee bit more strength in depth, boys would have been able to miss a game to get themselves fully fit. But with the money the gaffer spent, to challenge Rangers and Celtic right up to the last few games of the season was a brilliant achievement."

McCann sums up the lingering frustration at spurning an almighty opportunity to break an Old Firm stranglehold on the Scottish championship which, at the time of writing, is well into a fourth decade. "It's one of the biggest regrets in my career that we got ourselves into such a good position and let so many points slip towards the end of that season," says the winger, who went on to play for Rangers, Southampton and Scotland. "We lost against a Hibs side who were about to get relegated and drew at home to Kilmarnock, Motherwell and St Johnstone. If we could have got a couple of wins against the Old Firm, it would have changed everything but we just couldn't get over the line against them. But what really let us down was those results towards the end of the season against Kilmarnock, Motherwell, Hibs and St Johnstone. These teams weren't in our league as far as I'm concerned. They were nowhere near as good as us but we were probably just lacking that know-how.

"I've said many times in my media work over the years that you get a know-how when you win things. When I won titles at Rangers, I found that sometimes when games are going against you, there's still that belief that you've been there before and you know what's necessary to get over the line. I just think that Hearts side, as great as we were, we just didn't have that know-how because we hadn't won anything. I don't think it was anything to do with the pressure of failure from before because we didn't carry that burden as we were a new side. We carried the responsibility of trying to win something for a club that hadn't won something for a long time but the main thing we lacked, for me, was the know-how that the Old Firm generally possess. It was a real shame because, although we finished seven points behind Celtic, I'm telling you now, that Hearts side was every bit as good as the Celtic side that won the title. If we'd have won that league, I don't think anybody could have said we were lucky."

Cup Run

*"That was probably the only game we
found ourselves in a bit of trouble"*

The traditional end-of-season jaunt to Magaluf might have been a significantly less jovial affair for the Hearts players had their campaign concluded immediately after the final league game against Dunfermline Athletic. Plagued by galling thoughts of what might have been after missing out on a rare and golden chance to pip both Rangers and Celtic to the title, a bitter taste would surely have accompanied the many beers downed in the bars of the Majorcan party resort in the last week of May 1998.

Thankfully, Jim Jefferies' team had been spinning more than one plate in 97/98 and had given themselves one last chance to crown a memorable season with a tangible reward, the magnitude of which would override the disappointment caused by the unravelling of their bold bid to win the league. The Tennent's Scottish Cup final against Rangers, seven days after their closing Premier Division fixture, represented a lifeline for a group of players loaded with belief in their collective ability and driven by a desire to back it up in the form of glory. Hearts had earned this opportunity by capitalising on being drawn against lower-league teams in each of the four rounds en route to the final. "I wouldn't say it was easy but we certainly got a favourable draw," recalls defender Paul Ritchie. "We got a lot of good games at home, but we couldn't help that; you're not going to turn it down. To get to a cup final, you've got to beat the teams that are in front of you and I think we were very professional in the way we did things."

The journey began on Saturday 24th January with a third-round tie at home to Second Division Clydebank, a team Hearts had required a replay to see off at the same stage of the competition under Tommy McLean three years previously. While the Bankies of 1995 featured a 38-year-old Davie Cooper – with the legendary former Rangers, Motherwell and Scotland winger playing his last-ever first-team game that night at Tynecastle, just six weeks before he died of a brain haemorrhage – this time the most recognisable names in a side managed by Ian McCall were 37-year-old former Chelsea defender Joe McLaughlin and former Hearts full-back Fraser Wishart. Clydebank, who would go on to win promotion after finishing second in the third tier that season, arrived at Tynecastle on the back of a 15-game unbeaten run in all competitions.

Aside from Colin Cameron being dropped to the bench following a slight dip in his form and 22-year-old goalkeeper Roddy McKenzie starting in place of Gilles Rousset, who was laid low by flu, the Hearts team sent out to kick off their tilt at the 1998 Scottish Cup was arguably the strongest Jefferies could have picked. In a season featuring an array of sensational displays, the performance against Clydebank certainly wasn't one of their best, but they did enough to progress. After the visitors had struck the post through Davie Nicholls in the third minute, Thomas Flögel, who took Cameron's place in attacking midfield, eased the Tynecastle tension when he fired home the opener in 32 minutes. David Weir settled any lingering doubts about the outcome of the tie just after the hour by heading in a perfect free-kick delivery from Stephen Fulton, who was described afterwards by Jefferies as having been "the dominant force in the game". This 2-0 victory would represent the last time Hearts faced Clydebank before they disappeared from the Scottish professional set-up amid financial troubles a little over four years later.

While Hearts' underwhelming display had done little to warm the cockles of a crowd of 12,699 on a bleak January afternoon, word from across the city gave renewed reason for Gorgie cheer at full-time. On one of the rare occasions when both Edinburgh clubs played at home on the same day, those with transistor radios took great delight in informing their fellow supporters that John Millar had scored a double for First Division Raith Rovers in a 2-1 victory over Hibs at Easter Road. With the vibe after a low-key Hearts win always significantly enhanced by news of a popular former Jambo inflicting misery on the city rivals, "walking in a Millar wonderland" was the song of choice on the concourses of Tynecastle as supporters funnelled out the stadium towards the warmth of home or Saturday-evening hostelries. While Hearts' stretch of 42 years without winning the Scottish Cup was a source of ongoing frustration among their fans, their drought was less than half as long as that of Hibs, whose run without the old trophy had just been extended to 97 years at a time when they were sitting rock-bottom of the Premier Division. "No fan-fare but it's better than being a Hibees supporter today" was the unsubtle headline above the Hearts match report in Monday's Edinburgh Evening News.

The fourth-round draw was even kinder to Jefferies' side as they landed a home tie against Third Division Albion Rovers, the lowest-ranked team left in the competition. Managed by Billy McLaren, who had a brief spell as a Hibs player in the early 1980s, Rovers' most recognisable player was 33-year-old defender Ronnie Coyle, who had been a team-mate of Cameron's in Raith Rovers' revered 1994 Coca-Cola Cup-winning side. With Hearts expected to dominate possession, holding midfielder Stefano Salvatori was given the day off as Jefferies switched from his favoured 4-3-3 to go with two wingers in a 4-4-2 formation. This meant Jose Quitongo, who had been used predominantly as a substitute in his early months at Tynecastle, came in for only his second start for Hearts after scoring a stoppage-time equaliser in the league match against Celtic the previous weekend. At right-back, 21-year-old David Murie was handed what would be his only start of the season in the absence of Gary Locke, who missed out through illness, and Dave McPherson, who was out with a minor injury. "It was a hiding-to-nothing game for us," says Murie. "We were expected to win comfortably."

Played on St Valentine's Day, the tie proved more awkward for Hearts than most had anticipated, with Rovers holding firm for an hour before Quitongo made the breakthrough with a header in the 61st minute. Cameron put the game beyond doubt with a penalty five minutes later and then Quitongo ran clear of a stretched Rovers defence to add his second of the day and make it 3-0 with a couple of minutes left. "It was a difficult game," recalls the Angolan. "Albion Rovers played well in the first half and we missed a lot of chances. We were just happy to get the goals and go through because in the cups, no matter what team you are playing, anything is possible."

With five of their ten Premier Division rivals – Aberdeen, Hibs, Motherwell, Dunfermline and Kilmarnock – having been eliminated in the third and fourth rounds, Hearts were entitled to feel satisfied at progressing to the quarter-finals, even if it had been at the expense of two part-time teams. "Clydebank and Albion Rovers at home were tricky games for us because every Hearts fan went to those games not giving the opposition any credit and expecting us to win by three or four," says Locke. "It's always been like that at Hearts but it's usually not that straightforward. We didn't play brilliantly in the first two rounds but in the end we had too much for both teams."

Ahead of the draw for the last eight, Hearts supporters were hoping to avoid a trip to Glasgow to face Rangers or Celtic, with a home tie against one of the three First Division sides still in the competition – Dundee, Falkirk or Ayr United – the clear preference. As had been the case in the previous round, they hit the jackpot by landing a home draw against Ayr, the lowest-ranked remaining team. Managed by Gordon Dalziel – another of Cameron's Coca-Cola Cup-winning teammates from Raith – Ayr featured a familiar face in their squad in the shape of Ian Ferguson, a striker who had scored ten goals for Hearts in a two-year stint at Tynecastle between 1991 and 1993. With the exception of the injured Stephane Adam, Jefferies was able to send out a near-full-strength team of Rousset, Locke, Weir, Ritchie, Naysmith, Cameron, Salvatori, Fulton, Flögel, Hamilton and McCann. In front of a crowd of almost 16,000, Hearts – given a fright when Ayr's Laurent D'Jaffo hit the post early on – took a ninth-minute lead through a lovely finish from Ritchie with the outside of his left foot. It proved to be the defender's only goal of the 1997/98 season and was arguably the best of his career. "It was certainly right up there as one of my best," says Ritchie. "I think my header for Scotland against the Czech Republic (in a Euro 2000 qualifier in Prague in 1999) was a decent goal as well but for a centre-back that cannae play, the touch and finish wasn't too bad!" Hearts looked in total command when Flögel headed in the second in the 16th minute, but Ferguson pulled one back just two minutes later. Ayr's hopes of rescuing the tie suffered a significant blow when they had the experienced Derek

Anderson sent off for aiming a kick at Hamilton just before the break. Hearts eventually went on to make the scoreline more emphatic as goals in the last half-hour from Fulton and Hamilton – after a comical blunder from Ayr goalkeeper Kristjan Finnbogason – sealed a 4-1 victory. "It was another tricky one," says Locke. "We were 2-0 up and battering them and then big Fergie scored against the run of play to get them back in it. But just with the extra quality we had in the team, we ended up getting a third and then a fourth."

Hearts were joined in the semi-final draw by Rangers, Celtic and Falkirk. Although they had drawn their two previous meetings with the Old Firm, the First Division side were the opponents most supporters wanted; and once again they got their wish. For the third round in succession, Hearts were paired with the lowest-ranked side left in the competition as they were drawn against Falkirk, the former club of Jefferies, Billy Brown, Weir and Fulton. Just the previous year, Weir had been at Ibrox to support the Bairns in their Scottish Cup final defeat by Kilmarnock. Similarly, Falkirk had in their ranks three former Hearts players in Scott Crabbe, David Hagen and Neil Berry. In addition to the personnel links between the teams, the other main talking point was where the game would be played. With Hampden out of commission due to the redevelopment of the main stand, Hearts were eager to ensure that Easter Road wasn't considered as they didn't deem it big enough to accommodate all of their supporters. Edinburgh City Council had written to the Scottish Football Association proposing Murrayfield as a potential venue, but in the end Ibrox was selected after Celtic won a ballot to host their semi-final against Rangers at Parkhead the following day.

Falkirk went into the semi-final engulfed by turmoil after a debt of £1.5 million forced them to enter provisional liquidation (or what is now known as administration) just two weeks before the meeting with Hearts. With the club's future in genuine jeopardy, the Bairns players were well aware of the importance of trying to reach the final to generate a much-needed revenue boost. If this counted as any kind of additional motivation to Alex Totten's side, they were also driven by a desire to make the final in honour of their physio Bob McCallum – a former colleague of Jefferies – who had died after collapsing in the Brockville dressing-room just three months previously.

Hearts started the match without two key players through injury in the shape of captain Locke and deputy skipper Fulton, who was otherwise an ever-present throughout the 1997/98 campaign. Grant Murray, who was in the midst of a rare run of six consecutive starts, filled the right-back position, while Dave McPherson, who had endured an injury-ravaged campaign, started on the bench alongside Quitongo and Lee Makel, who had arrived at the club three weeks previously. Falkirk's starting XI included Berry, Crabbe and 35-year-old former Hibs winger Kevin McAllister, while Hagen started on the bench. "It was good going to Ibrox and having the majority of the crowd behind you rather than against you for a change," says McCann of an afternoon in which Hearts' supporters made up the bulk of an attendance of 31,587.

Despite seeing their team open the scoring after just six minutes, when Adam knocked in a Hamilton cross at the Broomloan end, any expectations of a smooth afternoon in Govan failed to come to fruition. "After I scored early on, I thought we would be alright," says Adam. "But very strangely, after that we didn't play our best and Falkirk challenged us quite a lot."

Locke, who had been invited to help Jefferies and Brown prepare and cajole the team on matchdays during this particular injury lay-off, was watching on anxiously from the dugout, praying his team-mates would earn him the chance to be able to lead Hearts out in the final. "That was probably the only game in the run to the final where we found ourselves in a bit of trouble," says Locke. "Kevin McAllister was brilliant. I wouldn't say they outplayed us but we looked a bit nervous that day. I think it was just a mixture of the expectation on us, the boys being desperate to win something and Falkirk being under slightly less pressure than us because they were from the league below."

As Falkirk sought to cancel out Adam's early opener, McAllister was giving 19-year-old left-back Naysmith the most difficult afternoon of his fledgling career. At that point, Jefferies must have wished he had the more experienced Neil Pointon to call on off the bench. The manager tore into Naysmith at half-time, with Hearts players on more than one occasion having since recounted the story of how the manager had the youngster pinned up by the throat with "his feet dangling in the air". Jefferies dismisses this tale, adamant that it has grown arms and legs with the passing of time. "It's absolute nonsense, that one," laughs the manager. "I've heard it claimed that I said if we lost the game, it would all be Gary's fault. I would never say that to a player. Yes, we pointed out what he needed to do better but the suggestion that I had him by the scruff of the neck is just nonsense. Everybody always tries to make things sound better and more dramatic than they were."

Regardless of how they were delivered, Jefferies' half-time instructions appeared to have a positive effect on Naysmith, who coped slightly better after the break against a player described afterwards by Totten as having the best individual performance he had ever seen. "The gaffer obviously didn't think Gary was getting tight enough to McAllister," laughs Locke. "I had sympathy for wee Gaz, though, because I've been there before where, as a full-back, you find yourself up against a winger who's at the top of their game and they just give you a roasting. That's what happened that day; McAllister was sensational and Gary didn't have the best of games."

With Cameron hindered by an ongoing pelvic problem and Flögel having what he himself describes as an "absolutely shite" performance, Hearts made a double substitution midway through the second half, with Makel and Quitongo introduced in place of the struggling midfield pair. "We weren't at it at all, which was strange for us," says McCann. "I wouldn't say it was down to nerves, I think it was mainly down to how Falkirk played, and that probably made it a harder game than we expected."

Just as Hearts looked like they might be about to hold on for a barely-deserved victory, McAllister capped his incredible display by arcing a sensational 20-yard strike high beyond the helpless Rousset with five minutes left. As Falkirk's fans celebrated, the Edinburgh club's shellshocked supporters sensed a return of the type of semi-final despair they had become accustomed to in the nine years prior to Jefferies' arrival. Chairman Leslie Deans, watching from the directors' box, had his head in his hands. "With five minutes left, I'd have been relieved to have come back for a replay," he recalls. The players, too, could feel the tension. "When Falkirk scored, I thought we were in trouble because they had been putting us under pressure," says Adam. "I was worried we were going to throw it away. The main thing I remember was the pressure because everybody expected us to get to the final. As players we expected to get to the final and we felt we deserved to get to the final because of the season we had had. But we certainly put ourselves under pressure. Thankfully we ended the game well which was the most important thing."

Hearts, wary of a late sucker punch from their crisis-hit First Division opponents, summoned fresh impetus in the dying moments, with McCann the driving force. In the 89th minute, the winger, who had been kept quiet for most of the game, was released down the left by a pass from Adam and skinned the veteran Berry before crossing for the French striker to force in his second of the match. McCann then sealed a 3-1 win himself in stoppage-time when he left Berry in his slipstream once more and clipped the ball home. "I think Falkirk thought they were going to go on and win it after they scored, but we had the ability to turn the heat on and open teams up," the winger explains. "When teams left space against us, that's when we were at our best. I remember just getting the ball and going by Neil Berry. I always knew Stephane was quick enough to keep up with me and that he'd be in the middle of the goals, so I knew once I'd gone past Neil that I just had to clip it into the area and take out (goalkeeper) Paul Mathers, who was coming towards the near post, for Stephane to tap it in. When I stuck the third past Mathers, I went down on to my knees behind the goal and I knew we were in the cup final. What a feeling that was."

Hearts learned the following evening that they would play Rangers in a cup final for the third time in two years after the Ibrox side defeated their city rivals 2-1 in the other semi at Celtic Park through goals from Ally McCoist and Jorg Albertz. With Hampden still unavailable, the match would take place at Celtic Park – the first Scottish Cup final to be staged there since 1993 – on Saturday 16th May, a week after the last league fixture. That would also be the same day as the FA Cup final between Arsenal and Newcastle United, meaning the Scottish and English showpiece matches would be played on the same day for the first time since 1992, when Rangers beat Airdrieonians 2-1 at Hampden and Liverpool defeated Sunderland 2-0 at Wembley on 9th May. "Once the dust settled and we realised we were in the final, we were all discussing our prospects and there was no doubt among the boys that we could win it," says McCann. "We knew we were a better team than the one that had run them close in the Coca-Cola Cup final the season before so we were full of confidence."

Hearts certainly hadn't been at their best in any of their first four Scottish Cup matches, but ultimately had scored a creditable 12 goals and conceded just two en route to the final. Fulton was buying into the notion among the club's embattled but increasingly optimistic supporters that this might finally be Hearts' year. "Things seemed to be going in our favour," he recalls. "We couldn't have asked for an easier run to the final. All our games were at home against teams from lower leagues and then we had Falkirk in the semi. You start to think it might be written in the stars."

Build-up

*"The Hearts board in 98 never
quibbled about a penny"*

Shortly after Stephen Fulton had returned home from helping Hearts defeat Dunfermline Athletic 2-0 on the last day of the league campaign, his sister-in-law, Ashley, arrived at his house in Cumbernauld armed with her hairdressing kit. The midfielder's three young sons – Jay, Dale and Tyler – watched on with a mixture of intrigue and amusement as their aunt set about dying their father's hair peroxide blond. This was to be Fulton's eye-catching new look for the following weekend's Scottish Cup final. When he rocked up at Edinburgh Airport the next morning to meet the rest of the squad ahead of their pre-cup final trip to the Midlands, Fulton – as was so often the case – found himself getting ribbed by his team-mates. "Me and Jose Quitongo had a wee agreement that we'd get our hair done if we got to the final but he backed out of it!" Fulton explains. "I don't know why I did it because I'm not actually one who likes the limelight and dying your hair blond kind of goes against that." Quitongo was also teased by the rest of the squad as he hadn't stuck to his side of the bargain. "I tried it and my hair turned ginger so I had to dye it back," the Angolan laughs. "Fulters actually suited that hair!"

The relaxed, upbeat mood in the Hearts camp the weekend before the final was in stark contrast to that of their opponents. As the players boarded their Sunday-morning flight to London Heathrow in good spirits, their Rangers counterparts – serial winners within Scottish football – were waking up to a realisation that, after nine successive years of league title glory, their dominance of the Scottish Premier Division was finally over; they had missed the opportunity to win a record tenth title in a row. While Hearts were beating Dunfermline in the Gorgie sunshine and rediscovering the verve and confidence that had eluded them for much of the previous month, Walter Smith's men were playing out a 2-1 victory over Dundee United at Tannadice which was rendered meaningless by the fact

Celtic defeated St Johnstone 2-0 at Parkhead to remain two points clear of the Ibrox side at the end of a remarkable league campaign.

Of course, until just four weeks previously, Hearts had also been heavily involved in this battle for the championship before their challenge fizzled out after the gut-wrenching 2-1 defeat away to bottom-of-the-table Hibs on Saturday 11th April. As everyone connected with the Tynecastle club could testify from their bitter memories of May 1986, if you're going to miss out on a league title, it's probably best that it doesn't happen on the last day of the season, the week before a cup final. "If we'd gone on to lose the 98 final, after the way we fell away in the league, I'd probably have been able to understand how Gary Mackay and Robbo (John Robertson) felt after losing the league and the cup in 86," Fulton acknowledges. "But even though we'd fallen away in the league, I had no doubt in my mind that we could pick ourselves up for the cup final. We never got enough points against the Old Firm to finish ahead of them but we had been close enough to them in most of our games. It wasn't like previous years when you'd look up at the scoreboard at Ibrox or Parkhead and see yourself 4-0 down. That Hearts team had something more about us so there was no fear going into it. It was the third time we were playing that Rangers team in a cup final in three seasons. The first time we got pumped off them, the second time we were a lot closer and so when it came to the third time, we were thinking 'right, this is the time we're going to do it'. There was a lot of pressure on Rangers as well. They had just lost the league and the team was all breaking up. I felt there were loads of factors in our favour."

With the benefit of hindsight, it seems fair to surmise that it was something of a blessing in disguise for Hearts that their title bid was effectively ended with four league games still to play, allowing just over a month in which to dust themselves down and recover, both mentally and physically, ahead of the final. After losing at Easter Road, and slipping four points behind both Rangers and Celtic with four games remaining, they were left with only one realistic prize to shoot for and all their eggs duly went into the Scottish Cup basket. "After we were out of the title race, we were able to put all our focus and energy on the cup final," says midfielder Thomas Flögel.

As galling as it was at the time, Hearts effectively had five weeks before the defining match of their season in which to banish the deep disappointment of missing out on a title they felt for long periods of the campaign was within their grasp. The last four league matches were basically an exercise in trying to restore some spark and poise to a team which had lost its mojo around Easter time. Gary Naysmith, Stefano Salvatori, Paul Ritchie, Flögel, Stephane Adam and Colin Cameron, who was battling a pelvic problem, all sat out at least one of the four season-closing fixtures as players were given the opportunity to recharge batteries and refocus minds after the strain of a three-way title battle ultimately proved too much. When Hearts lost 3-0 at home to Rino Gattuso-inspired Rangers in their penultimate home match, just three weeks before the final, it was hard to see how the hosts could take any positives from it. On the afternoon of Saturday 25th April, after witnessing their beleaguered team lose three or more goals to their cup final opponents for the third time in four meetings, 13,000 demoralised Hearts fans filtered out of Tynecastle fearing the worst about their upcoming rematch with the Ibrox side. Crucially, though, Jefferies and Billy Brown were able to use this setback – their last defeat of the season – to help them plot a path to glory.

"I remember vividly going to see Jim on the Thursday before the last league game against Dunfermline, so nine days before the cup final," recalls football journalist Graham Spiers, who was writing for the Scotland on Sunday newspaper at the time. "I always got on well with Jim; he seemed to take a shine to me for some reason. I said to him 'look Jim, I need to come and see you to preview the final. Can I have half an hour with you by myself?'. That was probably a bit selfish of me because he was doing loads of other media stuff to preview the final. It was at the end of the working day, possibly about 4.30pm. I arrived at the traditional pre-re-built Tynecastle main stand and he took me into his office. Jim was a bit cagey at first but then he said something along the lines of 'I don't know if I should tell you this but I've been speaking to Billy (Brown) about it and we've decided to do something totally different for this final'. Hearts had been unable to get a result against Rangers in each of the games against them that season so Jim and Billy were going to spend the next week in training working on a new idea and a new system. I remember sitting thinking 'gosh, this is quite revealing stuff' and Jim joked at the end 'what the hell have I been telling you?'."

Although the main part of Jefferies' work in the closing weeks of the league campaign revolved around trying to raise morale levels within his squad while pondering team selection and tactics for the final, there were plenty other things to be taken care of ahead of the big day; most notably, how they were going to spend the week leading up to the final. "The board of directors were brilliant for us in terms of the preparations," recalls Jefferies. "We had our disagreements at times but when it came to preparations for a game, I don't think they could have supported me any better. Preparation is huge. I remember when I was Kilmarnock manager and we lost 5-1 to Hibs in the 2007 League Cup final, I didn't think our preparations were as good as they should have been. Money was tight for Kilmarnock at that time and you can't do all these nice things for nothing. But the Hearts board in 98 never quibbled about a penny. They said to us 'we've got to get this right sometime and we don't want to lose out through a lack of preparation'. They gave us everything we required and all they wanted in return was the Scottish Cup! We did it sensibly – we didn't go over the score – but we knew we'd left nothing to chance."

On the recommendation of Scotland manager Craig Brown, Jefferies decided to take the squad to the Midlands, where they would spend the early part of cup-final week working on the new gameplan – alluded to by Spiers – at the impressively-maintained training fields of the National Farmers Union Mutual Headquarters on the outskirts of Stratford-upon-Avon. The club duly booked for the squad to stay from Sunday to Tuesday at the Forest of Arden Hotel and Country Club near Birmingham and then the Tuesday night at the Ettington Park Hotel in Stratford before their return flight to Edinburgh on Wednesday afternoon.

A squad of 20 made the trip south: Gilles Rousset, Roddy McKenzie, David Murie, Grant Murray, Dave McPherson, David Weir, Ritchie, Allan McManus, Naysmith, Neil Pointon, Salvatori, Lee Makel, Fulton, Cameron, Flögel, Quitongo, Neil McCann,

Robertson, Jim Hamilton and Adam. The one notable absentee from the travelling party was captain Gary Locke, who stayed in Edinburgh for extensive treatment on a knee problem as he attempted to make a miracle late recovery in time to be involved in the final. Upon arrival at Forest of Arden – a salubrious golf resort set within 10,000 acres of ancient woodland – on the Sunday afternoon, some of the players enjoyed a round of golf with Jefferies and his backroom staff at the complex, while others – including Weir, Fulton and Quitongo – chose to watch the final day of English Premiership action on television; with Arsenal having already won the league, this was a day most notable for Everton fans invading the Goodison Park pitch after a 1-1 draw with Coventry City saw them avoid relegation at the expense of Bolton Wanderers. Having played a match the previous day, some of the players also visited the on-site spa and swimming pool to unwind.

That evening Jefferies and his backroom staff enjoyed a beer together in the hotel as they crystallised the instructions they were about to start imparting to their players the following morning. The manager had a strong idea by this point of what his starting XI would be. He was already resigned to the likelihood that Locke – his first-choice right-back – would miss out, while he was hopeful that key duo McCann and Cameron would be fit enough to start despite their own injury issues. Regardless of which personnel would be available on the day, however, Jefferies was clear in his mind about exactly how he wanted to approach the game; and it involved a notable change of tact. "We had generally played 4-3-3 most of the season and got great credit for our attacking play as we ran Celtic and Rangers close," says Jefferies. "But in our first meeting when we got down south at the start of the week, we told them that we'd be working on a different gameplan. We read out the facts because for all the plaudits we'd had that season, the best we did against Rangers was a draw at Ibrox and we had lost 13 goals in the four league games against them. We'd been losing an average of three goals per game against them and we told the players we couldn't afford to give them a three-goal start this time.

"We'd always attacked Rangers but they were a great team who had proved they could handle it and had the players to punish us, as they did on a few occasions. We thought if we let them come on to us, we could handle it, especially with the players they had available to them. The main threats for Rangers around that period had been Paul Gascoigne, Brian Laudrup and Jorg Albertz. Gascoigne had left by that point, Laudrup was playing his last game before going to Chelsea and Albertz was suspended after getting sent off in the last league game against Dundee United. Albertz missing out was a big thing for me because he had been digging them out of a lot of difficult situations with free-kicks and long-distance shots. The likes of Ian Ferguson, Stuart McCall and Rino Gattuso were great players but they weren't necessarily players who would hurt you. We said 'look, if we can keep it tight and make it hard for them, we could maybe hit them on the break rather than the other way about'. We'd had enough praise that season for the way we had played but I said to the players that I don't think anyone will care how we play in this game if we win the cup."

From shackle-free 4-3-3, Hearts were preparing to go into their biggest match of the season playing a functional, safety-first 4-5-1 formation. "The gaffer explained very early in the week which way he wanted us to play, so we were ready," says goalkeeper Rousset, who had full faith in Jefferies' approach. "I didn't really think too much about the change of tactics. I had so much respect for Jim and Billy that they could have asked me to play up front and I'd have done that. I had no problem with us being more defensive. I just thought 'okay, no problem, let's go for it'."

Jefferies was keen to keep his players on their toes, so delayed naming the starting XI until Wednesday, with the substitutes announced on the day of the game itself. The first man given confirmation of his involvement in the squad was 33-year-old club legend Robertson, who had fallen down the pecking order and was alert to the likelihood that this would be his last match as a Hearts player. "Nobody knew what the team was but I pulled Robbo aside at the start of the week and told him he was going to be a sub," says Jefferies. "Although he wasn't in the team, he was happy that he wasn't being left out of the squad altogether."

Following friction with certain sections of the press throughout the season, and with Jefferies keen to ensure a degree of privacy for his players, the Edinburgh Evening News was the only media outlet allowed to accompany Hearts to England, albeit Hazel Irvine of the BBC would be given access to training on the Tuesday. On the back page on Saturday 9th May, the capital's local paper took great delight in proclaiming to its readers that "The club have banned all newspapers, radio and television from their English headquarters – except the NEWS!". Martin Dempster had been the paper's Hearts correspondent since shortly before Jefferies' appointment and had struck up a strong rapport with the manager and his players. It remains a source of pride to the journalist that he had earned the trust of Jefferies enough to be granted exclusive no-holds-barred access to the team on what would be such an historic week. "That was such a special few days in my career," says Dempster. "The training facility there was absolutely fantastic and I was part of the whole thing that week which was a real privilege. I think the only thing I didn't get to be part of was the meeting they had to discuss what the win bonus would be in the final, which was totally understandable. The fact they gave that sort of permission for me to be there, I think said a lot about the relationship that myself and the paper had with Hearts, and Jim and Billy in particular at that time. I was able to watch all the training sessions, have lunch with them and I had a round of golf with Jim and some of his staff at Forest of Arden. I got great access to the players and it was a fantastic thing to be part of."

Dempster watched on with fascination as Jefferies tried to instil a more defensive mindset into a team accustomed to playing free-flowing attacking football. "They had played Rangers four times that year and lost three of them," says the journalist. "Rangers had their number so Jim and Billy knew they had to come up with a system that gave them a chance to compete and beat Rangers. That was basically 4-5-1, and they worked really hard on it those few days in England."

While the Hearts players were being put through their paces down south away from the public glare, excitement levels were being ratcheted up among their supporters back in Edinburgh. The last of the club's 22,000 tickets were snapped up from the ticket office, while Jambos flocked in their numbers to the club shop to grab some merchandise for the big day. "It was a crazy week," recalls Clare Cowan, a childhood Hearts fan from Broomhouse who had just become the club's retail manager a few months previously. "The shop was going like a fair. People wanted anything they could get their hands on: wigs, foam fingers, scarves, t-shirts, you name it. The shop stayed open later and there was just such a buzz about the place; it was brilliant."

Well aware that the club's struggles to win silverware had become a big talking point within Scottish football, the Hearts players were happy to be away from the hullabaloo as they focused on the task at hand. "I think it was the right thing for us to go away in the week leading up to it rather than being up in Scotland for the whole week," says Fulton. "Especially round about Edinburgh, you knew there was a sense of tension whenever Hearts were going to a semi-final or a final. I could detect it and I hadn't been at the club for a particularly long time. Apart from Robbo, none of us had played through 1986 and all that but it was still a stigma associated with the club. Although most of us weren't Hearts supporters we had all developed an affinity with the club. Some of the guys had lost the two previous cup finals against Rangers and most of us had lost the previous one. I was well aware of the reputation Hearts had of being the bridesmaids and things like that. I remember well the day Hearts lost the league in 86 because I was away with Scotland Schoolboys and big Alan McLaren, who was a Hearts fan, was there. He was pretty much in tears. From then on, it was all about how Hearts would let their bottle crash. The only way you're getting rid of that reputation is by winning something."

Striking the balance between keeping the players focused and relaxed was of huge importance to the management team. "It was a big week for us," recalls assistant manager Brown. "We went away to get away from all the furore back home, with the papers all talking about Rangers and how many cups they've won and stuff like that. We wanted to go away somewhere, keep ourselves quiet and concentrate on preparing for the game. We prepared really well. There were certainly no drinking sessions that week, that's for sure."

After a double training session on the Tuesday, the squad checked into Ettington Park – a peaceful 19th-century country house with peacocks roaming perfectly-manicured lawns – and the players enjoyed a laugh together as they attempted to play some croquet, with Robertson proclaiming himself the top performer. The jovial mood was added to when Quitongo was ambushed by a group of teammates in the hotel grounds and stripped of his wacky all-in-one Lycra running suit, which he had been given by a sponsor. Fulton duly squeezed into the little Angolan's outfit and larked around on the grass, to the amusement of his colleagues. "It was revenge for him not dying his hair, but wee Jose's gear was a bit skintight on me!" recalls Fulton. "I was left with just my pants on," laughs Quitongo. "It was so funny."

Spirits were further raised later that evening when word reached the squad that Hearts' youth team, managed by Peter Houston, had won the BP Youth Cup for the first time in five years after a side containing future first-team mainstays Scott Severin and Robbie Neilson defeated Dundee United 2-0 in the final at Tynecastle in front of a crowd of 3470. "I was at Tynecastle on my own taking my youth team and all the boys and the coaching staff in England were waiting for reports from the game," recalls Houston, who would otherwise have been in Stratford helping Jefferies and Brown prepare the first team. "The phone call after the game to tell the boys in England the news that we'd won was great."

The success of the club's youngsters was overshadowed somewhat, however, when it emerged that chief executive Chris Robinson had been accused of calling angry Hearts supporters "parasites" after they questioned him outside the stadium about why their season-tickets weren't valid for free entry to the Youth Cup final. On the front page of Wednesday's Evening News, Robinson was pictured remonstrating with three supporters above the headline "I'm sorry for ticket row". The chief executive admitted calling those he had become embroiled with "petty" and "pathetic" but strongly denied branding them "parasites", even though the Evening News photographer backed up the supporters' claims that this was the word he had used. While Robinson battled in vain to calm this unwanted storm just a few days before his club's biggest game of the season, there were several nuggets of good news which helped nurture a generally positive vibe throughout the week for Hearts' players and supporters. In a huge boost to the club, Ritchie, who was due to run out of contract in the summer and had been linked with Newcastle United and Aston Villa, put the finishing touches to a new two-year deal down in Stratford while his defensive sidekick Weir got confirmation on the Wednesday that he had been included in the Scotland squad for the World Cup in France the following month. This news was slightly soured for Hearts by the fact none of Cameron, Ritchie, McCann or Fulton – all of whom had been in the Scotland B squad and touted as potential contenders – made the cut. Salvatori, being interviewed by Dempster for the Evening News, was baffled by the squad announcement. "I'm delighted for David but why have Steve Fulton, Neil McCann and Colin Cameron not been picked as well?" the Italian wondered. "Fulton, in particular, has had a fantastic season and I can't believe he is not going to France. Yet Craig Brown has decided to take some players who have not even been playing for their club. That would never happen in Italy."

Any disappointment for Cameron, Fulton, McCann and Ritchie over not making the Scotland squad was offset when Jefferies told the players what his cup final starting line-up would be on the Wednesday morning, before they left the Midlands to fly back to Edinburgh later that day. Rousset, McPherson, Weir, Ritchie, Naysmith, Flögel, Salvatori, Fulton, Cameron, McCann and Adam were the eleven men who would be leading Hearts into battle. "The team selection was difficult," recalls Jefferies. "It was picked so we could play that 4-5-1 system but also have enough legs to get at Rangers when we got on the ball. It was all about getting the right players in the right holes. Every manager in the world has put players in positions they're not totally comfortable playing but every player in that final was comfortable in the position they were playing. The back four virtually picked itself. With Lockey out, Slim (McPherson) was always going to play. Rangers had people like Richard Gough and Lorenzo Amoruso so we needed that height for set-plays and things like that. Davie was a good player with experience and you need that in cup finals. We had a few youngsters in the team and Davie had played in cup finals before so he'd have been a difficult player to leave out. We had a few options at right-back. Flögel could play there and Grant Murray had played there, but with Davie being an ex-Rangers player, I knew nothing would faze him.

"The most difficult one was leaving Jim Hamilton out because he was a goal threat who was great in the air. I think most people probably expected us to play with our usual three of McCann, Hamilton and Adam, perhaps with Adam playing in off the right. That would have been a more attacking team. But rather than putting Adam and Hamilton together through the middle, we decided to put Adam through the middle on his own, where he could get in behind and run on to things, and Flögel out on the right. Thomas was a disciplined player and we felt that would give us a good balance with him and Neil out wide and three midfield players. It was set up to effectively be a five-man midfield when we didn't have the ball. We didn't want to take away their attacking instincts but we just wanted to play in a slightly more pragmatic way."

The substitutes, although not named until the Saturday, would be strikers Robertson and Hamilton, along with Murray, the homegrown 22-year-old Hearts fan who had made only 12 previous starts for his boyhood club. "Grant could play as a defender or in midfield if somebody like Salvatori had got injured," Jefferies explains. "He had come in late in the season and never let us down. He was a steady Eddie; a good competitor who was very disciplined and just got on with his job. People like Lee Makel, who was great for us, wee Quitongo, who had played in the earlier rounds, Allan McManus and Neil Pointon were all in the frame. I wish I could have stripped them all but we only had three subs so you try and pick players who can cover you in different positions, and Grant could do that. He was there if we needed him."

Jefferies and his team were in buoyant mood by the time they arrived home on the Wednesday evening following a hugely positive and productive stint in Shakespeare country. "The spirit down in England had been fantastic," says Adam. "There was no sense of pressure. I think that few days in England was when we really started to believe we were going to win the final. Jim and Billy spoke about the tactics and we worked really well. There was quality in the training, lots of goals being scored, and everybody was having a laugh. You could feel there was a real confidence in the squad. It was a very important few days. My feeling when we travelled back to Edinburgh was that we were going to win that cup."

Adam's recollection more than two decades on tallies with the vibe that was evident at the time. In his Evening News cup final diary from England, Ritchie had written on the Tuesday that "I don't mind telling you that I already have a picture in my head of Steve Fulton, with his bleach blond hair, going up to lift the Scottish Cup". This theme of Gorgie bullishness was continued the following day when Jefferies was quoted as saying he had "a gut feeling about Saturday" and was "definitely detecting a genuine belief among the players". While respectful of the Rangers threat, there was certainly no hint of Hearts being intimidated by their more illustrious opponents. "We were all so confident," recalls Weir. "Jim and Billy always made you believe you could win any game, particularly a big game or a one-off game. You always went in with the belief that you had the capabilities of winning. Rangers had just lost the league and were on a wee bit of a downer so we felt we had a chance, there's no doubt about that. We were confident and excited."

On the Thursday, the players had a light training session at Tynecastle before carrying out a series of interviews with various journalists on the pitch and in the stands as the team staged their official pre-cup final media day. On the eve of the match, Hearts received yet more positive news as Ritchie landed the Bell's Premier Division young player of the year award while Jefferies was named as Bell's Premier Division manager of the year. On the Friday afternoon, the Hearts squad, loaded with belief and overnight luggage, boarded the coach – driven, as always, by Alan "Scooby" Scott – and headed along the M9 to their pre-match base, the Dunblane Hydro. "By the end of the week, Jim and Billy had done a great job preparing us for the final and had given us the belief that we could win it," said McPherson. Following a squad meal and the usual exchange of banter in the hotel lobby, the players retreated to their bedrooms primed for glory. The rooming combinations – as had also been the case down in England earlier in the week – included: Rousset with Adam, Weir with Fulton, Quitongo with McKenzie, Ritchie with Cameron, Flögel with Salvatori, Murray with Naysmith, and Hamilton with McCann. "Bonding together as a group and having that whole build-up to a cup final was pretty special for me because it was the first time I had experienced it for a Scottish Cup final," says McCann. "It was the showpiece match at the end of the season, you're in it, you know everybody's going to be watching, the media attention is huge, you're playing a Rangers side at the end of an era; it had all the ingredients and it was just a huge game to look forward to."

The Big Day

*"We had lost twice in maroon so we
thought we'd try something different"*

As they awoke on their day of reckoning, with rays of mid-May morning sunshine gleaming into their hotel rooms, the Hearts players were in no doubt about the size of the opportunity awaiting them. Throughout the 1997/98 season, and particularly in the week leading up to the Scottish Cup final, Jim Jefferies and Billy Brown, aided by long-serving striker John Robertson, had been hammering home what it would be like if they could bring silverware back to Gorgie for the first time since the League Cup triumph in 1962.

Jefferies was so ferociously driven to be the man to end the long wait for glory that he spent time subtly "brainwashing" his players – particularly the foreigners previously unaccustomed to the unrivalled passion of Scottish football – into believing they could achieve something uniquely special in Edinburgh. "I would sit for hours with them in small groups over a coffee or whatever just talking about how big a club Hearts were and explaining that any success that came their way would be like nothing they'd ever experience anywhere else," says the manager. "You just had to get that message across and get them to believe it, and they did. It was mostly just the foreign boys I'd have in these wee meetings because I was trying to sell them the journey that they were going to go on. You just hope they take it on board and that it comes true. It wasn't a big deal but all these wee meetings were worthwhile in terms of making them believe they had something worth striving for."

The message was ratcheted up in the week leading up to the final by those who knew the club best. "When you had someone like John Robertson at the club, he knew what it meant and he let everybody know what it would mean and what would happen to us if we won something," says midfielder Colin Cameron. "He was at it all week, talking about the opportunity we had to become legends."

When the squad gathered for breakfast on Saturday 16th May, Jefferies, surveying the room and bumping into them at the buffet, could detect a sense of determination and confidence among his players. "Watching them at the breakfast table and just speaking to them, I could tell they were up for it," says the manager. After a short wander around the lush surroundings of the Dunblane Hydro – a far cry in setting from the bedlam into which they would be pitched just a few hours later – the players returned to their rooms to relax and flick through the Saturday newspapers before getting changed into their cup final attire. Having come up short in previous finals wearing traditional dark suits, Hearts went for a fresh look on this occasion: eye-catching fawn suits, with white shirts and maroon and cream-checked ties. "I was responsible for sourcing the infamous suits," says Clare Cowan, manager of the club shop at the time. "I remember Jim and the players decided they wanted to go for something a bit different. As everyone knows, footballers are a superstitious bunch; they hadn't won in the previous finals so they wanted to try wearing something different. I presented them with the options and that was the one they chose. I remember hunting the country to get those ties because they weren't Hearts ties. I'm sure they were from River Island so I had to go round all the River Island shops in places like Falkirk and Stirling to ensure I had enough because each shop only stocked about six. Everybody still speaks about the suits, I think because they were so different as opposed to a navy or charcoal suit."

Suited and booted, the players headed down to the hotel restaurant for their pre-match meal shortly before midday. Any nervous tension as the big kick-off drew ever closer was eased by jovial interventions from Neil Pointon, who was recording most of the build-up on a camcorder. As one player enquired how long it was until departure time, David Weir could be heard saying "the arses are twitching". After lunch, the squad gathered in a function room in the hotel before boarding the bus for the 33-mile drive to Celtic Park. While the passing of time and the natural change in trends has painted the fawn suits in a less flattering light, the players – many of them sporting sunglasses – clearly felt they looked the part as they boarded the Park's of Hamilton team coach. "When you see some of the footage from Neil's video, some of the boys were loving themselves when they got on that bus," says captain Gary Locke. "In the finals before that we'd just gone with normal black suits. But at the time, as much as you wouldn't say it now, the beige suits were kinda fashionable back then. Everybody got to have a look at them before we picked them. They weren't that bad at the time but now everybody wears a skinny suit and the young team don't even wear socks with their suits. On that day, we genuinely all felt like we were cool as... As much as the suit gets hammered now, we all felt like we were looking alright. We certainly weren't as bad as the Liverpool boys in the cream suits a few years previously!"

As 90s hits such as Angels, by Robbie Williams, and Mysterious Girl, by Peter Andre, played on the coach sound system, the players started to tune into match mode. "When we left the hotel to go to the stadium, you could see in the eyes of the guys just how determined they were," says goalkeeper Gilles Rousset. "I thought 'this is for us today'."

By this point, Hearts supporters' buses were descending on Glasgow's sun-kissed east end en masse, with thousands of the battle-scarred maroon army already several beers deep as they sought to calm pre-match nerves. "Hearts, Hearts glorious Hearts...", "We have played in south Morocco, we have played in the USA...", "Hello, hello, we are the Gorgie boys", "Jim Jefferies' barmy army", "There's only one Rousset" and, of course, "Hibs are going down" were just some of the songs belting out from the pubs and social clubs within the vicinity of Celtic Park in the hours leading up to kick-off. Dozens of supporters gathered to greet the team coach as it rolled up to the stadium's main entrance shortly before 1.30pm. The players made their way to the home dressing-room and then headed out to get a feel for the pitch. "The nerves'll be going here," mused Pointon, who hadn't made the 14-man squad but was in fine spirits nonetheless. At that point, the stands were empty barring stewards and a couple of workmen who were sitting sunbathing in the work-in-progress West Stand. A few Hearts players joked that the construction staff in question would have told their wives they wouldn't make it to the match because they were "grafting all day".

Circa 2pm, confirmation of the Rangers team arrived with Hearts management. In the final game of his glittering seven-year reign as manager of the Ibrox club, Walter Smith would be sending his team out in a 3-5-2 formation: Andy Goram in goals; a back three of Sergio Porrini, Richard Gough and Lorenzo Amoruso; a defensively-minded midfield five of Joachim Bjorklund, Stuart McCall, Rino Gattuso, Ian Ferguson and Stale Stensaas; with Brian Laudrup roaming in a free role in support of Gordon Durie up front. Ally McCoist, Ian Durrant and Craig Moore were the three substitutes. For seven of the 14 – Goram, Bjorklund, Gough, McCall, Laudrup, McCoist and Durrant – this would be their last match as Rangers players. "I was surprised McCoist didn't start," says Jefferies. "He had been in and out at that time so there was no guarantee he would play, but we certainly expected him to start because he was a goalscorer. Their two full-backs (Bjorklund and Stensaas) weren't renowned for getting forward so they basically started with five defenders; that was a bit of a compliment to us. With Rangers playing the three centre-backs, I think that was a sign they were expecting us to go with Jim Hamilton and Stephane Adam up through the middle because that's generally what we'd done in the league games."

Marco Negri, who had finished as the Premier Division's top scorer despite being sidelined by an eye injury for most of the second half of the season, didn't make the Rangers squad, while Swedish midfielder Jonas Thern and Alec Cleland also missed out, along with Jorg Albertz, who was suspended following his red card in the final league match against Dundee United the previous weekend. This meant the Ibrox side's starting line-up was missing their three highest-scoring players from the season: 36-goal Negri, 15-goal Albertz and 14-goal McCoist. In addition, Laudrup's influence had diminished to the extent that the Dane had scored only five goals in 1997/98 compared to the 20 he notched the previous season. The departure two months previously of Paul Gascoigne, who had become plagued by injury and off-field issues, also made the Rangers team that started the 1998 final look notably less daunting on paper than the versions that had put Hearts to the sword in the two finals in 1996. "Especially with everyone preparing to leave, we certainly didn't have the same edge or the same energy as we had in 1996," concedes Rangers assistant Archie Knox. "We were coming to the end of our dominant spell. Walter and I were leaving, a lot of the players were leaving, and I think that just took the edge off us, especially at the tail end of that season."

Jefferies had been ramming home the message all week that Hearts would "never get a better chance to beat one of the Old Firm in a cup final", and the players bought into it. "Rangers had just lost the league for the first time in nine years, they had won no trophies that season and lots of players were leaving the club, along with Walter Smith," says Rousset. "The big thing for me was the suspension of Albertz because he had made a big difference in the matches between us in the league. He scored lots of goals, he was a danger at free-kicks and he was a very important player so it was great news for us that he was out. We knew also that there was no Gazza because he had already left and Laudrup was leaving, so we felt we had a big chance."

Although Rangers were 4/9 favourites to lift the trophy with bookmakers, the fact Hearts were just 13/8 highlighted that this was a well-balanced final on paper. Indeed, just before kick-off, Sky Sports pundit and former Celtic and Scotland striker Charlie Nicholas tipped Hearts for victory, pinpointing their "pace" as a potentially decisive factor.

Once the Hearts players returned to the dressing-room to change into their warm-up kit, it was time to get down to business. Pointon duly turned the camcorder on himself and said "the Jambos are ready for it, let's fucking go" as he ended his pre-match recording. Like coiled springs, they bounded out the tunnel at 2.10pm to begin their warm-up, almost 20 minutes before the Rangers players emerged on to the pitch. "I remember Walter mentioning to me after the game that he couldn't believe how quickly our players were out for the warm-up because it was such a scorching day," recalls Jefferies. "Our players were out about ten past two but he didn't put his out until about half two because he didn't want them knackered. He probably had a point but that just shows you how keen our boys were to get out and get a feel of the ball and get their minds on the game."

Peter Houston, the youth-team coach who would help out with the first team on matchdays, was the man charged with putting the players through their paces before kick-off. "My claim to fame from the 98 final is that I took the warm-up," he says. "Our boys were young and fit but I decided to do the warm-up in the shaded area in front of the main stand because it was so warm; it was red hot. The boys could have gone out and played without a warm-up because they were flying. The biggest thing for me was to try and calm them down and slow them down a bit because they were so hungry and ready to come out the traps; they were just desperate to play. It was a test for me to get them in the shade, watch what I was doing with them and not give them too much because the sun would have taken it out their legs. My goodness, we had a team that were hungry as hell that day."

By the time Hearts' warm-up drew to a close, the stands were filling up with supporters and the atmosphere was reaching fever pitch. "At about 2.45pm, I left the boardroom and went down to the dressing-room to have a brief word with Jim," recalls Hearts chairman Leslie Deans. "As I went down, I walked down the tunnel to have a look. As I came out the tunnel I looked across to that hugely imposing north stand at Parkhead and it was absolutely packed with Hearts supporters twirling their scarves and singing. When I went inside I said 'Jim, psychologically, we're not away today because the first thing the players will see when they come out the tunnel is 22,000 Jambos cheering their heads off'. It was just a little thing but psychologically I felt that was going to help."

In a further change of approach from Hearts, who had worn maroon in their previous two finals against Rangers, the Edinburgh side had elected to wear their away kits: white shirts with maroon trim, maroon shorts, and white socks with maroon turnovers. "When we talked about it, we said 'every time we go to a cup final we wear the club colours, why don't we change it and go with our white away strip for a change?'," explains Jefferies. "We had lost twice in the maroon so we thought we'd try something different. As it turned out, white was the perfect colour to wear on a scorching hot day."

Looking immaculate and ready to shine, the Hearts players – led out by a proud Jefferies – arrived on to the Celtic Park pitch to a wall of noise and colour just before 3pm. There was the blue, red and white of the Rangers fans in the main stand and the east stand behind the goal, and the maroon and white of Hearts in the north stand. It was t-shirts all round, except for Hearts defender Paul Ritchie, the only outfield player on the pitch wearing long sleeves. "When we came out the dressing-room, the Hearts fans were right across from us and it was scorching. What a feeling!" recalls McCann, emphasising the sense that this would be a perfect day on which to win a cup final.

The pre-match notion that Hearts had been straining at the leash was endorsed by the remarkable start they made. Once referee Willie Young blew his whistle, Thomas Flögel and Adam took kick-off and the Frenchman knocked it back to captain Fulton just outside the centre circle. The ball was moved out to the left-back area to Gary Naysmith, then inside to Ritchie, who stepped out of defence past Laudrup and played the easy ball wide to Fulton. Hearts' captain was clattered to the floor by Ferguson inside his own half just as he knocked it back to Naysmith, who in turn played it long up the left channel for the ever-willing Adam to chase down. Gough and Porrini came out to the corner in Rangers' right-back area to pressurise the Frenchman and force him away from danger. The Italian – the first Rangers player to touch the ball – made a half-baked clearance straight into the path of Fulton who had picked himself up off the floor and trotted up the left flank to try and support his team-mate. The peroxide-blond midfielder, midway inside the Rangers half and out near the left touchline when he received the ball, stepped away from the oncoming Ferguson and drove – with pace, poise and power – towards the penalty area. Just as he tried to skip into the box, Fulton fell to the ground under the dual challenge of Porrini and Ferguson, who had been giving chase. While Porrini's sloppy attempt to make a tackle was just outside the box, Ferguson clipped the Hearts man right on the edge. It was close enough to the 18-yard line to be debatable about whether it was actually inside the box, while some felt Fulton had gone down too easily in any case, but referee Young was in no doubt as he pointed emphatically to the spot. With just 29 seconds having elapsed and only six of the 22 players on the pitch having had a touch of the ball, Hearts had a penalty kick. "I wouldn't usually be thinking about driving at the opposition that early in the game but a wee gap just opened up and I went for it," recalls Fulton. "Some Rangers fans claimed I dived but two of them brought me down! I wasn't a diver. I'd just look like a big daftie if I tried to dive. I don't think anybody could have labelled me a diver. For me, it was definitely a penalty."

Cameron, the team's penalty taker, was stunned to get the chance to open the scoring before he had even touched the ball. "One thing's for sure, if it had been the last minute you wouldn't have seen Stevie Fulton making that run," jokes Cameron. Jefferies had full faith in the little midfielder to deliver amid the tension. "Mickey had stuck a few away for us so I had every confidence in him but it was a brilliant penalty considering how early it was in a cup final," says the manager. "Sidefoot; powerful; bang, right in the top corner. Even if Goram had gone the right way I don't think he'd have had a chance of saving it."

By the time Cameron's spot-kick hit the net, there were 90 seconds on the clock. It was the quickest goal in a Scottish Cup final since Derek Johnstone famously scored for Rangers against Hearts before 3pm in the 1976 showpiece. Hearts had 88-and-a-half minutes (plus any added time) in which to try and maintain their lead. Crucially, they had been working meticulously on soaking up pressure throughout the week leading up to the match. "We were very lucky that we got a penalty in the first minute and scored it, so the tactics worked perfectly," says Rousset. "If it had been the opposite way and we'd lost a goal in the first minute, we'd have had to chuck the tactics out the window."

Although there was still plenty of work to do, Hearts – willed on by a delirious support – felt this was their moment. "You get a feeling it's going to be your day when you get a penalty in the first minute," says Jefferies. "Obviously plenty can still happen after that but I think getting that goal so early just gave us that wee bit extra will to play the way we wanted, to hold on to the lead and try to hit them on the break. Scoring the first goal always suits your plan but if you score as early as we did, it probably makes you sit back a wee bit more than you intend to do. If we hadn't have scored in the first minute, we'd have probably been a bit more attacking."

For the remainder of the first half, Hearts barely threatened the Rangers goal. Equally, however, the Tynecastle side were generally able to keep their opponents – who had the majority of possession – at arm's length. Rousset had to make three saves to keep out long-distance shots from Gattuso, Laudrup and Amoruso, who also drove a free-kick well wide just before the break. The only time Hearts looked in any kind of trouble defensively in the first half was when they allowed Laudrup a shot from 12 yards out which came off the outside of Rousset's right-hand post. In a season when Hearts were renowned for their attacking verve, this was a day when their more defensive-minded players – specifically the back four plus Rousset and midfield enforcer Stefano Salvatori – were required to come to the fore. "Our defence had been outstanding all season but I felt sorry for them at times because we were such an attacking team that we probably left them a bit exposed," says

Jefferies. "In the cup final that all changed. We restricted Rangers to very few clear chances."

Unsurprisingly, Rangers made a change at the break, with McCoist sent on in place of Stensaas. Centre-back Porrini moved across to left-back as the Ibrox side switched to four at the back. The 35-year-old Scotland striker brought a renewed threat to Rangers' play and he spurned a couple of decent chances from inside the box in his first six minutes on the pitch. Just as the veteran's presence was starting to make Hearts look slightly vulnerable, however, the Edinburgh side doubled their lead in the 53rd minute. After Durie had been caught offside, Rousset launched a free-kick deep into the Rangers half and Flögel ducked out of the way to let it bounce through towards the edge of the penalty area. Amoruso thought he had the situation under control but was unaware of Adam, who burst round the outside to chest the ball away from the dithering Italian and take the ball into the box. The Frenchman, drifting wide of goal, hit a firm angled shot on the bounce across Goram, who got his right hand to it but could only watch in despair as the ball nestled in the net. Adam raced away ecstatically towards the corner flag in front of the Hearts supporters who could scarcely believe what they were experiencing. 2-0 to The Bridesmaids, as they had become tagged within Scottish football after losing their previous five cup finals. "Stephane was really quick up in his mind as well as across the ground," says Cameron. "Amoruso clearly thought he could let the ball bounce through him and he'd mop it up, but Steph anticipated it and managed to get in and nick it away from him. He was the type of striker who, when he gets into that position, would hit the target nine times out of ten. If it had been half a foot higher, Andy would probably have got a better hand on it but Steph kept it low enough that Andy was only able to get a wee bit of a hand on it and it ended up in the corner. We weren't even an hour into the game and we were two up; you couldn't have written it any better."

Hearts were in a state of euphoria. "The nerves eased a lot when we got that second goal," says McCann. "When Stephane scored we all ran over to him and that was the moment you're thinking 'right, we're going to win the cup, it's ours'. I knew Rangers would come at us hard but I was confident we wouldn't give up two goals."

Even in the media section of the main stand, there was a state of giddiness unfolding after Adam's goal put clear daylight between the teams. The Scotsman newspaper journalist Mike Aitken, a Hearts supporter "with a neutral exterior", was sitting alongside the Edinburgh Evening News' Hearts correspondent Martin Dempster, a boyhood Rangers supporter who had become a Jambo "by osmosis", according to Aitken. Both of these journalists place covering the events of 16th May 1998 as a career highlight. "When Adam gathered that ball from Rousset and whacked it into the corner of the net, my left leg went into Martin's right leg," says Aitken. "It was a bit like when you're speaking to people on Zoom, it doesn't matter what you're wearing down below as long as you're smartly dressed from the waist up. We were both perfectly calm from the waist up but our legs were dancing under the table. We knew that was the key moment in the game because it was going to be very hard for Rangers to come back against that terrific young Hearts defence."

"We shall not be moved" sang the Hearts support, now sensing glory. Having been under the cosh before Adam's goal, the Edinburgh side were suddenly invigorated. Indeed, they had a great chance to make it 3-0 just two minutes later when Flögel met a Fulton free-kick at the far post and headed straight into the grateful arms of Goram. "I should have scored," says the Austrian. Had that gone in, it would surely have spared Hearts' supporters the anguished finale that ensued as Rangers came on strong in the last half hour. "We knew it was going to be the Alamo from then on," says Cameron.

Rousset made a brilliant point-blank save to deny McCoist and Hearts' defence had to be fully concentrated to stop the likes of Durie and Laudrup finding a way through as the Ibrox side, who sent on the more attack-minded Durrant in place of McCall, started to crank up the pressure. Although it was a collective effort in which Hearts' entire team had to muck in and do the dirty work, McCann could sense his defensive colleagues were in their element as they won headers, made crucial tackles and interceptions, and generally worked as a unit to keep the ball away from their goal. "The defence was brilliant that day," says the winger. "All the guys that played across the back were simply outstanding. Sometimes when defenders are just asked to defend, they enjoy it. A lot of the time boys like Slim (Dave McPherson), Davie Weir and Gary Naysmith would like to step out of defence and join in attacks, but the way we set up that day meant they all had to defend, and that's essentially what those boys were all good at. In a weird way, they probably all enjoyed that. The boys at the back were brilliant."

As the match ticked past the 75-minute mark, it was clear several of the Hearts players were starting to feel the effects of a gruelling afternoon chasing and harrying high-quality opponents in searing heat. Jefferies opted to make his one and only substitution of the match in the 78th minute when he sent on Jim Hamilton in place of Adam. "Ideally, I didn't really want to make any substitutions at that stage because I was confident that with the players we had on the pitch we were going to see it through," says Jefferies. "But so many of our players were out on their feet so I felt I had to make one. Stephane was the obvious one to take off because he'd done so much work up there on his own. And when it came down to Robbo and Hammy, we felt that Hammy, with his aerial ability, could help us in other areas of the pitch rather than just as a striker."

Jefferies was becoming increasingly confident that his team were going to keep Rangers at bay, but that theory was dashed with nine minutes left when McCoist got in between Ritchie and Weir to latch on to a through ball from Gattuso before firing clinically beyond Rousset from just inside the box. "The way we were defending, I couldn't see us losing a goal," says Jefferies. "I said to Billy (Brown) with about ten minutes left, if we can get through the next five minutes I think we'll see it out, but just as I spoke, McCoist scored. After that, you start thinking 'here we go again'. But something told me the back four weren't going to let it slip that day."

Having put so much energy into the game, the prospect of being pegged back and taken to extra-time didn't bear thinking about. "We feared the worst when McCoist did what he always did and sniffed a goal out," says Cameron. "It was a great finish, to be fair. At that point there was about eight minutes left plus another 20 minutes of injury-time! You're thinking 'we need to hang on, we need to hang on' because I'm sure I won't be the only one who felt Rangers would have gone on and won it if it went to extra-time. We'd given everything."

Hearts' supporters – several thousand of whom had been at Dens Park 12 years earlier to see their team capitulate the previous time such tantalising opportunity knocked for their team – were gripped by anxiety. "When Rangers scored, I think there was probably a feeling of 'oh fuck, here we go again'," says Fulton. Gary McWhinnie, a diehard Hearts fan from Woodburn and a close friend of Gary Locke's, was 22 at the time. "I always remember when McCoist scored to make it 2-1, I couldn't believe what I was seeing," he recalls. "You're talking rows of Hearts fans, it seemed like hundreds, just getting up out their seats and walking down towards the exits. I was wondering what was going on. Five minutes left in a cup final, Hearts are winning, I'm asking my brother Allan 'where's everybody going?' As much as I was nervous and on tenterhooks myself, I couldn't believe the amount of people that were disappearing. I decided to get out my seat, walk down to the front and into the concourse area to see what was going on. As I went through the gangway, I've never seen anything like it, it was rammed with Hearts supporters. They were mainly older, guys in their 40s and 50s, with their heads in their hands. There were folk in tears with five minutes of the game left and they couldn't bear to watch the rest of the game. I couldn't believe it. I came back out into the stand because as much as it was horrible, the most nerve-wracking thing ever, I had to see the last few minutes of that game. I went back up to sit with my brother and I remember thinking 'there are hundreds of fans out there who are going to miss the moment the referee blows the whistle if we win this cup'. It was crazy but they had obviously had so many bad experiences following Hearts, particularly 1986 which so many guys of the generations above me had been unable to get over. It was an incredible scene."

Hearts managed to weather the storm for the next five minutes or so, but it looked, for a split-second, as if their dream was about to unravel in the 86th minute when McCoist tumbled into the box under a challenge from Weir after Durie had flicked the ball in behind the Hearts defence. Given that McCoist had fallen almost three yards inside the box, it looked a certain penalty in real time. Mercifully for Hearts, referee Young instead deemed that the foul had taken place outside the penalty area. "Well the referee didn't think it was a penalty which is the main thing, so whether it was or it wasn't, it doesn't really matter to be honest," laughs Weir.

There was certainly no such light-heartedness at the time. "That was definitely the scariest point," says Hamilton. "If that was a penalty, Rangers would have probably gone on and won the game because the momentum was with them." McCann recalls having to order Hamilton to pull himself together. "When Coisty got brought down, I was running back because I knew it was only a free-kick that had been given," says the winger. "But I remember running past big Hammy and he had his head in his hands. He thought it was a penalty, so I'm shouting 'Hammy, get fucking back, it's a free-kick, get in the wall'."

With Amoruso having spurned several free-kick opportunities throughout the match, Laudrup was given the chance to try his luck from a central position on the 18-yard line. To the almighty relief of every Hearts supporter, the Dane's meek attempt deflected off Salvatori in the defensive wall and ran behind for a corner. Rousset, having a commanding performance between the sticks, was inspired by the resolve of those in front of him. "We could feel the pressure but to be honest Rangers didn't really create many chances," he says. "We were lucky with the penalty decision with Coisty and they put some crosses into our box and tried some strikes from distance but, honestly, they never created much. We defended really well. Davie Weir and Ritch were outstanding."

Most of the Hearts players were running on empty as the match ticked agonisingly towards stoppage time. "Coming to the end of the game in heat like that, you're mentally exhausted more than anything," says Fulton. "For big periods of the game we were just chasing and tackling and concentrating on trying to be in the right positions so it was hard going. I think I'd started to cramp up in both legs. I was shouting to the boys, telling them not to give me the ball but you just go into autopilot at that stage. I think a few of us would have been cooked for extra-time."

Stoppage-time felt like extra-time for the Hearts players. The board displaying the amount of added time wasn't implemented until the World Cup in France a month later, so anxious fans had to guess how long would be added on. It was the most excruciating four minutes and 28 seconds of most of their football-following lives, and the players were feeling the effects as well. "The last five minutes felt like an hour because there was so much pressure from Rangers on our goal," says Flögel. "We were like a marathon runner going through the last kilometre; we were falling over."

Crucially, Weir was one of the few players in the Hearts team still going strong deep into stoppage time, and just shy of the 94-minute mark the centre-back had to make a brilliant challenge eight yards from goal to stop Porrini firing in what would almost certainly have been an equaliser. Seconds later, Durie blazed high over the bar from outside the box and the pent-up Jefferies – who had been joining the 22,000 Hearts supporters in hollering at Young to blow for full-time – clenched his fists as if his team had just scored another goal. Rousset took his time before pitching his bye-kick over towards the main stand as Young's whistle – with the ball in mid-air – finally brought one of the most momentous matches in Hearts' history to an end. "I had the last kick of the game and at full-time I fell down on my knees and I thought 'that's it, we've done it'," says Rousset.

After 36 trophyless years, Heart of Midlothian had withstood the pressure and won the 1998 Tennent's Scottish Cup. "At full-time, I erupted ten feet in the air out of my seat," says Deans. "Not what a chairman should do perhaps, but what the hell, it was the way I felt. It was a release, an explosion of joy because Hearts had beaten a top-class Rangers team and were no longer the bridesmaids."

Celebrations

*"All I could see on the pitch was empty cans
and the remains of the takeaway food"*

"The gaffer and the boys from Edinburgh had told us what it would be like if we won and they certainly weren't talking shite. It all came true," says Hearts mid-fielder and Scottish Cup-winning captain Stephen Fulton. From the moment the final whistle sounded at Celtic Park, a mixture of delirium, disbelief and Dario G gripped everyone of a Hearts persuasion. "I ended up on my knees cuddling Neil McCann and after that we were jumping on each other and hugging each other," recalls Fulton. "Neil was just the closest person to me at that moment but without getting soppy about it, looking back it was pretty poignant because we'd also gone to the same school (St Stephen's High School in Port Glasgow) and I was in his big brother's year."

As a small number of jubilant supporters invaded the pitch to celebrate, some of the players, having put so much into the game, required time to process the magnitude of what they had achieved. "I have to say I needed ten minutes to let my emotions come out," says Thomas Flögel. "At full-time you could see all the joy from the supporters but I needed a few minutes to realise what we had done. It was just unbelievable." Amid the bedlam, players tried to seek out loved ones in the stands. "For me, it was such a relief when the whistle went, and then the jubilation set in," says defender Dave McPherson. "I looked towards my son, who was in the directors' box, and then I was looking towards the supporters. It was incredible to see the relief and joy on their faces, almost like they couldn't believe what had happened."

While most Jambos were savouring the moment, Hearts' unstripped players, in-cluding Gary Locke, Neil Pointon, Allan McManus and Jose Quitongo, had become embroiled in a dispute with an over-zealous official. "All the boys who weren't stripped were in the tunnel area at full-time waiting to get on the pitch and this trumpet from the SFA said 'you can't go out there lads'," says Locke. "He refused to let us on the pitch but luckily the gaffer came over to do an interview with (BBC reporter) Chick Young so that helped. Chick was great: he was hammering the boy and trying to help us get on the pitch. There was a bit of a commotion and then eventually Chris Robinson came down and said there wouldn't be a trophy presentation if they didn't let us on the pitch because we were part of the team. It seemed like a good five minutes or so before we actually got on the pitch and it was just brilliant; one of the best moments ever. I went to give all the boys and the management team a cuddle."

Having been a peripheral figure on the day, club captain Locke was invited by matchday skipper Fulton to share in trophy-lifting duties on the Parkhead pitch. The end result was peroxide-blond Fulton, in his white Hearts strip, and Locke, sporting fawn suit and curtains hairstyle, simultaneously hoisting the old trophy, adorned with maroon ribbons, into the bright blue Glasgow sky in one of the most beautiful sights many of those present will ever have witnessed. "If Lockey was fit, he'd have been the captain so I just felt it was the right thing to do to ask him to lift the cup with me – it wasn't a big deal to me," Fulton explains. "Although, to be fair, he could have fucking let me get a hold of it instead of grabbing it himself!"

As the triumphant Hearts players celebrated on the pitch with the trophy, many of the Rangers fans, who were bidding farewell to several of their own heroes, stayed behind to applaud their conquerors. "The Rangers players were absolutely different class at the end; they were very nice to us," recalls Rousset. "And so were their fans; many of them stayed behind to see us lift the trophy. My wife told me that when the whistle was blown at full-time, all the Rangers board turned to the Hearts board, shook their hands and clapped them."

Dario G's France 98 song, Carnaval de Paris, blared from Celtic Park's sound system as Hearts' long-suffering supporters, with dry mouths and tears in their eyes, tried to soak in as much of this historic occasion as they possibly could. Stefano Salvatori, with a Hearts scarf tied around his head, broke off to give an impassioned interview with Sky Sports. "This is fantastic," said the much-loved Italian midfielder. "Congratulations to my team, my staff and our supporters. A fantastic day. After 42 years, Hearts win the Scottish Cup. Fantastic, very happy."

Mark Donaldson, a boyhood Hearts supporter from Penicuik who was in his early years as a broadcaster for Radio Forth at the time, recalls being one of the first people to interview Jim Jefferies after the match. "We got access to the trackside so we got Jim at the mouth of the tunnel just before he went inside to do the rest of the press," says Donaldson. "When I put the microphone to his mouth, I knocked his glass of champagne over and it went all over his suit, but he didn't give a toss. He was jubilant. It was weird for me because it was the best day of my life following Hearts but there was a part of me that was envious of mum and dad being in the Hearts end because I'd spent pretty much ten years following Hearts home and away before I started working in the media. I wasn't able to be a proper fan during the match but I was certainly a fan on the Saturday night back in Penicuik."

When supporters started to filter out of the stadium to make their way back to Edinburgh for a party, the victorious team headed inside for beer and champagne.

The dressing-room gradually got rowdier and rowdier as more players started to return from outside. Legendary striker John Robertson, who had been an unused substitute, immediately went round the room kissing all his team-mates and thanking them for helping him secure the first medal of his career. "18 years," he said, pointing out how long he'd waited for this moment as he proudly pushed his prize in front of Pointon's camcorder. A few moments later, Jefferies, Billy Brown and Locke arrived in the dressing-room. Assistant manager Brown, holding the trophy in his right hand, bellowed "fucking magnificent, lads", as Jefferies went round shaking hands with each one of his heroes. Chief executive Robinson – at a time when he hadn't yet become persona non grata at Tynecastle – was in the cramped dressing-room getting his hands on the trophy and soon the whole squad were bouncing to Carnaval de Paris, with Salvatori, usually one of the more reserved members of the squad, dancing jubilantly with both arms aloft while wearing nothing but a pair of pants. The Hearts party was only just getting started.

Amid the humidity and the mayhem, the players got showered and dressed back into their cup final suits before making their way upstairs to the Celtic Park lounge for a celebratory drink, where they were joined by some magnanimous Rangers players. When the victorious Hearts squad filtered out of the stadium, they were met by an army of jubilant Jambos who had gathered at the main entrance eager to show their appreciation as each player or member of the coaching staff made their way back on to the bus for the journey home. Departure was delayed, however, as both Fulton and Rousset had been summoned for a routine drugs test. "The problem was that I had a wee in the dressing-room and then I got asked to go for a drugs test," says Rousset. "When I got to the drugs test room, I couldn't do another wee so I had to drink something. I just picked up a bottle of champagne and a tea cup because there were no glasses around. Because it was hot, I had only my suit trousers on. I had no top or shirt on; I was topless in the room waiting for the drugs test. It took me a while to be able to go to the toilet and by the time I eventually did it, I was completely drunk. When I went back to the dressing-room, the boys had already left to get on the bus and all I could find was my jacket and my tie. I had no idea where my shirt was so I went back on the bus with just my suit jacket and my tie. When I got on the bus, the boys were worse than me because they had drunk a lot while they were waiting for me!" Fulton was in a similar state as he got on the bus. "By the time I'd come out the stadium after my drugs test, I'd had a few cans of beer and some champagne," says the midfielder. "I'd just played a game and hadn't had anything to eat. I was pie-eyed pretty quickly. We all were."

Prior to setting off, Jefferies, who was one of the last on the bus, stood at the front with a bottle of lager in hand, and proudly surveyed the scene as the squad of footballers he had assembled over the previous three years revelled in their glory, singing Hearts songs, guzzling beer and creating memories to last a lifetime. "I'll never forget that bus journey home," says Cameron. "The fact we were held up a bit waiting for Gilles and Stevie didn't help in terms of the state of us by the time we got to Edinburgh. When we came in through Sighthill, it started off as wee dribs and drabs of people waiting for us, and the closer we got there were lines of people; and then there were lines and lines of people; then you couldn't see the pavement. There were people hanging out their windows everywhere. It was amazing scenes, it really was. The bus on the way home was definitely a highlight of it all for me."

Hearts fans had descended in their thousands on the Gorgie area to welcome back their heroes. "As we came along through Sighthill, I've got a vivid memory of an elderly couple, perhaps in their eighties, standing out the front of their hedge clapping us," says McCann. "It was emotional to see that. As we got closer to Gorgie, it just kept getting busier and when we got to the start of Gorgie, all you could see was a sea of maroon and white. You're thinking 'my god, look at this'."

On a glorious sunny evening on the Gorgie Road, the chip shops and off-licences were doing a roaring trade as Jambos sought to refuel following an emotionally and physically draining day. With pavement space at a premium, many clambered up on to scaffolding, traffic lights and bus shelters to ensure they would be well placed to catch a glimpse of the coveted Scottish Cup in its first moments back in this part of Scotland since 1956. The players, too, wanted a better vantage point of this remarkable scene. Not content with being the goldfish inside the bowl, some of the cup-winning heroes – led by McCann – started climbing through the skylight towards the back of the bus and on to the roof. "We were just playing the Hearts song and banging the windows and then I decided 'right, I'm going up'," says McCann.

By the time the bus was trundling slowly past the old TSB Bank next to the entrance of the Gorgie Stand, a dozen players were on the roof, soaking up the adulation and the champagne of the crowd. Among this number were Quitongo and Jim Hamilton, who could be seen crawling along the roof on all fours to join Robertson and McManus, who were perched on the front of the bus, legs dangling over the windscreen. "I remember a few folk at the front of the bus shouting 'no, don't do that, don't do that' and I was like 'nope, I'm going up'," says Hamilton. "We just wanted to be out there and be a part of it. I remember wee Jose, who didn't even drink, was dancing about and he nearly fell off. We were out there just doing things that you'd probably never do in the rest of your life. We just got caught up in everything."

Fulton couldn't resist following his colleagues out through the skylight. "The gaffer shouted me and Lockey down to the front of the bus with the trophy but I just left Lockey with it and went up on the roof," says Fulton. "People just kept jumping out in front of the bus and we were up there, dancing about like big daft boys. It was crazy. We knew there were going to be people waiting for us, but Jesus Christ, the amount of people that were there, and just trying to get through the crowds, it was incredible."

Not everyone was up for going on the roof, though. "Nae fucking chance was I going up," says Rousset. "I left that to the others; I would have fallen off." McPherson was of a similar mindset to his fellow 34-year-old. "I was a wee bit more sensible, so I left that to the crazy ones," laughs the former Scotland defender.

For several players, being on the roof of the bus is one of the standout memories of the weekend. "I wish I could have frozen that moment when we were on top of the bus on the Gorgie Road with thousands of people out there celebrating," says Flögel. "I never want to forget it." As the coach turned on to McLeod Street, the crowds roared with approval from all sides. "It was just an incredible journey back from Celtic Park," recalls defender Paul Ritchie. "When we popped the sun roof out and were standing on top of the bus and seeing the amount of people that were there, it really was incredible. That's the one thing that really sticks out for me from the whole weekend."

The crawl along Gorgie Road and on to McLeod Street wasn't quite as enjoyable for Hearts' long-serving coach driver Alan "Scooby" Scott. "It was an absolute highlight of my life to have driven that team home from Celtic Park," he says. "Most of the journey home was exhilarating, really enjoyable. But as we got closer to Tynecastle I was genuinely worried that somebody was going to get seriously hurt. We had police horses in front of us for part of the route, but as soon as they went three feet in front of us, there were people running between the horses and the bus. By the time we'd turned on to McLeod Street, the horses had moved quite a bit ahead of the bus. The police on foot were panicking because the crowds were surging forward and they were struggling to push them back. There weren't enough officers to do it; they were just getting overwhelmed. When we eventually got round to the front of the old office at Tynecastle, I've never been so relieved. When the barriers got shut behind us, I thought 'thank heavens for that'."

"Scooby" was able to relax and enjoy himself for the rest of the evening as he parked his bus and headed into the Gorgie Suite – which had only opened a few months previously – for a party with the victorious Hearts team, club staff, family members and some former players. As they made their way off the bus amid frenzied acclaim, every player bar the tee-total Quitongo was under the influence of alcohol. McPherson, Fulton, Weir and Locke were all in a giddy state as they were interviewed by the BBC's Hazel Irvine before heading inside for more drink. Rousset, meanwhile, had been reunited with his shirt at some point on the journey home. "When I watched Neil Pointon's video back, I realised I had my shirt in my hand when I got off the bus, so someone must have given me it on the way home," he laughs.

Chris McPherson was nine years old at the time and having been at Celtic Park earlier in the day to watch his father Dave help Hearts make history, he recalls joining the rest of the players' family members on a coach back from Glasgow to Tynecastle to be part of the celebrations. "I think we spent about an hour waiting outside the ground because they hadn't opened the Gorgie Suite by that point so we were all hanging around outside the old education building that used to be there and there was obviously loads of police around, there were barricades up and there were a lot of supporters trying to get round," recalls Chris. "I was with my friend and we were stood there waiting and then I remember the bus coming round the corner and there were all these players on top of it which I thought was extremely funny. I stood at the door waiting for my dad to get off the bus and that's when the interviews with Hazel Irvine were happening. That was the first time I'd spoken to him since the game finished. I'd waved to him from the stand at full-time but I didn't get to see him until the team got back to Edinburgh. He'd had a few drinks by that point and he basically said 'I told you we'd win son, I dunno what you were worried about'. I think I was just like 'that was amazing, that was amazing'."

Throughout the evening, several members of the squad took some time out from the party in the Gorgie Suite to head out on to the Tynecastle pitch for fresh air and momentary reflection. "There was an awful lot of drinking going on," says young McPherson, recalling the night through the eyes of a primary-school kid. "Me and my friend from school were sat together at a table and it felt like a great big school disco; I remember the disco lights, the big buffet with party food, sausage rolls, cake and things like that. There was a lot of dancing and it went on quite late. I remember Sportscene came on and everybody started watching the highlights and cheering when the goals went in. I think my friend's dad picked us up about midnight and we were told to get to sleep because we were going to have another big day on the Sunday."

With the crowds having dispersed to pubs and street corners all around Gorgie to continue the party after welcoming the players home, the joyous vibe in EH11 lasted into the small hours of the Sunday morning. When the official party wound down in the Gorgie Suite, players moved on to drinking establishments elsewhere. Some headed over to Robertson's pub – owned by the striker – just round the corner from the stadium, while others drifted towards Bar Roma, the lively Italian restaurant in Edinburgh's west end owned by a Hearts-supporting Italian family and popular with the players and management. "A lot of the players came back at the end of the night and we were all there until about 3am," says Nadia Di Giorgio, who had been at Celtic Park to support Hearts earlier in the day and is the daughter of Bar Roma owners Mario and Beatrice Cugini. "For my family, it was a privilege that they came to Bar Roma on such a special day for Hearts. They had food and drinks and everybody had a great time. The players were helping clear up the plates at the end of the night; nobody wanted to let the night end."

Diehard supporter Derek Ferguson recalls bumping into Stephane Adam as the cup final goal hero headed along Dalry Road towards the city centre. "I was down on my knees kissing his feet," says Ferguson, who was 39 at the time. "I bumped into Stephane a year or two later and he remembered that moment."

More than two decades later, few of the players can remember where they actually slept on their first night as bona fide Hearts legends. Jefferies and some of the players – including Weir and McCann – stayed at the Caledonian Hotel; Hamilton and Locke have vague recollections of crashing at Robertson's house in Fairmilehead; and Cameron and Ritchie don't have a clue where they ended up. "It's all a blur for me because we were all so inebriated," says Ritchie. As much as he enjoyed himself at the time, Locke admits, with hindsight, he would have preferred to have kept himself more compos mentis. "I just wish I wasn't so drunk because there was so much to take in," he says. "I think the majority of the boys would say the same because we had a ridiculous amount to drink and there are parts of the night I just can't remember."

Thousands of supporters all across Edinburgh and the Lothians were in the same boat as Locke as they celebrated a moment they thought they were destined never to see. Needless to say, there were severe hangovers on the Sunday morning as Jambos awoke for the next phase of the celebrations. Indeed Jefferies was one of those suffering, the manager having told the story on more than one occasion of when he emerged from the Caledonian Hotel in the morning to go and get some painkillers from the chemist on Shandwick Place and he bumped into an elderly Hearts fan bedecked in maroon and white. As Jefferies asked him if he had enjoyed his day, the man in question – without looking up to see who was addressing him – muttered "see that Jim Jefferies – God bless him" and kept on walking, oblivious to the fact he had just been talking to his triumphant team's manager. "I don't think many people got much sleep that night," laughs Hamilton. "And then we obviously had to be at the City Chambers on the Sunday for the open-top bus parade."

Taxis were laid on to transport the bleary-eyed squad to the Royal Mile for a civic reception with Edinburgh's Lord Provost, Eric Milligan, shortly after midday. "Eric, a well-known Hearts supporter, had the manager, the team, myself and the other directors in his function suite and he brought out a bottle of vintage champagne which he said he'd only open on a special occasion," recalls chairman Leslie Deans. "This was indeed a special occasion, and the champagne was very nice as well. From there we went down The Mound on the open-top bus on what was an absolutely baking hot day and then enjoyed the slow procession back to Tynecastle."

Estimates ranged between 100,000 and the slightly more fanciful 250,000 with regard to how many people had come out to line the sun-kissed streets between the City Chambers and Tynecastle, with the week-to-week diehard Hearts supporters joined by many who were simply eager to experience the rare thrill of seeing an Edinburgh club parade one of Scotland's major trophies through the capital city. "Although I was a minion compared to some of the people on that open-top bus, I'll never forget those scenes as we came along Princes Street," says coach Peter Houston. "Even though I was a No.3 on the coaching staff, winning the cup with Hearts was a brilliant memory that I'll take to the grave with me. The faces of the Hearts fans at seeing their team finally win something was a sight to behold."

Players and management were joined by staff and family members aboard the top deck of the white Lothian Regional Transport open-top bus. "LRT says well done Hearts" was the slogan above the driver's windscreen, while an Edinburgh Evening News-branded banner which read "Hearts Scottish Cup winners" hung over the front window of the top deck. As had been case the previous night in Gorgie, supporters perched on anything they could clamber aboard in order to get a better view of their heroes. "Jim Jefferies had told me what it would be like but I genuinely never expected it to be like that, with all the streets so full of people," says Flögel. "I didn't even know so many people lived in Edinburgh. It was bigger than anything I'd experienced in Austria. It was a real sense of joy. I had never felt this before."

McCann, who returned to Hearts for a second spell in the Noughties, experienced this victory parade twice, but insists 1998 was on a different level. "I did the parade in 2006 again but obviously I wasn't fit for the cup final against Gretna," he says. "I always say it was nothing like 98. There was just something different about 98."

Broadcaster Donaldson remains proud to have got the chance to be aboard the bus, mingling with legends as they took the acclaim of the huge crowds. "I was so lucky on the Sunday to be basically the only Hearts fan on the open-top bus who wasn't affiliated to the football club," he says. "It came about due to a relationship I had with Dougie Dalgleish, the press officer at the time, and before the final I asked him if I could get on the bus to broadcast if Hearts won the cup. There was no club media at that time. I was set up at the back of the bus and I got Jim and some of the players to talk to me for the radio. I was really happy to be on that bus but I knew I didn't really belong there so I tried to be as unobtrusive as possible. I just wanted to enjoy the journey. It was something special, it really was. The exclusivity factor of being pretty much the only Hearts supporter on that bus not associated with the football club, I'll never forget it. It made up for not being able to celebrate like I would have liked at the game on the Saturday. The only down-side – like everything that weekend – is that it went by too quickly."

As the bus made its way through the crowds, another 17,000 people were packed into Tynecastle awaiting the players' return to the stadium. The youth team even got their moment in the limelight as they were introduced on to the pitch to take the congratulations of the full house just days after their BP Cup win in front of a little over 3000 people at the same venue. For 17-year-old Robbie Neilson, the thrill of being part of such a momentous occasion had a motivational effect. "Tynecastle was packed that day and it was a great experience to be involved in," recalls Neilson, a future Hearts captain and manager who followed in the footsteps of the 1998 legends and won the Scottish Cup as a player in 2006. "I was only 17, just in the door a couple of years, so it was inspirational for me to see. The club had laid on a bus for us to go to the final at Celtic Park the previous day and I remember we were sitting high up in the stand on a beautiful sunny day. We came back to Tynecastle that night and saw the crowds lining the streets. When you see such a phenomenal outpouring of emotion from the supporters, it whets your appetite and makes you want a piece of it for yourself.

"We were very lucky to get that chance to be involved in it and go on the pitch on the Sunday because back then Hearts probably only had about 30 players in total between the first team, the reserves and the youth team, so everybody was in it together. I was training with the first team occasionally and played with most of those guys in the reserves, so we all knew each other; it was really tight. Even though we were on the ground-staff at the time, Jim and the senior players all made us feel part of it. I used to travel through every morning with Fulters. These guys took the young players under their wing and looked after us. It was a good place to grow up as a young player at that time."

When the first-team players came out the tunnel of the old main stand one by one, sporting specially-made white t-shirts with the word "champions" embla-zoned on the front, the decibel levels soared. Salvatori bowed to all four stands as he made his entrance. It was a joy for the players who had children to be able to bring them on to the pitch on their weekend of glory. "My weans were only wee tots – two, four and six – so they don't really remember much about it but it was bloody tremendous for me," says Fulton. "You've got your three wee boys running about and all these people in the stands cheering you on to the park and going daft for you. Just tremendous. I've still got photos with them on the pitch at Tynecastle."

While the official celebrations died down towards teatime, for many the partying continued into Sunday night and beyond. Gary McWhinnie and Derek Ferguson, two aforementioned supporters, had never previously crossed paths until they began forging a close friendship inside Tynecastle's centre circle on the Monday night after the final. "I'd been out drinking on the Monday with my mates because we didn't want the celebrations to end," recalls McWhinnie. "We ended up back in Gorgie and at the end of the night, my mates had disappeared and I was on my own and just had this idea that I wanted to sleep on the Tynecastle pitch. I went and climbed into the stadium from the Gorgie Road end, along the Wheatfield Stand and down the stairs on to the pitch. I lay down on the centre circle and I've no idea how long I'd been asleep but I got woken up by these two guys who clearly had exactly the same idea as me. When they came over I think they thought I was a dead body. They woke me up and said 'what are you doing here?'. I said 'well, this is where I want to be'. They had come in with a carry-out and some food and they had a wee music system, so it seemed like they had pre-planned it.

"The three of us were sitting there having a bevvy and something to eat with a bit of music playing, talking about the game, talking about the team, talking about the experience of the weekend. It was surreal. The next thing I remember is waking up to bright sunshine. It must have been about 6am and the other two boys had done a bunk. All I could see on the Tynecastle pitch was empty cans and the remains of the takeaway food. My heart was going like mad, thinking 'I'm gonna get in severe trouble here'. I just got up and bolted, ran up the stairs of the Wheatfield, out the concourse and back out over the wall on to Gorgie Road. I jumped on the No.3 bus back to Dalkeith and as I got home around 8am, my mum was waiting worried sick because she had no idea where I was. She wouldn't believe that I'd slept on the Tynecastle pitch and she went berserk. I bumped into Fergie at an away game the following season. I couldn't remember what he looked like but he came over to me and gave me a cuddle and introduced himself to me as the guy who slept on the pitch with him. From that moment on, we've been really close and we try and meet up for a pint as often as we can before games."

Ferguson, who was 39 at the time, admits it was a "daft" episode but has no regrets. "It was three days of madness after the game," recalls Ferguson. "We had an all-day session on the Monday and towards the end of the night, me and my pal Greg Hamilton decided we were going to go and sleep inside Tynecastle. I lived on Gorgie Road at the time so I nipped back to the house and took a duvet, and we got a carry-out and a kebab. We climbed into Tynecastle thinking we were the only two dafties going to be there and found Gary lying on the centre spot. We woke him up laughing and then decided we'd move down to the penalty spot where Robbo had broken the scoring record the year before. We stayed there pretty much all night until the seagulls started attacking us. It was just a spontaneous decision so we could keep it all going because I'd had the best three days of my life up to that point. I was nearly 40 so climbing into a football stadium maybe wasn't the brainiest thing to do when you look back on it but it was brilliant at the time."

As these mad Jambos were waking up on their field of dreams, their heroes were preparing to travel to Majorca for a week-long end-of-season party in Magaluf. The majority of the Hearts squad flew out on the Tuesday although Rousset, who had gone the previous summer, decided to give it a miss and headed back to France instead. "I went the year before and had a great week but it was too much for an old Frenchman," he laughs. "Too wild for me."

Given the circumstances, the 1998 renewal was always likely to be even more raucous than previous jaunts to the Balearic island. "We'd just won the cup so it was bedlam," recalls Fulton. Two of Rousset's team-mates soon found out why the goalkeeper had declined the opportunity to return to Magaluf after the Scottish Cup triumph. Quitongo, who has never tasted an alcoholic drink in his life, recalls why he felt compelled to make a hasty departure. "I lasted two days because at 10am everybody was steaming!" he laughs. "I was having to look after them all, I was like the babysitter. I said 'no way Jose', so I went to the airport and got myself a flight home. The boys had great fun though." Adam found himself in a similar predicament. "I only stayed three days," smiles the Frenchman. "It was too much beers for me. After three days I went to see Lockey and said 'skipper, I'm off', then took a taxi to the airport and caught the first flight to Paris!"

Locke feels the end-of-season trips were key for team-bonding, although he understands why some of the foreign players found it something of a culture shock. "Stephane just liked a nice meal and a few glasses of wine but when he got to Majorca, I think he realised he was gonna have to drink a wee bit more than that, so him and Jose left a wee bit earlier," says Locke. "Every year we went to Magaluf it was chaos, but that trip in 98 was extra special because we'd just won the cup and we met a few Hearts fans over there. One of them actually spent pretty much the whole week with us! When we bumped into Rangers and Celtic fans there, they were great with us and they congratulated us. You get familiar with the boys that own the bars and the owner of Sinky's was a Rangers man but he was delighted for us. It was just a nice end to the season, a chance to get away with the boys and abuse your body for a week. It was a brilliant laugh and something the boys always looked forward to."

One particular incident on the beach almost ended with Hearts' cup final captain going up in flames. "Fulters had been to the toilet and when he came out he'd wrapped himself in toilet roll to look like a mummy," recalls Locke. "One of the boys set him alight. Luckily we were at the beach so he was able to run in the sea. At the time, when you're away with the boys and you've got a few bevvies in you, it's a great laugh. But when you look back now, that could have been more dangerous than what it was. You wouldn't get away with that now. That wasn't the type of thing that happened every day, but we did have a great laugh as a group."

Antics like this were perhaps why Jefferies and his coaching staff decided to stay in a separate hotel to the players on their annual trips to Magaluf. Not that the manager didn't enjoy letting his hair down. Jefferies and his staff met up with the players at various points on the trip while they also quaffed champagne with the Dunfermline Athletic management team of Bert Paton, Dick Campbell, Iain Campbell and Jimmy Bone. Paton had a brief spell as a coach at Hearts in the late 1970s when Jefferies was a player and the pair had remained close. The Pars manager had been quoted in the newspapers on the eve of the last league game of the 1997/98 season saying he would "rather have seen Hearts win the title than Rangers or Celtic".

Jefferies also bumped into Hamilton Accies manager Sandy Clark in Magaluf and this allowed him the chance to enjoy a poignant chat with one of his recent predecessors at Hearts, with Clark having been in charge at Tynecastle in the 93/94 campaign. "Sandy came over to congratulate me and it was a really nice moment," recalls Jefferies. "He sat with me and told me how envious he was of me because I'd done something he would love to have done. He didn't mean it in a bad way; he meant it in the right manner because he had been at Hearts shortly before me and he knew exactly what it would have meant to be the first person to win something after that length of time. He said exactly what I had been feeling before I actually won it. Hearing a guy who had been in my position just a few years previously speaking like that was one of the things that made me realise the magnitude of what we'd achieved."

Stephane Adam

*"I remember the tears on people's faces,
people crying, people screaming..."*

Passion and pride are the prevalent emotions accompanying Stephane Adam's gentle French lilt as he is invited to recount the moment he scored arguably the most significant goal in Hearts' history. "I remember it well," he says, casting his mind back to the halcyon point of his football career. "Because it doesn't happen a lot, you always remember this type of situation. When Gilles Rousset kicked the ball forward and it bounced, I was running behind (Rangers defender) Lorenzo Amoruso. I knew he was unaware of me because he was quite confident and was taking it easy. He wasn't moving fast enough; he didn't know I was at his back, so I knew this was my chance. When I chested the ball down, it took it quite far over to the side of the box; I knew I had to shoot early so the angle didn't go too tight. I gave everything I had to shoot the ball across Andy Goram. I knew it was going in even though Goram touched it. There was too much pace on the shot for him to stop it."

Adam's strike put Hearts 2-0 up on Rangers in the 1998 Scottish Cup final as the embattled Edinburgh club sought to end their longest post-war run without silverware. "From that point, all I remember is the energy and the noise coming from the crowd," continues the Frenchman. "That's something I will never forget. I went down on my knees in front of the stand and all my team-mates came over to celebrate; absolutely fantastic. I could just feel the energy and the noise and see the joy on the people's faces. I remember the tears on people's faces, people crying, people screaming, people jumping around. Honestly, the energy I received from that moment, I can still feel it. It will be with me for the rest of my life."

The fact that Rangers pulled one back later in the game meant Adam effectively got the winner. It remains the only time since George Wilson secured a 1-0 victory over Third Lanark in 1906 that any Hearts player has had the honour of scoring a decisive goal in a Scottish Cup final. Things could have been so different for Adam and Hearts, however. In one of the most significant "sliding doors" moments in Hearts' journey to Scottish Cup glory, city rivals Hibs failed in a bid to sign Adam in March 1997. "It was near the end of my second season at Metz and my contract still had a few months to run, but I had the opportunity to go on trial with Hibernian," Adam explains. "They were in a bad position in the table and were looking for a striker. I went to Edinburgh for about three days and played a friendly against Dundee. Jim Duffy and Jackie McNamara (senior) were the Hibs coaches at the time and they were keen to sign me but Metz were looking for quite a lot of money considering I had just a few months of my contract remaining and Hibs weren't in a position to pay it. I wasn't too keen to sign for Hibs to be honest; they were in a bad position, so I was quite happy Metz didn't let me go there. I wanted to finish the season with Metz and see what options I had when I came out of contract."

While no Hearts striker is ever likely to punish Hibs for not signing them as much as the legendary John Robertson did, Duffy was entitled to rue the fact he couldn't land Adam when he was sacked as Hibs manager at the start of February 1998 following a 6-2 defeat at Motherwell which left the Easter Road side four points adrift at the foot of the Premier Division. At the same time, Adam and Hearts sat joint top of the table. "We had a couple of French guys in on trial at the time and Stephane scored as a trialist in a bounce match we had organised," recalls Duffy. "He had a good physique, a really positive attitude and a good work ethic. When you get a striker who really puts in a shift, you know that the worst you'll get is 100 per cent effort. We tried to get him in but unfortunately we didn't succeed."

At the point of his Hibs dalliance – a couple of months before Hearts made their move for him – Adam was 27 and had spent his entire career in his homeland following a football-orientated upbringing in the city of Lille in northern France. "As far back as I can remember, I always wanted to play football," says Adam. "I've been involved in football since the moment I was able to stand on my two feet. My father, Albert, was an amateur football player and his job was to take care of a football complex – a stadium and training facility – in Lille. That was like my garden, I was basically born on a football pitch."

Adam mixed playing football with going to watch Lille, the club he started supporting in the 1970s. He cites Dusan Savić, a Yugoslavian centre-forward, and the long-serving Plancque brothers, Stephane and Pascal, among his favourite players as a kid. After playing for Lille's youth teams from age ten to 15, Adam landed the chance to go to the French FA school of excellence for three years: two-and-a-half years at the Vichy academy in central France and then six months at Clairefontaine where he was part of the first intake of young players to the renowned performance centre south-west of Paris. In his short time there, he helped Clairefontaine win the prestigious French Under-19 Cup (Coupe Gambardella) by defeating Beauvais in the final in May 1988, ten years before his ultimate glory day. Adam then returned to Lille to sign a professional contract when he was 18, although he didn't make a single appearance for his boyhood club. "I was involved with the first team but I never got on," says Adam, who subsequently dropped into Ligue 2 to kickstart his career. He would spend six years in France's lower leagues, representing four different clubs between 1989 and 1995: Louhans-Cuiseaux, Orleans, Creteil and Amiens.

Playing outside Ligue 1 in the early 1990s meant he never got the chance to cross swords with countryman Rousset, his future friend and Hearts colleague. "I knew of Gilles when I was in France because he was an internationalist," says Adam. "I actually remember when I was a young boy (in 1983) watching the Coupe Gambardella final between Sochaux and Lens in Lille before a Lille first-team game. Gilles and Stephane Paille (another future Hearts player) were playing for Sochaux that day. They were still young so they weren't that famous at the time but I became very aware of Gilles when he was playing for Sochaux, Lyon, Marseille and the French national team."

Adam's two years with Amiens, a club he initially joined in the third tier in 1993, proved particularly fruitful as he helped them win promotion in his first season and was their top scorer in 1994/95 when they finished ninth in Ligue 2. The standout moment of that campaign for Amiens was a 2-1 home win over eventual title winners Marseille, who had been relegated from the top flight in 1994 following a match-fixing scandal. Adam's exploits with Amiens earned him a crack at the top flight in the summer of 1995, when he was signed by Metz, who were embarking on the most buoyant period in their history. "I had been one of the top scorers in the second division but to go from Amiens to Metz was a big step forward for me," says Adam. "Metz were a team with big ambitions at the time. They wanted to play in Europe and fight for the title."

Adam's Metz team-mates included Robert Pires, who would go on to star for France and Arsenal; Cameroon internationalist Rigobert Song, who went on to play for Liverpool and West Ham United; and Freddie Arpinon, a midfielder who joined Hibs in 2001. His Ligue 1 debut came, aged 26, in July 1995 as a starter in a 2-0 home win over a Lens side featuring Jean-Marc Adjovi-Boco, who would go on to become an Edinburgh rival of Adam's two years later when Duffy signed him for Hibs in summer 1997. The highlight of Adam's time at Metz came towards the end of his first season when they won the French League Cup – one of only four major honours in their history at the time of publication – by defeating Lyon on penalties in the final in front of 45,368 spectators in Paris on 6 April 1996. That was the same day Hearts beat Aberdeen 2-1 in the Scottish Cup semi-final. Adam came on as a 35th-minute replacement for the injured Patrick M'Boma and scored one of the penalties in the shootout following a goalless draw. "That was my first trophy as a professional footballer and it was at the Parc des Princes against Lyon so I've got fantastic memories of it," says Adam.

In Adam's two seasons at Metz, they finished fourth and fifth in Ligue 1, ensuring qualification for the UEFA Cup each time. The striker made 51 appearances in total in all competitions – 24 as a starter – and scored six goals: three in each season. "Metz were a team in form at the time and I was lucky enough to play with Robert Pires; it was a fun time," says Adam. "I had to fight for my place in the team because we had good attackers like Pires, M'Boma and Cyrille Pouget, who were all quite big names. I learned a lot at Metz and my game improved in this period, which is one reason I think I had the chance to come over and play for Hearts later on."

Adam had the option of a contract extension at Metz as he approached his 28th birthday in May 1997 but, having been unable to establish himself as a regular starter, he had made up his mind to try his luck elsewhere. "I had a few offers from France and abroad so I had a choice to make," he says. "I was 27, nearly 28, and I had played in the second division and the first division in France so I felt it was the right time for me to go abroad and discover something new."

Hearts manager Jim Jefferies became aware of Adam in the wake of his visit to Hibs and he and assistant Billy Brown took advantage of a free weekend for his team in late April 1997 to travel to northern France in the hope of watching the striker in a Ligue 1 match at home to Auxerre. "Metz is right up next to the Luxembourg border," says Jefferies. "We flew into Strasbourg and Stephane's wife actually picked us up at the airport because his agent wasn't able to do it, so we drove to Metz and found out Stephane wasn't even on the bench! He'd been coming back from a small injury so wasn't included in the squad. No trip's a waste of time, though. We got to meet Stephane after it and talked to him about Hearts and the possibility of joining us. I said 'if you're really interested, why don't you and your agent try to arrange for Metz to let you come over for a few days?'."

Adam travelled to Edinburgh at the start of the week leading up to the final game of the 1996/97 season, at home to Rangers. "I played in a closed-doors friendly and, straight after the game, Jim Jefferies offered me a contract," says Adam. "I went back to France, spoke to my wife and spoke to my agent. Hearts had built up a very good team and according to Jim and Billy were looking to challenge Celtic and Rangers, so it seemed like the right club at the right time for me. I flew back to Edinburgh on the Saturday of the last day of the season to sign my contract. It was the day Robbo got the scoring record against Rangers. It was the first time I discovered Tynecastle and the atmosphere and passion of the Hearts supporters. When I came on the pitch at half-time to be presented to the crowd, I felt like the people were happy to meet me and that there was an expectation around me signing, which I was quite happy with. I could feel the expectation, and that gave me a lot of motivation to come back and do my best and also gave me the knowledge that I'd signed for a big club."

Adam attended Prestonpans Hearts Supporters Club's end-of-season awards dinner on the Saturday evening after the Rangers game and then returned home to France to prepare for the first foray abroad of his football career. "I came back to Edinburgh in mid-June for pre-season and I was made very welcome from everyone at Hearts," he recalls. "I enjoyed it from the start. We had a crazy pre-season, very different from what I'd experienced in France. We didn't touch the ball very much! We ran a lot in the first week; we went to Murder Hill (a steep sand dune) in Gullane which was very tough. The first few weeks I was staying in a hotel and I was really tired; most of the time I was just training and sleeping."

Adam and Thomas Flögel were the only two new arrivals of summer 1997, and both needed time to find their feet. The Frenchman came on as a substitute for the last 17 minutes of the opening league game away to Rangers and set up Colin

Cameron's consolation goal in a 3-1 defeat; he scored his first for the club in his fourth appearance when he secured a 2-1 win away to Raith Rovers in the Coca-Cola Cup before being sent off 14 minutes later for a tussle with Danny Lennon; and he got his first league goal in his sixth Premier Division appearance when he notched the third from close range in a 3-0 win away to Kilmarnock in late September. "It took me probably a couple of months to settle into the Scottish game and the way we were working at Hearts," he says. "It took me about a month into the competitive games until I started to show my best."

Apart from his cup final winner, Adam's most memorable contribution in his maiden season at Hearts came in late November when he scored a hat-trick in a 5-3 win at home to Kilmarnock: a brace of headers and a trademark run in behind the opposition defence before firing beyond goalkeeper Dragoje Lekovic. "That game was on the Sunday because Scotland were playing Australia in the rugby at Murrayfield on the Saturday; I remember that because me and Gilles went along," says Adam, who enjoyed watching rugby from a young age. "The Kilmarnock game was crazy; a very open game between two attacking teams looking to score goals. We were 1-0 down again, but we came back into it. There were defensive mistakes from both teams but we were the better team. It was my first hat-trick for Hearts. I'd scored a few hat-tricks in France, but Robbo told me he never scored a hat-trick in a (top-flight) league game for Hearts, so I knew it was a good achievement. It was a fantastic day for me."

In addition to his goals, Adam's workrate, intelligence and pace earned him the respect of supporters and team-mates. "Stephane was very important for us because he just ran all the time," says Rousset. "He would go in behind defences and he could create space for the other guys in our attack and for guys coming from the midfield. Because he never stopped running, he was very hard for opposition defenders to handle."

After his hat-trick against Kilmarnock, Adam had to wait another three months for his next goal, when he struck in the 4-2 win at Motherwell in February. He finished his first season in Scotland with eight league goals. Although he was never as prolific as Robertson in Gorgie, Adam brought an extra dimension to Hearts' attack. "Stephane was terrific," says Jefferies. "He was very intelligent and played on the shoulders of defenders. Anything over the top or in behind, he was very quick. He made intelligent runs and he was a good finisher. He was also very unselfish."

All these qualities made Adam the perfect candidate for the lone striker role when Jefferies decided to change to a 4-5-1 formation for the cup final against Rangers. The confident Frenchman was unfazed by the prospect of flying solo against a batch of high-pedigree defenders such as Richard Gough, Lorenzo Amoruso, Joachim Bjorklund and Sergio Porrini. "It wasn't new for me to play up front on my own because in France I used to play quite often as a lone striker, so it wasn't a problem for me," says Adam. "I liked to run, I liked to play on my own, to go in behind defences, so my style suited this role and this kind of tactic. I knew I would have a lot of running to do but I knew I'd have the support of Colin Cameron, Neil McCann, Thomas Flögel and Stevie Fulton. I wasn't scared of playing against guys like Bjorklund, Gough, Amoruso and Porrini. It was a cup final against Rangers so I knew I would be up against big-name players but that was no problem for me. I knew that playing against that strong Rangers defence I would get very few chances but I was always confident I would get at least one chance to do something. My focus was to move and create spaces, put them under pressure and wait for the right chance to come along. I knew if I got a chance, I would need to take it properly but, honestly, I was very confident before the game."

It all came to fruition in the most perfect fashion imaginable in the 53rd minute when Adam pickpocketed the dithering Amoruso and drove into the penalty area before firing an angled shot beyond the despairing Goram to put Hearts 2-0 ahead and on course for glory. "The goal was my first chance of the game," says Adam. "After that I had another half-chance when Dave McPherson put a header across the goal and I was only a few inches away from touching it, but the goal was the proper chance I was waiting for. I knew it would come. We had played well that season and challenged Celtic and Rangers for the league and throughout that season I learned a lot about Hearts' history. I knew they hadn't won anything for a long time. The supporters and the people connected to the club would speak to you throughout the season and say 'guys, we have to win something, please win something for us'. And then when I scored that goal to put us 2-0 up against Rangers, I was thinking 'ok, this could be our day'. The supporters had been so good to me from the start, and when I scored my goal, I thought 'something special is happening for them'. I stayed focused after my goal, though. I remember after we celebrated, I said to Stevie Fulton 'this is ours, we can't give it up'. I knew we still had to fight hard. We had to stay concentrated; we had to be strong defensively and work together as a team."

After 78 minutes, Adam – who had put in a tireless shift in the Glasgow heat – became the first and only Hearts player to be substituted in the final. "Stephane was very unselfish and he did a selfless job for the team in the final," says McCann. "He ran up there all day himself."

With 12 minutes plus stoppage-time remaining and Hearts leading 2-0, Adam was no longer able to influence his team's bid for glory. "It was very stressful when I was substituted because I was off the pitch and could not do any more in the game," he says. "I went to the dressing-room because I didn't want to watch the last ten minutes. I remember the game where we played Rangers at Ibrox a few months earlier and we had been 2-1 up before Jorg Albertz scored a free-kick in the last minute. I didn't want to see this happen again. I went back to the dressing-room and stayed in the corridor. Just at the entrance of the dressing-room was Gary Locke, Neil Pointon and some of the other guys who weren't playing. I didn't watch the last ten minutes but when the final whistle went I was straight back out on the pitch. The other guys in suits weren't allowed on at first but because I still had my strip on they let me back on straight away. The first guy I saw was the physio, Alan Rae. I jumped in his arms. I wasn't thinking too much at that point about the fact I had scored the goal. I was more interested in celebrating with my friends and team-mates because we had such a good relationship together and we had worked so hard. It was fantastic to celebrate altogether on the pitch with the energy coming from the supporters. That was the main focus at that time, just to be happy, celebrate together and enjoy the moment."

When the dust settled, Adam knew he had achieved something career-defining. "It wasn't the most spectacular goal I scored but it was certainly the most important for lots of reasons," says the Frenchman. "It was my first year at Hearts, my first year in a foreign country; I was at a big club with great supporters who were waiting for their moment of glory so I'm very proud and happy to be the man that scored that goal and put my stamp in club history. I won two cups in my career but the one with Hearts was the best by far. Winning the cup with Metz was fantastic because it was my first trophy but the passion from the supporters and stuff wasn't as big and didn't compare to winning it with Hearts. Because of the situation and because Hearts is a club with passionate people connected to it, the feeling and emotion was much bigger with Hearts. It was certainly the best moment of my football career."

The magnitude of the Frenchman's intervention in Hearts' history is underlined by the fact some supporters named their babies after him. David Kennedy was one of them, as he decided to call his son – born three weeks after the cup win, on 9th June 1998 – Adam. The striker is humbled at having Hearts supporters named after him. "Adam is in his 20s now and we speak together on social media occasionally," says Stephane. "When he says his name is because of me, it is very funny; it's amazing. This is why I feel proud. When this kind of thing happens, you realise you did your job well and you did something special."

The Kennedy family feel honoured to have developed a bond with the man who scored – in the minds of many – the most important goal in Hearts' history. "I had to persuade my wife Jane to call him Adam but she was happy to go with it in the end," says David, a Howgate-based Hearts fan who grew up in Morningside. "If Adam had been a girl I'd have hoped to go with Stephanie but that might have been a harder one to get Jane to agree to! I wrote to Stephane the week after Adam was born to congratulate him and tell him I'd named my son after him and he sent us his training top, signed and with a lovely letter. Sadly we lost the letter when our house got flooded in 2000, but Adam's still got the training top up in a frame in his bedroom. Adam is absolutely obsessed with Hearts and although he's not able to remember Stephane playing, he's well aware of what he did for Hearts and takes a lot of pride from being named after him; it means a lot to me as well. Stephane follows us and engages with us on social media. He just seems like such a nice chap."

Rousset, the striker's closest friend from his time at Hearts, can vouch for this. "I didn't know Stephane personally before he came to Hearts; I just knew him by name," says the goalkeeper. "But I am very close to him; he's a great guy and we still speak to each other now. The same as me, he fell in love with Scotland, with Edinburgh, with Hearts, the fans and the rest of the boys. He's Hearts-daft."

Adam departed Hearts in May 2002, having made the last of his 130 appearances for the club two days before his 33rd birthday in a 3-2 home defeat by Livingston. Injuries took their toll in his final two seasons at the club, and after scoring 22 across his first two campaigns, he ended up with a total of 33 goals from his five years in Gorgie; a tally not reflective of his overall contribution to Hearts. As a result of his exploits on 16th May 1998 and the fact that his spell at Tynecastle was the longest he spent with any club, Adam will be "a Hearts supporter for life". He has certainly emerged as one of the club's most impassioned former players on social media: expressing dismay over the way Hearts' controversial demotion to the Championship in 2020 was handled by the authorities; tweeting that Hearts would be the "only club" that could bring him back into football when a supporter enquired if he fancied returning to Gorgie as a coach; branding Tam McManus "a clown" after the former Hibs striker got himself into a fankle while attempting to compare how the two Edinburgh clubs had dealt with the financial challenges encountered at the onset of the coronavirus pandemic; and posing in Hearts' 2019/20 black third strip on the 22nd anniversary of his cup final winner. "I've got a feeling of pride because I went to Scotland and I showed people they were right to have confidence in me and give me the chance to play for this football club," he says. "I feel like I gave Hearts something back and I am proud of this. I'll be connected to the club for life now. I still follow the team, I've got plenty of friends in Edinburgh and I come over as often as possible and I make sure I go to the Hearts game when I'm over. I am still in contact with a lot of people connected with the club and I feel like I am part of the Hearts family."

In the summer of 1995, Jim Jefferies and Billy Brown arrive from Falkirk to take the reins at Tynecastle.

Gilles Rousset, who was guilty of a handling blunder early in the second half, Neil Pointon and Alan Lawrence after the 5-1 Scottish Cup final defeat by Rangers in May 1996.

Stefano Salvatori gives the thumbs up alongside compatriot Pasquale Bruno in Bar Roma.

Salvatori keeps his eye on the ball during a pre-season win at Berwick Rangers in July 1997.

With spirits high in the Hearts camp in the week leading up to the 1998 Scottish Cup final, Stephane Adam, Stefano Salvatori, Thomas Flögel and Lee Makel share a joke at the team's training camp in Stratford.

Hearts players celebrate Neil McCann's opener in the 2-2 draw with Rangers at Ibrox in February 1998.

In the hours after the cup win, fans gather on Gorgie Road and clamber on scaffolding as the party begins.

Following his transfer from French club Metz, new signing Stephane Adam is unveiled to the supporters at half-time of a 3-1 league win over Rangers at Tynecastle on the last day of the 1996/97 campaign.

Gilles Rousset, Jim Hamilton and Neil McCann toast the Scottish Cup win the following day at Tynecastle.

Hearts' LRT open-top bus crawls through a sea of sun-drenched supporters as it passes by Gorgie Farm.

Jim Jefferies, the architect of Hearts' cup success, enjoys a lap of honour at Tynecastle on the Sunday.

With his new, peroxide-blond hairstyle, Stephen Fulton previews the 1998 cup final.

Fulton is interviewed on the Celtic Park pitch in the aftermath of the 2-1 victory.

Salvatori and Gary Locke have a laugh ahead of the Cup Winners' Cup clash at Real Mallorca in October 98.

Stefano Salvatori jumps for joy after scoring at Dunfermline in December 1997, the Italian's only goal for Hearts.

At Hearts' training camp in England in the week of the final, midfielder Salvatori limbers up for the big day.

Salvatori takes a break from training at the Braids in Edinburgh to chat with team-mate Dave McPherson.

David Weir, scorer of the second goal, goes up for a corner in the 2-0 third-round win over Clydebank.

The fourth round against Albion Rovers, Jose Quitongo heads home the first of his two goals in the 3-0 win.

Jim Hamilton smashes home from close range near the end of the 4-1 quarter-final win against Ayr United.

The 3-1 semi-final win over Falkirk, Stephane Adam bundles the ball home late on to put Hearts back in front.

Rangers players slump to the Celtic Park turf ahead of the 1998 Scottish Cup final trophy presentation.

Ibrox legends Ally McCoist and Richard Gough console each other after their last appearance for Rangers ends in defeat by Hearts.

The man who scored the all-important winning goal in the cup final, Stephane Adam is all smiles as he spots someone in the crowd at full-time.

Lord Provost and Hearts supporter Eric Milligan reads all about the cup triumph in his copy of The Pink.

Jubilant Hearts players dance on the roof of their team bus in Gorgie after climbing through the skylight.

With the club's long trophy drought finally over, Hearts supporters celebrate in the stands at Celtic Park.

Jose Quitongo keeps Hearts' title dream alive with a late, late equaliser against Celtic in February 1998.

After waiting 18 years to get his hands on some silverware, the 1998 Scottish Cup triumph reduces Hearts legend John Robertson to tears.

With the Scottish Cup in one hand and his daughter, Jade, in the other, Robertson enjoys the party at Tynecastle on the Sunday afternoon.

The first day of pre-season training in July 1997, and new recruit Stephane Adam is bringing up the rear.

Gary Mackay
consoles a tearful
Paul Ritchie following
Hearts' 5-1 defeat by
Rangers in the 1996
Scottish Cup final.

Six months later and
Mackay is again
the one comforting
Ritchie, this time after
the 4-3 Coca-Cola
Cup final defeat, also
against Rangers.

Flanked by Gary Locke and John Robertson, it's third time lucky as Ritchie gets his hands on the Scottish Cup.

Summer 1996, new signings Jeremy Goss, Neil McCann and David Weir are unveiled in Gorgie.

Hearts winger McCann puts in a man-of-the-match performance in the Coca-Cola Cup final.

The day after the cup win, Jose Quitongo and his son, Jai, arrive at Tynecastle to continue the celebrations.

Thomas Flögel and Stephane Adam were the only new faces to arrive at Hearts in summer 97 as Jim Jefferies went for quality over quantity.

With 90 seconds of the 1998 final gone, Colin Cameron's penalty beats Andy Goram.

Hearts' 78th-minute substitute Jim Hamilton tussles with Rangers defender Lorenzo Amoruso.

Bedlam on the touchline as the Hearts bench celebrate the final whistle at Celtic Park on 16th May 1998.

Sealed with a kiss, manager Jim Jefferies and his assistant, Billy Brown, get their hands on the silverware.

Sparking a run of five league wins in a row, Neil McCann secures a 1-0 victory against Hibs in August 1997.

February 1998, Gary Naysmith scores against Aberdeen at Tynecastle to keep Hearts joint top of the table.

Colin Cameron congratulates Jim Hamilton on his early goal in the 1-0 win against Dundee United at Tannadice in March.

The day the title dream died, Kevin Harper scores Hibs' winning goal at Easter Road.

Dave McPherson takes on Aberdeen's Eoin Jess in the penultimate league game of the 1997/98 season.

Dressed in gear thrown from the stands, strikers Jim Hamilton and Stephane Adam celebrate the cup win.

Hearts supporters pack Gorgie Road as Sunday's open-top bus parade makes its way to Tynecastle.

November 1997, Gilles Rousset and Stephane Adam join a fourth year French class at George Heriot's School.

Hearts' newly-crowned cup legends clamber through the skylight and on to the roof of the Park's of Hamilton coach that had just transported them back along the M8 from Celtic Park to Tynecastle.

As some of the players started to wave flags and dangle their legs off the side of the vehicle, these images were captured from the window of Hearts supporter Derek Ferguson's flat on Gorgie Road.

Club captain Gary Locke and Hearts' skipper for the day Stephen Fulton share trophy-lifting duties.

Huddled behind boards bearing the sponsor's logo, the Hearts squad celebrate their cup win at Celtic Park.

Basking in the sun and the glory, a proud Jim Jefferies crouches in front of some of his players and staff.

Colin Cameron, scorer of the opening goal, sits on John Robertson's shoulders as he shows off the trophy.

Dave McPherson

*"People say never go back, but I seemed
to make a mockery of that theory"*

There was no more decorated player in Hearts' 1997/98 squad than Dave McPherson. The 34-year-old defender had won three Scottish Premier Division titles, four League Cups and one Scottish Cup over the course of his two stints with Rangers, the club he grew up supporting. In addition, McPherson had represented Scotland 27 times, including at two major tournaments: the World Cup in Italy in 1990, where he started all three matches against Costa Rica, Sweden and Brazil, and the European Championships in Sweden two years later, when he once again started all three, against Netherlands, Germany and CIS (Soviet Union). For too long, however, there was a glaring omission from his impressive CV: he hadn't won anything with Hearts, the club at which he had spent more than half of his career and made over 300 appearances during two separate spells. The long-awaited Scottish Cup triumph in 1998, achieved as underdogs and with his Hearts-supporting son Chris watching from the stand, therefore, means every bit as much to McPherson as anything he accomplished while playing for boyhood club Rangers. "I'd won a number of trophies at Rangers but I was always desperate to win something at Hearts," says McPherson, who first moved to Tynecastle in 1987, rejoined the Ibrox club in 1992 and then returned to Gorgie in 1994. "Going back to my first spell at Hearts, I don't know how we didn't win anything because we had a really good squad and went close a few times. When I went back to Hearts the second time, I was just desperate to win something. Having spent more or less ten years at Hearts and captained the club, I knew time was running out for me to win something so it was a special moment to break the mould and win the trophy in 98."

By the time he eventually got his crowning moment at Hearts, McPherson – nicknamed "Slim" due to his rangy 6ft 4ins frame – was in his mid-30s and at the end of a season heavily disrupted by knee problems. Indeed, so peripheral was the popular defender for long periods of the campaign, the final against Rangers was the only match of the cup run in which he actually played. While everyone else who enjoyed game time in the final had featured in at least three of the four earlier rounds, McPherson wasn't in the squad for the victories over Clydebank, Albion Rovers or Ayr United and was an unused substitute for the semi-final against Falkirk. "The cup final was the only game I played but when you look back, the majority of people won't remember the other games; they'll just remember the final because it's the most important one," says McPherson. "I had a lot of niggly injuries that season and it was frustrating to be out when the team was doing so well because you always want to be part of it. There were some games where I felt my experience might have helped make a wee difference. I was lucky that I didn't have any serious injury problems in my career but when you get to the age I was, it becomes harder to keep yourself at peak fitness. Even though I had my injuries that year, I finished it off with a Scottish Cup winner's medal. It doesn't matter how many games you've played in, there's not a better way to finish the season than being involved in the Scottish Cup final and winning it. It's always the game everyone remembers."

It is certainly the game McPherson's son remembers most. Aged nine, Chris McPherson – a Jambo from the moment he first took a proper interest in football in 1995 – got to experience the unique thrill of watching his favourite team win the Scottish Cup with his own father playing a key role. Too young to recall his exploits with Scotland and Rangers, Chris's main source of pride regarding Dave's distinguished playing career derives from memories of watching with delight from the Celtic Park directors' box as he lifted the Scottish Cup as a Hearts player. "I'm proud of him for being part of something that made so many people so happy," says young McPherson, 31 at the time of publication. "For as long as they live, everyone at that game will be able to tell you the name of every player that played that day, and it's a really nice thing to know your dad was involved in something as meaningful as that. I just wish that I'd been able to see him win more things. I would love to have seen him play at the World Cup; that would have been like the height of pride. But as a Hearts supporter, I take a lot of pride from the fact my dad is part of my club's history."

This is endorsed by the fact McPherson and the rest of the 1998 Scottish Cup-winning heroes were inducted to Hearts' Hall of Fame in 2018 although Chris feels his dad might have been worthy of inclusion prior to this on the basis of being a cup winner who sits – at the time of publication – 20th on Hearts' all-time appearance chart. "We've reflected on the cup win together more in the last few years since he got put into the Hall of Fame with the rest of the team," says Chris. "I've always found it slightly strange, just from a personal point of view, that he hasn't been inducted to the Hall of Fame as an individual. With winning the trophy and, statistically, with the number of games he played, I think he's just as deserving as a lot of players – maybe moreso than some – that have been put in."

It says much about what McPherson accomplished in his 20-year career that he is in the Hall of Fame at two of Scotland's biggest clubs, with Rangers having inducted him in 2014. Born in Paisley and raised in Pollok, where he attended Crookston Castle Secondary School, McPherson first embarked on his journey with Rangers when he joined as a 16-year-old in 1980. He made his first-team debut under John Greig as a 17-year-old in a 1-0 League Cup win at home to Brechin City in September 1981 and started to make his presence felt the following season before becoming a regular in his early 20s. Team-mates at Ibrox in this period included Jim Stewart, a future Hearts goalkeeping coach; Kenny Black, Jim Bett, Sandy Jardine and Sandy Clark, all of whom McPherson would go on to play with at Tynecastle; and Tommy McLean, who would become his manager at Hearts in the 1994/95 campaign. "Davie was a top player," says Clark, who first linked up with McPherson in 1983 when the defender was 19. "My first real memory of Davie was playing in the 1984 League Cup final (when Rangers beat Celtic 3-2 courtesy of an Ally McCoist hat-trick). We were missing a few players so Jock Wallace put Davie wide left in a midfield four! He was only 20 but he had an absolutely brilliant game. He was a big skinny drip but he was a really good footballer."

After winning the League Cup with Rangers in both 1984 and 1985, McPherson savoured his first league title as a 23-year-old in 1986/87. His delight at the end of that season was soured, however, when he returned from holidaying in Spain to be informed that manager Graeme Souness, who had replaced Wallace in 1986 and was eager to freshen the team up with his own signings, had sanctioned the sale of he and fellow Rangers defender Hugh Burns to Hearts. The Tynecastle club paid £500,000 for the pair, with McPherson – who cost £400,000 – becoming Hearts' record signing at the time. "I won the league, I didn't miss any games and I scored nine goals but then all of a sudden I was sold," says McPherson. As angry as he was with Souness at being cut loose from his boyhood club, McPherson set about taking his game to a new level at Hearts under co-managers Alex MacDonald and Jardine, his old Rangers team-mate. This move also reunited the mulleted defender with striker Clark. "By the time Davie got to Hearts, he had developed into a cen-tre-half with real quality," says Clark. "He was a ball-playing Alan Hansen-type. Him and Craig Levein played together at the back and they were different class."

In two of his first three seasons at Tynecastle, Hearts finished in the top three of the Premier Division, with McPherson – who prided himself on trying to play football from the back and carried a goal threat at set-pieces – one of their key men. Aged 25, he captained the Edinburgh side to their famous 1-0 UEFA Cup quarter-final victory at home to Bayern Munich in February 1989 before they lost the second leg 2-0 in Germany. McPherson made his Scotland debut two months later in a 2-1 victory over Cyprus in a World Cup qualifier at Hampden, and a little over a year later he was off to Italia 90 – along with team-mate Levein – as one of Scotland manager Andy Roxburgh's first-choice defenders.

The move to Hearts proved to be the making of McPherson as one of the coun-try's top centre-backs in the late 1980s and early 1990s. Although Rangers are still the club he supports, he enjoyed so much career fulfilment in Gorgie that he will always maintain a strong affiliation with Hearts. "I was brought up not far from Ibrox, I was taken to Ibrox as a kid and I joined Rangers as a schoolboy, a bit like how Gary Locke and Gary Mackay were brought up as Hearts supporters," says McPherson, explaining his Rangers background. "You're not just going to change your mind overnight about who you support but I'm sure if Gary Locke or Gary

Mackay had spent ten years at Rangers – like I did at Hearts – they would have an affinity with the club. Particularly in my first spell at Hearts, I was attending supporters' club events every Saturday night, so that brought me close to the fans and I had a really good bond with the supporters which I still have to this day."

McPherson's star was constantly on the rise throughout his first spell at Tynecastle and in his fifth season (1991/92), he captained Joe Jordan's Hearts side to second in the Premier Division before heading off to Sweden for Euro 92 as Scotland competed with the continent's elite nations at the finals for the first time since the tournament began in 1960. Just like at the World Cup two years previously, the Scots lost two matches and won one as they made a group-stage exit. McPherson, aged 28, performed so well at Hearts that Rangers, who had won four league titles in a row at that point, moved to buy him back that summer for a fee of £1.3 million. Rangers manager Walter Smith, who replaced Souness a year earlier, admitted it had been a mistake to let the defender join Hearts in the first place. He spent two-and-a-bit years back at Ibrox and helped Rangers win five of the six domestic trophies available to them in that period. They won the treble in 1992/93, with April 93 a particularly notable month for McPherson as he scored in a 2-1 Scottish Cup semi-final win over Hearts at Celtic Park, won what would be the last of his 27 Scotland caps in a 5-0 mauling by Portugal in a World Cup qualifier in Lisbon, and had his hopes of winning the Champions League dashed at the penultimate hurdle when Marseille pipped Rangers by a point to top Group A and set up a showdown with AC Milan in the final in Munich. In the following season, the defender helped Rangers win the league and League Cup double before they lost to Dundee United in the Scottish Cup final after goalkeeper Ally Maxwell had smashed his clearance from a McPherson passback against Christian Dailly, allowing Craig Brewster to tap in the game's only goal. McPherson started the 1994/95 season at Ibrox but was on his way back to Tynecastle for a second spell in October 94 as part of the deal that took 23-year-old defender Alan McLaren – with whom he had played alongside for both Hearts and Scotland – to Rangers. Having enjoyed his previous five-year stint at Tynecastle, the 30-year-old McPherson was happy to return to Edinburgh in a move which saw him reunited with his former Rangers team-mate McLean, who was in his early months as Hearts manager. "Going to Hearts the first time turned out to be a great move for me so I was excited when I got the chance to go back the second time," he says. "It was an easy decision. I never looked upon joining Hearts from Rangers as a step backwards, I always looked upon it as a step to the side, a chance to go somewhere I could make myself a better player. There's not many better places to do that than Heart of Midlothian Football Club. People say you should never go back but I seemed to make a mockery of that theory in my career."

In one of the few highlights of Hearts' grim 1994/95 season, McPherson produced a superb performance – featuring a goal and a trademark marauding run from defence which set up Kevin Thomas to score – in a 4-2 Scottish Cup victory over Rangers at Tynecastle in February 1995. There was no hint of divided loyalty as McPherson celebrated his headed goal against his former club with clear delight just four months after leaving Ibrox.

After McLean was replaced by Jim Jefferies in summer 1995, every Hearts player was at risk of being phased out as the new manager set about shaking things up. "That happens at all football clubs, as I found out when Graeme Souness got rid of me at Rangers after we'd won the league," says McPherson. "Jim tried to bring some freshness in with the younger players. He was very good in the transfer market and he managed to build a really good squad of players."

While long-serving colleagues like Levein, Mackay, Neil Berry, John Colquhoun, and Henry Smith had run their course at Hearts, McPherson was one of the few players to survive the Jefferies cull. Indeed, he was the only first-team player the manager inherited in 1995 who went on to play in the 1998 Scottish Cup final. "Davie was just a good player to have in your team," says Jefferies. "He could play anywhere, he could defend, he could get forward, he had good composure. He'd played for Scotland and Rangers and had quality. He read the game great and was good in the air; he had everything you wanted in a defender."

Having been a prominent player in every one of his eight seasons at Tynecastle prior to 1997/98, McPherson – described as "an absolute gentleman" by Austrian team-mate Thomas Flögel – is entitled to feel he had earned the stroke of fortune that allowed him to come in from the periphery at the business end of an injury-interrupted campaign just in time to land the glory he had craved in a Hearts jersey. After being restricted by a knee issue to playing just a few minutes of his own testimonial match against Rangers at Tynecastle in July 1997, the veteran was sidelined until January 1998, when he made his first appearance of the campaign in the 3-2 win away to St Johnstone. In total he made just ten starts in the league, his lowest count of any of the ten seasons he spent at Tynecastle. When it was confirmed that club captain Gary Locke wasn't going to be fit for the final, McPherson, who started each of the closing three league games and chipped in with three goals from mid-March onwards, was the most experienced and obvious candidate to line up at right-back, a position that had been shared by Allan McManus, Locke and Grant Murray – among others – earlier in the campaign. Although McPherson was predominantly a centre-back, he had all the attributes required to play on the right. "When I started at Rangers I was a centre-back but I think because I was good on the ball some managers would play me at right-back," says McPherson. "Fitness-wise, I could get up and down the pitch quite well. Right-back wasn't my favourite position but that doesn't matter when you've got a chance to win a cup. I had to mark Brian Laudrup that day so I knew I would have to be at the top of my game."

Having only followed Hearts for three years prior to the 1998 final, McPherson's son was accustomed to the Tynecastle side struggling against Rangers. Chris and his classmates in primary four at George Watson's – encouraged by their Hearts-supporting teacher, Mr Robertson – made "good luck" cards for his dad ahead of the final, and Dave had told his son beforehand that he was confident this would finally be Hearts' day. Chris – like many more seasoned Jambos – was far from convinced. "Even though I was only nine I could sense the tension because in the three years I had been going to Hearts games, I'd only seen us beat Rangers once," Chris recalls. "I'd missed the two wins we had in 95/96 because I was still too young to go to away games or midweek games. I'd never seen us beat Rangers apart from the last game of the previous season when John Robertson broke the scoring record, but even then that game felt like a bit of a testimonial for Robbo because Rangers had already won the league. I'd been brought up with the belief basically that Rangers are the best team in the country and they are one of the best teams in the world; that's how it was portrayed in the Scottish media at the time. Hearts were seemingly an afterthought as it was all about Walter Smith's last game; it was almost accepted that we wouldn't win this game. Before the game, my dad told me we were going to win. I said 'oh, but we've not beaten Rangers all season' and he replied 'this is different, this is the one that matters and we're going to win this one'."

Even though he was no longer club captain, and hadn't been a regular in the 1997/98 campaign, there was a lot of responsibility on McPherson's 34-year-old shoulders going into the final. He was the oldest outfield player in the starting XI by almost four years; he had played a lot more games for Hearts than anyone else bar substitute Robertson; he was the only player who had played at a major international tournament; he had won more trophies than anyone else; and he was the veteran member of a back four which also included a 22-year-old (Paul Ritchie) and a 19-year-old (Gary Naysmith). McPherson duly revelled in the Celtic Park sunshine. "As the oldest player in the team, I felt like I had a responsibility to help other guys deal with it and keep everybody relaxed," says McPherson. "We had good defenders in there and we had a bit of experience with myself and Gilles (Rousset). Everything felt right, the team felt right. It was a glorious day and it helped that we got off to a flier. Getting that goal so early probably helped us a lot in terms of taking the pressure off, especially the boys who hadn't won anything before. I think it probably made a lot of people realise 'hang on a minute, we can win this'. From a personal point of view, I thought I played really well; I enjoyed it. I had a run up the park in the closing stages and I don't know where I got the energy from because I was on the Hearts supporters' side, where the sun was beating down, so it was roasting hot. My fitness throughout my career was always pretty good but it was certainly tested that day. I think what kept me going was just looking at the Hearts fans who were all the way up my side of the pitch in the second half. The supporters carried us through that day, especially in the last 20 minutes or so. Everything just went perfect on the day."

Aged 35, McPherson left Hearts a year later to join Australian club Carlton with 364 competitive appearances and 32 goals to his name over the course of his two five-year spells at Tynecastle. For a man who was accustomed to winning things at Rangers, he cherishes the fact he also has a piece of silverware and memories of that glorious weekend in May 1998 to illuminate his brilliant decade of service with Hearts. "I probably didn't realise before the final just how big it would be if Hearts won something, but you certainly knew after the match just how big it was," says McPherson. "The scale of it was just incredible. It made me a bit emotional actually. Going back to my time at Rangers, you got the post-match celebrations on the pitch where the supporters are going mental, which was always brilliant; I expected that with Hearts as well. But what you never got at Rangers was the journey back to the stadium on the Saturday night after the game, with all the crowds greeting you when you got back, and then the bus parade through the city the following day. It was a real eye-opener, just incredible. It's a weekend I'll never forget."

Neil McCann

*"We knew Neil would usually be out of
our price range. We got him for a song"*

Between 1998 and 2003, nobody had a firmer grip on the Scottish Cup than Neil McCann. In the six stagings of the competition within this period, the winger from Port Glasgow got his hands on the old trophy a remarkable five times: once with Hearts and on four occasions with Rangers. McCann is in no doubt about which of these triumphs means most to him. "The one with Hearts in 1998 was the best by far, no question," he says. "I won two Old Firm cup finals and one of them was when (Peter) Lovenkrands scored with the last kick of the ball to win 3-2 (in 2002). I played in proper, epic cup finals, but everything involved in this one made it the best: the build-up, Hearts not winning it for so long, the group I was playing with, the fact it was my first Scottish Cup, beating a legendary Rangers side when every-body probably thought 'Hearts will choke again'. All of that blended in together, and then going back to Tynecastle on the bus after the game; that journey home is something I'll never ever forget. The Sunday was brilliant as well but the bus back to Gorgie on the Saturday is something that will live with me for the rest of my life. You can't do stuff like that in Glasgow and it's a shame because it was incredible with Hearts. It was just ridiculous."

The journey involved in getting to this point of glory, aged just 23, also added to McCann's sense of achievement. In the space of 18 months, the winger faced Rangers twice in cup finals at Celtic Park, and both brought very different outcomes. In the first – just four months after joining Hearts from Dundee – he terrorised the Rangers defence with one of the best performances of his career but ended up with only a Coca-Cola-branded 'man-of-the-match' mountain bike as reward fol-lowing a gallant 4-3 defeat in wintry conditions. "I kept the bike in my garage for a while and then I gave it back to Hearts many years later to auction off for their youth fund," says McCann. "It's nice when people talk about how well I played in

1996 but ultimately it means nothing. Mentally I took a lot from it in terms of it reinforcing to me that we weren't far away from potentially winning something, but in terms of being runner-up in a cup final, that means nothing."

Despite being at the same venue and against the same opponents, McCann's second final for Hearts – the 1998 Scottish Cup – proved to be a totally contrasting experience to the first one. This time there was no swashbuckling individual performance, no bleak November weather, and – most crucially – no "meaningless" consolation prize. Where previously the marauding left-winger had caused havoc for the Rangers defence, this time – in searing mid-May heat – he spent much of the game chasing, harrying and back-pedalling, trying to help out his full-back, Gary Naysmith. Notable forays forward were almost non-existent for McCann on a day when both sides adopted a more defensive approach. Indeed, Scotland manager Craig Brown – co-commentating on the 1998 final for Sky Sports – mused that Rangers, who had started with a back three and a defensively-minded midfield five, had been guilty of showing McCann "too much respect" before they tweaked their formation at half-time. The absence of space to thrive and personal accolades at the end of it mattered not a single bit, however, as McCann landed the first big prize of his career. "I ended up playing left-back at times in the 98 final," says McCann. "It took a lot of discipline from me and Thomas Flögel in the wide areas because it wasn't about attacking, it was about sitting in for a lot of the game and then trying to get up to support Stephane (Adam) as quickly as possible when the ball went up to him. It was about tracking back, doubling up on players and making sure we were doing our defensive duties. It was a really different type of game for me. It certainly wasn't one of my best games in an attacking sense, but I would say on a different level it was one of my best games because it was a totally different job I was asked to do. Sometimes in a team you've got to sacrifice what you're naturally built to do in order to get a result and that was a perfect example of a lot of us sacrificing parts of our natural game to follow team orders."

Making sacrifices was nothing new for McCann, who had devoted most of his young life to becoming a professional footballer. "I got picked up by Dundee when I was 12," says the winger, who went to St Stephen's High School in Port Glasgow, the same catholic secondary attended by his Hearts team-mate Stephen Fulton, four years his senior. "I went and trained a couple of nights a week with Dundee up at Springburn (in northern Glasgow). Jocky Scott and Drew Jarvie would come down and coach us and occasionally we'd get to go up to Dens Park to get a bit of an experience up there training with the club. In between training with Dundee, I'd be playing for my school team, my boys' club and the district team all the way through to when I left school. My mum and dad were massive for me because they were at every juvenile game and took me to all my training sessions. As much as it was a big thing for me to make it as a footballer, I think it's just as big for your parents who have supported you all the way through."

In order to fulfil his potential as a footballer, Eddie and Mary McCann had to let their boy leave the family home and move up to Dundee when he was signed on a YTS (youth training scheme) by the Tayside club as a 16-year-old in 1990. McCann moved into digs with a local couple, John and May Gardner. He would be joined in the Gardners' home a few years later by Jim Hamilton, when the big striker moved down from Peterhead to sign for Dundee in 1994. "I've got so much to thank John and May for and I'm sure Hammy would be of the same mind," says McCann. "They were brilliant, they were like second parents to us. They let us rest, they fed us great, they created a home from home and they were so welcoming to our families when they came to watch us play. For a young boy leaving home to go into another household and be so comfortable, that was dynamite."

In addition to learning to live away from home, a teenage McCann had to adapt to training with fully-fledged professional footballers. "Gordon Wallace was the manager when I signed on a YTS," says McCann. "I went on to a small ground-staff but I was rubbing shoulders with the first team and training with guys like Stevie Frail, Stevie Campbell, Albert Craig and Billy Dodds, which definitely helped me. I used to clean Billy Dodds' boots. There were some great professionals there. I was 8 stone 13 at my first weigh-in at Dundee when I signed at 16; I was like an empty packet of crisps. I could survive in the training because I was quick but I knew physically I had to develop so I got myself doing weights. You didn't have any strength and conditioning staff back then so I just had to work away in the gym myself and try and catch the eye while playing for the reserves."

McCann's first couple of years at Dundee were spent predominantly playing for the second string and finding his feet in the professional environment. He eventually earned himself a debut when he started a Premier Division match at home to Airdrieonians in March 1993, aged 18, under Simon Stainrod. Jim Duffy, who had returned to Dens Park from Partick Thistle in summer 1992, was Dundee's player/assistant manager at the time and would take over from Stainrod as player/manager in autumn 1993. Duffy was the man under whom McCann really started to thrive as he established himself as a regular in the 1993/94 season. "Pretty much from the moment I set eyes on Neil I thought he was a player who was destined to play at a high level," says Duffy. "He had a really exceptional start to his career in terms of catching the eye and being really positive but then after that teams started to double up on him. He got really frustrated with that for a few months because he couldn't get the ball so much and couldn't get as many one-v-one situations. I had to take him aside and say 'look, that's a compliment to you'. I told him that because they were doubling up on him, that would free up the other side of the pitch for someone like Paul Tosh, so he was still doing a job for the team. Because he was young, he wanted to impress so he got really frustrated when he wasn't getting the ball so much. He just had to learn from it.

"Whereas now wingers come in off the flanks to leave space for full-backs, Neil was an out-and-out winger who liked to play on the touchline. We'd look to get the ball to him as much as possible and let him get at defenders. As well as his pace and a phenomenal attitude, he always had brilliant delivery on the run. That was a big thing because a lot of wingers have a poor final ball but even when he was 18/19, Neil's final ball was really good. That's what made him stand out at an early age because so many wingers can beat a man then shank their cross into the stand or fail to beat the first man. Neil could whip it in or stand it up on the run and under pressure from defenders. He was a brilliant kid, his mum and dad were down to earth and kept him grounded. He was one of the fittest boys you've ever met in your life, he could run all day, and he was quick as anything; he also had real talent. I had no qualms whatsoever about Neil; I always felt he would go and play at a very high level."

McCann scored his first goal in a 3-0 win over Kilmarnock in March 1994 but Dundee finished bottom of the Premier Division and were relegated at the end of his first full campaign in the first team. He spent the remaining two seasons of his Dundee career in the First Division but had some particularly eye-catching moments in the cup competitions: in October 1994, McCann scored the winner in the Challenge Cup semi-final win away to Dunfermline Athletic before Dundee lost to Airdrie in the final; in August 1995 – on the same day that Hearts were defeating Alloa Athletic in Jefferies' first competitive match in charge – McCann scored four in a 6-0 win away to East Stirlingshire in the Coca-Cola Cup; in the quarter-final of the same competition, he scored a penalty in a shootout victory over Hearts following a remarkable 4-4 draw at Dens Park, then scored a sublime late winner in a 2-1 semi-final victory over Airdrie at McDiarmid Park before being hindered by injury in the 2-0 defeat by Aberdeen in the final at Hampden. "I ruptured my thigh on the Thursday, played on the Sunday and ended up getting taken off injured in 70-odd minutes and being out for a few months," he says of the first major final of his career. McCann was also a regular for Scotland Under-21s and made a particularly notable impact in a 2-0 win over Portugal at the Toulon tournament in 1994 as part of a side also featuring his future Hearts captain, Gary Locke. Celtic and Blackburn Rovers were among a raft of clubs linked with the highly-regarded young winger. "Once I broke into the team at Dundee, that was me, I never really looked back," he says. "I ended up staying in the team until I left the club. By the time I made my debut, I'd been training with the first team for a while so the transition was actually pretty smooth. Once I got in, I just wanted to make as much of an impact as I could and I ended up getting picked for Scotland Under-21s. Dundee was a brilliant stage for me in my development; the grounding I got there was perfect. Towards the end, though, I felt like it was getting to the stage I had to move on. I'd been linked with a number of clubs and nothing really happened. I felt my form was dipping a wee bit. Maybe I let the speculation get to me at times. I'd been involved with Dundee since I was 12 and as my contract was coming to an end, I felt I needed a change and I wanted to go and test myself at a higher level."

It was a surprise to many that Hearts were the club that landed McCann when his contract expired in summer 1996. "I remember meeting Kenny Dalglish at Gleneagles when he was manager of Blackburn and we discussed Neil," says Duffy. "It might have been a bit of a jump for him to go to a club at that level straight away. A number of clubs were in contact regarding Neil and although they didn't put any money on the table, it made me aware that clubs were keeping tabs on him. Eventually Hearts secured his services. No disrespect to Hearts because they're a big club, but I was actually a bit surprised they got him because I thought he might have gone to one of the Old Firm or down to England. I think maybe some clubs hesitated to go for him because of the league he was playing in, so fair play to Jim; he made a brilliant decision to take him to Hearts."

McCann was just about to turn 22 and had been all set to sign for Austrian side Sturm Graz under freedom of contract, which would have meant Dundee losing out on a fee. Duffy, eager to ensure his club got some compensation for the loss of their star man, contacted Jefferies to make him aware that he could land one of the hottest young prospects in Scotland for around £200,000, although the fee wasn't properly settled until a tribunal a year later after Stuart Callaghan, who was supposed to head to Dens Park as part of the initial deal, ended up staying at Tynecastle. "We were very fortunate to get Neil," says Jefferies. "We knew he would usually be out of our price range. It was just a bit of good fortune that Jim Duffy phoned me to say he's about to board a plane to Austria and asked if I'd be interested. I said 'yeah, but could we afford him?'. We got him for a song really compared to what his value was."

McCann was thrilled to get the chance to remain in Scotland. "I was getting a really good deal in Austria," recalls McCann. "I hadn't been over there but I was close to getting on a plane and heading over. Then my agent told me Jim Jefferies was interested in taking me to Hearts. I thought 'that's perfect' because I didn't particularly want to go abroad. I went to speak to Jim at Tynecastle and I knew as soon as I spoke to him I wanted to sign. The money was nowhere near what I'd have got in Austria but I just saw it as a brilliant platform, a great opportunity to step up and play at the next level. I knew I would improve under Jim. If Jim hadn't come in, I'd have 100 per cent signed for Sturm Graz. I was really pleased that he did because I just fancied it. I knew the club and I knew what they were trying to do. As soon as I spoke to Jim, I knew this was for me."

After making his debut – the same night as fellow new signing David Weir – as a substitute in a pre-season friendly against Porto, McCann made a crucial contribution in his first competitive appearance for Hearts when he came off the bench in a Coca-Cola Cup tie at home to Stenhousemuir in mid-August and equalised within seven minutes of entering the fray. Following a 1-1 draw, he then scored a penalty as his new team won the shootout. "It was a big season for me because I wanted to go to Hearts and make an impact," says McCann. "I remember making my debut against Stenhousemuir; it was a warm night and I thought 'this is a brilliant place to play'. Straight away I felt comfortable in the group of players we had. The squad we had really complemented my game. The way Jim wanted to play was all about speed and attacking football, which suited me."

This was never more evident than in the Coca-Cola Cup final against Rangers, four months after his arrival, when McCann was the best player on the pitch despite Hearts losing 4-3. The winger had only just returned to the team in the 0-0 draw at home to Hibs the previous weekend after missing six games, including the semi-final victory over his former team Dundee, through injury. "A lot of people have said it was one of my best games ever, never mind in a Hearts jersey," says McCann. "I felt unstoppable, particularly in the second half. I've never watched the full game back, but I've seen highlights of it. I should probably sit down and watch it some time. It was good, it was one of those games where I just wanted the ball at every opportunity because I felt I had the beating of firstly Alec Cleland and then after he was taken off at half-time, it was Craig Moore. Charlie Miller was helping them out and Joachim Bjorklund would also come out to help but it was a game where I was in a vein of form where I didn't care who I was coming up against, I just felt I could go past them and try and get ammunition into Stephane Paille and Robbo (John Robertson). We should have won that final, I've no doubt about that. We were every bit as good as Rangers that day, if not better."

By the end of his first season at Hearts, McCann could be delighted with his contribution in helping his new team finish fourth in the Premier Division. He chipped in with nine goals, including an 82nd-minute winner at home to Hibs in March 1997. "It was a horrible day at Tynecastle and I smashed it high into the net after a really good move involving Neil Pointon," says McCann. "I've got pictures of my career through the years and one of my best ones is that moment after I scored and the veins were popping out my neck. What an unbelievably good feeling." As well as making an impact on the pitch, McCann swiftly became a prominent member of the Hearts dressing-room, with he and Hamilton branded "Pinky and Perky" by veteran Robertson due to their penchant for winding up team-mates. At the end of August, in the fourth league game of the 1997/98 campaign, McCann made it back-to-back Edinburgh derby winners for himself when he produced a deft finish with the outside of his left foot to secure another 1-0 triumph over Hibs – this time at Easter Road – and kickstart a run of five consecutive Premier Division victories which took Hearts to the top of the table. "Wee Mickey (Colin Cameron) just lifted it over the top and I ran on and hit it with the outside of my boot into the far corner," says McCann. "I remember wheeling away round by the Hibs fans with my ear cupped just to rub it in because I'd been getting a bit of stick from them. I actually found myself in that central striker position because Jim gave me the freedom to come in from the left. That's how attacking we were, that I could go in and join in with the strikers. That's why I loved playing under Jim. He and Billy took me to another level because they encouraged me to be a real attacker and not just an out-and-out winger."

McCann – described as "a flying machine" by assistant manager Brown – was a key man in the Hearts side that chased the double in 1997/98, getting the team up the pitch quickly and notching 13 goals in all competitions. "Neil was a terrific signing," says Jefferies. "He wasn't the biggest or the bulkiest but don't underesti- mate how strong he was; he could compete with the best of them. For somebody of his height, he was also very good in the air; he had a great spring on him. He was built for speed though; he was mostly about pace and delivery. Never mind the goals he scored, he got numerous assists as well. I think back to the Scottish Cup semi-final against Falkirk and it was the pace of Neil that won it for us that day. He laid one on for Stephane Adam and scored one himself. Falkirk couldn't cope with him in those few minutes."

In the lead-up to the 1998 final, it was a concern for Jefferies when McCann be- came an injury doubt. "I carried an injury into that preparation week in England and it was because of my own stupidity," admits McCann. "This just sums up how competitive we were as a group: me and Fulters – from the same area, obviously, and both competitive boys – were both in the running for an award in one of the newspapers (based on player ratings) going into the last game of the season against Dunfermline. I think we were neck and neck and one of us would have got player of the year. Jim Jefferies said to me 'I'm not going to play you, I'm going to rest you to save you for the cup final'. I said 'no chance, I want to play because me and Fulters are going for this prize'. So I played in the game and I remember in the second half I turned on the outside of my foot and I got a heavy tackle and hurt my knee pretty badly. I couldn't tell Jim it was bad so I carried on until half-time and I soon knew it was a bad one. I saw the physio and the doctor and they thought I'd just strained the lateral ligament on the outside of my knee. It was absolute stupidity because I was sore and couldn't train for the first few days when we went down south. There was a point where I'd effectively ruled myself out which would have been an absolute shocker considering I'd just played for a stupid award in the paper. I think Fulters ended up beating me as well because I got subbed at half-time! Towards the end of the week I trained and declared myself fit but I had to take a lot of painkillers to play in the final. I remember passing the anti-inflammatories about with Mickey before the match and the two of us were popping them like Smarties. We were both sore, but there was no way we were missing that game, otherwise we'd have got the famous story the gaffer always gave us about how he once played when his big toe was hanging off. The pain didn't affect me in the game. Once you're full of the tablets and adrenalin you don't feel anything. When I eventually went to get my knee checked, I'd actually knocked my bone out of place a wee bit."

By that point McCann had become a Scottish Cup winner after digging deep to help Hearts secure their famous 2-1 victory over Rangers. "Neil had been outstanding in the 1996 Coca-Cola Cup final, the best player on the pitch," says Jefferies. "But in 98, he had a different job to do and he got forced back because we scored so early. We wanted him further up the pitch but he gave great support to young Naysmith because he was always there and available for him. We actually thought about putting Neil up through the middle when Stephane Adam was coming off because he would have run the legs off any Rangers defender, but we'd have lost that balance we had on the left-hand side."

McCann was in his element as he celebrated this remarkable triumph and hoped there would be more glory days to come in the maroon of Hearts. He was gone within six months, however, as Rangers' new Dutch manager Dick Advocaat paid £2 million to trigger a release clause and take him to Ibrox in December 1998, shortly after he'd returned from injury and at a time when Hearts were struggling to build on their success of the previous season. "Listen, I had no intention of leaving Hearts," he says. "I could have left after the cup final, I had a few clubs interested, but I signed an extension because I loved it at Hearts. The bid Rangers made was too good for Hearts to turn down. Of course, Dick Advocaat was making a lot of new signings so it was an exciting challenge for me to go to Rangers at that time. But what I was so happy about is that the club got a huge transfer fee for me to allow Jim to go and rebuild. I remember sitting in his office the night I signed for Hearts and I said to him I'd repay him. I signed for very little and the club got a lot of money for me. I was pleased to get the club some money because they gave me the chance to go and play in front of those Hearts fans and to take my career to the next level, and that's something I'll always be thankful for."

McCann's move along the M8 was vindicated by the fact he played regularly for Rangers and won nine trophies: three league titles, four Scottish Cups and two League Cups. His triumph with Hearts means as much to him as anything he achieved in the game, however. "I'm blessed to have won ten major trophies and the Scottish Cup was a lucky tournament for me," says McCann. "When your career finishes, you think 'actually I played in a lot of finals'. I ended up winning five Scottish Cups and two League Cups, but it's only when you finish your career and you see that some players have never played in a final – never mind won a cup – that you realise how lucky you are. I wasn't taking them for granted though, especially not the Scottish Cup finals because they felt really special for me. Winning the cup with Hearts is right up there in terms of everything I achieved in football, but it's hard to quantify exactly what the best moment of my career was because I also scored two goals for Rangers to win the league at Celtic Park for the first time in their history (in 1999), and making my Scotland debut and also scoring three goals for Scotland was pretty special."

McCann won 26 caps for Scotland, the first of which came as a late substitute in a goalless draw away to Lithuania in September 1998: his only full international appearance as a Hearts player. It still rankles that he didn't earn a place in the squad for the World Cup in France a few months prior to that. "I was really disappointed not to make the World Cup squad because I had a great season and scored 13 goals for Hearts," says McCann, who started both Scotland B internationals in the run-up to France 98. "I got called up in the September afterwards so in one respect I was close, but I thought I could have sneaked into the squad." He gave the shirt he wore on his international debut to a man he felt indebted to. "Jim Jefferies got my first Scotland jersey because I believe he was a big part in me becoming an internationalist," says McCann.

Scotland manager Brown valued the winger's game intelligence. "Neil was a clever player who could identify weaknesses in the opposition full-back," he says. "If he was slow on the turn and had no pace, Neil would just zip past him. If he was right-footed, Neil would go on to the defender's left foot. Basic stuff, but some wingers don't think along those lines; they just go out and play and don't analyse a situation. Neil was an intelligent footballer."

Jefferies recognised this as well and helped get him a foot on the coaching ladder when he was manager of Dunfermline in 2012. "It didn't surprise me that Neil went on to have the career he had because he was one of our top signings," says Jefferies. "He's a terrific lad. He's a football fanatic who's had a good career as a pundit with Sky. I knew all about his enthusiasm for the game and that was one of the reasons I got him in for a bit of coaching with Dunfermline, which he did voluntarily before I managed to get him a role. That gave him a bit of grounding before he stepped up to manage Dundee."

McCann is the only man who left Tynecastle after the 1998 Scottish Cup triumph and subsequently returned for another stint as a Hearts player, after he rejoined the club in January 2006 following two-and-a-half injury-disrupted years with Southampton. It meant he was at Hearts when they won the Scottish Cup in May 2006 but he played no part in the run after sustaining a serious injury just 23 minutes into his first game back at the club, away to Kilmarnock. "I've got a huge affinity with Hearts," says McCann. "I went back to Hearts and ruptured my knee ligaments on my debut and then I came back from that and had a double leg-break so injuries soured my experience of the second spell but it was nothing to do with the club itself. I had other options to stay in England when I left Southampton but I always wanted to come back to Hearts because of the affinity I had with them which was all cemented because of what happened in 1998."

Gary Locke

*"He would have captained Scotland
if it wasn't for the injuries"*

In the 76th minute of a tense showdown with title rivals Rangers at Ibrox on the last day of February 1998, Hearts skipper Gary Locke received a pass from Neil McCann midway inside the opposition half and chipped the ball up the right channel. Joachim Bjorklund moved across to the hosts' left-back area and appeared to have the situation under control as he shepherded the ball towards the bye-line. The Swedish defender, anticipating a goal kick for his team, clearly hadn't bargained on a diehard Hearts supporter – driven by a determination to become the first non-Old Firm captain to lift the Premier Division trophy since Aberdeen's Willie Miller in 1985 – refusing to give up on what appeared to be a lost cause. Displaying a level of commitment that has epitomised his lifelong association with Hearts, Locke sprinted forward, slid in full pelt on Bjorklund to stop the ball rolling out of play and hooked it back into the path of Stephane Adam, who had the simple task of squaring it for Jim Hamilton. The big striker got the glory as he knocked the ball gleefully past Andy Goram from a few yards out to put Hearts 2-1 up, but the goal – later cancelled out by Jorg Albertz's deflected, stoppage-time equaliser – owed everything to Locke's tenacity. It was a prime example of why he was so highly valued by Jim Jefferies and Billy Brown, and why he was Hearts' main right-back for the guts of 1997/98, until having his season effectively ended by a knee injury sustained in the very next league game: a 1-1 draw at home to Kilmarnock in mid-March. "I got to the ball first and as I planted my foot I just felt my knee," says Locke, recalling the moment his season suddenly started to unravel. "I knew I'd given myself a bad one. The following day I was on crutches. I got a scan and it came back saying I'd nicked a bit of my cruciate and I'd have to get an operation to get a bit of the cartilage shaved. I knew then I would be out for a good few weeks, depending how well the rehab went."

Cruelly for Locke, it didn't go well enough and he ended up having his participation in a cup final wrecked by injury for a third time in the space of just two years as he failed to recover in time for the 1998 Scottish Cup final. The significant consolation on this occasion, however, was that, aged just 22, he got the chance to be the focus of one of the most iconic moments in his boyhood club's history when he was invited by Stephen Fulton, his close friend and cup final captain, to share the privilege of raising the trophy to 22,000 euphoric Hearts supporters after the 2-1 victory over Rangers. It was the perfect ending to a "headmixer" of a week. "It was an unbelievable moment to lift the cup as captain, but moreso just as a supporter to see what it meant to so many people," reflects Locke. "To see your mum, your dad, your brothers, your mates who you went to the games with, and all the rest of the boys so happy, that meant everything to me."

Youth Cup winner; rampaging young first-team right-back; Scottish Cup-lifting captain; Scottish Cup-lifting coach; manager of the first team; and, most recently, club ambassador: Locke has enjoyed the type of association with Hearts throughout his life of which most childhood Jambos can only dream. Despite this, there will always be a feeling when reflecting on his Hearts career – particularly that contrasting period of promise and pain in the mid-to-late 1990s – that things could have been so much more fulfilling for the maroon-blooded Bonnyrigg boy. "I was effectively denied three finals in the space of two years by injury, which was really tough to take," laments Locke. "I know I started the first one but I only lasted seven minutes." Brown, the assistant manager, takes the effect of knee problems on Locke's career to another level. "Gary Locke would have captained Scotland if it wasn't for the injuries," he states, with no hint of doubt in his mind. Brown's faith in Locke as a footballer is endorsed by the fact he was part of a management team, as No.2 to Jefferies, who handed him the Hearts captaincy aged just 20 in November 1995 and subsequently signed him for Bradford City in 2001 and then Kilmarnock 18 months later. Brown's bold assertion that Locke would have gone on to skipper his country doesn't seem particularly far-fetched when it is recalled that he was captain of Scotland Under-21s under Tommy Craig. Indeed, he was deprived of the chance to lead them out in a European Championship semi-final against Spain in May 1996 after tearing his anterior cruciate ligament in the seventh minute of the Scottish Cup final against Rangers at Hampden just ten days prior. The Scotland side Locke would have led into battle in Barcelona's Olympic stadium, in front of more than 15,000 people, featured Simon Donnelly, Christian Dailly and Jackie McNamara – all of whom went on to make the full squad for the World Cup in France two years later – as well as Steven Pressley, a future Hearts captain who went on to win 32 Scotland caps. Spain's team, incidentally, included a Real Madrid teenager called Raul.

Before injuries started taking their toll, Locke – fuelled by natural talent and a drive to succeed at the club he dreamed of representing as a little boy – was one of the most highly-regarded Scottish youngsters of the 1990s. A pupil of Lasswade Primary and then Lasswade High School, Locke's childhood revolved around football. It was clear from an early age that he was one of the standout players in Midlothian and as he moved from Panda Youth Club in Mayfield to Hutchison Vale Boys' Club in Edinburgh, he started to get invited to train with senior clubs including Dundee, Rangers, Celtic and Manchester United in his late primary and early high school years. Amid the period when he was making an impact at boys' club level, Locke would spend most of his Saturdays throughout the 1980s travelling to Hearts matches, home and away, on the Danderhall Hearts Supporters' bus – which picked up in his hometown of Bonnyrigg – with his father Danny and his two brothers, Jamie and Kevin. When he eventually got the chance to get involved with Hearts in the late 80s, Locke was ecstatic. "Gary signed for the club on a schoolboy form when he was about 13 so I knew him from an early age," says Sandy Clark, the former Hearts striker who was a youth coach when Locke first came into Hearts and then gave him his debut when he became first-team manager. "Once he started to get to the stage of coming in to train with the younger full-time players when he was 14, 15 you could see he was a really good player. He was Hearts-daft, he had great talent and he was desperate to be a footballer.

"I remember shortly after Joe Jordan took over as first-team manager (in September 1990), Gary would have been about 15 and Joe wanted to know about all the young players at the club and wanted to see them play. At that point Gary was struggling with his physical development, just growing pains. Because of the growth spurt, he was going through that stage where instead of being a solid, fit young player, he looked like a lanky, skinny boy who had no co-ordination. In the games Joe came to watch, he wasn't playing anywhere near the way he could because of this. I fought Gary's corner big time and told Joe about the situation and told him he's a really good player, much better than he's showing at the moment. Joe, to his credit, totally took that on board and saw enough in Gary to give him the chance professionally and he signed on a YTS (youth training scheme). I think that proved to be a major bonus for the club and for Gary at the time."

As a 17-year-old, Locke – a central midfielder at the time – was a key member of the team that defeated Rangers 3-1 in the BP Youth Cup final at Ibrox under Clark in late April 1993. Within two weeks, after Jordan was sacked and Clark stepped up to take the first-team reins on a caretaker basis, Locke made his debut as a 43rd-minute replacement for Derek Ferguson, the club's record signing at the time, in a 3-1 defeat away to St Johnstone on the last day of the campaign. The following season, with Clark given the job permanently, an 18-year-old Locke set about establishing himself in Hearts' first team as he started 29 of their 44 Premier Division fixtures. Playing predominantly at right-wing-back, the teenager's performances – including a superb display in a memorable 2-1 home win over Atletico Madrid in the UEFA Cup – provided one of the few reasons for optimism in a difficult season which, although illuminated by Wayne Foster's famous late winner in a Scottish Cup tie away to Hibs in February 1994, was predominantly spent battling relegation. "Lockey was absolutely brilliant when I put him in the first team," says Clark. "He was always willing to play wherever you asked him to play. As a young player, apart from being a Hearts fan, he had an incredibly good attitude."

Like most Hearts youngsters at the time, Locke's progress stalled in the 1994/95 season after Clark was replaced by Tommy McLean, with the former Motherwell manager starting him in only three of the team's 36 league games. Locke was effectively frozen out in the second half of the campaign, restricted to just five appearances – all as a substitute – from the end of November onwards despite being available for selection throughout. "I don't think it was Gary's fault that he struggled under Tommy McLean," says Clark, who clearly wasn't enamoured with the way the young players were handled by his successor. "I don't think there was a lot of belief in the young boys at the club from Tommy. Thankfully they all survived that period and went on to have great careers."

For Locke, the arrival of Jefferies as McLean's replacement in August 1995 was the antithesis to the youth-stunting managerial change at Tynecastle the previous summer; a chance to reverse the damage. Having turned 20 in June 1995, he was swiftly back in the thick of it in pre-season under caretaker Eamonn Bannon – who had been McLean's assistant – and from the moment Jefferies walked in the door, Locke was on the road to reasserting himself as one of Hearts' main players. Although the team was struggling to pick up results, his quality, maturity and attitude impressed the new manager in the early months of his reign. Remarkably, after Hearts hit the bottom of the league following a defeat away to Falkirk in late October, Jefferies decided to make Locke the new Hearts captain ahead of a home match against Partick Thistle. Having only entered his 20s less than five months previously, Locke was effectively asked to become a leader of men, with the likes of John Robertson, Gary Mackay, Dave McPherson, John Colquhoun and Neil Pointon among a batch of team-mates in their 30s and boasting far more experience. "I remember it well because the gaffer pulled me into his office and normally when that happens and you're a young kid, you think it's because you've done something wrong," says Locke. "He sat me down and explained to me that he was going to change everything at the club. He felt the whole place needed change and basically said that the remainder of the 1986 team, who were all obviously heroes of mine, would need to be broken up and that he would be giving the young lads a chance. He just said 'you're young but I think you're good enough and I think you can handle it'. Being a big Jambo, I was obviously delighted. To be the club's youngest captain was a huge honour. I wasn't nervous about it, I was just buzzing to get back and tell my dad; that was probably the first thing that went through my head. On the morning of the game against Partick, I was thinking about how some of the boys would react to me being captain but I always had a great relationship with the older lads. I knew the likes of Robbo, Gary Mackay and Dave McPherson would be great with me because we were all great mates.

"Although I got plenty stick about being 'the gaffer's son' and all that, I think because of the way I handled the captaincy, I got a lot of respect from the older lads. I didn't get the captaincy and suddenly think I was in charge or anything like that. If I needed advice about something, I'd always ask the likes of Robbo or Gary Mackay what they would do. I loved the captaincy and organising things, but I probably didn't look at what a massive achievement it was at that age until later in my career when I started to look back on it and think about what it actually meant."

The decision to make Locke club captain coincided with a notable upturn in Hearts' form as they surged from bottom place to fourth. For the team and for Locke, 1995/96 was a positive campaign. "It was probably my best season at Hearts in terms of getting a good run of it," says Locke of a campaign in which he started 29 out of 36 league matches.

Prior to injuries becoming an issue for him in the very last game of that campaign, Locke's main source of niggle was the fact he didn't feel he got a proper crack of the whip in his favoured position. "Probably one of the things that bothers me slightly when I look back on my Hearts career is that I never really got a chance to play central midfield," he says. "That was always my position but when I went in under Sandy Clark I played right-wing-back in front of Alan McLaren. He used to just tell me to bomb forward and not worry about defending. But when Alan left and we eventually went to a back four, I went back to right-back. I would never have said I was a brilliant defender but I got better over the years because I knew I had to. I played a few games at centre-mid for Hearts, but I would have loved to have played more games in there. I think both Sandy and Jim liked the fact I could bomb forward and could cross the ball."

On one of the rare occasions when Locke was selected in central midfield, it ended in catastrophe. In the 1996 Scottish Cup final, the young captain was moved into a three-man midfield alongside Fulton and Mackay as Jefferies opted for a 5-3-2 formation. Just four minutes into the match, Locke fell awkwardly in the centre circle as he tried to close down Rangers' Stuart McCall. After a minute of treatment from physio Alan Rae, he got up and managed to play on for another two minutes before collapsing in clear distress as Brian Laudrup easily stepped away from him out near the touchline. As young Locke screamed in pain, team-mates Allan McManus, Pasquale Bruno and Paul Ritchie were on the scene to try and console him while the paramedics prepared the stretcher which would transport him from the pitch just seven minutes into a match he and his Hearts-supporting family had been eagerly looking forward to from the moment Aberdeen were defeated in the semi-final six weeks earlier. Paradoxically, the biggest game Locke ever got the chance to play in ended up giving him the worst day of his entire career. "I've never ever watched that game back," says Locke. "I was flying at the time and I'd just gone from the highest point to the lowest point."

The summer of 1996 was a "total nightmare" for Locke as he missed out on participating in the last four of the Under-21 European Championships and had to shelve plans to travel to England with friends to watch Scotland's full team at Euro 96. "I had to get a big operation because the cruciate wasn't such a common injury for footballers at that point in time and the rehab was nowhere near as advanced as it is now," says Locke. "It was just a battle to get back fit."

As if to exacerbate Locke's plight, he missed out on the Coca-Cola Cup final against Rangers a little over six months on from his dire day at Hampden. After more than eight months on the sidelines, he returned to action in a 5-0 Scottish Cup third-round victory at home to Cowdenbeath in late January 1997 and went on to start 14 of the last 15 games of the campaign. "I actually played quite a few games in the second half of that season but as any player will tell you, when you've been out that long and you've not had a pre-season behind you, you never really feel quite right," says Locke. Generating sustained momentum would prove difficult in the years after his horrific knee injury. Locke missed the start of the 1997/98 campaign after an Achilles problem disrupted his pre-season and had to wait to get back in the team as Hearts – with McManus holding down the right-back berth – started strongly in his absence. He made his first appearance as an extra-time substitute in the League Cup defeat away to Dunfermline Athletic in early September and eventually forced his way back into the starting line-up for a mid-week league game at home to the Pars at the end of October. Hearts won 3-1 and he was a regular from then until March, starting 17 out of 22 games in that period. "I played quite a lot that season," says Locke. "I missed the start of the season through injury but once I got in I played pretty much every week. I felt over the season I contributed a great deal. It wasn't just on the pitch, I felt I played my part in keeping the team close-knit by making sure we went go-karting and went for food with each other and things like that. There were loads of things I did that I felt benefitted the team that season. Having said that, we had loads of big characters at the club so my job as captain was pretty easy."

Having played for inferior Hearts teams in the years prior to his injury, it was a joy for Locke to be part of the swashbuckling side of 1997/98. "Honestly, it was great playing in that team," he says. "We were an entertaining team, albeit possibly a bit gung-ho at times, and I loved it. When you got the ball, you always had plenty options because all the boys were playing with so much confidence. I had Davie Weir playing just inside me, then I had Fulton and Cameron in the midfield and Stephane Adam's runs were a joy to play behind because you knew exactly where he was going to go."

Whether he was on the pitch or not, Locke was always a prominent voice in Hearts' dressing-room. "Although he missed parts of that season because of injury, Lockey was a very important member of our team because his personality was so infectious," says McCann. "When a player goes into a new club, it's really important that they get an understanding of the make-up of the club and what it's all about, and Lockey never let that miss with anyone that came into Hearts. He was just a really good team-mate to have about the place. Even when he was injured, he was never overly downbeat. You could tell he was frustrated because he wanted to be part of it, but he knew he was part of it. You didn't need to be on the pitch to feel part of our dressing-room and what we were doing. Lockey was vital because he was woven into the fabric of the club. That's important, in particular for the guys who maybe don't understand the history of the club and how long it had been since Hearts had won something."

When he sustained his injury against Kilmarnock in March, Jefferies and Brown were keen to ensure their inspirational captain remained heavily involved with the team at the business end of the season. In the matches that followed, even though he was unavailable for selection, he would be in the dressing-room and in the dugout on a matchday. "I remember Lockey was injured for the semi-final against Falkirk but he was in the dressing-room with the big coaches' jacket and he was in and about people, cajoling them, geeing them up, giving them support or whatever it may be," says McCann. "Even though he didn't play that day, he was very much part of it. That was good from Jim and Billy to use him like that."

As soon as Hearts defeated Falkirk 3-1 in the Scottish Cup semi-final, Locke was in a race to be fit for the final six weeks later. It was one he initially appeared on course to win, especially when he returned to action for the third-last league match of the season at home to Rangers on 25 April and played the full 90 minutes of the 3-0 defeat. However, Locke had an adverse reaction in the following days and wasn't deemed fit enough to make the trip to Aberdeen on the penultimate weekend of the league campaign. "The manager said I'd play in the final if I could prove my fitness and I was pushing myself really hard, constantly getting treatment and running on it," recalls Locke. "I knew I needed to be fit enough to play maybe 45 minutes of the last league game against Dunfermline if I was to have a realistic chance of playing in the final but I didn't make that and I didn't go to England with the squad at the start of the week. I stayed behind to get treatment but I just didn't feel good at all, I knew I was struggling. Midway through the week, the manager got in touch to ask how I was and I just had to be honest and say 'look, I'm not making this'."

At that point, a demoralised Locke had to draw on all the qualities that had prompted Jefferies to appoint him captain in the first place: in particular, strength of character, maturity and a genuine desire to do the best by Hearts. A chance meeting with former team-mate McLaren at Straiton Retail Park earlier that week had helped put things in perspective. On the Wednesday leading up to the cup final between his present and former clubs, Scotland and Rangers defender McLaren – with tears in his eyes – officially announced that he was retiring, aged just 26, due to injury. As gutted as Locke was over his own situation, he had the relative solace of knowing that – unlike McLaren – he would at least get the chance to play again at the start of the following season. In his Edinburgh Evening News column on the eve of the final, Locke wrote: "In truth, I'd say I'm 85-90 per cent fit at the moment, but it wouldn't be fair to anyone else in the squad if I let my heart rule my head and the manager decided to put me on the bench. I might only last five or ten minutes and that is the last thing Jim and Billy would want, especially in a game like this. The main thing is that Hearts win tomorrow."

Jefferies remains impressed with the selfless manner in which his young captain dealt with what was another huge setback in his career. "We gave Lockey every chance to prove his fitness, but that situation just shows how much of a Hearts man he is," says the manager. "Some boys might have said they were alright and just hoped they could get through it but Lockey knew how important it was that everybody out there was fully fit."

Even though he wouldn't be playing, Locke – as both captain and supporter of the club – was well aware he had a duty to help his team-mates prepare as best they could in the days and hours leading up to the game. "Fair play to Lockey because after what happened to him in 96, it would be totally understandable if he was destroyed inside about missing out in 98 but he never let that show in the lead-up to the game," says Fulton. "He was always there to cajole the boys and keep the spirits up; there was no sign of him moping about or anything. It seemed like he'd just managed to get rid of his player's head and just went back to being a supporter who wanted his club to win the cup."

Putting Hearts before himself has always come naturally to Locke. "I'm a huge

Jambo anyway so there was never any danger of me thinking about myself and going in a huff about not playing," he says. "I just wanted to see us winning the cup. Don't get me wrong, I was absolutely gutted at missing it because I genuinely felt we were going to win that final, but the most important thing was to get behind the boys and support them as much as I could. The gaffer told me he wanted me in the dressing-room and about the place in the lead-up to it to help get the boys up for the game, so that's what I did. I stayed with the team on the Friday and I just went to that game full of enthusiasm and acted as if I was going to be playing. I was as lively as I always was in the dressing room. I tried to do everything I would normally do."

After a handshake and a hug with each of his team-mates in the dressing-room before kick-off, Locke – the only member of Hearts' squad who missed the final through injury – headed up to the directors' box, along with others who hadn't been selected in the 14-man squad such as McManus, Pointon, Jose Quitongo and Lee Makel, his pre-match room-mate. After playing in two of the earlier rounds at home to Clydebank and Ayr United – he missed the Albion Rovers tie through illness – there was nothing more Locke could do to influence his team's chances of winning the trophy. "We were sitting behind the directors so we were surrounded mostly by Rangers fans in the main stand," explains Locke. "I had a great view of the Hearts fans in the stand opposite though. I actually wish I was sitting in the Hearts end because I'd have got a bit of a suntan before Magaluf. We were sitting in the shade. It was so nerve-wracking watching it. I was like any fan: the last ten minutes were horrendous; I could hardly watch. I remember when it got to about 90 minutes me and the rest of the boys went downstairs to the tunnel area and we were watching the last bit of it on the TV because we wanted to get out on the pitch and celebrate with the boys. The injury-time seemed to last an eternity – it was horrific – but when Willie (Young) blew the final whistle, it was just sheer elation."

Locke and his unstripped colleagues were eventually allowed to join their victorious team-mates after an SFA official tried to stop them getting on the pitch, and the captain swiftly got caught in a wave of emotion. "You just get carried away with the whole thing," he says. "I actually wish I could remember those moments a bit better because I was just so carried away. I was high as a kite. Everybody was so emotional. I was a boyhood Hearts fan who had never seen us win anything so I was in tears; it was just so special."

Having been on the periphery for most of the afternoon, Locke got to be centre stage when the trophy was handed out. "I had no idea that Fulters had decided I would be lifting the cup if we won it," he says. "I vaguely remember thinking 'I can't wait to see us lift this cup', and then Fulters said 'no, you're captain, you've been through a lot the last few years and we know what this means to you, so you're lifting it'. I told Fulters that he was the captain and he should lift it, but he was adamant I was doing it with him. That just sums up the type of guy he is. It was a moment that will live with me forever although I get haunted by it now because of the hairstyle and the suit! As disappointing as it was not to play, it was a great honour to be the captain of that team. It was particularly special for me that it was that group of boys because we had a bond that year that I've never really had in any other team I've played."

Jefferies took pride and satisfaction from the sight of two of his team's most important players sharing in such a significant moment. "It just shows you the camaraderie in the team that it was Stevie Fulton's decision to invite him up to collect the trophy with him," says the manager. "He and Gary got on terrifically well. It was a great gesture from Stevie."

Despite lifting the trophy as club captain, Locke didn't get a medal in 1998. He is entirely at ease with that, and insists that fond memories are all the confirmation he needs that he was part of the club on two separate occasions in which they won the Scottish Cup. "I played two games in the run so I played my part, but I didn't feel I deserved a medal in 98," he says. "For me, you need to do something in the final to deserve a medal. It would be great to have a medal, don't get me wrong, but I don't need a medal to say I was involved; you just need to look at the photos of me lifting the cup to know I was involved."

There are few more devoted and genuine Jambos to have ever played for Hearts than Locke, who – even when not employed by the club – has attended every game he possibly could, home or away. "Lockey is Hearts through and through," says Pointon. "For him to be the guy who finally got to lift the Scottish Cup for Hearts was just amazing."

With 189 appearances to his name over seven-and-a-half years in the Hearts first team, 25-year-old Locke took the opportunity of a fresh challenge when Jefferies, who had left a couple of months previously, offered him the chance to join him at English Premiership side Bradford at the start of 2001. After 18 months at the Yorkshire club in which he was a regular in a side featuring Benito Carbone, Eoin Jess and Stuart McCall, Locke followed Jefferies back up to Scotland to sign for Kilmarnock where he spent seven years before persistent knee problems eventually took their toll and forced him to retire at 34. As much as he enjoyed his time at both Bradford and Killie, there is little doubt about where his best days as a footballer came. "Being at Hearts was the most enjoyable period of my career," he says. "Being a Jambo growing up, all I ever wanted to do was play for Hearts and see them win a trophy. To be involved in all of that, it's something nobody can take away from you."

Locke played under Jefferies and Brown at all three of his clubs, and he then joined them on the coaching staff briefly when he retired from playing at Kilmarnock, before the trio – with Locke as first-team coach – returned to Tynecastle in January 2010 to steady the ship following Csaba Laszlo's exit. More than two decades on – and after being reunited at Tynecastle in summer 2020 when the legendary manager took on an advisor role at a time when Locke was club ambassador – Jefferies retains huge respect for the man who captained his Hearts side to such impressive effect in his early 20s. "He was such a popular lad in the dressing-room," explains Jefferies. "I knew his worth on that side of it which is why I took him to Bradford and Kilmarnock and why I still wanted him involved when he finished playing. He was tailor-made to be involved in the backroom staff with a view to hopefully being a manager himself. He eventually got that chance at Hearts but in very difficult circumstances (in 2013, as the club lurched towards administration at the end of Vladimir Romanov's turbulent reign as owner). Every job Lockey does for Hearts, he does it with enthusiasm and gives 100 per cent."

After Jefferies had been replaced as manager by Paulo Sergio in August 2011, Locke stayed on in a coaching capacity and got the chance to be involved in a second major triumph with his boyhood club when Hearts demolished Hibs 5-1 in the 2012 Scottish Cup final. In light of Locke's largely positive experiences in the Edinburgh derby as a player and as a coach, Sergio lent heavily on the Midlothian man for advice in the lead-up to that Hampden showdown, and several players have cited his presence as a key motivational factor. "Of the two Scottish Cup victories I was involved in with Hearts, I actually felt I was probably more deserving of a medal in 2012 because I was heavily involved in the tactics and the set-pieces, one of which we scored from," he says. "I did a lot of homework about the Hibs team and I felt I contributed a lot to that day. It gives me immense satisfaction to have been involved in Hearts winning two Scottish Cups, especially when you consider so many fantastic players over the years weren't able to win anything with the club."

Colin Cameron

*"As I'm taking my run-up,
cardinal sin, I changed my mind"*

Colin Cameron had been enjoying a sensational season for Hearts until discomfort in his pelvic area first began to surface in February 1998. "It started as a little ache and as each week progressed it got worse and worse, to the point where I'd miss a couple of days' training and then train Thursday and Friday and play on the Saturday," explains the little midfielder. "It then got to a point where I was only training on the Friday, and playing on the Saturday. You can't keep going like that."

As the pain started to take its toll in early spring and medics struggled to diagnose the problem, Cameron – who had nine goals by mid-February and was deemed one of Hearts' main men – became a diminished force just when his team needed him most as they entered the critical phase of their bid to win the Premier Division title and the Scottish Cup. Having previously started every league game of 1997/98 bar the opening-night defeat away to Rangers, the influential 25-year-old had to sit out the damaging home draw with Kilmarnock in mid-March. Although he was able to return to face Dundee United and Celtic away in the next two games, he lasted just 66 minutes of the Scottish Cup semi-final against Falkirk and missed the home game against Motherwell four days later, when his team's title bid started to unravel. In a desperate attempt to try and keep the dream alive, Jim Jefferies fielded Cameron in the Edinburgh derby the following Saturday, but it was clear he was in need of a rest as his team lost 2-1 to bottom-of-the-table Hibs in mid-April. With four weeks to go until the cup final, it swiftly became a case of how Hearts could get their key midfielder in a fit state to face Rangers at Celtic Park in what was shaping up as their season-defining match. "Once we got through the semi-final against Falkirk, and after we had fallen a wee bit behind Rangers and Celtic, the physio and Jim and myself made a decision to try to manage me and limp through to the final, really," says Cameron, who played only one of the closing four league fixtures: a 2-2 draw at Aberdeen on the penultimate day of the campaign. "The match at Pittodrie was pretty much the one where we tested out whether I'd be fit to play in the final. I had some local anaesthetic put into my pubic bone before the warm-up. I did the warm-up but still didn't feel great so I got another couple of jabs put into it. I got through the game and it went well, but for the next week I could hardly walk. It was horrendous. My stomach felt like it was getting pulled apart. I couldn't raise a walk, let alone a run. But the main thing was that we knew I could still get through 90 minutes. Before the last game against Dunfermline I went to see the club doctor and I got a Cortisone injection in my pubic bone with a six-inch needle. I sat out that game and then I went to Stratford with the team and was able to train fine for most of the week. I felt really confident at that point and I felt like the Cortisone had done the trick."

There was still time for some pre-match fret, however. "On the day before the final, at the end of the last training session at Tynecastle, I started to feel the pain again, and I thought 'oh, shit'," says Cameron. "I was really anxious at that point. I was worried it was going to get worse and I'd wake up on the day of the final and not be able to walk, the way I'd been the previous week. Thankfully it wasn't like that. It was just a wee dull ache so I knew that with a few injections I'd hopefully get through it. I'd really missed my football in those few weeks I'd been out and I think the adrenalin of the build-up to a cup final probably helped take my mind off the pain. It was a bit of a worry but once I woke up on the morning of the game I knew I'd be able to get through it. It was only one game, and it was a cup final, so we basically just had to do exactly the same as we did for the Aberdeen game two weeks previously in terms of injecting local anaesthetic into it four times before the game to try to numb it."

Thankfully for every Hearts supporter, Cameron won his battle to start the final, although he had no time to feel his way gradually into the match. In the opening minute, he found himself preparing to take a penalty against Andy Goram, the country's outstanding goalkeeper for most of the 1990s, at the end in which a mass of Rangers fans were seated after Stephen Fulton had been fouled just 29 seconds in. "When he goes down, you're thinking 'it's only the first minute, we're not going to get that' but the ref points to the spot, so you're thinking 'brilliant, we've got a penalty'," says Cameron. "Then I remember I'm taking it. People say 'you must have been nervous', but I never really had time to be nervous. Straight away I'm thinking 'what am I going to do with it?'. I always used to say to myself 'pick your spot, don't change your mind, pick your spot, don't change your mind'. I put the ball on the spot, I stepped back and I was standing there looking at Andy Goram and I thought 'he's the type of person who'll have looked at penalties I'd taken that season'. I'd taken three penalties that season and scored them all. As I'm taking my run-up, cardinal sin, I changed my mind. I would normally have put it to Andy's bottom right, where he actually went, but at the last minute, I just opened my foot up and put it high to the opposite side. It was the first time I'd changed my mind and thankfully it was the right thing to do."

As the ball hit the net with 90 seconds on the clock, Cameron had already made a significant mark on the final. Given the fitness issues he was battling, the fact he was able to last the full, gruelling 94-and-a-half minutes in searing heat was as much a triumph for the former Raith Rovers midfielder as his ability to outfox Goram from the penalty spot. "I got another two injections of local anaesthetic at half-time," he says. "Had the game gone to extra-time I don't think I would have been able to play on, both in terms of the pain and fatigue. It was a hot day, we were under the cosh and I was feeling it, so I was thankful we were able to hold on."

The alcohol consumed in the days of celebrations afterwards helped dull the lingering pain from Cameron's exertions in the final. The fact he hadn't made it into the full Scotland squad by that point meant – unlike team-mate David Weir – he didn't have participation at the World Cup in France to look forward to in the weeks after the cup victory. "I certainly felt, had I been fully fit, I'd have had a chance but I think my injury probably cost me any chance," says Cameron. It wouldn't be long before the midfielder was off to Paris, however.

Although he was able to play in the Scottish Cup final, the issue that had wrecked his chances of helping Hearts sustain their title challenge and which had forced him to pull out of the Scotland B international against Norway at Tynecastle in April – possibly his last real opportunity to impress Craig Brown and push his way into the World Cup squad – hadn't gone away. "I decided to do nothing over the summer, which wasn't like me because I always liked to keep myself ticking over," says Cameron. "I would always have two weeks of total rest and then after that I would get myself back into some sort of shape because I knew Jim and Billy liked their tough pre-seasons and I had to be ready for it. But because of the issue with my pelvis, I had total rest that summer to try to make sure I was right. The very first day back we were up at the Braid Hills and even in the walk-jog warm-up I could still feel it."

After the final in May 98, Cameron didn't play another match until late February 99, when he came on as a substitute in a 2-0 home defeat by St Johnstone. A week later, he started in another 2-0 home defeat, this time against Aberdeen, and had to be replaced in the second half. He didn't properly get up and running until April – when he memorably inspired Hearts' late-season escape from relegation – after visiting highly-regarded Paris-based osteopath, Philippe Boixel, who had treated French World Cup winners Bixente Lizarazu and Zinedine Zidane as well as the wife of Hearts goalkeeper Gilles Rousset. "It took us three-quarters of the season to get to the bottom of it," says Cameron. "I had a double hernia operation but that didn't help. I rehabbed and came back from that but I still had the pain.

"When Gilles recommended Philippe, I went over to Paris and ended up spending almost a week with him. He did a test in his office where I stood still with my eyes closed and my hands out and was asked to take 20 steps on the spot. When I opened my eyes, my body had turned about 90 degrees. He said 'right, do it again', but this time he folded a bit of cardboard and put it in one side of my mouth and got me to grip it in my teeth. This time I'd hardly moved when I opened my eyes. He said 'there's the problem' – on one side of my face, the muscles were tight the whole time so over several years my whole body had been knocked out of sync, culminating in my pelvis being the weakest part. He said I must have been kicked or banged on that side of my face when I was a kid and my muscles were tight the whole time because of it.

"I was with Philippe for five days and I had an hour session first thing each morning and an hour at night, and in between I got stretching exercises and I spent time with the masseurs there. They basically just battered me and stripped my muscles back: stomach, back, hamstrings, glutes, calves, the lot. It was agony. I'd go in at 9am and finish at 5pm. I'd go back to the hotel, get something to eat and go to my bed; I was knackered. But after all the struggles I'd had over the previous year, I was back playing within two weeks of seeing Philippe. I wasn't cured for good though; I don't think there was a proper cure for what I had. I had a gum shield made and that helped with my face but I had to keep going over to see him once a month for years after that. It was basically like a MOT where he would manipulate me back into shape. It was pretty brutal because I'd fly out the night before, then fly back the day after seeing him. I didn't get to enjoy much of Paris because I was just in the hotel, visiting Philippe and then flying home. It was a means to an end, just something I had to do to keep playing. Hearts were really good with me; they knew that to get me playing, I had to go. And then when I signed for Wolves (in August 2001) I made sure I had it in my contract that I went over once a month. After I left Wolves, it became more difficult. Coventry and MK Dons wouldn't send me over so I went a few times of my own accord. When I came back up to Scotland to sign for Dundee (in 2008), I had an osteopath called Stuart Barton, and he was the closest I could find who could match what Philippe could do, so I went to see him from then on."

Having found himself in a similar predicament to that faced by Hearts' Austrian midfielder Peter Haring two decades later, Cameron is indebted to Boixel – "a fantastic guy" – for swiftly identifying his issue and allowing him to have another two excellent years at Tynecastle; seven years in the English Midlands with Wolverhampton Wanderers, Coventry City and MK Dons; and then a further eight years back in Scotland with Dundee, Arbroath, Cowdenbeath and Berwick Rangers, for whom he made his last senior appearance a week after his 43rd birthday in October 2015. In addition, Cameron won 28 Scotland caps, the first of which came as a late substitute in a friendly victory away to Germany in April 99, just a matter of weeks after his first visit to Boixel. Almost 25 years as a senior professional and 28 appearances for his country: Cameron would gladly have settled for that outcome when embarking on his career with Raith, the team he has supported since he first got into football in the late 1970s. "In the early part of my life, I used to stay in the centre of Kirkcaldy but when I was about ten we moved to Links Street, so I was literally 2-300 yards from Stark's Park," says Cameron, a former pupil of Balwearie High, the same school, incidentally, which Hibs' 2016 Scottish Cup winner Lewis Stevenson attended. "James Joyce, my friend's grandad, was the boot man and through him we were in and around the club when we were really young. I remember we used to sneak in under one of the fences to get into the games; we used to get in trouble for that. I became a ballboy and eventually I joined them on a S-Form. Raith were really good in terms of giving me the opportunity to get my foot on the ladder. I'm eternally thankful to them. Frank Connor was manager when I signed my S-Form and then Jimmy Nicholl came in and transformed me from a striker to a midfielder, which was the making of me."

Even at an early age, the diminutive Cameron – who became known affectionately as "Mickey" because of his resemblance to Mickey Mouse – offset his lack of stature with a ferocious competitive spirit. "I joined Raith as player-manager in November 1990 and in summer 1991 I was given the opportunity to make the club full-time in some way," says Nicholl, recalling how he helped set young Cameron on his route to stardom. "I was allowed 12 full-time players – six professionals and six YTS (youth training scheme) boys – and wee Mickey was one of the young lads that got in full-time. That's where it all started for him. At 16, 17, first of all you look at their ability and then you look at how they're going to develop physically. Ordinarily with Mickey, you might look at him and think 'Jesus Christ, I hope he grows', but in Mickey's case, I never thought that because he was so tenacious. Despite his size, playing against bigger opponents didn't faze him at all. He had a big heart, so I never worried about him being intimidated by people bigger than him."

Before establishing himself in Raith's first team, a teenage Cameron had loan spells at Junior clubs Lochore Welfare and Kelty Hearts as well as a stint with Irish side Sligo Rovers. By the time he entered his 20s in late 1992, he was ready to feature regularly for Nicholl's team. "Mickey's energy levels were remarkable, he would just run and run all day," says Nicholl. "If we were attacking and a move broke down, you would just see him turning round, getting the head back down and racing back into position. I could never remember him taking a break during play. He was a clever player who could play balls round the corner and things like that, but he just loved getting beyond strikers or arriving in the box from deep to get on the end of things. His goals from the middle of the park were just brilliant. He loved playing behind Ally Graham and Gordon Dalziel and getting beyond them, which is a very rare thing now for midfielders. I just told him to concentrate on getting into the box, getting beyond the strikers and trying to get 10-15 goals a year. That type of midfielder is always going to draw attention from other clubs. With the determination, commitment and dedication he had, you knew he was always going to make a step up from Raith at some point. It takes more than ability to make it as a footballer, you've got to have the right character and temperament, and Mickey had it all. When I went to Cowdenbeath as manager, that's why I brought him in as assistant (in 2010) because I knew about his determination to win a game of football and get the best out of others round about him."

Cameron enjoyed great success at his boyhood club, most notably when he scored in the penalty shootout to help Raith stun Celtic and win the 1994 Coca-Cola Cup final at Ibrox. The following season, Rovers faced the mighty Bayern Munich in the UEFA Cup and took the lead in the second leg in Germany on the last day of October 95 before losing 4-1 on aggregate to the eventual winners of the tournament. On the evening Cameron and his Raith colleagues were enjoying themselves in Bavaria, Hearts languished bottom of the Premier Division. Just five months later, Cameron – with 42 goals to his name in 168 appearances for Rovers – was given the chance to leave his boyhood club and sign for the Tynecastle side, who had moved into contention for a top-four finish and were in the last four of the Scottish Cup. "Near the beginning of that season I had a trial down at Leicester, where Mark McGhee was the manager," recalls Cameron. "I spent a week down there, it went really well and although nothing came of it, it just gave me a little taster of things. Towards the end of that season Jimmy pulled me in and said Hearts were interested in signing me. They had pretty much agreed a fee, with John Millar going the other way. I went to Tynecastle and spoke to Jim Jefferies. He showed me around the place, told me how he was looking at the team moving forward and said he felt I'd be an integral part of that team. I was very impressed with what he had to say. A few weeks previous to that, Aberdeen had been on the phone to Raith and wanted to sign me. But with Aberdeen it was basically a case of them putting the offer on the table to my agent, telling him what they were offering me and asking if I wanted to sign. I asked if they were inviting me up to talk to them first and get a look around and my agent said 'no, that's the deal'. I wasn't comfortable with that. If that was the way they wanted to work, I didn't feel they would be the right club for me. I turned Aberdeen down and then when Hearts came in for me and I spoke to Jim, it was a totally different feel. I felt really comfortable and I was excited by the possibilities.

"I had spent five years in and around the Raith first team so I felt it was the next step on the ladder to further my career. At Raith we were very up and down in terms of getting promoted and relegated and promoted again. When Hearts came along, I felt they were an established top-four/five club. The experience of playing in Europe with Raith had excited me and I felt with Hearts I'd maybe have more opportunities to be able to do that. The other thing I was thinking about was that if I went to a club like Hearts and continued progressing, I'd have a possibility of breaking into the Scotland squad at some point. It was a big decision to leave Raith Rovers but it was the right decision because I felt I needed to go to a bigger club to further my career. It was as simple as that. Look at Hearts' fanbase, they're a bigger club; it was a step up and I felt it came at the right time in my career, age-wise."

Cameron was 23 when he sealed his move to Tynecastle at the end of March 1996, a few days before the Scottish Cup semi-final victory over Aberdeen, a match for which he was cup-tied. His impact in a Hearts jersey was swift. The little Fifer made his debut in a 2-0 midweek home win over Rangers and scored the opening goal in a 3-1 win away to former club Raith in his second game, which was played in front of a reduced number of Hearts supporters as Stark's Park was in the process of being redeveloped. Cameron was also on target in the 1-1 draw at Motherwell in the last league game of the campaign, meaning he had scored twice in his first four appearances. "I think those games and goals at the end of the season gave the fans something to look forward to in terms of what I might be capable of in the years after that," says Cameron, who felt good about his move to Tynecastle despite watching from the stand as his new colleagues crashed to a 5-1 defeat at the hands of Rangers in the 1996 Scottish Cup final. "When I first joined, there were some really good, experienced players that I looked up to. I wasn't a youngster but I was still relatively young and I certainly wasn't a seasoned professional, so to have the likes of Gary Mackay and John Robertson there was a big help. They were good role models and they made me feel comfortable really quickly. There were also a lot of good youngsters coming through such as Allan McManus, Paul Ritchie, David Murie, Grant Murray, Gary Locke and Gary Naysmith, so there was a good blend. There were a lot of exciting things happening and Jim also added some experienced players from different countries which was difficult to do back then. It's a lot easier and more common to bring in foreign players to Scottish football these days because you have (scouting and match analysis company) Wyscout and all that, but if you look at the players Jim brought in, they were all guys who could improve the club and who wanted to win things."

In his first full season (1996/97) he was the only player to start every one of Hearts' 46 games in all competitions as they finished fourth for the second year running and lost 4-3 to Rangers in the final of the Coca-Cola Cup, the tournament Cameron had won just two years previously with Raith. He finished as the team's second-top scorer (behind Robertson) with 11 goals, two of which came in his first Edinburgh derby: a 3-1 win at Easter Road in September 96. This would be the first of four seasons in which he would hit double figures for Hearts from midfield. "Mickey was one of the best players in the league when he was at Hearts," says Jefferies. "He moaned all the time but that was because he was a winner; he was a fantastic guy to have in the team. Whenever he lost the ball, my God, he never hung about and felt sorry for himself. He just went and tried to win it back again; he was a terrific competitor."

Cameron continued to be one of Hearts' main men as they mounted their strong title challenge in 1997/98; in the eyes of many, he was the key player in Jefferies' swashbuckling team. "Wee Mickey was exceptional," says Neil McCann. "He was the player that allowed us to play the way we did. As soon as the opposition put their focus on any of our attackers, Mickey could come from deep. He was really important to us. If I was pushed, I would probably say he was the most important player in the 97/98 team because he gave us goals, he had a great engine, he was tenacious in the middle of the park and he really complemented Fulters and Stefano (Salvatori) in midfield. He was a really important part of the jigsaw for us because he could break so quickly and effectively from the middle of the park."

Stephane Adam relished having Cameron in support of him. "Colin was a big guy in the team, the link between the defence and the strikers," says the French forward. "He was a fantastic box-to-box midfielder. Colin was probably the player I would pick out as the most important in our team."

While Cameron's injury-enforced absence towards the end of the campaign was damaging for Hearts, his return to action in the penultimate league game away to Aberdeen seemed to have a galvanising effect on Hearts in the lead-up to the Scottish Cup final. "I always say that, as well as Jim and Billy getting the system right in the final, the key was Mickey Cameron coming back in for the Aberdeen game because he was such a big part of that team," says Martin Dempster, the Hearts correspondent for the Edinburgh Evening News in the mid-to-late 1990s. "All season long, just with the drive that he had in the middle of the park, he was a key player, and I felt the timing of him coming back gave the team a real psychological lift."

Despite his own stresses over his fitness in the lead-up to the first Scottish Cup final of his career, Cameron detected a bullish vibe among his colleagues. "You could sense in the dressing-room and the tunnel before the game that everybody was fully focused," he says. "We knew our gameplan and we were confident. Not overly, obviously, because we were playing Rangers but we knew if we could stick to our gameplan and play to our potential, we could definitely beat them in a one-off game. I just felt it was meant to be for us that day and that feeling was pretty much epitomised when our hearts were in our mouths and they didn't get that penalty at the end after Ally McCoist went down. We got a good bit of luck that day in terms of the penalty we got in the first minute and the fact they never got that penalty late on. Either or both of those decisions could easily have gone the opposite way."

Cameron remained at Hearts for another three years after the 1998 triumph and established himself as one of the finest midfielders to grace Tynecastle for several decades. In August 2001, after more than five years at the club and with Craig Levein having replaced Jefferies as manager towards the end of 2000, Cameron – by this point club captain and firmly established as Hearts' most important player – felt the time was right to move on. It underlined how impressively he had performed for Hearts that, despite being only a couple of months shy of his 29th birthday, he was sold to Wolverhampton Wanderers for a fee of almost £2 million. He left with 59 goals to his name from 189 appearances. "Craig had said he wanted to build the team around me but I was honest with him: I felt I needed a change," says Cameron. "I'd been at Hearts for nearly five years and I was getting a bit bored of playing the same teams four times a season. I felt it would have been detrimental to my performances if I stayed so I expressed an interest in going down south."

After earning legendary status at both Raith and Hearts, Cameron continued his trend of excelling wherever he went as he became a firm fans' favourite at Molineux, where he scored 25 goals in 188 appearances and helped Wolves win promotion to the English Premiership in 2003. He has a particular achievement to define his spells at each of the three main clubs he represented in his long and distinguished career. "For me it's really hard to pick one moment in my career where I can say that's the best I ever felt," he says. "Winning the Coca-Cola Cup with Raith Rovers – a small club – against Celtic and me being a local lad, that will probably still go down as my best achievement. But it's hard to say that because I then went to Hearts and helped them win the Scottish Cup for the first time in 42 years, which was a massive thing. And then I went to Wolves and went up to the Premiership through the play-offs which was also phenomenal. The other highlight for me was every time I pulled on the Scotland jersey. Those four things are all very close for me in terms of career highlights."

Although Raith will always be his first love, Cameron – who had his baby daughter Megan on the Tynecastle pitch the day after the Scottish Cup triumph – regularly returns to watch Hearts, where he is forever guaranteed a warm reception. "It's always nice to be remembered fondly by your supporters; as a player that's what you aspire to do," says Cameron. "You try to be successful, you try to win things and you try to have a lasting effect on the people that mean the most, and that's the people that come through the gates to watch you. To still get talked about fondly by Hearts supporters after all this time is very humbling."

The Nearly Men

*"Hazel Irvine gave me the video camera
and said 'record whatever you want'"*

Amid the exhilaration, there were some individuals who would have been entitled to take a few moments to rue their own personal misfortune as Hearts won the Scottish Cup. None moreso than Neil Pointon. Had the fates not conspired against the popular Englishman midway through the 1997/98 campaign, it is not beyond possibility that he would have been the man to lead the team out as captain for their date with destiny. Instead the left-back, who had established himself as a firm fans' favourite in his first two years in Gorgie and started the two previous finals against Rangers, found himself consigned to the role of matchday videographer.

With the team built predominantly around an exciting clutch of Scots and a smattering of impressive Europeans, it is easy to forget that the rugged and dependable veteran from the Nottinghamshire mining village of Warsop Vale was the skipper for the first half of the season. With club captain Gary Locke and Dave McPherson both missing the start of the season through injury, and Gary Mackay – who had worn the armband on occasions in the absence of this duo in the 96/97 season – having departed the club, Jefferies chose Pointon to take on the responsibility of leading the team. "Jim said he wanted me to be captain because Lockey was still young, he was coming back from his injuries and they didn't want to put too much pressure on him with him being a local boy and everything that goes with that," recalls Pointon.

Despite turning 33 in November 1997, Pointon held his own in this swashbuckling side, starting 18 of the first 20 league matches – the two he missed were due to a minor injury – as Hearts surged ahead of both Rangers and Celtic at the top of the Premier Division. Although teenager Gary Naysmith had impressed in his fleeting appearances in place of Pointon over the previous year or so, there was no obvious sign in the early months of the 1997/98 campaign that the former Everton,

Manchester City and Oldham Athletic player was about to be phased out. Four simultaneous events around the turn of the year, however, combined to play a part in Pointon's remarkable fall from prominence at a club he grew to love: a newspaper article, a chastening 45 minutes in an Edinburgh derby, an untimely suspension and the emergence of a driven 19-year-old ready to seize his chance. He pinpoints a newspaper interview – sensationalised, in his view – in which he revealed his intention to return to England at the end of the season as the main contributor to his demise. Pointon recalls Jefferies being irked by the tone of the article and indicating then that his days as Hearts' captain and first-choice left-back would be coming to an end. "I had recently got married and me and my wife had sorted things out to go back down to England at the end of that season because I wanted to finish my career in England and get a contract somewhere with the possibility of going into coaching at the end of it," explains Pointon. "I got interviewed around Christmas time, when I was captain, about how we were doing well, top of the league and things were going great. I was asked by the reporter if I was looking to get a new contract and I let my guard down and said 'no, I think I'm going to go back to England with my wife'. Unfortunately, the headline the paper went with was something along the lines of 'Pointon drops bombshell and quits'. When I went into the club the next day, Jim pulled me in and asked me what was going on. I hadn't seen the paper at that point and Jim told me it said I was quitting. I told him I wasn't quitting, I just wasn't looking for a new contract because I wanted to go back down the road to settle back in Wigan and raise a family. Jim didn't like what I'd said and I didn't like the way it was portrayed in the paper. That was pretty much the killer for me. It was unfortunate but I didn't have any regrets about what I'd said because I've always been an honest guy."

It didn't help that, at the time of the interview, Pointon was about to serve a three-match suspension after a booking in the 5-2 home defeat by Rangers just before Christmas took him through the disciplinary points threshold. Furthermore, in his last match before serving the ban, the Englishman endured a torrid second half at the hands of the rapid Hibs attacker Kevin Harper as the Easter Road side came roaring back from 2-0 down to draw 2-2 at Tynecastle on New Year's Day. And as if to exacerbate Pointon's situation, in the first game he missed through suspension, Naysmith replaced him at left-back and produced a man-of-the-match display which featured a stunning goal in a 3-2 Monday-night victory away to St Johnstone. The 19-year-old went on to make the jersey his own thereafter, with Pointon appearing only twice more for Hearts: as a starter in the 1-1 draw at home to St Johnstone in April and as a late substitute, in what would be his farewell appearance, in the 2-0 home win over Dunfermline Athletic in the final league match of the season. The Englishman – who didn't make the matchday 14 for any of the five Scottish Cup matches – is philosophical about the unfortunate chain of events that led to him being a peripheral figure on one of Hearts' greatest days. "Gary went on and wrote his own piece of history and I was left on the sidelines but that's how football goes," he says. "If I'd played, we might not have won the cup. It's all ifs, buts and maybes. Me and Jim finished on great terms and we still keep in touch."

Pointon loved his time at Tynecastle and still felt he could have contributed in the closing months of the season, a notion lent credence by the fact he would go on to start 52 games for a Walsall side who enjoyed one of the best seasons in their history in 1998/99 by finishing above Manchester City in England's third tier and winning promotion to the old First Division. As soon as his intention to move on had been made public, however, Jefferies immediately started planning for life after the Englishman as he attempted to land Twente Enschede's Rab McKinnon in January before the 31-year-old former Motherwell left-back eventually agreed a pre-contract with the Tynecastle club for the start of the 1998/99 campaign. Pointon, meanwhile, saw a proposed loan move to Wigan Athletic fall through in March, so he was left to see out the season playing occasionally for the reserve team while acting as both mentor and deputy to the burgeoning Naysmith until his contract expired after the cup final.

"I was frustrated because I wanted to play but I knew why it had happened and that I'd probably been too honest and said the wrong thing," he acknowledges, referring to the newspaper interview. "Me and Jim had a discussion about it and he basically said he would keep me on board and use me if he needed me and I agreed that I'd try to help Gary as much as I could. I think when Jim was asked about me not being in the team, he just said 'well Neil's made his decision to go back down the road and we're looking to the future'. Which they were, because the average age of the whole team was coming down drastically. The likes of Allan McManus, Paul Ritchie, Neil McCann and Lockey, as well as Sticky (Allan Johnston) who had left by that point, had all been in the team. I actually remember Hearts being compared to the Liverpool Spice Boys (Robbie Fowler, Steve McManaman, Jamie Redknapp et al) because of all the young lads in the team.

"I wouldn't say I was at the peak of my powers at that point but I knew what I was good at and I knew how to avoid putting myself in a situation where I might be overrun or exposed. Gary was probably quicker and fitter than me by that stage but I knew all the tricks of the trade defensively. If I'd signed a new deal at Hearts, I'd have still been capable of having another two or three years playing at a decent level but it was just a case of planning for the end of my career. My wife had her own business in Wigan. I'd seen many footballers go off for football and their wife can't go with them and it ends in divorce, and I didn't want that to happen."

Pointon knew that barring any late-season misfortune befalling Naysmith, he wouldn't be involved in the final. He was, however, given a role of sorts when Jefferies asked him if he fancied recording the day with a camcorder on behalf of the BBC. The Englishman duly played his part by ensuring Hearts supporters can relive their team's big day by viewing raw behind-the-scenes footage on YouTube. "We were on our way down to England for our pre-cup final getaway and Jim pulled me aside and said that Hazel Irvine at the BBC had asked if one of the players could do a video diary of the day and he felt I was the man to do it because I was a bit of a joker and would be comfortable sticking a camera in the lads' faces at any point," recalls Pointon. "I said 'yeah, I'm up for that'. Hazel gave me the camera with about 20 cassettes and said 'record whatever you want and we'll edit and cut it up' although I don't think they ever cut it up! I think they just pretty much left it as I'd filmed it! It was a smashing little hand-held camera. The players were more than happy to be recorded and we had some laughs with it. I was able to take the mick out of them and take their minds off the game.

"Jim wanted certain things recorded. He said to do a little bit at the hotel and a bit on the bus but once we get back into the dressing-room before the game that's when the business starts and the recording stops. He didn't want the pre-match instructions on the video but he said, depending what the mood is, I could record in the dressing-room afterwards. So after we got back in the dressing-room, it was a case of grab the bag with the camera and let the celebrations begin. The camera was getting passed about quite a bit on the way home after the game so I've no idea who else had it. After the parade on the Sunday, I returned the camera and the BBC did whatever they did with it. I think it was a good few years later that the whole video actually started to come out on YouTube.

"I grew up watching the FA Cup when they would show the players eating their breakfast and then you'd have a camera on the team bus on the way to Wembley. I remember being on the Everton team bus on the way to the 1986 cup final when I was injured and there was a camera crew on the bus but that all kind of stopped as the years passed, so it was great to get the chance to film all that side of it for the Hearts fans. Even though I wasn't playing and had fallen out of the picture, I was delighted to be filming it and be part of the day. I would have paid for my own ticket to be there if I had to because I still felt part of the club. I had nearly three superb years at Hearts and I don't regret anything."

Another victim of unfortunate timing was Mackay, the dyed-in-the-wool Hearts supporter who became the club's record appearance holder. After playing a whopping 640 competitive games in almost 17 years at Tynecastle, Mackay departed for Airdrieonians in March 1997, shortly after turning 33 and a little over a year before Hearts would go on to finally win the silverware that had eluded him throughout his time in Gorgie. Having lost three finals and missed out on the league title in such agonising fashion in 1986, Mackay – who had captained the team in the 1996 Coca-Cola Cup showpiece – had to settle for being among his fellow Hearts supporters when the team eventually banished their 36-year trophy drought. "I'd taken a bus from what was the Wheatsheaf pub in Edinburgh with all my mates and Tosh McKinlay had organised a bar for us in Rutherglen before the game," Mackay recalls. "We walked from there to Celtic Park; it was a fair walk but it was a beautiful day. We were sitting quite low in the stand near the corner at the end where Stephane Adam scored. There was certainly no disappointment at not being involved but, as somebody who had been through so many near misses over my 17 years as a Hearts player, I'd be lying if I said there wasn't a wee pang of envy at seeing these players – most of whom I'd been team-mates with the previous season – achieve something I'd tried my best to do but never been able to manage.

"Gilles (Rousset), Lockey and Stevie Fulton were the players in that team I was really close to and obviously Robbo, who I had a closeness with on and off the pitch that had been built up over years and years. My only disappointment on the day was Robbo not getting any minutes on the pitch. Having been the bridesmaids so often before that, I was just delighted for everyone involved but as an ex-player, I'd have swapped a lot of things for the medal these guys all picked up. The teams that I had played in just hadn't been good enough on the day but these guys were and I had to appreciate that.

"At the end of the game I was euphoric, high as a kite. I wanted to run on the pitch. I just wanted to thank the guys for what they had done. Knowing them all and how hard they had tried, thinking back to the 5-1 game two years earlier and Lockey getting carried off, thinking of all the tears that had flowed so many times after all the near misses in the years before, this time I had tears of joy in my eyes. When they were going round the pitch with the cup at the end, a couple of the players spotted me in the stand and came across for a hug.

"Myself and Vicky, my wife at the time, were invited along by Billy Brown to the function in the Gorgie Suite in the evening, which was lovely, but I didn't stay particularly late. It was a big gathering but I probably felt a little on the periphery because essentially I was there as a Hearts supporter and not as a Hearts player. I was delighted to get the chance to congratulate a few of the guys, but, as delighted as I was, in all honesty, the whole day was probably just too much for me emotionally. Any time I bump into any of these guys there is a respect for each other as players but there is a respect from me to them for what they achieved in a Hearts jersey."

The significance of Mackay – known to team-mates as "Kai" – missing out on this moment wasn't lost on Fulton. "The only galling thing for me about winning the cup was that Kai had just left a year before," he says. "I can actually remember walking round the park with the cup after the game, spotting Kai in the crowd and trying to get him to come on the pitch with us. I wish he'd have still been at the club, even if he was just on the bench like Robbo (John Robertson). Although Robbo would have been desperate to get on the pitch, at least he got a winner's medal, and I'd have liked Kai to have got that as well."

Jose Quitongo was so often the life and soul of the party during his time at Hearts but the wind was temporarily removed from the charismatic Angolan's sails when he learned that he hadn't made the 14-man matchday squad for the big occasion. Despite his popularity at Tynecastle, the little winger was never a regular starter under Jefferies and was mainly used as an impact sub. Having only failed to make the squad for three of the previous 30 matches after arriving from Hamilton Accies a few months into the season, however, he looked a good bet to be starting on the bench, especially since he had played in each of the four rounds on the way to the final – three times as a sub and once as a starter. The first hint that he might not be involved came when he was dropped from the squad for the penultimate league game of the season away to Aberdeen, a day when most of Jefferies' main men – including 12 of the cup final 14 – made the cut. "I had played in every round on the way to the final and been in the squad for almost every game since I joined so I was very disappointed when my name wasn't in the 14," Quitongo reflects. "That's football though – things like that can happen. I never complained. I didn't speak to the manager about it. I was a player who never complained about things so I never had a problem with managers.

"If I was playing, great, I play, but if I wasn't playing I just accepted it and tried to get back in the team the next time. That's the way I was. I was disappointed not to play but delighted that we won. In football you need to be prepared for every possibility. The manager picks the team he feels is best to win the game and you have to respect that. Hearts is a very big club, so just to be part of that team was amazing. I can't complain about anything. It was a special time in my career. Even though I didn't play in the final, I still feel like I played my part. I played in all the other rounds, I was part of that team. I was part of everything with the lads. It was great fun. The celebrations were amazing. The next day when we went on the open-top bus, oh my God. All the people in the streets, amazing!"

Another player disappointed not to make the squad was Allan McManus. The 23-year-old defender had played the full 90 minutes of the Scottish Cup final two years previously and was an unused substitute in the 1996 Coca-Cola Cup final. After making seven consecutive starts in all competitions early in the 1997/98 season at right-back, Paisley-born McManus lost his place to Locke in late October and barely featured thereafter. He made only one start after the turn of the year and that was effectively a farewell outing at home to Dunfermline on the last day; albeit it served to raise McManus's hopes that he might make the cup final 14. "I played the last game against Dunfermline and I remember that game well because I was thinking to myself 'I've got a wee opportunity here just to try to catch the gaffer's eye and maybe squeeze into the cup final squad'," says McManus. "I remember coming out of that game thinking 'I was excellent today, I might have just done enough to squeeze in'. I went from thinking I had no chance to thinking I had a slight chance of getting on the bench. So when the gaffer read out the team I was disappointed, but even still I was right behind the boys. Myself and Lockey were very tight and I spent the whole game sitting next to him. The two of us were going absolutely crazy for 90 minutes in the directors' box. It was a hard game to watch. Any professional footballer will tell you that if you don't get on the pitch, you don't feel you've played your part, but to have been involved in the squad for three years before that and get to celebrate with some of the best people I've been fortunate enough to play with, it meant a lot. The whole club celebrated together. To feel what the fans and the whole city felt that day is something that will stick with me forever."

McManus – predominantly a centre-back – was a regular starter for more than half of Jefferies' first season in charge as he broke into the team a few months after his good friend and youth-team colleague Paul Ritchie in late 1995. Ultimately, however, he was unable to reach the required levels to maintain his status as a regular beyond his breakthrough season and – with 55 appearances to his name – he left the club to join Morton in summer 1998. "It's not until you come out of the game and you look back that you realise what an absolute honour and a pleasure it was to be part of Hearts at that time and get that grounding from the youth team all the way through to playing in the first team," says McManus. "As a young boy, it was something special to get the opportunity to play alongside so many proper Hearts legends like John Robertson, John Colquhoun, Dave McPherson and Gary Mackay. By the time we got to 97/98, the gaffer had brought some top-quality players in. If I'm being honest with myself when I look back, I don't think I was mentally tough enough at that stage to do what was required to keep pushing and compete with guys like David Weir and Paul Ritchie, who both went on to play for Scotland. I look back and say there's no shame in not being able to play more regularly in that team because I wasn't at the same level as those guys, but at the same time I think looking back at myself I could certainly have worked harder to up my game and try to work my way back in. I've absolutely no regrets though. To look back on the quality and stature of players I couldn't get in ahead of, I don't think there was any shame. There were only three subs allowed back then so if you weren't in the XI, you could very quickly find yourself out the squad entirely. You're never comfortable being out the team but sometimes you just have to respect that there are better players who are going to get in ahead of you."

Lee Makel, Roddy McKenzie and David Murie were the other notable members of the 1997/98 squad left out of the 14-man pool for the final. As a boyhood Jambo who came through the ranks and struggled to establish himself in the right-back position before eventually dropping into the lower leagues, Murie takes satisfaction from the fact one of his 14 senior appearances for Hearts came in arguably the most famous cup run in the club's entire history. Then aged 21, Murie played the full 90 minutes of the fourth-round victory over Albion Rovers and relished being part of the squad in the build-up to and aftermath of the final. "Obviously I'd have loved to have played more often, but it was a big honour for me to even play a small part in the run," says Murie. "I made the squad that went to England before the final, which was great. I think, realistically, if I was to have had any chance of being involved in the final, it would have been as the third sub but Grant Murray got the nod. It means a lot to me that I was involved in the whole thing, especially as a Hearts supporter."

David Weir

*"I always say Davie Weir
is son-in-law material"*

While the Scottish Cup victory in 1998 was the career pinnacle for many in the Hearts team, it represented something of a floodgate-opener for David Weir. In the years following the Tynecastle club's momentous triumph, no player from Jim Jefferies' squad went on to achieve as much in the game at club or international level as the classy Falkirk-born centre-back. Weir moved to Everton just nine months after lifting the trophy with Hearts and spent eight years in England's top flight, playing regularly and performing to a high standard; he made 269 appearances for the Merseyside club and was a highly-regarded captain under both Walter Smith and David Moyes. Thereafter, he spent five years with Rangers in which he played in the 2008 UEFA Cup final, aged 38, and won eight trophies: three league titles, two Scottish Cups and three League Cups. He replaced Barry Ferguson as captain of the Ibrox club in 2009 and, aged 41, played his last-ever game in a Champions League qualifier against Malmo in 2011, 13 years after his glory day with Hearts. "Winning the cup with Hearts was the biggest moment of my career at that point, there's no doubt about that," says Weir. "It was my first Scottish Cup final and with Hearts not having won a trophy for so long, it was really important to me; it was a great experience and a great memory. I went on after that to play in the English Premier League and won trophies with Rangers so I was very lucky in terms of what I did, but winning the cup was a great moment; one of the best moments of my career."

Weir was the only one of Hearts' heroes of 1998 who went on to play at a major international tournament when he appeared at the World Cup in France just weeks after winning the cup with the Tynecastle side. While team-mates Paul Ritchie, Neil McCann, Colin Cameron and Gary Naysmith soon followed him into the international fold, Weir had the distinction of making it into Scotland's Hall of Fame by virtue of winning 69 caps, the first of which came at home to Wales in

June 1997 and the last of which was won at home to Spain in October 2010. This left him as the oldest player – at 40 years and 116 days old – ever to have appeared for the national team. "Davie Weir is one of the best players Scotland has had in the last 30 years," says Craig Brown, the man who gave him his international debut and took him to France 98.

Brown's namesake, Billy, the assistant manager who worked with Weir at both Falkirk and Hearts, echoes the former Scotland manager's sentiment. "David Weir was cool, calm and collected; one of the top centre-backs, in fact one of the top players that this country has produced for a long time," he says. Superlatives for Weir are not hard to find. "Davie was one of the best centre-halves I ever played with," says Cameron, the midfielder who joined Hearts a few months before Weir in 1996.

There is a clear sense of respect and admiration from those who played along-side him. "Davie's still someone I look up to," says Naysmith, who was a team-mate of Weir's for the best part of a decade with Hearts, Everton and Scotland. "I roomed with him at Everton and with Scotland and we got really comfortable with each other, to the extent that he'd go to sleep with nothing on or when I was in the shower he'd just come in and go to the toilet. He's a great big guy who had a fantastic career. I don't speak to him as much as I should, but as soon as we meet, it's like we've never been apart. He's one of my closest mates in football and one of the people I most look up to. If he says anything to me now, I'm still of the mindset: 'right, big Davie's telling me something here, I need to listen'."

Weir was a late bloomer, however. While most of his team-mates made their debut in the senior game as teenagers, the defender – who played initially for Grahamston Boys' Club and then Dunipace Boys' Club – had been unable to establish himself with any professional club, despite a brief spell training with Celtic, and was resigning himself to the likelihood that he wasn't good enough to make it as a footballer. As he came to the end of his time as a pupil at Woodlands High School in Falkirk, his parents, David and Janet, were encouraging him to get a job in a bank. Young Weir felt there was something else out there for him, something more exciting. His big break came in 1988 when he was scouted while representing the Scottish under-18 schoolboys at a tournament in Skegness and offered the chance to go on a four-year football scholarship at the University of Evansville, Indiana. Brought up in the Shieldhill area of Falkirk, Weir had never been on an aeroplane before and hadn't previously considered moving abroad; he was suddenly enthused, however, by the prospect of pursuing a football career in America. Aged 18, he flew Stateside on his own to begin a hugely fulfilling life experience which he credits with giving him the grounding required to go on and prosper in professional football. Indeed, he would probably have been inclined to remain in America if there was an established outdoor league in place at that point, with Major League Soccer not coming into play until 1996. Instead, he returned home to Falkirk in 1992 and – buoyed by the progress he had made and the confidence he had gained in his four years in Indiana – set about trying to get his foot on the ladder in the UK. "America didn't have an outdoor league at the time – they only had an indoor league – so I came back to Scotland and wrote to a lot of English clubs with a view to going down there," says Weir. "I had a trial lined up with Leeds United for when they were due to start back for pre-season, but in the meantime I was back living with my mum and dad. My dad – unbeknown to me – got in touch with Falkirk to see if I could go in and train with them as they started back a wee bit earlier. Bill Parker, who was a scout there, remembered me from before I'd gone to America so he spoke to Jim Jefferies who allowed me to go in and train. So probably within three weeks I was offered a contract at Falkirk. I had really enjoyed it – I loved training full-time with the first team – so I signed the contract. I started to play in the reserve games and in training I was just trying to work my way up and get a bit of confidence from Jim and Billy and the players."

With regular centre-back Joe McLaughlin missing through injury, Weir was given his professional debut in a 1-1 draw with Dundee United at Brockville in October 1992, aged 22 and a half. "David was up against Duncan Ferguson and he had him in his pocket," recalls Jefferies. From then on, he never looked back. Weir would often play right-back in his early years in the Falkirk side, but whatever position he played, his quality was evident. "He was outstanding for us at Falkirk," adds Jefferies. The Bairns were relegated in Weir's first season in the team but bounced back at the first attempt by winning the First Division title – as well as the Challenge Cup – in the 1993/94 campaign. By the time Weir helped the Bairns finish fifth in the Premier Division in Jefferies' last season in charge, several clubs were monitoring his progress, with Rangers manager Walter Smith among those taking an interest. "I enjoyed my time at Falkirk," says Weir. "It was obviously an introduction to professional football and it was a quick learning curve. We were playing in the Premier Division and we also had a season in the First Division trying to get promoted, so it was a really pressurised situation. I enjoyed the environment, I enjoyed the culture we created and I enjoyed the kind of relationships we developed in the dressing-room."

After Jefferies left in 1995, however, Weir's form dipped as Falkirk were relegated again following a poor season under John Lambie and then Eamonn Bannon, the former Hearts player. Aged 26, the defender was eager for a new challenge. "I was just really keen to leave at that point," he says. "I felt I had overstayed at Falkirk. I had options to leave before that but it just didn't quite happen. When Jim and Billy were still at Falkirk, they probably didn't want me to leave and made it harder for me to leave. Then when they left I lost my direction a wee bit. I didn't enjoy it as much with John Lambie being there and then Eamonn Bannon for a short period of time so I was desperate to move, to be honest."

Having initially stopped Weir leaving Falkirk, Jefferies acted swiftly when he learned he might be able to bring the wantaway defender to Tynecastle in the summer of 1996. "When I got the Hearts job, Davie and Steve Fulton were two of the first players I had my eye on signing," says Jefferies. Hearts weren't the only club keen to recruit Weir, but the presence of Jefferies and Brown gave the Tynecastle side a clear advantage. After mulling over his options, Weir agreed to move to Hearts in a straight player swap deal which saw out-of-favour duo Brian Hamilton and Craig Nelson head to Brockville. "I had interest from Hearts, Hibs, Aberdeen and some English clubs as well," the defender explains. "I wanted to go and enjoy my football again and I knew with Jim and Billy that I would enjoy it. I knew what the culture and environment would be like. Hearts are a big club so it was a real step up for me but it was exciting. I spoke to some of the other clubs out of courtesy but my mind was made up in terms of wanting to go to Hearts. I've always been like that throughout my career; I knew where I wanted to go and when I wanted to go, and my mind was made up very quickly. Jim and Billy being there was the main factor if I'm honest, but even now I still consider Hearts the biggest out of those three clubs. If I was advising somebody to go to Hearts, Hibs or Aberdeen, I would advise them to go to Hearts because, in my opinion, they are the third-biggest club in Scotland."

Weir took the step up to Hearts in his stride. "I wasn't daunted going into Hearts," he says. "There were big characters like Craig Levein, John Robertson, Gary Mackay and Dave McPherson, who had been top players internationally and domestically, but I was ready for that. I wasn't a kid; I was 26 when I moved, so I'd been round the world a wee bit. I'd been in America and I'd played a lot of games for Falkirk so I wasn't intimidated. I'd like to think I was just respectful of those guys' careers and let my football do the talking rather than worrying about too many other things."

Stephen Fulton knew better than any of the Hearts players what to expect from Weir after spending a season with him at Falkirk. "Big Davie was never the quickest but you just couldn't get the better of him," says Fulton of his friend and regular room-mate. "That became even more apparent when he went to Rangers at the end of his career. He could play centre-back, he could play in a back three, and he could play right-back because he could get forward and join in the play. He was also a bit of a nasty bastard without you thinking he would be because everybody sees this big quiet, placid guy. There was certainly a determination there to be a winner, and I think he proved that with the career he had."

In his first season at the club (1996/97), Weir was Hearts' star man and was nominated for the Scottish PFA player of the year award, which was won by Celtic's Paolo Di Canio. The defender started 43 of his team's 46 games in all competitions as they finished fourth in the league, while he also chipped in with an impressive eight goals, including one in the 4-3 Coca-Cola Cup final defeat by Rangers. The Ibrox club were credited with an interest in Weir towards the end of the season, and Hearts responded by putting a £3 million price tag on his head. "Big Davie was a gentle guy and was very intelligent; on the pitch, he oozed class, confidence and composure," says team-mate Cameron. At the end of a fruitful first campaign in Gorgie, Weir made his Scotland debut in a 1-0 friendly defeat by Wales at Rugby Park in June 1997. "One of the reasons for moving to a bigger club was to try to open that door with Scotland and that happened when I was at Hearts," says Weir. "So to play in a cup final and to be playing international football at the end of my first season was a good sign that I'd made the right move. In terms of finishing fourth, Hearts would bite your hand off to be up there now (in 2020) but that was kind of expected at the time, that was the benchmark. The first season was okay, but the normal expectation was to be better and to be closer to the top."

That certainly happened the following season as Hearts maintained a strong title challenge until mid-April before letting it slip in the last six games. "There was definite improvement that season," says Weir. "The players got better and Jim and Billy probably instilled more of what they wanted in everyone. We had a good blend of experience and energy and we had really good talent in the team, so it was a really exciting time. We genuinely felt we had a chance of winning the league, which would have been great, but we just never quite had enough to get to where we wanted to be. You really can't criticise the group, though, in terms of the performances we had and the attempt we made to win the league."

Weir started 43 of the team's 44 games in all competitions in 1997/98 and scored three goals, including Hearts' second in the Scottish Cup third-round victory over Clydebank. His most important intervention in the whole season, however, came in the cup final against Rangers when he capped a brilliant individual display by making a critical challenge eight yards from goal to stop Sergio Porrini equalising for the Ibrox side in the fourth minute of stoppage-time. "That was an unbelievable block from Davie," says fellow defender Naysmith. At a time when most of his team-mates were running on empty, that moment epitomised Weir's determination to be a winner. "It was backs-to-the-wall towards the end but that's the nature of trying to win a cup," says Weir, who went on to win five finals as a Rangers player. "You need to defend well and you need a wee bit of luck. We had a good team and we had a good gameplan. We got ahead early on in the game which helped and we defended well and got that bit of luck – there's no doubt about that – but I think we deserved it."

Weir had little time in which to savour the victory as he was the only Hearts player selected by Scotland to go to France for the World Cup, which kicked off just three-and-a-half weeks later. As a result, he didn't travel to Magaluf for the end-of-season party with his triumphant Hearts team-mates. The defender had received confirmation of his inclusion in Craig Brown's squad on the Wednesday prior to the final. "I was probably established in the squad by that point because I'd been in it consistently for a year, but I certainly wasn't established in the team," says Weir. "I was hopeful of being included in the squad but I wasn't assured of it so it was a big thing for me when I found out I was definitely going to the World Cup."

Weir didn't feature in the opening match of the tournament – a gallant 2-1 defeat by Brazil in Paris – but Hearts fans watched on with pride as he came on as a substitute for Colin Calderwood in the second match against Norway in Bordeaux and set up Craig Burley for the equaliser in a 1-1 draw. Weir's contribution in the last half-hour was enough to earn him a starting place for the following match: a 3-0 defeat by Morocco in Saint-Etienne which ended Scotland's participation in the tournament. "I used to say to my players that the best pass in football is the one between the opposing left-back and the left-centre-back because often the left-centre-back was right-footed and the left-back was left-footed so if you put the ball between them they'll both usually be defending it with their weaker foot," explains Scotland manager Brown. "Lo and behold, the only goal we scored from open play in the World Cup in France came when Davie Weir played a great ball into that area for Craig Burley to run on to. When you gave Davie information like that, with an explanation, you could guarantee he'd take it on board and try to do it. Davie was a smashing footballer: totally reliable, totally consistent, good in the air and good on the ground. You couldn't fault him. He had a wee issue with Berti Vogts (Brown's successor as Scotland manager who publicly criticised Weir's performance after the infamous 2-2 draw with the Faroe Islands in September 2002) but I know whose side I'd have been on in that dispute because Davie's the salt of the earth. I always say Davie Weir is son-in-law material; he's highly intelligent and such a decent guy."

Weir's impressive progress in his first two years at Hearts, allied to his status as an established Scotland internationalist who had played at a World Cup, meant it was always going to be hard for the Tynecastle side to hold on to him, especially with his contract due to expire in summer 1999. When Smith, by now the Everton manager, showed an interest in signing him in February 1999, at a time when Hearts were struggling near the bottom of the league, Weir – approaching his 29th birthday and with a burning desire to play at the highest level possible – forced through a cut-price £200,000 transfer to Goodison Park. Although Jefferies was disappointed at the time, Weir – whom he recruited at two separate clubs – will always stand as his best-ever signing. "Davie wasn't the quickest but he didn't need to be because he read situations better than anybody," says the manager. "His anticipation was great, he had real composure, he was a great calming influence and he could also come out of defence and play a pass. He was top quality."

Weir – with 117 appearances and 12 goals to his name in just over two-and-a-half years – departed as one of the classiest centre-backs ever to play for Hearts and remains so highly thought of at Tynecastle that he was in the frame to return as director of football in summer 2020. "Big Davie just went from strength to strength throughout his career," says Ritchie, his defensive partner throughout his two-and-a-half years in Gorgie. "He was a gentleman off the pitch but as a footballer, he was tough; he was a proper player. He looked after himself and that all shone through with how successful he was when he moved on and how long he played. He was someone I looked up to; it was an absolute privilege to play with him."

John Robertson

*"It meant the world to the boys
to see wee Robbo get his medal"*

There was no more poignant sight after Hearts' Scottish Cup triumph in 1998 than a visibly emotional John Robertson raising both arms aloft, with the trophy grasped securely in his right hand. As the club's record league goal-scorer turned round to show this most coveted of prizes to all sides of Celtic Park, he pressed his left hand gently on his heart, and muttered to the skies "that's for you, dad" in a touching tribute to his beloved late father – a Hearts supporter, also called John – who had passed away while Robertson was just 14.

This was the moment the diminutive striker had craved throughout his goal-laden 18 years at Tynecastle, and it came in what proved to be his very last weekend as a Hearts player. Dave McPherson, his close friend and longest-serving team-mate at the time, stood in the background applauding, well aware of the magnitude of what he was witnessing as Robertson's status as a titan of the club's history was endorsed with the sheen of silverware that had hitherto eluded him. "I was delighted for Robbo," says defender McPherson, eight months older than Robertson. "To play to the level he did for such a length of time and not win a trophy would have been difficult for him to take; it would have stuck in his throat. It looked like that was going to happen because Hearts were always 'the nearly men' through mine and Robbo's time at the club, so I was absolutely delighted he got that moment at the end of it all. You could see after the game what it meant to him, and that certainly meant a lot to me."

The Scottish Cup was the icing on the cake for 33-year-old Robertson, who had already secured his place in the highest echelon of Hearts legends. A year previously, he had become the club's top league goal-scorer of all time after a double in a 3-1 home win over Rangers took him two ahead of Jimmy Wardhaugh. Robertson ended up only seven goals short of the all-time Hearts scoring record in all competitions set by his father's hero, Willie Bauld, who, remarkably, scored more than a quarter of his 278 goals in European ties. Robertson remains Hearts' second-highest appearance holder, with just eight fewer than the 640 accumulated by his long-time team-mate Gary Mackay. It seems fair to surmise that if Robertson hadn't defected to Newcastle United for a seven-month stint in 1988, he could quite feasibly have been sitting at the very top of both Hearts' all-time scoring and appearance charts. "If you're mentioning the greats in Hearts' history – Bobby Walker, Tommy Walker, Alfie Conn, Willie Bauld, Jimmy Wardhaugh, Dave Mackay and Alex Young – then John Robertson is in there with all of them," says Mike Aitken, who followed the striker's Hearts career closely from start to finish in his role as a sports journalist for The Scotsman newspaper. "I've just reeled off seven or eight of the greatest players who ever wore a maroon jersey and John's the only one from the more modern era that you would include in that category. There have been some others who were fantastic players – Donald Ford and Willie Hamilton were big favourites of mine – but in terms of accomplishment, I think Robbo's the only one up there with the others I mentioned."

Robertson, an Edinburgh boy who attended Parsons Green Primary School and Portobello High, agreed to join Hearts in September 1980 – a month before his 16th birthday – but only after former Hibs owner Tom Hart had fatefully blown the chance to land the burgeoning young striker when he put him under pressure to sign for the club immediately at a time when he had hoped to have another night to mull things over with his family. Robertson, initially of a mind to sign for Hibs, was unimpressed with the Easter Road club's heavy-handed approach and instead opted to join Hearts, one of several other British clubs who had been tracking him through his schoolboy years, which he spent predominantly with Salvesen Boys' Club and Edina Hibs Boys' Club. Aged 17 – two months into Alex MacDonald's reign as manager – Robertson made his Hearts debut when he replaced Gerry McCoy in the 78th minute of a First Division match at home to Queen of the South on Wednesday 17th February 1982. Although Hearts won 4-1, they were enduring a malaise at the time, so only 2397 spectators were present on the night one of the club's greatest-ever players took his first steps in professional football. That 12-minute cameo represented the only occasion in which Robertson would play in the same side as his big brother Chris, who scored the first goal that evening and ended his two-year spell with the club a few months later, before John made his next appearance. "My dad didn't get to see either of us playing for Hearts but he would have been the proudest man in Edinburgh that night," said Robertson in the John Robertson Story video documentary, released in 1992.

The teenage Robertson started to make his presence felt in the 1982/83 campaign as he scored 21 goals – including three hat-tricks – to help Hearts win promotion to the Premier Division as runners-up in the First Division behind St Johnstone. "I was at John's first game and I just saw something in him from a very young age," says Aitken. "You didn't need to be the most prescient of football writers to look at John Robertson and think he's a good player; it was blindingly obvious."

His scoring stats were remarkable from the moment he started to settle in the first team. After his excellent breakthrough campaign in the second tier,

Robertson posted tallies of 20, 13, 25, 19 and 31 goals in his first five seasons as a Premier Division player. His 25-goal haul in 1985/86 was crucial to Hearts' famous but futile bid for the title, while his 31-goal return in 1987/88 was the best of his career and helped Hearts finish as runners-up for the second time in three seasons. That was also the first campaign Robertson and McPherson played in the same team. "Robbo was one of the top Scottish strikers of his era," says the defender. "He was a natural penalty-box striker; he didn't do a great deal outside the box but any time it went in the box, he'd be there trying to get on the end of it and score a goal. He was a similar type to (Rangers legend) Ally McCoist; both of them were lethal penalty-box strikers. They weren't so interested in creating chances for anybody else but you knew if you got the ball anywhere close to them in the box, there was a good chance it would be a goal. I remember, particularly in my first spell at Hearts, we'd go up for corners and basically if I or any of the other defenders flicked it on at the front post, Robbo would invariably get on the end of it to put it in the net. I played against Robbo when I was at Rangers and also in training at Hearts. Outside the box, I wasn't too troubled by him because I knew he wasn't big enough to beat me in the air, but inside the box, you had to be aware of him because his movement was excellent. He always got in front of defenders really well and knew how to throw them the wrong way. He always seemed to be in the right place at the right time but that wasn't all about natural ability; he worked hard in training on his movement and his finishing. He was always wanting to improve and the end result was an incredible scoring record."

Aged just 23 and a half, and with an astonishing 129 goals to his name in his first five-and-a-bit years in Hearts' first team, Robertson was sold to English top-flight side Newcastle United for £625,000 in April 1988, a month before the end of the most prolific season of his career. The move to England's north east came about after he was unable to agree a new contract at Tynecastle, with chairman Wallace Mercer branding the striker's wage demands "obscene". At Newcastle, he became a team-mate of Dave McCreery, who would soon follow him back to Tynecastle; Michael O'Neill and Darren Jackson, who went on to play against him in Edinburgh derbies for Hibs in the early 1990s; and Brazilian internationalist Mirandinha, among others. Robertson's time at St James' Park didn't go to plan, however. He suffered an untimely injury early in the 1988/89 campaign after a promising pre-season and was often played out wide, which was never going to suit a player whose game revolved around penalty-box poaching. With no competitive goals to his name, and Willie McFaul, the manager who signed him, having been sacked after a poor start to the season, Newcastle offered Hearts the chance to buy him back for £750,000 in December 1988. After a brief discussion with his own family, Mercer was left in little doubt that he simply had to find a way to bring this once-in-a-generation striker back home to Gorgie. "Our family lived and breathed Hearts when I was growing up, so when dad had to make big decisions about the football club he would often discuss them with us around the dinner table," recalls Iain Mercer, son of the former Hearts owner. "When this particular chat came up about John potentially coming back from Newcastle I was only ten at the time, but I remember saying to dad that he couldn't afford not to bring John back. I think that resonated with him. It was just a throwaway line, but it soon became part of folklore that it was my decision, as a ten-year-old, to bring John back to Hearts!"

Because Newcastle were asking for a higher fee than they had paid for Robertson just eight months previously, the Tynecastle club required financial assistance to make the transfer possible, so Hearts supporter Ramez Daher, an Edinburgh-based fruit and veg distributor from Lebanon, helped fund the deal to bring him back to Gorgie. "We've missed John," said chairman Mercer, when he arrived back at Hearts. The feeling was mutual. Upon returning to Tynecastle, Robertson scored four goals in the second half of the 1988/89 campaign and swiftly got back into the habit of hitting double figures when he netted 22 in the 1989/90 season. He was rewarded with a long-awaited and well-deserved Scotland debut when, aged 25, he scored in a 2-1 win over Romania in a Euro 92 qualifier at Hampden in September 1990. A month later, he made it two goals in two games for his country with a penalty in a 2-1 home win over Switzerland. Despite his remarkable form at club level over such a sustained period, however, Robertson won only 16 caps and did not make the squad for any of the four major tournaments Scotland qualified for while he was in his pomp: Mexico 86, Italia 90, Euro 92 (which he missed out on through injury) and Euro 96. "Compared to now, Scotland had a really good batch of strikers at the time," says Ewan Murray, a Hearts supporter and sports journalist who became a friend of Robertson's. "Ally McCoist would have been his main rival in terms of the Scotland set-up, then you had the likes of Steve Archibald, Graeme Sharp, Mo Johnston, Charlie Nicholas, Robert Fleck, Gordon Durie and Brian McClair. There were loads of really good centre-forwards in the late 1980s and early 90s. Sixteen caps really didn't reflect Robbo's performances for Hearts."

Even when MacDonald – the manager under whom he scored 157 times – left Hearts in autumn 1990, Robertson remained ruthless in front of goal. There were further returns of 16, 20, 15, 12, 14, 14 and 19 as he maintained an incredible record of hitting double figures every single season in which he played regularly for Hearts. In total, he breached the 20-goal mark in six different campaigns at Tynecastle and netted double figures a whopping 14 times. For context, at the time of publication, no Hearts player has hit 20 goals in a season since Robertson last achieved the feat under Joe Jordan in 1991/92, while Stephane Adam, Jim Hamilton, Colin Cameron, Mark De Vries, Paul Hartley, Andrius Velicka and Rudi Skacel are the only Hearts players since the legendary striker to have notched double figures in back-to-back seasons. Robertson – who scored 27 goals (ten per cent of his Hearts total) against Hibs alone – was exceptional on so many levels. "You don't get players that stay at one club as long as he did any more, and on top of that you don't get players who score as many goals as he did for one club any more," says journalist Murray, a starry-eyed young supporter when Robertson was in his prime. "He did it season after season after season. Although the team in the late 80s was really good, I always felt if he'd played for a more successful team than Hearts, he'd have scored even more goals. He scored regularly even when Hearts weren't doing so well. When you're a young supporter you tend to identify with strikers anyway, but Robbo was the pin-up boy for Hearts fans for years. I think the other players recognised that because his goals dug the team out of so many holes and won them so many points over the years. Hearts have had some good forwards over the years but it's a bit of a frustration among supporters that we've never had anyone that's got anywhere close to the level of reliability that Robbo brought."

In addition to the goals he scored for Hearts, Robertson was a fine ambassador who represented the club with distinction off the pitch. "I got to know John very well over the years," says Aitken. "I liked the fact that, when Wallace Mercer tried to take over Hibs and merge the clubs (in 1990), John was brave enough to stand up and say 'no, I don't think that's right'. He was a football person through and through. There was a spell when John wrote a column for The Scotsman which I used to ghost write for him and one of the things I liked about John was that he was so knowledgeable about football in general. If I suggested an idea for a column for him, he would run with it and I would get ten minutes of good chat out of him no problem. I just really liked him as a footballer and as a person."

As a young Hearts supporter who had grown up in awe of Robertson in the 1980s, Gary Locke found it a privilege to become a team-mate of the striker in the early 90s. "I was starstruck for the first six months I played with Robbo," says Locke, who went on to become captain of a side containing Robertson in the mid-90s. "He was my hero growing up; I idolised him as a kid, I had posters of him on my wall."

Robertson's last season as Hearts' main striker proved to be 1996/97 when his 18th and 19th goals of the campaign – both scored in a 3-1 final-day victory at home to champions Rangers – took him two ahead of the great Wardhaugh as Hearts' all-time record league scorer. Former Dundee centre-forward Hamilton, more than a decade his junior, and new French recruit Adam took over as the most prominent strikers at Tynecastle in 1997/98, with Robertson restricted to just 11 starts and six goals in all competitions. As a player who needed games to maintain sharpness, the veteran went out on loan to Dundee for a month in late February 1998 and scored one goal in four appearances for the First Division leaders before returning to his parent club for the run-in to the Premier Division title race. Robertson's 271st and final goal for Hearts – fittingly, perhaps – came against Hibs, albeit in a 2-1 defeat at Easter Road in April 98 which effectively ended the Tynecastle side's bold bid to win the league. "It was a shame he was coming towards the end of his career and we didn't get to play more often together," says Adam, who was unveiled to the Hearts supporters on the day Robertson eclipsed Wardhaugh's scoring record. "I think his style of play and my style of play could have been a killer if we had played more often together. Even in the season we had together, you could see his quality; he was a goalscorer, always in the right place at the right time. A little bit of space for him and he scored. You could tell this guy was a killer in the box. With my style of play, making a lot of runs and creating space for him, I think we would have made a fantastic partnership."

In the previous two finals under Jefferies, Robertson had been a substitute for the 5-1 thrashing by Rangers in May 1996 and had started – and scored – in the 4-3 defeat by the same opponents six months later. When he featured in each of Hearts' closing six league matches of the season after returning from Dundee and was restored to the starting line-up for the last two matches – away to Aberdeen and at home to Dunfermline Athletic – it raised the possibility that he might have timed his run right to start the 98 final against Rangers. Jefferies, however, had decided on a formation that would require only one hard-running centre-forward, and Adam duly got the nod. The manager pulled Robertson aside early in the week at the club's training camp in England and broke the news to him that he wouldn't be starting but would be in the 14-man squad as one of the three substitutes. "Robbo had played in a few games before the final in a new position just behind the striker and we felt he'd done well there," says Jefferies. "He was outstanding in the last league game against Dunfermline. But that wasn't the way we wanted to play in the final. If we'd played that way against Rangers, we'd have potentially left ourselves short in other areas. I didn't put him on the bench for sentimental reasons at all; I did it because he genuinely was in my thoughts to play, and I think he appreciated that. He was great about it. He had experienced a lot of heartache with missing out on things so he just wanted to be part of something successful."

Robertson, wearing the number 15 shirt, didn't see a moment of game time in the final as Jefferies opted to make only one substitution – Hamilton for Adam – during a fraught finale in which Hearts held on for victory. "Robbo was stripped and ready if we needed him, but the way the game was going, there was nothing really needing changed," says the manager. "Hamilton was the obvious one to put on for Adam because we knew late on they would pile high balls into our box so we needed Jim's height to help us deal with set-pieces, and his first touch was actually a headed clearance from a throw-in. I thought about putting Robbo on to waste time but, with Hammy already being on, that would have left us with two up front when we were trying to see the game out. Even though he didn't get on the pitch, he goes down in the record books as being part of that squad. People made more of it because of all the adulation he had from supporters and everybody would have loved to have seen him on the pitch but that doesn't come into it when you're trying to win a cup. Robbo, to his credit, understood the situation."

Despite not getting on, Robertson celebrated Hearts' momentous triumph as joyously as any of the players. In the dying moments of the final, he and fellow substitute Grant Murray stood anxiously on the sidelines pointing instructions to their colleagues, willing them to see out victory. When the full-time whistle went, Robertson and Murray jumped into a huddle of unbridled delirium with the management team. It wasn't long before the veteran striker was in tears as he took the acclaim of an adoring Hearts support and savoured a moment he feared he would never get to experience. When he returned to the dressing-room, he thanked his team-mates for earning him his first-ever winner's medal. There was no hint of disappointment at not playing any part in the match. While other 30-somethings like McPherson and Gilles Rousset stayed inside the team bus as it made its way along Gorgie Road on the Saturday evening, Robertson was up on the roof with the younger players, initially sitting alongside Allan McManus with his legs dangling over the front windscreen and then dancing jubilantly with Hamilton and Jose Quitongo. When the party in the Gorgie Suite ended, Robertson took some of the players over to his pub on Gorgie Road to continue the celebrations. The following day, as he emerged from the City Chambers before the open-top bus parade, the 33-year-old – dressed in a suit, shirt and tie but looking slightly worse for wear – punched the air ecstatically with his right hand. Robertson was then asked in a television interview to sum up his emotions. "I was unashamedly crying yesterday and I make no bones about it; that's how much it meant to me," he said. "My dad died when I was 14. He was a big Hearts man and he saw Conn, Bauld and Wardhaugh bring the cup back; now his wee boy's brought it back for him. I'm delighted."

More than two decades on, Robertson maintains that it was all about putting side before self. "There's no contrasting emotions at all for me," he said in a Facebook Live interview with Scottish football events company The Longest Forty during the coronavirus lockdown in April 2020. "My full thing at the time was for Hearts to win the trophy. Whether I played or not, whether I made the 14 or not, was irrelevant. It was about the club winning the trophy. To be honest, I didn't feel I'd be involved because Jim had gone with Stephane Adam, Neil McCann, Thomas Flögel and Jim Hamilton for most of the season and I had been a bit-part player. He put me out on loan in March to Dundee to get match practice because Hearts were still in the title shake-up and he wanted me for the run-in. I came back and played in a few games and when it came to the final, I thought 'mmm, not sure whether I'm going to be involved'.

"To be fair to Jim, we'd gone down to Stratford-upon-Avon and on the Monday he pulled me in and said 'look, I'm going to put you at ease, you're going to be on the bench'. But Colin Cameron had been out through injury for a while and Jim told me we were going to be playing this new 4-5-1 formation so to watch what happens because if Mickey didn't make it, I'd be playing in his position (behind Adam). That took a lot of pressure off me; I felt far more at ease knowing I was in the squad. People say it would have been great if he'd thrown me on for 30 seconds. Would it have been great if he'd thrown me on for 30 seconds? Yes, of course it would. But it was about winning the trophy. I didn't care, I was as delighted as anybody. The big thing for me when I look back is that all the fantastic team-mates I had – Henry Smith, Walter Kidd, Tosh McKinlay, Craig Levein, Gary Mackay, John Colquhoun, Jimmy Bone, Sandy Clark, Scott Crabbe, Wayne Foster, Neil Berry, Ian Jardine and many more – didn't manage to win a trophy with Hearts, and they would have deserved that. It was fantastic to finish up with that final little piece because it would have been a massive regret if I hadn't won anything with Hearts."

Journalist Murray believes an appearance on the pitch from Robertson would have been the only thing that could have enhanced the experience of 16th May 1998 for Hearts supporters. "I think Robbo genuinely is comfortable with the situation; he's certainly never suggested otherwise to me," he says. "He lived through a lot of the lows and sampled a lot of those bad moments that the club had so he understood the significance of Hearts winning a cup after all that time better than anyone. I think he meant everything he said about 1998 being about Hearts rather than himself. But from the outside, I think every Hearts supporter will have a little tinge of sadness that he didn't get on to play. It was just down to circumstances that there wasn't an opportunity to put him on. It was fitting and unbelievably appropriate that he finished with a winner's medal at least, but I think if you wanted a perfect day, Robbo would have played some part in it. You can't criticise the manager for anything he did – that's not the point – because everything he did was proven correct, but there is a little bit of sadness that Robbo didn't have any involvement."

After 632 appearances and 271 goals in maroon, Robertson was able to depart for Livingston later that summer content that he had finally capped his 18 years at Hearts with glory. Although he didn't get on in the final, the veteran striker made the matchday squad for three of the five rounds and came on as a second-half substitute in the victories over Clydebank and Albion Rovers. "It meant the world to the boys to see wee Robbo get his medal," says Stephen Fulton, the cup final captain. "For him to be Hearts' record goalscorer and not win anything at the club, it would have been a tough one to take. Although he didn't play on the day, I don't think anybody could begrudge him his medal."

Locke, in a similar predicament to Robertson in terms of being a prominent figure who didn't kick a ball on cup final day, was thrilled for his boyhood hero. "I was buzzing for Robbo," says Locke. "As a player, he always took time to help me, even going back to when I was an S-Form about 13 or 14. I was at Dens Park as a fan in 1986 and I was only ten at the time and I felt horrendous, but to have been a player missing out on the double, I can't imagine how that would have felt for Robbo; to see him getting the medal that he had waited for all his career was absolutely superb."

Aitken embraced with Robertson outside Tynecastle's old main stand when the team arrived back from Glasgow on the Saturday evening. "I was just so pleased for him because nobody deserved it more," says the journalist. "It would have been sad if his career with Hearts had ended without him winning something. For me, it was the highlight of the day that John was part of it."

Paul Ritchie

"My kids bring it up all the time; they're like 'oh, look at you ya big baby'"

Three minutes into stoppage-time in the 1998 Scottish Cup final, Paul Ritchie thundered ferociously into a 50/50 challenge with Rino Gattuso and thumped the ball high into Celtic Park's main stand for a Rangers throw-in. The pent-up Hearts defender's momentum caused him to clatter into the Italian midfielder and the two had something of an altercation. As Ritchie calmly retreated to focus on defending his penalty area at this critical end-of-match moment, 20-year-old Gattuso – a future World Cup winner with Italy and two-time Champions League winner with AC Milan – was visibly riled. The little Italian, a fierce competitor who would go on to earn himself the nickname "Rhingio" (The Growl) in his homeland, tapped the right side of his head with his finger, implying that Ritchie – with whom he had also clashed earlier in the match – was a loose cannon. Gattuso wasn't the only Rangers player the 22-year-old Hearts centre-back got under the skin of that day. Just a few minutes before the late flare-up with Gattuso, the usually mild-mannered Ally McCoist jumped up in a rage and ranted furiously at Ritchie after he was the victim of a robust challenge from behind by Hearts' burgeoning home-grown defender.

"That was me all over," says Ritchie. "As much as I respected the players I played against, I was never going to back down. I had an opportunity to play for my team that I'd supported as a boy so there was no way I was going to let anybody run over the top of me. Watching the game back, there were one or two naughty challenges from myself but that was me: I always gave 100 per cent. Nobody could ever question my hunger, desire, attitude and application when playing for the jersey. Yeah, I had a few run-ins but that was all part and parcel of my game."

Ritchie's strong spirit endeared him to managers, team-mates and supporters. "Paul was a dog," says Peter Houston, a coach at Hearts when he was emerging as one of Scotland's top defenders in the late 1990s. "He maybe wasn't the greatest ball-playing centre-back but he was hard as nails."

Ritchie's will to win was evident long before he started making his presence felt in Hearts' first team in 1995. In April 1993, aged 17, he was part of the first Hearts side to win the BP Youth Cup when they beat Rangers 3-1 at Ibrox in the final. "That was one of those special groups that don't come along often in football," says Sandy Clark, the former Hearts striker who became the first-team manager just a week after coaching Ritchie's team to Youth Cup glory. "They were an incredible team. We had a lot of good flair players and scored a lot of goals but defensively we were absolutely brilliant. We had three at the back: Grant Murray as sweeper and Paul Ritchie and Allan McManus either side of him as centre-backs. One of my memories of Paul is Alan Rae, the physio, talking to me some time after the BP Cup win and he said it was like having two Alsatians (Ritchie and McManus) with a Rottweiler (Murray) behind them. That always stuck in my mind and it summed those boys up. Paul was a really determined boy with a really good character. He was a ferociously committed defender; hard but fair."

How does Ritchie feel about being compared to a "dog" and an "Alsatian" by two of his former coaches? "The dog analogy is fair," Ritchie chuckles. "I was limited as a footballer. I wore my heart on my sleeve. I was playing for the club I loved. There were no airs and graces with me; I knew what I was good at. I was a good defender, I worked hard, I kept things simple and I basically did as I was told by my managers and the players around me."

By focusing on his wholehearted, aggressive playing style, there is a danger of doing a disservice to one of the best centre-backs ever to emerge from Hearts' youth ranks. From the early months of Jim Jefferies' reign in 1995, Ritchie was a regular in the team for the best part of four-and-a-half years before his magnificent performances earned him international recognition with Scotland and took him to a level whereby it was only a matter of time until – like several of his Scottish Cup-winning colleagues – he left Hearts for more lucrative pastures. "Paul had a great attitude," said Clark. "And there was no doubt about the quality he had as a defender. Once he got in the first team, his career just took off."

Ritchie's desire to prosper while wearing maroon was in-built from an early age. Although he grew up across the River Forth in Glenrothes, his father, David, was originally from Edinburgh and his grandparents lived in Corstorphine. His grandfather, William, was a Hearts supporter and took young Ritchie to his first match in the early 1980s. From then on, he was hooked on Hearts, and remains so to this day. His passion for the club intensified in his early teenage years when, as one of the standout footballers of his age-group in Fife, he got the chance to sign schoolboy forms with Hearts aged 13. He would train twice a week at Saughton Enclosure and then travel on the Glenrothes and Kirkcaldy Hearts Supporters' bus to watch the first team on a Saturday. "Once I got to about 14 years old, my parents let me go by myself to watch Hearts," he explains. "I used to go to every home and away game with these older teenagers and other guys on the supporters' bus. At that time Hearts weren't particularly successful but the support the team had was incredible. Hearts have been through a hell of a lot of turmoil in my lifetime

– there's been a lot of highs and also a lot of lows – but as a young kid who loved football, just going to watch your heroes playing and being part of that environment was fantastic."

As a pupil at Glenwood High School, Ritchie was the subject of interest from big clubs in England and would often travel south for trials during school holidays. In the lead-up to his 16th birthday in August 1991, Hearts made their pitch to Ritchie's parents and secured him on a YTS (youth training scheme). Scotland legend Joe Jordan was Hearts' first-team manager at the time, with Clark looking after the youths. Rubbing shoulders with his boyhood heroes such as John Robertson and his fellow Fifer Craig Levein was a thrill, while he enjoyed the camaraderie of being part of a close-knit ground-staff carrying out chores around a ramshackle, predominantly-terraced Tynecastle. "When I was young and first went into Hearts, I never really thought about playing in the first team because when I was on the ground-staff it was just so good to be there," says Ritchie. "The first team felt so far away at that point because you were still playing in the youth team, which was effectively the third team. You weren't even guaranteed to play in the reserve team at that point. The drive to make it was always there though. The grounding that we all got in those YTS apprenticeship years was exactly what we needed and what I think helped get most of that youth team into the professional ranks because Sandy was a taskmaster. At that point, we were only there to facilitate the first-team players. We'd spend hours on end at Tynecastle cleaning up, something that's never done now. To clean the stadium, wash boots, do the laundry, clean toilets and all the other normal every-day jobs that were part of it, it was really, really tough. But looking back, it definitely gave me the drive to be successful in the game and played a big part in helping me grow as a football player and as a human being. I'm grateful for everything we got at Hearts in those early years."

Ritchie – who played as a striker in his early teens before Clark identified that he was best suited to centre-back – got his reward for his graft on and off the pitch when he was part of the Youth Cup-winning side alongside Murray, McManus, Kevin Thomas, Gary Locke and David Murie at Ibrox on 29th April 1993. Just a few days later, after Jefferies' relegation-bound Falkirk side defeated Hearts' first team 6-0 at Brockville, Jordan was sacked and replaced, initially as caretaker and soon on a permanent basis, by a 36-year-old Clark. This would, temporarily at least, enhance Ritchie's prospects of breaking into the first team. Within three months of Clark taking the reins, the defender was given his debut when, a few weeks before his 18th birthday, he was sent on as a half-time substitute in Henry Smith's testimonial match at Tynecastle against an Everton side featuring Maurice Johnston. That was, incidentally, one of the few occasions Hearts wore their popular Inter Milan-style blue and black-striped away kit. Ironically, Scotland striker Johnston would be a team-mate of Ritchie's by the time he made his next appearance for Hearts' first team. With former Manchester United defender Graeme Hogg, £300,000 signing Jim Weir, and Scotland pair Levein and Alan McLaren all vying for slots in Clark's three-man defence, Ritchie was content to continue his development in the youth and reserve teams throughout the 1993/94 season, safe in the knowledge that the first-team manager was aware of his qualities and had genuine intention of promoting him when the time was right. In the last week of May 1994, following a difficult league campaign in which they became embroiled in a relegation battle, Clark took Hearts to Canada for the Hamilton Cup, a four-team tournament in Hamilton, Ontario, in which Celtic, Aberdeen and Montreal Impact were the other three sides involved. In a travelling party predominantly made up of senior players such as Smith, Robertson, Gary Mackay, John Colquhoun, Neil Berry and Maurice Johnston, Clark displayed his faith in the young players at the club by taking teenage quartet Ritchie, McManus, Locke and Thomas along with 20-year-old pair Gary O'Connor and Allan Johnston across the Atlantic. Eighteen-year-old Ritchie played the full 90 minutes of both games – a 1-1 draw with Celtic and a 2-0 victory over Montreal – and returned home anticipating greater first-team opportunities in the 1994/95 campaign. The timing wasn't right for Ritchie, however. Just as Hearts were getting back from Canada, Chris Robinson and Leslie Deans were completing their takeover from previous owner Wallace Mercer, and within a matter of days Clark was unceremoniously sacked by Robinson. "In Sandy, I had somebody that believed in me," says Ritchie. "Unfortunately, he didn't last long as manager."

Clark's replacement – in a move that almost proved fatal to Ritchie's Hearts career – would be Tommy McLean, the highly-regarded former Motherwell manager. McLean clearly didn't have the same belief in Hearts' young contingent as his predecessor, with striker Thomas the only one he seemed to rate. Allan Johnston and Locke, who had been thriving under Clark, made just 15 starts between them under McLean, while Ritchie and McManus were pushed towards the exit door. "I didn't get a look-in under Tommy," recalls Ritchie. "He had his own ideas and opinions, and he did not like me one bit, as a player or as a person. I remember one reserve game at Partick Thistle when he gave me stick for having my hair too short. 'Your hair's too short, make sure you grow it. And by the way, every time you win the ball just give it to Allan Johnston cos that's all you can do'. That stuck in my throat, I always remembered that. When you hear that sort of stuff, that's when you realise it's personal. I found it really difficult under Tommy. If he had lasted any longer, I think a few of the young boys would have been moved on elsewhere and contracts not extended. I was fortunate that he got the sack. It was unfortunate for him but very, very fortunate for me and for the club, in my opinion. I knew what I was good at and I knew I was limited in certain aspects, but as a young player, it's all about finding the right person to believe in what you're good at."

After McLean was sacked at the end of a grim season spent battling against relegation, Jefferies' appointment in the summer of 1995 signalled the start of a far brighter period for Hearts and their young players. "As soon as Jim and Billy (Brown) arrived, I got a positive vibe from them," says Ritchie. "They knew a lot about everything that had gone on at the club before they arrived. We'd been written off by the previous manager but I think they knew that because we'd won the Youth Cup and competed with Rangers and Celtic at that level, they had a good group of young players with hunger and desire they could call on."

In Jefferies' fourth league game in charge, a 20-year-old Ritchie finally got the competitive debut that he craved when he started at home to Celtic in late September. It didn't go to plan for the young centre-back as he was deployed at left-back in a 4-0 defeat. "I think from that day forward Jim knew I was never going to be a left-back!" laughs Ritchie. He got his first chance as a centre-back a fortnight later when he started in a 3-1 defeat away to Kilmarnock and then, following a three-game absence, his Hearts career effectively took off at the start of November when he was pitched in alongside Italian debutant Pasquale Bruno in a 3-0 home win over Partick Thistle. From then on, he was a regular starter. "Paul had been three or four years at the club in the reserves but never got a chance," says Jefferies. "I gave him his debut and once he got in he grabbed his chance. He wasn't the biggest centre-back but he was fantastic in the air, he had great spring. He was a great tackler and was very quick. Paul was all about aggression and his speed got him out of trouble at times. He wasn't the greatest at using the ball but we didn't need him to do that; we just wanted him to give it to the nearest man."

By the turn of the year, Ritchie had been joined in the first team by McManus, with the young duo playing either side of former Juventus and Torino centre-back Bruno in a three-man defence. "Pasquale helped Paul a lot," says Jefferies. "He was at the back end of his career and I put Ritchie and McManus in beside him in a back three and he taught the two of them how to play centre-half."

Ritchie felt reassured by the presence of 33-year-old Bruno beside him. For a player compared to a dog, it was perhaps apt that he spent the majority of his first season in the first team learning from a man who had become known in Italy as "O'Animale" (The Animal) due to his aggressive playing style. "Playing beside someone of Bruno's calibre was fantastic," said Ritchie. "He looked after me and McManus and basically gave us a really good grounding in how to become a professional centre-back. He was hard as nails but a very nice man. It was perfect for me and McManus. We basically did all his running and he mopped up behind us. Being relatively young in the first team, you always want some experience round about you so having Pasquale next to me and also having guys like Gilles Rousset and Dave McPherson there was a big help."

Ritchie adapted quickly to life in the first team and started every match from the beginning of November to the end of the season. This period coincided with Hearts climbing from bottom place in the Premier Division to fourth while also reaching the Scottish Cup final for the first time in a decade. "I felt at home in the first team quite quickly," says Ritchie. "It's every young boy's dream to play first-team football, especially for the team you support as a kid. I think the more often you do that, you grow in confidence. I'd obviously had those ups and downs through the early stages of my career, so to get a little bit of stability, a bit of trust and understanding from the manager, and knowing that somebody believed in me, I gained a bit of confidence and it built from there. I wouldn't say I was a naturally confident boy though; I was a worrier and probably a bit fearful. Jim and Billy were big characters and as much as they loved us as young players, the demands that they put on us were high, so there was a fear of letting them down. You knew that if you didn't do it week in, week out, you could be out the team, out the club and potentially out the game. It was more a fear factor that drove me forward rather than me being a particularly confident player.

"I think there was a general progression for me once I got into the first team. There were always going to be games where you got found out a little bit because you were playing against some top quality players. When you go up against Rangers and Celtic as a young man in your early 20s, it's difficult because you're talking about the best in the country. It was tough at times and it certainly wasn't a case of having a fantastic game every week, but I thought my progression was generally going really, really well. I think I was a good, solid player and I felt I fitted nicely into what Jim and Billy were trying to do."

Within 14 months of his first-team debut, Ritchie had played in two cup finals, both of which ended with the young defender in tears. He was demoralised after the 5-1 Scottish Cup final thrashing by Rangers in May 1996 and devastated after the same opponents edged a thrilling Coca-Cola Cup final 4-3 just six months later. "There are pictures everywhere of me crying after both those games," says Ritchie. "My kids bring it up all the time; they're like 'oh, look at you ya big baby'. Losing so heavily in the first one and so badly in the second one, they both hurt just as bad for different reasons. The first one was a really difficult day to be involved in – a real doing for a young player – and in the second one we gave a fantastic account of ourselves and on a different day could have won."

Losing nine goals in two cup finals was character-building for the young defender, but the main sign of his progress was that he had established himself as a regular in a Hearts team on an upward curve. In between those two finals, he was one of four Hearts players sent off in an infamous 3-0 defeat at Ibrox; the subsequent suspension brought an end to 40 consecutive starts for Ritchie. Upon serving his ban, he was swiftly restored to the team alongside David Weir, who had arrived from Falkirk in summer 1996 to become his new defensive sidekick and mentor. "We were always looking to improve and Davie effectively came in for Allan McManus, and Pasquale was getting older at that point, so Davie just slotted in and was good enough to give us the opportunity to go to a back four," says Jefferies. "Paul Ritchie learned a lot from Pasquale and then carried that on by having a great partnership with Davie."

The fact McManus, nine months older than his close friend and similarly highly-regarded at youth-team level, was struggling to stay in the team on a regular basis highlighted just how well Ritchie was progressing. "I think Paul was just ahead of me in terms of the attributes you'd look for in a centre-back at that time and probably had a wee bit more focus," said McManus when asked what Ritchie had that he didn't. "The more games you play breeds more confidence, and Paul probably had more confidence in his own ability than I did. If you look back, we were only 21, 22 years old which is still very young to be involved with the players we played with and play in the games of the magnitude we played in. Sometimes I found it quite tough to cope with, whereas Paul seemed to cope better than myself. He was a fantastic player even at that young age. Paul was strong and aggressive in the air; he was a proper centre-back."

Ritchie turned 22 just a few weeks into the historic 1997/98 season – his third in the first team – and by that point he was viewed as one of the top defenders in the country. His partnership with Weir was fundamental to the team's impressive dual challenge for the Premier Division and Scottish Cup. "Paul had been learning from David, who had a bit more experience, and they became a fantastic partnership; arguably the strongest in the country at the time," says McManus, who played right-back in the early months of the 1997/98 campaign before losing his place to Locke.

Weir feels he and Ritchie were a perfect combination of assurance and aggression. "I think we complemented each other well," says Weir. "Paul was quick, athletic and aggressive whereas I was probably better with the ball than Paul so he was happy for me to have the ball more and he liked the contact. I wasn't scared of contact either but I just thought it was a good relationship in terms of the balance we had. I was right-sided, he was left-sided. We had good qualities and we worked well together."

While Weir was Hearts' standout defender in the 1996/97 season, Ritchie was arguably the team's most consistent centre-back in 1997/98, particularly in the second half of this double-chasing campaign when Weir was hindered slightly be a knee problem. Ritchie started 42 of Hearts' 44 matches in all competitions and his solidifying presence was clearly missed when he sat out the damaging home draw with Motherwell in April through injury. His form was so impressive that he started both of Scotland's B internationals against Wales and Norway in March and April respectively. When he was singled out for praise by Scotland manager Craig Brown after the Wales game, it raised hopes that he might step up and follow Weir – five years his senior – into the full squad in time for the World Cup in France that summer. Ritchie was linked with Newcastle United and Aston Villa and was widely deemed unfortunate not to win the Scottish PFA young player of the year award in April, with 19-year-old team-mate Gary Naysmith, who had only established himself in the team from January onwards, landing the prestigious accolade instead. Even Naysmith was "completely shocked". The left-back said at the time: "I was sure Paul Ritchie was going to get it. In my opinion, he should even have been in the running for the main award." Ritchie eventually got his deserved recognition when he was named Bell's young player of the year on the eve of the Scottish Cup final. Landing awards, being the subject of transfer speculation and gaining international exposure was part and parcel of being a young player at Hearts under Jefferies' tutelage. "It was a compliment that we were all getting linked with other clubs and touted for Scotland, but I think we all handled it well," says Ritchie. "It was a great confidence boost, but I was happy at Hearts at that time."

Ritchie's sense of contentment at Tynecastle was endorsed by the fact that, with his stock level soaring, he felt compelled to sign a new two-year contract in the week leading up to the final. He capped his sensational campaign with a brilliant individual display as Hearts frustrated Rangers at Celtic Park and generally restricted the likes of Brian Laudrup, Gordon Durie and Ally McCoist to half-chances for most of the afternoon. "We showed fantastic character in the final," says Ritchie. "It was a real team effort. It was important that we managed to get ourselves 2-0 up because that second half was like the Alamo. Collectively, we kept them to a minimal amount of chances but we certainly rode a thin line a few times. It was just great to get over the line and win something. As brilliant as it was for us, seeing the joy of all those supporters who hadn't had any success for a number of years was the biggest thing to take away from it for me."

After achieving legendary status at his boyhood club aged just 22, Ritchie went on to make his full Scotland debut less than a year later when he replaced Colin Hendry in the 64th minute of a 1-0 friendly victory over Germany in Bremen. Ironically, having failed to make the squad when his club were challenging for the Premier Division title, the centre-back earned the first of his seven caps at a time when Hearts were battling relegation towards the end of a wretched 1998/99 campaign. Ritchie's reputation remained intact despite Hearts struggling to build on the glory of 98 and it became increasingly apparent that, as he headed towards his peak years, he was likely to be following the likes of Weir and Neil McCann out the exit door. "Paul was a fantastic player for Hearts and deserved all the accolades that came his way; he thoroughly deserved to go on and play at a higher level," says McManus.

The manner of Ritchie's departure, however, didn't go down well with supporters. Having seen former team-mate McCann flourish following his move to Rangers a year previously, the defender had his head turned when the Ibrox club – mindful of the fact he was in the final year of his contract – made a low-ball offer for him which was rejected in the early months of the 1999/2000 campaign. The unsettled Ritchie, who didn't feel Hearts would be able to match the financial packages on offer elsewhere, intimated to Jefferies that he planned to leave Tynecastle when his deal expired at the end of the season. The manager decided he could no longer build his defence around a player who was preparing for a future away from the club and duly allowed Ritchie to join Bolton Wanderers on a six-month loan in December 1999. Ritchie – to the disappointment and anger of many Hearts supporters – ended up signing for Rangers under freedom of contract in the summer of 2000. Bizarrely, he didn't make a single appearance for the Ibrox club under Dick Advocaat and was sold just 70 days later to Manchester City for £500,000. More than two decades on, Ritchie regrets the way it all panned out. "It was a difficult situation for me," he recalls. "As a professional you're only in the game for a certain period of time. The opportunity to play for Rangers and all of the other clubs that were interested in me was flattering. I didn't actually get an offer to turn down from Hearts because I think they knew they couldn't compete financially with the clubs that were interested at the time. The money in the game nowadays is far greater than it was back then. It's not about being greedy but in football you're one bad injury away from retirement so as a human being in any walk of life, if you get an opportunity to increase your livelihood and look after your family, you've got to seriously consider it. That's what happened with me, and that's ultimately what happened with all the other players who left Hearts for bigger clubs. Hearts are still a massive club in their own right but when you compare them to any club in the top flight in England, it's a different level. It's just part and parcel of the food chain.

"Hearts at that time were in a difficult period. They'd just brought in some foreigners (Fitzroy Simpson, Gordan Petric and Antti Niemi) who were on substantially more than the local boys. They turned down an initial bid from Rangers for me and then they decided they couldn't offer me a contract that they thought I'd be willing to stay for. They never actually offered me a new contract; they didn't want to compete financially with other clubs. I was very disappointed to leave Hearts but Jim was up front and honest; he said if I didn't plan to be there long term, he couldn't play me short term because he had to build for the future, so that Christmas I went to Bolton for six months.

"I loved it at Bolton and then I went to Rangers. Looking back with hindsight, sometimes you realise you made the wrong decision. That just looked like a business transaction from Rangers, and it left a bitter taste that my boyhood club didn't get any money for me and Rangers, who only had me for 70 days, did. There was nothing I could do about all that but it wasn't nice because I love Hearts. I got a bit of stick from some supporters for turning my back on the club but I thought at the time it was a good opportunity, both financially and from a football point of view. Unfortunately, it didn't work out that way."

Ritchie's career didn't unfold the way he had hoped after leaving Tynecastle. Only one of his seven Scotland caps came after he had officially departed Hearts in summer 2000: a 4-0 friendly defeat away to Wales under Berti Vogts in February 2004 at a time when he was playing for relegation-threatened Walsall in England's second tier. Prior to that, he had two seasons in the English Premiership with Manchester City in which he made 27 appearances – 17 as a starter – alongside the likes of Shaun Wright-Phillips, Shaun Goater, Paulo Wanchope, Alf-Inge Haaland and, for a couple of months, George Weah, before playing out the final year of his contract at Maine Road with loan spells at both Derby County and Portsmouth in 2002/03. The defender returned to Scotland with Dundee United shortly before his 29th birthday in summer 2004 and occasionally captained the Tannadice team, but he never quite rediscovered the consistency and contentment he enjoyed when making 162 predominantly impressive appearances under Jefferies at Tynecastle. "I'd have loved to have stayed longer at Hearts but football's a short career so you've got to make what you think is the right decision at the time," says Ritchie. "I thought it was right to leave Hearts at that time because I had a young family to look after, but looking back now it was probably not the right decision. If you asked me now if I'd make the same move: 100 per cent no, I wouldn't."

As a key member of one of the finest Hearts sides since the 1950s, any animosity from supporters over the nature of his departure has long since subsided. Ritchie is one of the most prominent Hearts-supporting former players on social media and is a regular at matches with his Jambo sons, Jordan and Dylan, whenever he returns to Scotland from his base in the USA. By virtue of events on 16th May 1998, his place in the history of the club of his heart is secure forever. "I am very, very fortunate and honoured to have played for Hearts, particularly at that time because it was a fantastic environment and a great place to be under Jim and Billy," says Ritchie. "When I started playing football, it was a case of: Can you play for your country? Can you play for the team you support? Can you win something? I managed all three of those things. I think myself and all the other lads in that

98 team are very fortunate to have been part of something so special that made a mark in the club's history and is still spoken about to this day, especially every time the anniversary comes round. It's something nobody can ever take away from us."

Thomas Flögel

*"We went up the Braid Hills – that was
the hardest day in my whole career"*

When Thomas Flögel backheeled the ball nonchalantly over the head of Lorenzo Amoruso and then forced a corner off Richard Gough as his team led Rangers 2-0 in the 1998 Scottish Cup final, Craig Brown, the Scotland manager who was co-commentating for Sky Sports, remarked: "Flögel has been a revelation for Hearts today, an excellent signing by Jim Jefferies."

The prospect of such a scenario coming to fruition in the concluding match of his first season in Scotland would have seemed far-fetched to Flögel as he sat in his plush flat in Moray Place, in Edinburgh's New Town, during the opening months of his time at Hearts wondering what the hell he had signed up for. "Early on, I was thinking 'I have probably made a mistake coming here, I am not suited to Scottish football'," says Flögel. On his competitive debut for Hearts, away to Rangers on the first night of the season, Flögel – who had just turned 26 – suffered the ignominy of being substituted at half-time with his new team trailing 2-0. "I found that game difficult for a number of reasons," he recalls. "One was the language barrier: I couldn't understand the tactics from the gaffer and I wasn't able to ask. The gaffer was shouting from the sidelines and I couldn't understand what he was telling me. Even though I didn't understand how we were playing, I just thought I'd get by with my technique and it would work out okay. In pre-season, when we played against Hull City and other teams, the tactics were working nicely but that was pre-season. As a coach myself, I know that pre-season friendlies and competitive matches are simply not comparable.

"After ten minutes of the Rangers game, there were so many things going through my mind. I was affected by the pace of the game, the size of the crowd, the stadium. We didn't play well in the first half, we didn't play together, we weren't compact; we were too open, too far away from each other. I was just running around, chasing the backs of Rangers players. It was the best thing to take me off because I was struggling. It was hard to take because you think you're a good player, you get yourself on to a big stage like that and then you find yourself in a situation like that, substituted at half-time. I was sitting in the dressing-room for ages, I was so fucking frustrated. After that, I was thinking about what I would have to do to improve and whether I should even stay in Scotland. Should I go back to Austria? That was my thinking at that point."

Flögel didn't start a game for another three months. Although he had no burning desire to return to Austria in this period, he at least knew he could hold his own there; his homeland was his comfort zone. It was where he had developed his love of the game, encouraged by his father, Rudi, a highly-regarded Austrian striker who had won four league titles in a distinguished 14-year spell with Rapid Vienna and played 40 times for the national team in the 1960s. "I started to play football because of my father," explains Flögel, born and bred in Vienna. "I just lived for the sport. I always played with him when I was a little boy in the garden so he brought me into football. When I was at school he asked me if I wanted to play in a club so I said 'why not?'. Some of the boys I went to school with already played for Austria Vienna. I actually found it a bit boring at first but I kept going and I started to really enjoy it. I enjoyed all my youth teams. I was at Austria Vienna my whole career as a young boy and we smashed everybody in the league from seven years old until first team. We won the championship every year and I also played for the national team at under-15, under-16 and so on. I often got the chance to play for the generation above me. I had so many games in my youth career."

It wasn't lost on the football followers of Vienna that young Flögel was playing for the city rivals of the club where his father – who made his Austria debut in a friendly against a Scotland side featuring Hearts greats Alex Young and Dave Mackay in May 1960 – was one of the ultimate legends. "Of course this has always been a big issue for the people; they always asked me why I played for Austria Vienna when my dad played for Rapid," laughs Flögel. "It was just because of where we lived: Austria Vienna trained in the second district and I grew up – and still live – in the second district. Rapid Vienna was in a totally different district and when I was a young boy I wasn't able to go there every night and train until 7pm. In the early days, there was no underground back then so it would have taken me an hour to go there. My mother said no chance was I doing that when Austria Vienna was just round the corner and I could cycle to training with my friends. My father was fine with me playing for Austria Vienna."

When Flögel was 17 and knocking on the first-team door in September 1988, Austria Vienna were eliminated from the UEFA Cup by Hearts, with Mike Galloway's goal in the Ernst-Happel Stadion (known as the Praterstadion at the time) securing a 1-0 aggregate win for the Edinburgh side. Little did the young Viennese – watching on from the stand – know that, just under nine years down the line, he would be a team-mate of the 24-year-old Hearts captain, Dave McPherson, and that one of the agents facilitating his move to Tynecastle would be Brian Whittaker, who was playing alongside McPherson in the visiting defence. Flögel made his debut for Austria Vienna as an 18-year-old substitute in September 1989 and became a regular starter towards the end of the 1989/90 campaign. He capped his maiden season in the first team by winning silverware when he started the Austrian Cup final at the Ernst-Happel as his side won 3-1 after extra-time against a Rapid Vienna side featuring Andreas Herzog, who would go on to become Austria's most-capped player. Flögel swiftly forged a reputation as one of his country's top young players in the early 90s as he followed up his breakthrough campaign by becoming a key member of an Austria Vienna side which ended their four-year title drought by winning the Bundesliga championship three years in a row in seasons 1990/91, 1991/92 and 1992/93. Flögel also played in Austrian Cup triumphs in 1992 and 1994 in what represented a purple patch for his boyhood club. "Austria Vienna was a very successful time for me," says Flögel. "I won the championship three times and I won the cup three times. We always went to the second or third round of the UEFA Cup and then it was game over because we would come up against strong teams like Juventus, Barcelona and Arsenal."

Among his team-mates in those glittering early years of his career were Anton Pfeffer, Andreas Ogris and Peter Stöger, all of whom won more than 60 caps for Austria; Ralph Hasenhüttl, who went on to manage Southampton; Attila Sekerlioglu, who went on to be a popular player at St Johnstone; and Valdas Ivanauskas, who managed Hearts when they won the Scottish Cup in 2006. "Valdas was a very strong player," recalls Flögel. "We always had fantastic players in the team so it was really enjoyable to find my steps as a young player at Austria Vienna. The experienced players really helped me."

Flögel was making an impact at club and international level. Aged 20, he made his Austria debut in April 1992 when he started in a 4-0 friendly win at home to a Lithuania side featuring Ivanauskas. Within two years, he had seven full caps under his belt. Flögel ended up with 37 caps by the time his international career ended in 2003; just three fewer than his father. "It means a lot to me now that both me and my father played for the national team but it's not something I really thought about at the time," he says. "I wasn't thinking about my father's career when I was a boy, to be honest. I just grew up used to the fact he had been a footballer. I never had any issues with that although I found that some other people or players I played against used to try to wind me up by saying I was only playing because of who my father was. That was more motivation for me to play well. Some people in Austria actually used to call me Rudi because they thought I played similar to him. I've always been very proud of my father. Today, when I look back, it is a big thing that we both played for Austria because it isn't a common thing for a boy to make the same steps as his father in international football."

As the 90s wore on and Flögel entered his mid-20s, the attacking midfielder found he was starting to stagnate. His motivation levels and form dipped, his team stopped winning the title as Rapid Vienna and Austria Salzburg (now Red Bull Salzburg) took over at the top and he lost his place in the national team from 1994 onwards. "I'd won everything in Austria with this team and I started to settle and get complacent," he explains. "That's why I was falling out of the national team and dropping off a bit. Because of my own slackness, it got to a point where I wanted to move on but the problem was that I was still under contract and nobody wanted to pay money for me, so I couldn't leave."

After soldiering on for a couple of years, playing regularly but not to a level he was satisfied with, Flögel knew he would be leaving his boyhood club when his contract expired in summer 1997. The arrival of Wolfgang Frank to replace Walter Skocik as manager in April 97 helped give the midfielder his "appetite and enjoyment back" at a timely period in his search for a new club and he produced one of his best displays of the season when he scored the only goal of the game in a 1-0 home win over FC Tirol in May 97. Crucially for Flögel, Dundee United had a scout in the stand who had travelled to watch his Latvian team-mate, Vitalijs Astafjevs. "It wasn't a case of me wanting to go to a specific country," Flögel recalls. "Austria Vienna wanted to re-sign me but I just wanted to leave at that point. The club wasn't the problem; the problem was with myself because I just couldn't motivate myself. I needed a fresh challenge because I had won everything and I was too settled. I had talks with several other teams in Austria so I would probably have stayed in Austria if I hadn't been lucky and been scouted by Dundee United. They had come to watch a different player in my team. He didn't play well, but I played well and scored a goal. My agent (Eddie Bruhne) was sitting beside the Dundee United scout and he was asking 'who is the No.10?' It was just good timing for me. Dundee United invited me to come over and train with them in the summer and the rest is history."

Of course, Flögel didn't end up signing for Dundee United – who were under the charge of former Hearts manager Tommy McLean at the time – but his trial with the Tannadice club led him to Tynecastle. "Dundee United treated me fantastic but after a few days of my trial, I felt a little bored and confused because nobody had told me whether I was getting a contract or whether I should go home," says Flögel. "After a few days, I said 'you have to decide' because I can't wait for two or three weeks until you make a decision. I was a bit upset so I told my agent who was working together with Brian Whittaker (a Scottish agent at the time) and Brian said 'okay, I will see if I can get you into Hearts'. I didn't know anything about Hearts at that time apart from having vague memories of loads of guys in kilts being at the game they had played against Austria Vienna when I was 17. But I said 'okay, let me see what they're all about'. So after leaving Dundee United, we went to Edinburgh. I met Jim Jefferies and it was easy. He said 'yes, I am interested in signing you' and very soon he offered me a contract. That was the right way for me. I didn't want to train for several days and then somebody tells me there is no deal. I'm sure Jim knew I was a decent player by that point because it had been in the papers that I had been training with Dundee United. He had one more contract left and I got it so I will be thankful for that for the rest of my life because it was the best time of my football career."

Flögel had a good vibe about Hearts from the moment he met Jefferies. "I liked him straight away, especially because of his straightness," he says. "In Austria I had spoken to clubs and I never heard anything back from them. With Jim, it was all so much more straightforward. I remember when he first showed me Tynecastle; that was one of my most memorable days. I went through the tunnel and on to the pitch with Jim and my agent, and as soon as we got out there and I looked around, I said to my agent 'yes, I'm signing here'. Tynecastle was better than Austria Vienna's stadium at the time. It all felt right straight away. In the next few days, there were a few negative headlines regarding the Dundee United situation but that is the business; I was always looking for straightness but I felt they were fucking around. With Hearts there was none of that."

Flögel's transfer to Hearts owed plenty to the trust Jefferies had in Whittaker, who had played under him at Falkirk for two years in the early 90s after leaving Tynecastle in 1990. "There was no time to watch Thomas in a match or anything like that, so I asked Brian what he thought and he said he would be a fantastic signing," explains Jefferies. "To be sure, I asked if I could get him down for a few days. It said a lot for Thomas because he would probably have got an offer at Dundee United but he gave that up just to let us have a look at him because Brian had told him how big a club we were. Once you're in at a club it's hard to walk away if you know they're interested but Thomas clearly liked the idea of Hearts. It didn't take me long to make up my mind; I could tell after one training session that he was quality."

His ability was evident immediately to the rest of the Hearts players. "When Thomas came in, I remember in training thinking 'who's this guy?' because he was doing these big slide tackles, scissors kicks and overhead kicks," recalls Neil McCann. "He was technically brilliant, but just as importantly he was a team player."

In his first venture away from his home city, Flögel was eager to make a positive impression. "In one of my first training sessions we did a wee game; five against five, perhaps," he recalls. "It was very fast for me. It felt like they wanted to see what I could do. Me being an offensive player, I was always looking for the striker. I didn't know who John Robertson was at the time, but of all the balls I played through, most of them were to him. Robbo said to the gaffer 'he's a good boy'. It always helps when the experienced players have a positive opinion of you."

Flögel, accustomed to winning in Austria, wasn't fazed by the prospect of playing for a club whose resources were dwarfed by Rangers and Celtic. "I used to play for a big club in Austria where the target was always to win, win, win," he explains. "Win the championship, win the cup; there was no reason for me to change that mindset when I came to Hearts."

While his technical ability was never in doubt, Flögel struggled initially with the physical demands of Scottish football, to the extent that he was very close to giving up and going home. "I needed a few months to find my steps at Hearts because of the style of football and because of my own weaknesses," he explains. "I was struggling when I first arrived. I thought my technique and my quality would be enough, but it wasn't. Scottish football was different to Austria. All the foreign players will tell you the same, when the first tackle comes in from a young boy in training, the gaffer stands there and says 'welcome to Scotland'. It was hard for me; it was more physical than I was used to. In Scotland you need to be able to run your socks off and you need to have a good attitude. It doesn't matter if you can play football or not; the main thing you need in Scotland is heart and desire. That's what I really learned about being in Scotland, that you need to do it with your heart. This was something I had lost towards the end of my time at Austria Vienna. When you come up as a young boy, why do you play football? Because your heart tells you it makes you happy, you have passion for it, you want to score a goal. That's what I tell my players now as a coach and that was the biggest thing I took away from my time at Hearts. The technical side is good but the first thing is to play with your heart and give everything you have, not just for yourself but also for your team."

The warning signs were there for Flögel early on in pre-season. "I always remember we went up a hill, I think it was the Braid Hills, to do some running," recalls the Austrian. "That was the hardest day in my whole football career. The whole squad and the young boys went up the hill and the gaffer said we had so many minutes to complete the circuit. I thought it would be easy so I was just jogging at a relaxing pace and then I noticed the young boys sprinting. I was wondering why they were sprinting at first and then I realised it was because they needed so much time to get up the hill. I was one of the last boys to get back and I was really struggling. Then they started up with press-ups and then sprints up the hill. It got to a point where I thought 'it's game over'. I was seeing stars; it felt like I was running on drugs. By the end I was just walking. I had to lie on the grass for ten minutes afterwards. We had so many hard running sessions at Hearts. It was different to anything I experienced in Austria. It was just old-school running, but I needed that; I needed that kick in the ass. I became fitter in Scotland than I ever was in Austria."

The early months in Edinburgh were tough, both physically and mentally, for Flögel as he struggled for form and game time while awaiting the arrival of his partner Tina from Vienna. "I really loved being in a new country, I loved being in Edinburgh; I had a fantastic flat with a big garden outside," says Flögel. "I really wanted to stay there but I felt if it wasn't working out, I would have to move on. I didn't want to go back to Austria but I spoke to my agent and told him I didn't know what I was doing in Scotland. He told me to take my time and Jim Jefferies also said this."

In the 12 matches that followed his chastening debut at Ibrox, Flögel failed to make the 14-man matchday squad for five of them. His contribution in that three-month period between early August and the end of October, when Hearts were establishing themselves at the top of the Premier Division, was just seven substitute appearances, three of which came in the last five minutes. Flögel – who had also been getting game time in the reserve team – felt on the periphery at Hearts and was braced for a winter of discontent. "Near the end of October, I went to Jim Jefferies' office and asked him to let me go," says Flögel. "I said 'please, let me go, cancel my contract'. I was so frustrated. I felt if I wasn't playing at Hearts, I needed to go somewhere else. Jim said 'listen, be patient, you are getting better, you will get your chance'. He promised me I'd get my chance. Then, out of the blue, came the game against Aberdeen away which changed the whole situation for me. I hadn't been in the squad for the previous game (at home to Dunfermline) and I actually called my agent in the lead-up to the Aberdeen game and said 'please look for a new club for me because it's not happening for me here'. But then when Jim told me I was in the starting XI, I couldn't believe it. I didn't know how to react; it was a situation I wasn't expecting at that point. I played up front with John Robertson that day and everything just clicked for me. We played fantastically well, won 4-1 and I scored two goals. After the game, the first thing I did was phone my agent to say 'forget that phone call we had before, I'm staying at Hearts'."

Flögel went on to start the next seven games and, although he dropped out of the starting XI again over the festive period before flitting in and out of the side in the second half of the season, he had banished the turmoil of his early months in Edinburgh and started to feel like he could make a success of his move abroad. "I was wrong to look at it as a mistake joining Hearts in those early days," he reflects. "It was all about understanding what I had to do to make things better. At that point I could have gone under or I could stand up and fight for what I really wanted. Thankfully I learned to stand up and do what I needed to do to become more physical and become a better player. That was the point when I started to see things differently and I started to train harder. That was a very important point in my life and my football career. I needed time to adapt and thankfully Jim gave me that time. That was the key for me. I had someone believing in me and it made me stronger and I became a better footballer. After two or three months of playing for the reserves and coming off the bench for the first team, I started to find my steps. I needed to go back to zero, it was like a reset button. After the Aberdeen game, I started to play more regularly and that was all down to Jim Jefferies giving me the chance to take my time and find my steps."

Flögel found it a humbling experience to be in a situation where he wasn't considered a key man. "It was important for me to see that the team could function without me in those early months of the season," he says. "At Austria Vienna, I was winning everything and playing all the time so I thought I was the man. It was really important to find a different situation where I was having to think from the outside about how I could help the team."

From mid-December until the end of the 1997/98 campaign, Flögel started only five league games. He topped up his game time, however, by starting in each of the first four rounds of the Scottish Cup and scored two goals en route to the final: Hearts' first of the run against Clydebank and the second goal in the 4-1 win over Ayr United in the quarter-final. "I saw the cup as my chance to bring some good performances and show what I was capable of," says Flögel.

With every Hearts player fit for the final apart from captain Gary Locke, it was a surprise to many – including the man himself – that Flögel got the nod to start. Indeed the Austrian had been linked with German clubs Borussia Moenchengladbach and Karlsruhe a fortnight before the final due to the fact he hadn't been a regular starter in his first season at Tynecastle. Most anticipated that top scorer Jim Hamilton would start the season's showpiece match, while midfielder Lee Makel had started three of the closing six matches of the league campaign and, at that point, would have been deemed as likely a starter as Flögel, who had started just two of the final six league games. "I thought I wouldn't play because I had a bad game in the semi-final against Falkirk; I was absolutely shite," says Flögel. "Lee Makel came on for me in that game and I thought he might have started in the final. Another reason I didn't think I would play was because I hadn't had good experiences against Rangers. I didn't expect to start but I tried to give my best in training leading up to it and I thought 'we'll see what happens'. Then Jim named the team and told me I'd be playing. He told me what I'd have to do and that I'd be playing mostly against Brian Laudrup. This time, unlike the first day of the season, I could understand what he was asking me to do. It was tremendous when he told me I was playing; it gave me a massive boost. After my previous frustrations against Rangers, this was a chance for me to show the people I could do a lot better."

Flögel, who was an attacking central midfielder in his homeland, was used as a striker, a central midfielder and occasionally out on the right as he struggled to nail down a specific position in his first season at Hearts. In the 4-5-1 formation Jefferies had opted to go with for the final, the Austrian was deemed the ideal man to bring the right blend of defensive nous and attacking intent to the right side of midfield. "Our alternative option within the formation we had chosen to go with was Stephane playing in off the right and Jim up front," says Jefferies. "But Thomas was a very disciplined player and we felt he would be ideal for that position and the way we wanted to play."

McPherson, who was selected at right-back, was delighted to have someone of Flögel's intelligence playing in front of him against a formidable Rangers side. "Thomas was a great player to play with," says McPherson. "He was probably a bit underrated. Technically he was very good, he would work his socks off for the team and his delivery was very good when he had the chance to cross into the box. He was a quality player."

The 90 minutes in the Celtic Park sunshine would be career-defining for Flögel. "It was the best experience of my career and it was a turning point in my life," he says. "It changed my character, my attitude and my view on football. It was the best day of my life. The games against Rangers that season were milestones for me. The first one against them was a disaster and the last one was my turning point."

Flögel believes Hearts' Scottish Cup triumph – the pinnacle of his career – was the embodiment of team spirit and a collective desire to achieve something special. "Until fairly recently I had only seen highlights of the game, but then I watched the whole game a few years ago because I was interested from a coach's perspective to see what we really played like, how our tactics worked, how Rangers played, and things like that," says the Austrian, who went into coaching and management, predominantly in Austria's lower leagues, after retiring in 2006. "The big thing I can take away from that game and tell my players is that the most important thing in football is to run your fucking socks off. In modern football, a lot of the discussion surrounds tactics. But the reality is the most important thing is the basics like attitude, desire and workrate. That final in 1998 is a perfect example. We didn't play fabulous football but we worked hard. In this particular game, it was so important just to run and tackle, and try to do something together. It was impressive for me to watch it back. My performance was okay, I had some good moments and a big chance with a header which I should have scored, but when you win a game like that, it's not so important how well you played as an individual. As a group, we ran our socks off and we made sure we won that fucking game because we wanted to become legends. Jim Jefferies always said to us that if we won we wouldn't believe what it would be like, and he was right. The celebrations afterwards, I had never experienced anything like that before. I won the championship three times in Austria and it was great but it was nothing like what it was like in Edinburgh. What happened after that with the bus and so on, it was absolutely tremendous. The two or three days of that weekend will always stay in my mind. As a football player you always want to win something, you want to stand in front of 50,000 supporters; when I won the cup with Hearts, it felt like I'd reached this target. When you work hard for something in a job that you love and you achieve it, there is no better feeling. It's the best feeling in the world."

Jefferies' faith in Flögel in those testing early months was vindicated by the fact the Austrian contributed to one of Hearts' greatest days and went on to play 164 times in a five-year spell at Tynecastle. At the time of publication, Marius Zaliukas, the 2012 Scottish Cup-winning captain, is the only overseas player to have made more appearances for the club. "You've got to give foreign players time because in Scotland, when you get the ball everybody's on top of you," Jefferies explains. "In a lot of other countries, teams retreat and let you have the ball. Thomas was one who needed a bit of time to settle in but he became a great asset for us. I've been lucky to work with a lot of technically-gifted players but not many as good as Thomas. With Thomas's track record, we were fortunate that we were able to get him in at a good age and he was terrific for us. He was very professional and a great lad to work with. Whenever Hearts have got an event on, Thomas will invariably be there; that's how much he loved his time in Edinburgh."

After a six-year absence from the national team, Flögel's form at Hearts earned him a recall in March 2000 and he scored in a 1-1 draw with Sweden in Graz in his first game back. By the time he returned to Austria Vienna, aged 31, after leaving Hearts in 2002, Flögel had married Tina (in 1999), welcomed his son Alec into the world (in 2000), and developed significantly as a footballer, both at club and international level. "My best seasons at Hearts came after the cup final," he says. "I was building myself up towards that game and getting better all the time, and after that game I was a different player altogether; I was a better player physically and mentally. By the time I returned to Austria Vienna I was a totally different player to the one that had left five years earlier. I could play in any position: at the back, in midfield, up front. I won the title in my first season back in Austria and the people there told me I had become more physical and was more of a leader. I had a whole different playing style and I played with more heart. I remember when I scored the volley against Sweden (in 2000), that was the point when people started saying 'wow, look at him, look at the player he's become'. Hearts made me the player I was. I joined Hearts when I was about to turn 26, but, in hindsight, if I had the chance I would have gone to Hearts when I was 20."

Jim Hamilton

"Leaving Hearts was probably the biggest regret I had in football"

As Jim Hamilton performed his Elephant Man goal celebration in front of the away end at Tannadice on the afternoon of Saturday 21st March 1998, few Hearts supporters would have contemplated the notion of going into a big match without the in-form striker in the starting line-up. Hamilton had just scored a magnificent goal – lifting the ball deftly over the head of Dundee United defender Magnus Skoldmark with his left foot before rasping an emphatic half-volley with his right foot beyond goalkeeper Sieb Dijkstra – to secure a crucial 1-0 win over Tommy McLean's side and keep title-chasing Hearts within two points of Premier Division leaders Celtic. It was Hamilton's sixth goal in six games, his 12th in 14 league appearances away from home and his 14th league strike of the season. At that point, with seven games of the 1997/98 campaign to play, only Rangers striker Marco Negri and United's Kjell Olofsson had more Premier Division goals.

So, while it is entirely natural that the narrative of Hearts' Scottish Cup triumph revolves significantly around John Robertson's diminished role within the squad, Hamilton was the substitute striker who had more reason to rue the fact he didn't play a more prominent part in the final. Although that goal at Tannadice proved to be his last of the season, Hamilton finished as Hearts' top scorer with 15 goals in all competitions; two more than his close friend and former Dundee colleague Neil McCann. In addition, the 21-year-old centre-forward had a knack of scoring against cup final opponents Rangers. He had netted in both of his previous encounters with Walter Smith's side and had also struck a hat-trick against them in Dave McPherson's testimonial match at Tynecastle the previous summer.

Apart from a period through November and December in which he had been used predominantly as a substitute and become the subject of a bold but unsuccessful mid-season attempt from St Johnstone to try to buy him, Hamilton was a regular starter for Jim Jefferies in 1997/98 after joining Hearts midway through the previous campaign. Between the 3-2 win over Saints in Perth in January and the 1-1 draw at home to the same opponents in mid-April, he started 15 out of 17 matches in all competitions – including all four Scottish Cup ties en route to the final – and scored eight goals in that period. Two key factors conspired against him, however, when it came to handing out cup final starting jerseys. The first was that Hamilton had incurred an untimely three-match suspension as a booking in the 2-1 defeat away to Hibs took him beyond the SFA's 16-point disciplinary threshold and ruled him out of the last three league games, therefore denying him the chance to enhance his already strong case for inclusion. Secondly, in the weeks leading up to the big match, Jefferies had decided on a change of formation which involved only one central striker as opposed to his usual two. With the mobility of Stephane Adam preferred in this instance to Hamilton's more physical approach, the former Dundee striker was listed as a substitute alongside Robertson and Grant Murray.

"It was partly my own fault for picking up stupid bookings and getting myself suspended for the last few games," Hamilton acknowledges. "The manager obviously decided to go with one up in a different kind of formation and Stephane was the one who could run the channels, all that kind of stuff, so I could have no complaints. Obviously you're a bit disappointed when you don't start a final but because we had such a good team spirit, everybody was involved in it whether they were stripped or not, and that helped the situation. It was just about being involved."

Indeed, Hamilton found himself heavily involved in the most critical phase of the match when – unlike his two fellow substitutes, who didn't see any game time – he was summoned from the bench to help Hearts see out victory. With 78 minutes gone and Rangers cranking up the pressure as they sought to reduce their 2-0 deficit, Jefferies needed some fresh legs. The manager felt Hamilton was best suited to the demands of this particular moment and he was sent on in place of Adam, who – like most of his team-mates – was feeling the effects of a gruelling afternoon's work in the searing heat. Although supposed to be Hearts' most advanced player, Hamilton spent much of his time on the pitch in his own half, repelling crosses with his head and generally aiding a defence which, by this stage of the match, was under siege. The tone for Hamilton's valiant late cameo was set when, within seconds of bounding on to the pitch in enthusiastic manner, he made a towering leap just outside his own six-yard box to head clear a long Rangers throw-in. The anxious Hearts support responded with a loud cheer of relief and rapturous applause.

"To get on was amazing even though the last 15 minutes, or whatever it was when I went on, was a bit scary!" he reflects, alluding to the fact Rangers had several moments when they threatened to equalise after Ally McCoist had pulled one back in the 81st minute. "With maybe about half an hour to go, Jim told me to go and get warmed up because he was planning to put me on. Obviously Rangers were coming more and more into the game and playing the longer balls and Jim said I'd end up probably being more in the defence than up front in the last 15-20 minutes, which obviously ended up happening. So many people have commented to me over the years about the number of headers I won when I came on. It was just a great feeling to know that I was coming on to be part of it and to try to help the situation."

Hamilton's second notable moment in the match came when, just two minutes after his introduction, he picked up a booking for tangling off the ball with Rangers centre-back Lorenzo Amoruso. "That was part and parcel for me," he explains. "That was my problem sometimes, I got involved quite a lot. It was part and parcel of the atmosphere on the day and just getting involved in everything."

The striker's immediate involvement in the cup final highlighted a physical, combative playing style which was honed on the parks of Scotland's Highland League. Born and raised in Peterhead, Hamilton – whose father, also Jim, was a professional footballer for Aberdeen, East Fife and Dunfermline Athletic in the late 1960s and early 70s – was never going to be a shrinking violet given the gruelling, character-building grounding he experienced in the north east. "My dad's career was cut short with injury, so he landed up going into management in his early 30s," Hamilton, a former pupil at Peterhead Academy, recalls as he explains how he first started to emerge as a footballer. "When my dad was the manager of Peterhead in the Highland League, he took me in to train with them when I was about ten years old. I was just joining in with them in training, obviously getting kicked about all over the place, but it kind of toughened me up for what I had to do in the rest of my career. Then my dad moved to Keith as the manager and I landed up playing for them when I was about 15 years old against ex-professionals. That was when the Highland League was of a very high level so that toughened me up further.

"I remember playing a derby for Keith against Huntly in one of my earlier games and big Doug Rougvie, who had played for Aberdeen in the (1983) Cup Winners' Cup final, was playing for Huntly at the time. He was playing centre-half and, honestly, he kicked me up and down that park for 15-20 minutes at the start. He burst my head wide open, I came off and I says to them 'bandage me up, I'm going back on', and at the end of the game Doug Rougvie turned round and says to me 'by the way, you'll make it all the way because you've got that heart and the toughness, you've got everything that's needed to be a professional player'. I was an Aberdeen fan as a boy so to have someone who had won the Cup Winners' Cup for them against Real Madrid say that to me, it meant a lot."

Rougvie's words were proved correct. In January 1994, a month before his 18th birthday, Hamilton joined Dundee on a YTS (youth training scheme) following a successful trial. He made a swift impact at Dens Park as he earned himself a professional contract within a few months and made his debut for Jim Duffy's first team in a 4-0 home victory over Hibs in the penultimate game of the 1993/94 season, after Dundee's relegation from the Premier Division had been confirmed. "Jim Duffy and John McCormack (the assistant manager) were a breath of fresh air for me," says Hamilton. "They toughened me up. It was a good education being at Dundee and I felt it was a very successful time there; we had a really good side."

Player/manager Duffy, himself an unyielding centre-back, was impressed by young Hamilton's willingness to go in where it hurt. "Jim was a gangly boy, a composed finisher with a nice left foot on him, but the biggest thing about him was that he was competitive," Duffy explains. "He would get in about defenders. I think that spell he had in the Highland League was definitely good for him because he came to us with a really positive attitude and was fearless about playing against guys who were big and strong. He was really good in the air; he had that ability to get up early and hang there for that wee split second which could make all the difference. He was a really good team player who could get us up the pitch, flick the ball on and bring others into play. He wasn't the most prolific goalscorer but he was a good goalscorer. He did really well for us and I always felt he could play at a higher level because, particularly at that time, teams were always looking for that type of striker who could get you up the pitch."

Hamilton spent around two-and-and-a-half years in Dundee's first team, playing alongside the likes of Duffy, Ray Farningham, Dusan Vrto, Morten Wieghorst, Paul Tosh, George Shaw and McCann, who was 18 months older than him and slightly further on in his development as a professional footballer. "When I first joined Dundee, Neil was around the first team at that time," recalls Hamilton. "Within that summer of 94 I landed up moving in to digs with him so we stayed in the same digs for about two years before he moved to Hearts. We had a very close relationship. When I ended up moving to Hearts, me and him stayed round the corner from each other in Livingston so we travelled with each other until he obviously moved to Rangers. It was a very good relationship we had and still have."

Despite playing predominantly in the First Division, Hamilton got to experience some big occasions with Dundee. He came on as a substitute in the 1994 Challenge Cup final defeat by Airdrieonians at McDiarmid Park, and then started the 1995 Coca-Cola Cup final defeat by Aberdeen at Hampden after helping defeat Hearts in the quarter-final at Dens Park. With his star on the rise as he came to the end of his teenage years, Hamilton finished the 1995/96 season as Dundee's top scorer. In one of his last big games for the club, he scored in a 3-1 defeat by Hearts at Easter Road in the 1996 Coca-Cola Cup semi-final as Dundee were denied the chance to make it to the final for the second year in succession. "I wouldn't change anything about the way I started my career," says Hamilton, who scored 39 goals in total for Dundee. "Because Dundee gave me the opportunity, they'll always be very special in my heart. I had some great nights, scored a few goals and made a lot of appearances for them, and they obviously got me into the Scotland Under-21 set up as well so I've got very, very good memories from my time at Dundee."

The good times continued to roll when Hamilton got his big move to Hearts in December 1996. Asked how his £200,000 transfer to Tynecastle came to fruition, Hamilton laughs: "Neil always says he instigated my move from Dundee to Hearts, but don't believe him, right, if he does say it!"

Sure enough, McCann is quick on the draw. "I'm taking a bit of credit for big Hammy getting his move to Hearts," the winger proudly exclaims. "As a footballer, I thought Hammy was brilliant; he hung in the air like nobody else I ever played with. I went on to play with James Beattie, big Crouchie (Peter Crouch) and other fantastic strikers who were good in the air, but big Hammy was as good as any. I remember we were training and Billy Brown came up to me and said 'Jim Hamilton?'. And I went 'if you can get him, sign him in a minute, he'll be brilliant for us'."

Hamilton's ears pricked up when informed by McCann that his name was being spoken about by Hearts' management team. "After Neil left Dundee, we were always in contact with each other and he just says 'oh, I've been asked about you by Jim (Jefferies) and Billy (Brown)'," Hamilton explains. "Obviously I was still only 20 and I was thinking 'oh, this is really good' because I'd just watched the Coca-Cola Cup final at Parkhead when Neil was unbelievable. I'd seen a bit of Hearts at that time and I knew the way that Jim and Billy were trying to build the team with boys like Davie Weir, Neil and Colin Cameron, so it was nice to hear that they were talking about me. Neil had obviously put a good word in and he told me they were going to come and watch me. I must have impressed them because my agent contacted me and said 'there's been an offer made, what do you think?'. My first thought was 'yeah, I want to go, right away'. I remember going to Tynecastle and meeting Jim and Billy. As soon as I met them and heard their ambitions for going forward, and obviously having seeing Hearts in that cup final and stuff like that, I thought 'right, this is definitely the club I want to join'. I couldn't wait to get started."

Hamilton wasted little time getting his feet under the table at his new club. The 20-year-old scored his first goal in his third start for Hearts – a 4-1 home win over Motherwell on 28th December 1996 – and then endeared himself further to supporters by scoring a double in a 4-0 win away to Hibs in the following game on New Year's Day. "Obviously it was my first derby at Hearts, I'm new in the door, so the fans will be wondering how I'm going to get on and what's going to happen," says Hamilton. "That was actually Jim Duffy's first derby as manager of Hibs after he left Dundee so obviously with me having been with him for three years, it was quite weird. It ended up a really special day for me. By scoring two goals in the derby, the fans start liking you right away. That was a big help for me because it settled me right down. Obviously you're going into a new club, not knowing what's going to happen, so to get off to that kind of start was great."

Within a month of joining Hearts, Hamilton had scored five goals. Despite his fast start, he added only one more – in a 1-1 home draw with Dundee United in the Scottish Cup – before the end of the 1996/97 season. Nonetheless, considering he had barely played in the Premier Division prior to joining Hearts, he could be content with a haul of six goals in his first half-season in Gorgie. "I felt I improved quite quickly after moving to Hearts," he reflects. "Obviously I went to Dundee from the Highland League and even though I was there for almost three years, I was still a bit raw and I'd never really played in the Premier Division before. I'd played against Hearts and Aberdeen in the cup games, but not in a consistent manner so it was basically a case of trying to prove I was good enough to play at that level for Hearts. To get off to a great start really helped me because it was a big step up for me going there."

The presence of the legendary Robertson alongside him in the Hearts attack also helped Hamilton immensely in his early months at Tynecastle. Robertson ended that season as Hearts' top scorer with 19 goals. It would be the veteran's last as the main man in Gorgie. "Robbo was a massive influence on myself, just with what he'd done in his career, his experience and the knowledge he had," Hamilton explains. "Obviously you know Robbo, he disnae shut up; he's that kind of guy, he could talk for Britain. He would talk football all the time but his knowledge on it is incredible and he would take me on the training ground and do different stuff with me. Although other folk maybe played more than he did while I was at Hearts, he was a massive help in my career. Even when I left Hearts, he was hugely influential on me. Eventually, at the end of my career he was my manager at East Fife, so I've got massive respect for wee Robbo."

When Robertson started drifting on to the periphery at Hearts, Hamilton and Stephane Adam, who arrived from Metz in summer 1997, were paired together in attack for the majority of the memorable 1997/98 campaign. Neither player was found wanting, with both hitting double figures in their first full seasons at the club. "I think it helped that it wasn't just a case of everybody relying on me and Steph to score the goals," Hamilton reflects. "Mickey (Cameron) was in double figures, Neil was in double figures, and the likes of Stevie Fulton and Thomas Flögel were chipping in. Everybody was contributing so that helped us majorly, that the team didn't have to rely on just the two of us or Robbo coming in and scoring goals. I actually got more satisfaction out of assisting than scoring goals. Obviously it's nice to score goals but we were such a good team because we weren't reliant on just two or three of us to score the goals. It was a team effort."

Hamilton found it a thrill to partner Adam, a player with whom he felt he dovetailed perfectly in attack. "Stephane had loads of energy; he just wouldn't stop running," Hamilton explains. "He would be running the channels while I would be coming short. It was just a good mix we had. Everybody knows I wasn't the quickest of players. I wouldn't get in behind defences and stuff like that, but Stephane did the dirty work and got into good situations so that's why it became a very good partnership. That season we contributed a lot to each other's goals with assists; he maybe set up half my goals and I did the same with him. He was a very good finisher, he had everything. But the perfect word for him was definitely 'unselfish'."

It was, ultimately, Adam's goal in the 1998 Scottish Cup final that allowed Hamilton to savour his best moment in football, at the end of his best season in football. "When that final whistle went, it was just unbelievable to see everybody's faces; the players, the fans," Hamilton reflects. "It was a moment you could never take away from anybody. The atmosphere in that stadium that day was incredible, and it's something I'll never forget for the rest of my life. That whole season was definitely the most special season I ever had in my career."

Hamilton scored 31 goals in 94 appearances over the course of his two-and-a-quarter years with Hearts. "Jim wasn't the quickest but he had other great attributes," says Jefferies. "He was a goalscorer, difficult to play against, very good in the air. The players liked him because he could hold it up well. Just don't put it over the top and expect him to sprint on to it. But if he did have pace as well as all his other qualities, he wouldn't have lasted long at Hearts because he would quickly have gone on to a bigger club."

McCann has no regrets about endorsing his friend's credentials as a potential

Hearts striker. "I was so pleased Jim and Billy went and signed him because I thought he was a great player for us; he was a big reason why we were so successful," says McCann.

Despite growing up as an Aberdeen fan, Hamilton laments the fact he was persuaded to leave Hearts against his wishes when the Pittodrie club tabled a £300,000 offer for him in March 1999, less than a year on from the most momentous day of his footballing life. He is in no doubt that his spell in Gorgie was the most fulfilling of a career which spanned 17 years and encompassed stints with 12 of Scotland's senior clubs. "Hearts will always be the best place for me as a footballer," he says. "I have so many great memories, great friends I've still got to this day and so many connections there. Even though I was leaving to go to Aberdeen, the club I'd supported as a young boy, leaving Hearts was probably the biggest regret I had in football because the fans and the club were just absolutely amazing to me."

Gary Naysmith

"Glenn Hoddle, who played 3-5-2, wanted
me to be his middle man in midfield"

The great Alex Young remains the benchmark for any Loanhead boy embarking on a career in football, but Gary Naysmith – the second most famous player to emerge from the humble Midlothian town – made a pretty decent fist of following in the Golden Vision's hallowed footsteps. Indeed, the parallels between this esteemed pair – born 41 years apart but raised on the same pitches of EH20 – are notable. For starters, the two Loanhead natives were just 19 years old when they won the Scottish Cup with Hearts. Considering the Tynecastle club have – at the time of publication – won the tournament on just eight occasions in their entire history, it is remarkable that two teenagers from a town with a population of circa 7000 people achieved such a feat; Young did it in 1956 and Naysmith in 1998. The similarities don't end there: both players left Hearts to sign for Everton and also played for Scotland. While Naysmith would never claim to be in the same league as Young – one of Hearts' finest-ever players and the most revered in Everton's history – it is a source of pride to the Jambo fraternity of Loanhead that two of their own have made their mark in the club's history.

"Loanhead isn't a big place so to have two players from here taking such a similar path is incredible," says Frank Morton, a diehard Hearts supporter from Loanhead who has known Naysmith and his family since an early age and also got to know Young before he passed away in 2017. "I take a lot of pride from anything that's local to my area. Don't get me wrong, it's nice to have big-name foreign players at the club but I'd always rather have local guys than anybody else playing and doing well at Hearts. You can't beat seeing one of your own, especially someone who you get to know, putting the Hearts jersey on. I get a real kick out of that."

With Gary Locke and John Robertson on the periphery on cup final day in 1998, Naysmith was the only player from the Lothians who played in the Hearts team that defeated Rangers at Celtic Park. "That was the greatest day I've ever had following Hearts and for a young laddie from my area to be in that team, there's a lot of pride associated with that for me," says Morton.

David Murie was the other member of Hearts' 1997/98 squad who hailed from Loanhead although the right-back, who didn't make the matchday 14 for the final, never enjoyed the same level of prominence at Tynecastle as Naysmith, who was two years his junior. "I've known Gary since we were kids; we grew up near each other, we played in the same primary school football team (Paradykes) and we played in the streets and at the park together," says Murie. "He was always a standout. He never played full-back in those days, he played further forward. He was just a great talent with a great left foot so I'm not surprised he went on to have a career at the level he did. You can never guarantee that any young boy's going to make it but I'd have been surprised if Gary didn't because he was that good. He was well known at boys' club level; there was plenty interest in him when he was a young boy because he was an exceptional talent in his age-group."

Naysmith wasn't a rabid Hearts supporter in the mould of Locke, his fellow Midlothian boy and Lasswade High pupil, but he did have an affiliation with the Tynecastle club which helped sway him when it came to deciding which team he would join on a youth training scheme when he turned 16. "My dad (Andrew) was a big Rangers man and I went to a few games with him, but he worked on a Saturday so I couldn't get to a lot of their games," explains Naysmith. "So my uncle asked me to go and watch Hearts with him because he used to take my sister and my cousin. I sort of turned into a Hearts fan because they were the team I was going to watch."

With no shortage of options to ponder – most notably an offer from Chelsea, whose first team were under the charge of England legend Glenn Hoddle – a combination of locality and familiarity led Naysmith to Hearts. "I signed for Hearts as an S-Form when I was about 14 but I didn't really enjoy it so I left," says Naysmith, explaining his early years in football. "By the time I left school at 16, I had a couple of different options and it initially looked like I was going to go to either Chelsea or Hibs. When I had to decide, Hearts came back in for me. Dougie Dalgleish, who took me to Hearts in the first place, was affiliated with Tynecastle Boys' Club, where I played. Dougie said 'look, I know you didn't enjoy it the first time at Hearts, but we want you to come in full-time'. The thing that swung it for me was that the majority of my family were Hearts fans."

Snubbing Chelsea and the bright lights of London was a big decision, but given Tynecastle is just seven miles from his hometown, it was an understandable one for a family-orientated teenager straight out of school. "I was getting flown down at weekends to play with Chelsea's youngsters and watching the first team play, and I really enjoyed it," says Naysmith. "When I was down at Chelsea, Glenn Hoddle, who played 3-5-2, wanted me to be the middle man in the midfield; get the ball from the defence and start making things happen. He told me that from watching me, he'd have expected me to be in his first team within a couple of years. When somebody like that says something like that about you, it's a big thing. I'd probably have signed for them if they weren't so far away from home; I just wasn't ready to leave home at that point. Glenn was surprised I didn't sign for them; he asked if it was about money and stuff like that and I said 'no, I just think I'd be homesick if I came down'. From the way they were speaking, they certainly thought highly of me so I gave up a big opportunity to join Hearts."

Naysmith loved learning his trade at Hearts from the moment he signed for the club in 1995. As a free-scoring schoolboy who enjoyed being at the heart of the action, however, he was surprised when youth and reserve coach Walter Kidd suggested that he would be better served as a left-back. It proved an astute call as Naysmith soon developed into the best Scottish left-back of his generation. "My career was as a left-back but I never played left-back growing up," he states. "I was a centre-forward, a central midfielder or a left midfielder. I've still got trophies in the house that I got as a kid for scoring 100-150 goals a season. Until I went into Hearts full-time and Walter Kidd got a hold of me, I'd never played as a left-back. With the attributes I had, he thought I had the best chance of making a career as a full-back, so I went with it and he was proved right."

Naysmith is indebted to youth and reserve team coaches such as Kidd, a long-serving former Hearts right-back, Paul Hegarty and Peter Houston, as well as others in the backroom staff such as physiotherapist Alan Rae and sprint coach Bert Logan, who helped make his early years on the ground-staff so fulfilling. "Walter was my first youth coach at Hearts and I still meet him to this day because he lives in Loanhead," says Naysmith. "I still remember how hard but fair he was. He made us work hard and he'd check we were doing our jobs properly. If anybody didn't do it, he'd keep us all back until 5pm to get a bit of discipline into us. I remember him telling us he didn't want any defenders in his team wearing moulded boots, even if the pitch was rock hard. He wanted his defenders to have studs on and he generally taught us a lot of discipline. Guys like Walter, Heggy and Housty were great for me. It wasn't just the coaches though; people like Bert Logan and Alan Rae looked after me and helped me with things. That 12 or 18 months that I spent under all those guys helped shape my discipline and my beliefs. I learned a hell of a lot off them. Alan Rae played a big part in the team spirit we had; he was a maniac at times. He did a lot of work at the club, not just as a physio. I remember Alan up ladders fixing lights, fixing tumble dryers and helping out with the washing. Everybody just chipped in. We didn't have a great gym at the time but we made it work. I had some of my happiest times up in that wee gym (inside Tynecastle's old main stand). There were days when we'd finish our chores at 4pm but we didn't want to go home so we'd go up to the gym and play head tennis. On the YTS we all liked spending time with each other."

Naysmith spent part of his first year at Hearts playing youth football for Whitehill Welfare's Colts side on a loan basis, while he would also turn out for Hearts reserves. "When Gary went full-time with Hearts, me and him travelled into Tynecastle together," says Murie. "Even though he was a bit younger than myself and some of the other lads in the reserves, he didn't look out of place."

Naysmith believes it was his attitude that helped him make a strong early impact at Hearts. "When I first went into Hearts, instead of playing for the youth team, I went out on loan to play for Whitehill so I was playing for them on the Saturday and Hearts' reserves in midweek," says Naysmith. "We had a really strong reserve team, with guys like myself, Davie Murie, Grant Murray, Scott Severin, Robbie Horn, Grant McNicholl, John Paul Burns, Stuart Callaghan and Mark Bradley, and we'd always have a couple of first-team players dropping down to play with us, such as Stevie Frail, who was coming back from injury. When the first-team players dropped in, Paul Hegarty made sure they took it seriously because he knew we were putting in the effort every week. I remember playing against guys like (Rangers pair) Ian Durrant and Alexei Mikhailichenko in the reserves when I was 16/17. Billy Brown always says that me and Steven Naismith (with whom Brown worked at Kilmarnock) were the two youngsters he looked at and knew were going to make it at a good level, but I didn't ever feel like that about myself. I didn't see myself as the most skilful or technical player in my YTS group, but I'd like to think I was one of the hardest-working."

Naysmith's efforts were rewarded at the end of his first full season at Hearts when, aged 17, he made his debut as a 65th-minute replacement for Neil Pointon in the final league game of the 1995/96 campaign: a 1-1 draw away to Motherwell two weeks before the 1996 Scottish Cup final against Rangers. The other two substitutes that day were Robertson and John Colquhoun, two of the club's most iconic attackers and players almost twice his age at that point. "Of course I was nervous when I first started playing for Hearts' first team, but I wasn't nervous playing with the senior players because I knew them all quite well from training with them on a regular basis and most of them had dropped down to play with us in the reserves at some point," says Naysmith. "I never felt in awe of playing with them because they were always good with me and passed on advice when I was in the reserve team. Even though I was predominantly playing in the reserves, I regarded the first-team players as my team-mates because I was training with them during the week."

Naysmith had to wait another four months to make his second appearance, and what an occasion it was. In September 1996, just three days after Hearts had four defenders – Pasquale Bruno, David Weir, Pointon and Paul Ritchie – sent off in a 3-0 defeat away to Rangers, Naysmith was summoned to start in a makeshift back four alongside Allan McManus, Dave McPherson and emergency short-term signing Andy Thorn for a Coca-Cola Cup quarter-final at home to Celtic. Hearts won 1-0 after an extra-time goal from Robertson and 17-year-old Naysmith was named man of the match. "He was up against Paolo Di Canio and he barely gave him a kick," says Jefferies. In what was his first career start, Naysmith played with a level of assurance that defied all expectations. "He was just so natural in that area of the pitch and he seemed such a confident lad that nothing really fazed him," says Murie. "He made it all look so easy when he went into the first team."

After his heroics against Celtic, it was little surprise that Naysmith kept his place for the following match: a 1-1 draw at home to Motherwell. Thereafter, the teenager didn't appear again for another two months and he wasn't included in the squad for the Coca-Cola Cup semi-final against Dundee or the final against Rangers. "The Celtic game was a big one for me but the gaffer looked after me after that," says Naysmith. "I was in for two games, then I came out of the team for a wee bit."

Jefferies believes it was imperative that Naysmith – despite his quality – was nurtured slowly and carefully into the first-team environment. "I'm a big believer that you've got to take a young boy out when he's doing well, not when he's doing badly," says Jefferies. "Everything's new to them when they get in. They've got the enthusiasm, the adrenalin's going, it's fresh and the fans are behind them, but they usually hit a bit of a brick wall. I was fortunate that the likes of Lockey and Allan Johnston had already been in the first team and been taken out the team before I got there, but Paul Ritchie, Allan McManus and Gary Naysmith hadn't been through that. Even if you think they're too good to leave out, I feel you still have to think about taking them out. If you take them out when they're really struggling, they can worry about it and be on a downer so when they come back into the team, there's extra pressure on them. But if you take them out when they're doing well, they're bursting to get back in and they're desperate to prove you wrong because they think they've been hard done by. It tells you a lot about the player how they deal with that. I was fortunate in Gary's case that I had a first-class left-back in Neil Pointon who could come back in and play until Gary was ready."

Naysmith made seven starts in Pointon's absence in the second half of the 1996/97 season and remained largely on the periphery as Hearts made a scin-tillating start to 1997/98. Pointon was in command of the left-back jersey, with Naysmith – afflicted by injury issues and a form dip – restricted to just one ap-pearance in the first half of the season, when he started the 2-1 win at home to St Johnstone in November. "I was still round about the squad but I fell away for a wee bit because the gaffer didn't think I was training hard enough and felt I'd maybe let things go to my head; he was probably right," says Naysmith. It all changed for the youngster in January 1998 following a pep talk from Jefferies and Brown, as well as a couple of senior players, at the club's winter training camp in Portugal. With Pointon about to serve a suspension in the first game back away to St Johnstone, Hearts' management were weighing up whether to replace the dependable Englishman with Naysmith, an out-of-sorts 19-year-old left-back, or Murie, a right-back who possessed slightly more experience. "I didn't play much in the first half of the season but when we went on the winter break to Portugal, Jim and Billy had a talk with me and said I needed to get back to the level I was at in the Celtic game," says Naysmith. "I think they noticed that I'd worked hard on that trip and they put me in the team for the St Johnstone game. I scored that night and I didn't really look back after that; I pretty much made the position my own."

After scoring Hearts' second goal in the 3-2 win at McDiarmid Park with a mag-nificent dipping volley from the edge of the box, Naysmith ended up starting 20 of the closing 21 games of the season in all competitions, with Pointon barely playing again for the club. "There was a period when Gary wasn't having the best of times and it seemed like he might have been in danger of going under a little bit so guys like myself and John Robertson would have a little chat with him," says Pointon. "When he got back in the team, he was really positive and it all worked out bril-liantly for Hearts and for Gary. I was probably still a better defender than him at that time when he got in but he was probably a bit quicker and better on the ball than I was. If you look at modern football and how the role of the full-back evolved after 2000, Gary Naysmith was the ideal fit, as was proved by the career he went on to have."

One of the highlights of Naysmith's 1997/98 season was a sensational long-range strike in the 3-1 home win over Aberdeen in February. "Gary and Neil Pointon had been kind of fighting for the left-back position for quite a while," says Weir. "Neil was a really good, experienced player but Gary came in with his energy and his enthusiasm and he got forward really well. He made a really big impact in that season and was a big part of our success."

By the time the 1998 final came round, it would have been a surprise if Naysmith wasn't in the starting line-up. Indeed, when it came to team selection, the teenager was more concerned about whether his close friend Murray would be in the squad. A boyhood Hearts fan from Mayfield, Murray – like Naysmith, Murie, Locke and goalkeeper Gary O'Connor – was another of the young Midlothian contingent at Hearts in the 1990s. He became known at Tynecastle as "Bert" – the same name as his father – after O'Connor, a family friend from nearby Newtongrange, started addressing him as "Wee Bert". Naysmith, well aware of how much Murray loved Hearts, was desperate to see his room-mate involved on cup final day. The versatile 22-year-old had started ten games for Hearts in the 1997/98 season, including the Scottish Cup semi-final victory over Falkirk, but didn't get any game time in the closing three league matches. After a nervous wait, Murray – who joined Hearts after leaving Newbattle High School in 1992 and would depart the club in 2001 with 99 appearances to his name – got the nod ahead of his fellow defenders Pointon, Murie and McManus for one of the three substitute berths. "Bert is godfather to my oldest daughter, Nicole; that's how close we were around that time," says Naysmith. "Bert had played quite a few games in that season but was left out for a few games before the final. I knew earlier in the week that I was playing but I can honestly say I got just as much joy from when I found out Bert was going to be on the bench. He was a Hearts fan and I knew how much it would mean to him and his family to make the bench so I was absolutely buzzing for him when I found out he was one of the subs."

Naysmith was the first teenager to appear in a final for Hearts since 19-year-old Arthur Thomson played in the 3-1 defeat by Dunfermline Athletic in the 1968 Scottish Cup final, and the first to win a cup for the Edinburgh side since Billy Higgins, also 19, played in the 2-1 victory over Third Lanark in the 1959 League Cup final. Since 1998, Kevin McHattie, Jamie Walker and Dale Carrick have all appeared in the 2013 League Cup final loss to St Mirren aged 19, while 16-year-old Aaron Hickey started the 2019 Scottish Cup final defeat by Celtic. Playing in a cup final for Hearts is a significant accomplishment for any teenager, and Naysmith handled it impressively. "I got nervous before every game; whether it was the cup final in 98 or playing for East Fife v Montrose in my 30s, I got the same level of nerves," says Naysmith. "I liked having a certain level of nerves; if I didn't get them before a match, I'd wonder why I wasn't nervous. I liked being a bit nervous. Once the game started, I was one of the only Hearts players who had actually touched the ball before we scored the penalty. That goal was great because it settled us all down and gave us a foothold in the game. I've only watched it back once or twice but my mum kept all the paper cuttings and I got a lot of good marks. I didn't think I was brilliant; I thought I played decent but there were others on the pitch who played better than me that day."

Neil McCann, playing on the left wing, spent much of the cup final doubling up with young Naysmith to try to stop Rangers attacking down their side of the pitch. This pair would also go on to play together on the left for Scotland. "I didn't mind helping Gary out defensively and we always had a wee laugh and joke about that," says McCann. "I built up a good relationship with Gary on the pitch; he was very powerful going forward. He seemed to have no nerves whatsoever when he came into the team and I think a lot of that was down to the fact there were quite a lot of young boys sprinkled through the squad. But the biggest factor in him doing so well for Hearts was that he was a good player who could handle it; although I'm not sure he'd have thought football was for him when Jim Jefferies pinned him at half-time in the semi-final! You need to have big balls to play in a cup final as a teenager but Gary was superb."

As proud as he is of what he achieved in his football career, Naysmith admits his memories of 1998 are not as sharp as he would like. "It's certainly one of my career highlights but, to be honest, I can't remember too much about certain aspects of it," he says. "Until I watched Neil Pointon's video, a lot of the day had faded from my mind, but the more I've watched it back, things have come back to me. What I didn't realise until I watched the match back was how much Rangers battered us in the last 20 minutes; that had kind of faded from my memory. The fans will obviously remember all that because they'll have been biting their fingernails but I didn't remember that part of my day. I don't reminisce too much about it, to be honest. I took more satisfaction from the enjoyment that it gave other people, lifelong Hearts fans who had never seen them win a trophy and others who had waited 36 years to see them win another trophy; people like my sister and other family members. I was never one to look back and take a lot of pride from things. Don't get me wrong, I am very proud of it but it's not something I think about a lot."

After a form dip which led to Naysmith being dropped to the bench for four games towards the end of the 1998/99 campaign, he swiftly returned to his best in 1999/2000 and earned himself a Scotland debut in a 2-1 friendly win over Republic of Ireland in Dublin in May 2000. Although on an upward curve, 21-year-old Naysmith had no burning to desire to leave Hearts. With the club unable to offer him a new contract befitting of the form he had been showing since establishing himself as the club's first-choice left-back, however, they had little choice but to sell when the opportunity arose to cash in on him in October 2000. Naysmith initially looked destined for Coventry City, managed by Gordon Strachan, but Everton assistant Archie Knox, who was also No.2 to Craig Brown in the Scotland set-up at the time, got wind of his availability and told Walter Smith, the Goodison Park club's manager, they should move for the burgeoning left-back. A £1.7 million offer was accepted by Hearts and Naysmith, who had been psyched for joining Coventry, was informed he was off to Everton instead. After more than five years at Tynecastle, he departed with 120 appearances – 115 as a starter – four goals, a Scottish Cup triumph and a grounding in the game which would serve him well for the rest of his career. "Jim and Billy were fantastic for me in terms of putting me in at such a young age in front of somebody like Neil Pointon and then keeping me in ahead of Rab McKinnon when he came to the club (in summer 1998)," says Naysmith. "I wouldn't have had the career I had if it wasn't for everybody I worked with at Hearts."

Naysmith went on to make 155 appearances for Everton, although his progress was hindered in his later years at Goodison as a string of injuries took their toll before he joined Sheffield United in 2007. "Being at Everton for seven years was another career highlight," says Naysmith. "Not many Scottish boys go down to the English Premier League, especially a club of Everton's stature, and last that long. It's very difficult to do that, especially when you have the injuries I had."

Knox, who was part of the Rangers management team when Hearts beat them in the 1998 final, believes Naysmith vindicated his move south. "When Walter and I went to Everton, we felt we could get good value by adding players from Scotland, and Gary was one of those," says Knox. "When we were signing players for Everton at that time, we weren't signing them to come in as back-up, we wanted guys who could go straight into the first team and Gary was able to do that. He fitted in and did really well for Everton. He had energy, he was good in the air, a good passer and could get up and down the pitch. He had a great attitude; he was a winner."

These attributes helped him become Scotland's most pre-eminent left-back throughout the Noughties. Aged 30, he won the last of his 46 caps in a 2-1 World Cup qualifier at home to Iceland under George Burley in April 2009. "I don't think so much about the fact I got 46 caps for Scotland and that 45 of them were starts; I think more about the fact I didn't get to 50, and it irks me," says Naysmith. Craig Brown was so impressed with Naysmith that he signed him for Aberdeen as a 33-year-old, 12 years after giving him his Scotland debut. "I liked Naysmith very much," he says. "I'd be interested to see what he would cost in today's market because he had all the attributes for a left-back. He could defend and go forward, he was quick and he could compete; he was a warrior. I picked Naysmith for Scotland but I also signed him for Aberdeen towards the end of his career. Unfortunately he got an injury when he came to Aberdeen but even an injured Naysmith was motivational to the rest of the team."

After leaving Aberdeen in 2013, Naysmith was in the frame for a return to Hearts when Locke was in charge of the administration-hit club. A signing embargo prevented this happening and he joined East Fife instead, although he would eventually get back to Tynecastle for a spell as the club's loans manager in 2019/20. When a 37-year-old Naysmith kicked his last competitive ball as player/manager of East Fife in a Scottish Cup tie at home to Edinburgh City in November 2016, he had accomplished a playing career, spanning more than two decades, to be eminently proud of. "Once Gary kicked on at Hearts, he never looked back," says Murie. "You always want to see local lads go on to bigger and better things, and in terms of guys who grew up around me, there's not a better example than Gary Naysmith. To win the Scottish Cup with Hearts as a teenager, then go on and play for Everton and win 46 caps for Scotland, it's some achievement."

Stephen Fulton

"My dad told me to get my arse to
Tynecastle as quick as I could"

"Hearts in Paradise!" screamed the splash headline on the front page of The Pink, the much-loved sports newspaper which fans across Edinburgh would flock to buy on a Saturday night in order to catch up with the day's football results. On Saturday 16th May 1998, The Pink would represent a keepsake of a momentous achievement for Hearts as well as a source of confirmation for those intoxicated by drink and euphoria that what they thought they had witnessed at Parkhead earlier that day had actually happened.

In addition to being a nod to the state of utopia Hearts had found that afternoon, "Paradise" was also the word commonly used by Celtic fans to refer to Celtic Park. Stephen Fulton (he prefers his Sunday name to Stevie) would certainly have needed no explanation on this matter. As a west-coast boy who attended a Catholic secondary school in Greenock and emerged through the ranks at Celtic to impressive effect, Fulton could never have envisaged when flourishing in Billy McNeill's first team in the late 1980s and early 90s that his finest moment in "Paradise" would come in the colours of Heart of Midlothian, a fierce and long-standing rival of Celtic's. Indeed, when Fulton joined Hearts from Falkirk in 1995, there was some scepticism among supporters due to the fact he was perceived to be "a Celtic man". His association with Celtic wasn't lost on team-mates either. Upon arrival in the home dressing-room on cup final day in 98, it was a source of pre-match jesting among the Hearts squad, with Neil Pointon, who was recording the day's events on a camcorder, enquiring "where's the picture of the Pope, Badge?". Badge, of course, was a shortened version of the nickname "Baggio" which Fulton had bestowed upon him after being mentioned in the same sentence as the Italian superstar, Roberto Baggio, by McNeill following his emergence at Celtic. Gary Locke, Hearts' dyed-in-the-wool club captain, looked on with a mixture of amusement and mild disgust as his good friend Fulton muttered "Paradise" in banterous manner towards Pointon's camera. Manager Jim Jefferies, meanwhile, could be heard remarking to his peroxide blond playmaker that being back in such familiar territory "will take you back a few years".

While Fulton was understandably proud of his Celtic past, he was always intent on making sure that, having left Parkhead in the month of his 23rd birthday to join Bolton Wanderers in a £300,000 transfer in 1993, his career wouldn't be defined by his early years at his boyhood club. The closest he got to glory in his time at Celtic was when, as an 18-year-old, he was an unused substitute in the 1989 Scottish Cup final victory over Rangers, while he also started the 1990 Skol Cup final defeat by the Ibrox side. His fulfilling seven-year stint with Hearts, incorporating 240 appearances and illuminated by the day he led them to Scottish Cup glory, certainly ensured that, in his post-playing days, he would be able to reminisce about something more substantial than just a promising breakthrough in Glasgow's east end.

"When I look back on my career, my time at Hearts means the most to me," Fulton reflects. "Listen, I was at Celtic, came through as a young boy and any player will tell you that coming through with your mates as a young boy is one of the best times of being a footballer. I played 90 games (65 as a starter) over three or four years for Celtic. I was in and out, had good runs and bad runs. But at Hearts, I was there for seven years and in the team most weeks, playing in finals and winning the cup. All my best times as a footballer came at Hearts. If you look at my career, I wouldn't be much of a man if I didn't value my time at Hearts as much as my time at Celtic. Hearts are where I had my most enjoyable times and winning the Scottish Cup was obviously the pinnacle. I'm sure there will have been some supporters that didn't like me at the start but I felt I had a great relationship with most of the supporters by the time I left. I was gutted when I eventually left; I wanted another contract."

Fulton was 25 when the opportunity arose to follow Jefferies and Billy Brown from Falkirk to Hearts in 1995, a little over two years after he left Celtic. Eager to better himself in what would be the peak years of his career, the midfielder – encouraged by his father, Norrie – jumped at the chance to move to Tynecastle. "There was no doubt in my mind about signing for Hearts," he says. "I was always brought up with the west-coast mentality that Hearts were the wee Rangers but it was never going to be a problem for me as I wanted to go with Jim Jefferies anyway. The only trepidation was that I was perceived as a mad Celtic man, which I wasn't. I only started watching Celtic when I signed for them; I actually don't think I attended a senior game until the 1985 Scottish Cup final (when Celtic beat Dundee United). My dad was kind of a Celtic supporter but he played Junior football to a high level for teams like Pollok so that was what I grew up watching. I was more involved with that as a kid, watching my dad. I never grew up in amongst the bigotry and all that. My mum's a Protestant, my dad's a Catholic, so none of that meant anything to me. As soon as I told my dad Hearts were in for me, he told me about the size of the club and that I should get my arse through to Tynecastle as quick as I could. I'd played against Hearts before but it wasn't until I signed that I realised just how big a club they were. In my first few months at Hearts, I think if I wasn't doing so well some of the supporters would see me as a fenian this and a fenian that, but none of that stuff bothered me."

Fulton, who admits to smoking the occasional cigarette during his career, developed a reputation in some quarters for struggling with his fitness when not playing regularly, particularly in his early years. The midfielder believes this issue has been significantly overblown and feels several misconceptions formed around him during his playing days. "I probably did struggle with fitness at times but Jim Jefferies wouldn't have signed me three times if I wasn't fit enough for his team," says Fulton. "I would say I had to keep on top of my fitness. Billy Brown didn't like me taking too many days off because I could lose my fitness pretty quickly. Maybe when I got towards the end of my career, it became a bit of a struggle fitness-wise, but in the main part of my career there were no problems. A lot of times in football, a perception builds around people and it sticks. People thought I was slow but ask anyone and they'll tell you I was right up there with everyone in the sprints. There were a lot of labels that got stuck on me when I was younger. The Baggio thing, and also that I liked my fast food; things like that just stick to you. To be honest, it didn't bother me because I was playing every week. What people thought about me wasn't an issue for me."

Fulton took some time to find his feet at Hearts, but once he settled into his rhythm, he swiftly won over any critical supporters. "I didn't hit the ground running at Hearts," he admits. "At Falkirk I'd just had an operation and hadn't had much of a pre-season. I was a player who needed a pre-season. I needed games to get my fitness up. When I first arrived at Hearts we would win one week, lose the next and that's why the gaffer was changing the players as quickly as he could. As the team started getting better, I started getting better and the supporters started to warm to me."

Pointon made his Hearts debut in the same game as Fulton in October 1995 and could see similarities with one of his highly-regarded former Everton and Manchester City team-mates. "Fulters was a solid all-round midfielder who reminded me a bit of Peter Reid," says Pointon. "He could command a midfield. He loved a tackle and his passing was strong. He wasn't the quickest box to box but he had a good knack of being in the right place at the right time. He wasn't the greatest fan of certain fitness work in training; Jim used to joke with Fulters about his fitness. Fulters preferred the type of training where he could have the ball at his feet; he could do special things with the ball and he was capable of scoring some great goals."

David Weir was a team-mate of Fulton's at Falkirk in the 1994/95 season and would be reunited with him when he followed the midfielder to Tynecastle in summer 1996. The defender believes Jefferies and Brown – the management team who also took Fulton to Kilmarnock when he eventually left Hearts in 2002 – were key to getting the best out of him. "Fulters was always a top player," says Weir. "I played against him when he was at Celtic and he was one of the most talented players in the country, there's no doubt about that. It wasn't football that was the problem for Fulters in those early years, it was just probably staying fit, staying focused and actually getting consistency in his game. But when he was fit and available and mentally in a good place, then he was as good as there was in terms of ability. I think Jim and Billy got the best out of him at Hearts in terms of keeping him focused, getting him on the pitch and trying to keep him doing the things he was best at. At Falkirk, we saw it in flashes but I think Jim and Billy were still getting to know him and he was getting to know them. But when he went to Hearts he got a good level of consistency within his game and was in a really good team, a team that probably worked for him."

As well as bringing quality to Hearts' midfield, Fulton swiftly became a popular member of the dressing-room. "Stevie was a fantastic individual," says defender Paul Ritchie. "He was a madman on a night out. Him and Lockey were the two that fed off each other and gave the dressing-room the spark that it had."

With a nod to Fulton's occasional moments of unpredictability on a team night out, Locke still has his good friend's named saved in his phone as "Time Bomb". "When he had a couple of drinks he was the life and soul of the party," laughs Locke. "Monday to Friday, he was actually quite a quiet lad but when he spoke he was a really funny guy; his one-liners were brilliant. He was really influential on the pitch but he was brilliant for the dressing-room. He was just a great teammate; a great guy who would do anything for anybody."

By the time the 1997/98 campaign – his third as a Hearts player – got into full swing, Fulton was riding the crest of a wave. A week after his 27th birthday, he burst into the opposing penalty box to score in the first home league game of the campaign – a 4-1 win over Aberdeen – and went on to enjoy the season of his life. Several team-mates pinpoint Fulton as the individual most important to making that scintillating, history-making Hearts team tick. "I can't speak highly enough of Fulters," says midfield colleague Colin Cameron, who went on to play for Scotland and Wolverhampton Wanderers in the English Premiership. "I speak to people and they say 'you played with some great players, who was the best you played with? Was it Paul Ince?'. Well, believe it or not, for me it was Stevie Fulton. I say that based on what he helped me achieve on a personal level. Playing alongside him, I had the confidence that I knew I could get forward 90 per cent of the time and he would just sit. And I knew that if I made a run and he was on the ball, I'd always get a chance because his left foot was a wand. It would be good to look back on his 'pass completion' stats because he'd be up there with the best. His ability on the ball was second to none."

Described as having a "left foot like a tin-opener" by Peter Houston, the third member of Hearts' management team in 1997/98, Fulton's elegance and comfort on the ball was matched by few other players in Scotland at the time. "If I had to pick one player in our team, I'd probably say Fulton," says Locke. "I don't think he got the credit he should have got because he used to run the show at times. He would take the ball off you anywhere. I used to think I was good at taking the ball but with Fulters, it didn't matter how the game was going, he was always available to take the ball off you. Mickey (Cameron), for instance, wouldn't need to come short and try to get on the ball because he knew if he made a run forward, Fulters could get on it and play a 50-60-yard pass into his path. He was a great passer, and he was quicker and fitter than people gave him credit for. Over 50 or 60 yards he was as quick as anybody, it was more the long-distance running he struggled with, but he wasn't the only one that struggled with that."

Assistant manager Brown – who spent the best part of a decade coaching Fulton at Falkirk, Hearts and then Kilmarnock – believes the quality and movement of his Tynecastle team-mates played a big part in Fulton's sensational form in 1997/98. "Stevie Fulton was the boy that made it tick for us; he had fantastic ability," says Brown. "But what we gave Stevie was a picture of boys in front of him that could make runs that suited his array of passes. So, for instance, we had Colin Cameron who could break from the middle of the park and get in behind, we had Gary Naysmith who could overlap on the outside of him, we had Neil McCann wide left who was a flying machine that Fulton could play to, and he had Stephane Adam who was fantastic at making runs in behind. So he had the picture for the first time in his career that we gave him and that helped him pull the strings. He was a smashing football player but without Cameron, without Adam, without McCann, would he have been as good? I don't know, but we gave him that picture and he was brilliant.

"He'd done well for us at Falkirk which is why we took him to Hearts but I think, because he'd been at Celtic and played in a cup final when he was a teenager, he was happy to be back in the big time at a big club like Hearts. He had the temperament for the big time and I think that's what suited him, he rose to the occasion and the crowd at Tynecastle. Let's not forget, Stevie used to get a lot of stick at times from supporters but he could stand it. He thrived on the big-time atmosphere and he turned out a really good player for Hearts, one of the better midfield players they've had for a long time. But, as I say, without the other ingredients in the team he might not have been as good."

The significance of having dynamic team-mates wasn't lost on Fulton. "If I was playing well, the gaffer would just get everybody to give me the ball and then we'd have wee Mickey, Neil and Stephane all running in behind, Tam Flögel up there as well, full-backs bombing forward," he explains. "I had options all over the pitch."

Jefferies was delighted with the impact Fulton had at Tynecastle after becoming one of his first signings as Hearts manager. "Stevie was a great footballer, a strong boy who could take the ball and pass it well," said the manager. "The other players loved him, especially the likes of Mickey and Neil McCann because they knew if they made a run they would be 99 per cent guaranteed to get the ball exactly where they wanted it. They loved the service they got from him. Stevie maybe didn't always look the fittest but it never seemed to bother him. He was never out of position, he made the ball do the work. Look at some of the goals he scored for us, he wasn't just hitting them from 25 yards, he was getting forward into the box and he had the intelligence to know when to go forward. He certainly wasn't just a sitting midfielder."

Underlining how impressively he performed in the 1997/98 campaign, Fulton was one of the four nominees for the Scottish PFA player of the year award, alongside title-winning Celtic pair Jackie McNamara and Craig Burley and 32-goal Rangers striker Marco Negri. McNamara came out on top in that particular vote, while

Burley landed the Scottish Football Writers' player of the year award. "That was the best season I had in my career," says Fulton. "In terms of my own form, I had a few really good seasons on a personal level but that was probably my best. I maybe won more personal accolades from supporters' clubs and things like that in the seasons after that, but that was probably because the other players at Hearts weren't as good as they were in 97/98. When you factor in that we won the cup and challenged for the league, it all goes together to manifest in that season being the best of my career."

Starting with the fourth-round victory over Albion Rovers in February – the first game in which he got the honour of skippering Hearts – Fulton wore the armband whenever Locke missed a game through injury in the last three months of the season. With the club captain sidelined by a knee problem in the closing weeks of the league campaign, Jefferies chose him to lead the team out for the final. "I think he was picked to be captain because of the respect he had from all the players," says Locke. "The team spirit in that squad was fantastic – everybody got on really well and everyone respected each other – so in some ways I don't think it mattered who was captain. But I think Fulters probably got it because of his performances that season; he led by example with his performances. He wasn't a shouter and bawler but if you didn't give him the ball when the pass was on, he wouldn't be shy in letting you know about it. The two obvious reasons for giving him the captaincy were that he had the respect of everybody and, secondly, because that season he was the best midfielder in the league."

Jefferies believes his decision to make Fulton the captain for the final was vindicated by the fact he invited the injured Locke to lift the trophy with him afterwards. "The fans had really warmed to Stevie because he'd had a great season; his performances were outstanding," says the manager. "With Lockey being out, we looked at it and there were a few guys who could have been captain. Davie Weir could have handled it, Colin Cameron could have been considered and Dave McPherson would have been an obvious choice but I just felt picking somebody like Stevie, who was so popular with the players, was the right call. Asking Lockey to go and get the cup with him just underlined it. He was never asked to do that but that's the type of guy he is. That was his own decision because he knew that if Lockey was fit, it would be him who would be doing it. All the boys loved Stevie. He wasn't just a great player on the park, he was great in the dressing-room. Sometimes he could have you on edge as a manager, but I got some laughs from him because of the answers and expressions I got from him when I pulled him up for a few things. You need all different types of characters in the dressing-room. He's a great boy who I've always kept in touch with."

Although Fulton set the tone for victory by driving at the Rangers defence to win the penalty in the first minute, he concedes that he and his creative team-mates weren't at their best on a day when resilience, organisation and bravery proved to be among Hearts' most pre-eminent qualities. "In terms of my own performance, from my initial recollections, I thought I had a good game, but when I watched it back I actually thought I was pretty shite," he says. "For big periods of the game, Rangers battered us, but that's football. There were plenty times we battered teams and didn't get results. The way things worked out, we actually played better in the Coca-Cola Cup final the season before than in the final that we won."

Fulton felt his memorable campaign should have been extended by inclusion in the Scotland squad for the World Cup in France in the summer of 98. The midfielder, who had been heavily touted for a full call-up in the second half of the season, was one of four Hearts players to be selected for the B internationals against Wales and Norway in March and April respectively. Fulton played in the 4-0 victory over Wales at Broadwood Stadium but was denied a further chance to enhance his World Cup prospects when he had to sit out the 2-1 defeat by Norway at Tynecastle through injury. In the end, only two players – Celtic pair Jonathan Gould and Tosh McKinlay – stepped up from Tommy Burns' B team to win a place in Craig Brown's World Cup squad. Although he had spoken regularly about Fulton's qualities in the early part of 1998, raising hopes that the Hearts playmaker might join Weir in the squad for France, the Scotland manager instead selected the central-midfield quintet of John Collins, Burley, Paul Lambert, Scot Gemmill and Billy McKinlay. "Fulton was excellent when I had him in my Scotland Under-21 team," says Brown. "He obviously did really well at Hearts but he was unfortunate that we had an abundance of quality in his position." Fulton was called up by Brown for a Euro 2000 qualifier in Lithuania the following season but didn't get on the pitch. He would end his career with no full international caps. "I thought I had a wee outside chance of going to the World Cup that year," he says. "You know with international football you'll always have your mainstays, but I think you should also go for the guys who are playing the best at that particular time. That season I don't think any other midfielder in Scotland was playing better than me. I was thinking 'I've played like this for a full year and I can't get a chance with Scotland', so it was very disappointing."

While there was to be no dream trip to France for Fulton, he was able to head off on Hearts' celebratory end-of-season jaunt to the Majorcan party resort of Magaluf knowing that he had just become the first man to captain the Edinburgh club to Scottish Cup glory in 42 years. "At the time, being captain didn't mean that much to me, but looking back now I'm proud that I'll always be one of the Hearts captains that lifted the cup," he says. "I take immense pride from it. I'm usually one that likes to stay under the radar but I was fair proud that day, leading the team out in front of that huge stand of Hearts supporters. It was amazing. I loved my time at Hearts and that day was the pinnacle. I've had a lot of Hearts supporters say to me that that day was even more special to them than beating Hibs 5-1 in the 2012 cup final, which is hard to believe. But then when you think that we were the first team to do it for Hearts in 42 years, it's pretty special. Any time I'm through in Edinburgh or I run into a Hearts supporter, that weekend is what they want to talk about. If you don't want to talk about one of the happiest days of your life, you've got to be a bit of an eejit."

The Architects

*"Every player would have run through
a brick wall for Jim and Billy"*

Colin Cameron and Stephane Adam got the golden goals; David Weir, Paul Ritchie and Gilles Rousset made the vital blocks; and Stephen Fulton and Gary Locke lifted the trophy. There is little doubt, however, about the identity of the real architects of Hearts' Scottish Cup triumph in 1998. "Jim Jefferies and Billy Brown were the main reason Hearts won that cup," Peter Houston says of one of the most recognisable and long-serving managerial double acts Scottish football has seen. The players are of no mind to disagree with Houston's assertion. "Jim and Billy were instrumental," says winger Neil McCann. "They're the reason we were successful as a team."

They are two peas in a pod, born just a month apart at the end of the year 1950 and raised barely a mile away from each other: Jefferies in Wallyford and Brown just across the railway line in the Wimpeys estate in Musselburgh. As manager and assistant respectively, this trusty duo transformed Hearts from plodding relegation candidates to swashbuckling title challengers and history-making Scottish Cup winners within three years of their appointment at Tynecastle in 1995. "The thing about Jim and Billy is that they are two people but they are only one; they have such a good understanding between each other," says French striker Adam.

Heart of Midlothian's success story of 1998 effectively began when Jefferies and Brown first crossed paths on the playing fields of East Lothian in the 1960s. "Billy and I were close at the school," says Jefferies. "I was at Wallyford primary and Billy was at Pinkie so we'd play against each other at primary school age, about nine and ten years old. Then we went to Musselburgh Grammar together and we were in the same high school team." A special bond was formed that remains intact to this day. "From the moment we got to know each other, we were always friends," says Brown. "I left the school to sign for Hull City when I was 15, so I was away for a few years and in that spell Jim signed for the Hearts. But we kept in touch all the time."

For Jefferies, a dyed-in-the-wool Hearts supporter, it was the realisation of a dream when he got to sign for the club he loved after a stint as an apprentice motor mechanic in Musselburgh. "I used to play for my primary school in a Hearts strip even though that wasn't our colours," recalls Jefferies, who grew up idolising left-back Davie Holt and prolific forward Willie Wallace in the 1960s. "I got a Hearts tracksuit and a ball every Christmas. My brother supports Hearts, my dad was a Hearts supporter; all I wanted to do was play for Hearts. I signed for them in 1966 and then went full-time in 1969. I could have signed for other clubs but I wasn't interested; I just wanted to be a Hearts player."

Jefferies was given his debut, aged 21, by manager Bobby Seith in a top-flight match away to East Fife in March 1972 and went on to make 310 appearances for Hearts before joining Berwick Rangers, the only other senior club he played for, in 1981. The closest Jefferies got to glory as a Hearts player was in 1976 when he was part of the team, managed by John Hagart, that lost 3-1 to Rangers in the Scottish Cup final. The nadir was the infamous 7-0 thrashing at home to Hibs on New Year's Day of 1973, with Jefferies playing in defence. The 1970s was far from a vintage decade for Hearts, but Jefferies – who became captain – was a stalwart figure. "I remember playing against Jim for Dundee United at Tannadice and he gave me a real dull one," says Archie Knox, the assistant manager of Rangers when Hearts defeated them in the 1998 final. "I had to get stitches in my ankle at half-time. He was a tough, uncompromising player who had a terrific career."

Brown, meanwhile, returned from Hull in 1970 to sign for Motherwell and then in 1973 he joined Raith Rovers, where he played for five years before injury brought an end to his professional career at the age of 28 and led to him dropping into the Junior ranks with Newtongrange Star and then Musselburgh Athletic. "We probably didn't see each other quite so much socially for a period when we both got married, but we kept in touch," says Jefferies.

In the mid-1980s both men embarked on managerial careers in the non-league ranks: Jefferies with Hawick Royal Albert briefly and then Gala Fairydean, and Brown with Musselburgh. "I learned a bit about the pub trade while I was playing part-time for Berwick as I looked towards a life outside football," says Jefferies of the period in the early 1980s before his managerial career started to take off.

The Jefferies-Brown management team – which would span almost quarter of a century – was first formed at Berwick Rangers in 1988, a decade prior to their greatest day in football. "Like me, Billy was football mad; it was in his blood," says Jefferies. "He was in charge of Musselburgh Juniors for years and he phoned me when I was manager of Gala Fairydean and asked if we wanted a friendly. We played them at Fisherrow one night and I think we skelped them 6-1. I was due to meet him for a pint afterwards but he spent ages in the dressing-room giving his team absolute pelters. It was a cold night, it was just a friendly, we were a really good team, and he was laying into them. Billy's a winner, and the way he was that night told me that the spirit and fire in his belly was still there. When I first got the Berwick job, I was on my own in the dugout and I was thinking 'I need someone to bounce ideas off'. So I spoke to Billy and asked if he'd be interested in coming down to help and that's how we got together. We were sitting together in the dugout and taking the training together. We had known each other a long time and we both took different paths to get to Berwick but from then on we were a partnership."

Jefferies and Brown transformed Berwick from a hapless bottom-of-the-table side to one which finished fifth in Scotland's 14-team third tier in 1989/90, and they even oversaw a club-record 21-game unbeaten run. "We had great success at Berwick, turned things round there and then Falkirk came calling," says Jefferies. They followed up their prosperity at Shielfield Park with a hugely impressive five-year reign at Brockville, which featured two First Division title triumphs (1991 and 1994), a Challenge Cup win (1993), a 6-0 win over Joe Jordan's Hearts (1993) and a fifth-place finish in the Premier Division (1995). The fact they were a well-established management team, with almost seven years under their belt as a pair, was part of the appeal when Hearts moved to bring them to Tynecastle to sort out the mess left behind by Tommy McLean in August 1995. "I always took the view that managing a football team was a job for two and Jim and Billy complemented each other very well indeed in that regard," says Leslie Deans, who was a year into his dual ownership of Hearts with Chris Robinson when they headhunted the burgeoning duo from Falkirk.

By the time they took the reins at Hearts, Jefferies and Brown had developed a solid understanding with each other. "Of course we had rows and heated words, but it was never personal," says Jefferies. "Billy respected that I was the manager and would always have the final say. He learned very fast that I had a great instinct or gut feeling to do something that would often prove to be right. There were a few things I did that he was shocked about but they usually came off for us. He always knew I didn't want a 'yes' man who would sook up to me; I wanted him to tell me if he didn't agree with me and we would discuss it. If we couldn't agree, I'd always have the final say. The only times I went with Billy were if I wasn't 100 per cent sure myself. I would always ask Billy what he thought about things but if I was 100 per cent sure in my mind, I wouldn't change my decision. We were so close that we could say things to each other and it would never ever cause an issue between us."

Although they had the odd disagreement, Jefferies and Brown were generally on the same wavelength. "We worked very much as a partnership," says Brown. "Jim was the manager so he had the final say on everything, and quite rightly so. We used to debate things or we'd argue at times but we'd always come out with the right solution. I took most of the training and Jim watched, keeping his eye on everything. In my position, I was closer to the players than Jim was. That's how it's got to be; the manager can't be too close to the players. We always tried to foster a good dressing-room. If you can get the right types in your dressing-room, it makes your job so much easier. At every club we were at, we tried to do that and make it a happy working environment for everybody."

In an era before Hearts had a specialised scouting department or access to data analysis websites such as Wyscout, Jefferies and Brown's recruitment skills came to the fore. Spending less than £1 million in total on transfer fees and paying players generally between £700 and £1500 per week in wages, they built a team that – for one season at least – was on par with Celtic and Rangers, two clubs operating in a different financial stratosphere to everyone else in Scottish football. "I think our biggest asset was our player recruitment," says Brown. "That is the most important thing for a football club. If you don't get good players you'll never have a good team. It doesn't matter how good a coach you are, all the best coaches in the world are the best coaches because they've got good players. It took us three years to build the team that won the cup and it was a lot of hard work finding the right players. Me and Jim had a lot of good contacts and we were up and down the country and abroad looking at players, and eventually we ended up with a team to be proud of. Everybody looks at Wyscout or DVDs now, but we always did our homework on players. We went and watched them, found out about them, saw how they reacted to things that were happening on the pitch during the game. Jim and I generally liked the same type of player, and we liked players that could stand up for themselves. When we went to watch them, one of the questions was 'could they play at Tynecastle under pressure?' because Tynecastle is a hard place to play at; you have to have a pair of balls to play there. We knew people like Colin Cameron, Neil McCann, Stephane Adam, David Weir and Stevie Fulton, all those people that we brought in, would be able to handle that."

Getting "good characters" into Hearts was always the aim. "A big part of the job is having a good eye for a player," says Jefferies. "When you're Hearts manager, your judgment needs to be right. Teams are not just made up of players' ability and what they're good at; that's part of it, of course, but a big part of it is the type of character and person they are. You have to get the right vibes when you're watching them and talking to them. You don't get everybody right – nobody does – but as long as you get a bigger percentage of signings right than wrong you've got a chance."

Crucially, they managed to do this at Hearts as they boldly set about rebuilding a team which had slipped to the bottom of the table by the end of October in their first season at Tynecastle. "I was still at Falkirk when they beat Hearts 2-0 at Brockville and I spoke to Jim and Billy after the game and they were like 'you can see it for yourself Peter, we've no legs, no energy, no enthusiasm, we need to spark it up' and things like that," says Houston, who was a player and coach under Jefferies and Brown at Falkirk before following them to Hearts in 1996. "You've got to give Jim and Billy massive credit for the way they just ripped it up. It wasn't popular because Hearts fans, naturally, loved the likes of Gary Mackay, John Colquhoun and John Robertson, but there came a time when Jim had to gradually phase them out. Jim and Billy were very good at recognising that the team needed changed and needed more pace and athleticism. I arrived at Hearts around the time Weir, McCann and Cameron were coming in and then Jim Hamilton arrived after that. The whole complexion of the team changed pretty quickly."

Deans was thrilled with the impact Jefferies and Brown had. "They brought a professionalism to the club, they were popular and they were an excellent management team," he says. "At that time we still didn't have lots of money. We weren't in a position to spend £750,000 on a player, for example, as (previous owner) Wallace Mercer had done when signing Derek Ferguson from Rangers a few years earlier. But Jim was astute in his signings and he was picking up gems left, right and centre. Gradually we were building a squad that was getting better and better. I had a very good working relationship with Jim. We did fall out once or twice but we were very much on the same wavelength. As others have said, the most important relationship at a football club is between the manager and the chairman, and we certainly had that at Hearts. It made for a smoothness and a harmony and unity that was vital to the club."

One of the practical changes the management team made involved obtaining a new training area on the playing fields of Pinkie Primary School. This, of course, meant Brown helped prepare Hearts' legendary cup-winning team on the very same pitches he had played on as a schoolboy. "Pinkie became our main training pitch," says Brown. "When we first went into Hearts, we used to go round to Roseburn or wherever else we could find, and we'd sometimes train at Tynecastle, but we were like a team of nomads until I managed to get Pinkie fixed up. The groundsman there was great for us and we were well looked after by him. The pitches were great. It might not have been as salubrious as what they've got now (at Oriam) but we won the cup from there. Those were the pitches I played on as a boy so it was nice for me."

A training pitch overseen by Jefferies and Brown was no place for slackers. "Jim and Billy worked magnificently well as a team; the dynamic was brilliant," says Houston. "Day to day, Billy would train the players and one thing they both demanded was that they trained to a high standard. If they didn't, then all of a sudden I would see a senior first-team player walking towards me to train with the younger players because they had been sent over by Jim or Billy. If you dropped your standards, Jim was hard as nails that way and would chase them over to me."

The players were well aware of the need to ensure they were pulling their weight. "For his size, Jim is relatively softly spoken but Billy was the opposite; he was the wee Rottweiler growling and snarling at you in training," says midfielder Cameron. "Having said that, when Jim did get angry and raise his voice, which happened occasionally, we all stood up and took notice because we knew the shit was going to hit the fan. We tried to make sure that didn't happen too often. What happened at Hearts in that period, and the success we had, was mainly down to those two guys because it was them who moulded the team together. The two of them worked really well together; they bounced off each other."

Fulton, who also played under the pair at Falkirk and Kilmarnock, is in no doubt about their main qualities. "I think the biggest thing about Jim and Billy's management was team building," he says. "They knew how to bring different characters together to slot in next to each other. It's no coincidence we ended up with the midfield we had in 1998. Mickey (Cameron) scored the goals, I did the passing and (Stefano) Salvatori booted everybody! All our strengths were mixed together, and it was like that throughout the team. I think that was Jim and Billy's biggest strength; they had an eye for a player and knew how to build a team."

They also knew how to motivate their players. "The gaffer just got the best out of everybody," says Locke, who was appointed captain as a 20-year-old just a few months after Jefferies' arrival. "He was a great man-manager who had such a presence. When he came into the dressing-room, there was instant silence and instant respect from the boys. He had a great double act with Billy who deserves enormous credit as well for the huge part he played. The biggest compliment I can pay Jim and Billy is that I think every player in that team would have run through a brick wall for them. Don't get me wrong, if you were on the receiving end of a rant, fuck me, they were terrible. Some of the things they would say to you, you had to be thick-skinned to handle it. But they were very fair. If you were doing well, they were full of praise for you and if you weren't doing so well you'd get a kick up the backside. They were also good at getting the right types of people into the club. They wouldn't just bring anybody in, they would get boys in that they knew could handle playing at Tynecastle when things weren't going so well. They brought good people with good personalities and that's a trait lots of managers don't have. They always knew a good egg and that was evident in the way they built that Hearts squad."

Houston, who went on to become a manager himself, loved working alongside Jefferies and Brown as a coach, learning from them every day and also occasionally acting as peacemaker when they disagreed on team selection. "One of the funniest things for me about Jim and Billy was when they picked the team towards the end of the week, they sometimes couldn't agree on the subs," says Houston. "They'd maybe agree on the team but Billy would think a certain player should be on the bench and Jim would often have a different opinion. As matchday got closer, they would both speak to me about what my thoughts were on it and I felt like a pawn in the middle."

One man who was never spoken about as a potential substitute was Weir, who started every single Hearts match for which he was available. The defender had earned the trust of Jefferies and Brown during his time at Falkirk, where he loved working under them so much that he deemed their presence a key factor in his decision to move to Tynecastle in 1996. "They were exactly the same at Hearts as they were at Falkirk," says the defender. "I don't think they ever changed. Even now, when I speak to them or meet them they're exactly the same. They're good people and they're straightforward. They're straight talkers, they're very honest in terms of they give you an opinion whether you want it or not. They're very black and white; there are no grey areas with Jim or Billy and, for me, that's reassuring.

"They had a real method of how they wanted to work. They enjoyed rehabilitating players and, at Falkirk in particular, they brought players in who had probably gone off the rails a wee bit. Then at Hearts they started to buy some younger players like myself, Neil McCann and Colin Cameron, to add to the young boys already there like Gary Locke, Paul Ritchie and Allan McManus. They also had a good network abroad so they brought in some good international players as well. They were just kind of maximising all their avenues and they had a real good blend and a real good feel about the club. Whether it was Falkirk or Hearts, it was always enjoyable under Jim and Billy. It was always a good environment when they were in charge in terms of training being good and it being quite black and white in terms of how things worked. I loved working under them. For me, Hearts was just a progression on from Falkirk, but probably with slightly better players."

Craig Brown, the former Scotland manager, describes Jefferies and Brown as "excellent coaches, good guys who players wanted to play for". Striker Jim Hamilton would certainly endorse this statement. "I say to this day, when anybody asks me the question about the best management team I worked under, none come close to Jim and Billy," he says. "There were some very good managers in my time but Jim and Billy were the best I ever worked with. They had everything. They knew how to put an arm round somebody if they were struggling or give somebody a boot up the arse if they needed it. Their training was excellent. Just everything about them, I couldn't speak highly enough about them."

Asked if he was ever on the receiving end of a rant from either of them, Hamilton laughs: "I think everybody was at some point. Sometimes I needed a cuddle, sometimes I needed a kick up the bum, but they got the best out of me and I think they got the best out of everybody at Hearts, certainly for a couple of years at least. Obviously Celtic and Rangers are always going to have the extra finance but I think we definitely had the best management team at that time which is why we ended up with the team we had."

Hamilton, Hearts' top scorer in 1997/98, was one of the many players who benefitted from the fact Jefferies and Brown were hellbent on playing attacking football. "Jim and Billy's teams always attacked," says Weir. "We always tried to win the game and if we got it right on the day we had a chance of winning. That's what I was used to at Falkirk and that's how it was at Hearts as well with them."

Gary Naysmith can vouch for the positive mindset Jefferies was always eager to instil. "The gaffer hated me passing the ball sideways or backwards," says the left-back. "He absolutely frowned upon it. He wanted me to drive forward with the ball and if I couldn't do that, I was to pass it forward. He didn't like me turning back."

Perhaps Jefferies' adventurous approach to football was a reflection of the natural optimism he feels he possessed. "I always said to Billy that he was the biggest pessimist I'd ever worked with and his answer was that he wasn't a pessimist, he was a realist," says the manager. "People might not believe it but I was always the optimistic one, I always used to look on the bright side. I liked it that way, that he was a pessimist and I was an optimist. We laughed about it all the time."

Jefferies had every right to feel upbeat while in his pomp at Hearts as his managerial career was firmly on an upward trajectory. "I remember Jim being a very impressive Hearts manager in terms of team-building, signings and man-management," says Graham Spiers, a football journalist for the Scotland on Sunday at the time. "He reminded me a little bit of (former St Mirren and Aberdeen manager) Alex Smith in terms of his natural wisdom for football. In fact, I remember Alex Smith saying to me that the great thing about Jim Jefferies was that he'd learned about management and made all his mistakes out of the limelight at Gala Fairydean and Berwick Rangers. I thought 'gosh, that's right'. So by the time Jim got to Hearts, he'd been steeped in football, he'd done his apprenticeship and he'd learned the pitfalls of management. I think Hearts got a reasonably finished article in Jim Jefferies. I remember Jim as being a guy who had an instinctive football intelligence and

90-minute know-how; he had an intuitive understanding of what was happening on the pitch. Nowadays we fuss over tactics and strategies but I don't remember Jim being obsessed with all that. Although, having said that, it was very interesting that he decided to make a strategic change for the 98 final. As a human being, I really took to him. We were like chalk and cheese but I found him generous in spirit. He was incredibly helpful and considerate with his time. I found him a great guy."

So did Naysmith, despite the ferocious half-time dressing-down he was subjected to by Jefferies in the 1998 Scottish Cup semi-final victory over Falkirk. "Even when I see him now, I still address Jim Jefferies as 'Gaffer'," says the left-back. "Jim and Billy were brilliant for me. I liked everything about them. I liked their training. I liked the fact they didn't take any shit. They were just black and white. If you did well, they told you that. If you didn't do well, they didn't pull any punches."

This perfectly-blended management team made a long-lasting impact on all of the players they led to glory. "Jim and Billy will always be a massive part of my life," says defender Ritchie, one of several young players who made their Hearts breakthrough under Jefferies and Brown and who later gifted the manager the shirt he wore on his Scotland debut in 1999. "I'm very grateful for the opportunity they gave me to play for the team I supported as a kid. As players, they kept us on the straight and narrow, praised us when we deserved it and beat us down when they needed to. These type of people are what the game misses nowadays in my opinion. Jim and Billy were the main reasons that the team over that period in the late 90s was so successful."

Jefferies acknowledges football has evolved in a way that means some of the methods he used wouldn't work in the present day. "There were certain things I got away with in my day that I wouldn't even attempt to do now because it wouldn't be received well," he admits. The fundamental aspects of their management, however, ensured Jefferies and Brown enjoyed a longevity in the game rivalled by very few in what is an increasingly cut-throat profession. Indeed, Jefferies' five-and-a-bit-year reign at Tynecastle remains the longest anyone has managed the club in a single sitting since Alex MacDonald's nine-year stint in the 1980s. "It wasn't just their ability to pick a player or assemble a side, it was the whole way they went about their business as people," says McCann. "I love people who are winners. I can't be bothered with people who are just happy to be mediocre or just getting by, but Jim and Billy absolutely instilled a winning mentality in us. There would be some games we'd be winning and Jim would come in and go crazy because we weren't at it: for example, the 98 semi-final against Falkirk. That was the beauty of them; they demanded 100 per cent from us all the time. Sometimes you would have an absolute stinker but if you were leaving everything on the pitch they were alright with that. For me, that's a brilliant attitude to have for a management team. As a coaching partnership, they were superb. Billy was really good and probably doesn't get as much credit as he should because he took loads of the training. He was on the pitch every minute of every day, his training sessions were good and his demands were high. He was the coach and the gaffer would step in when he had to. As a partnership, you'll struggle to get two better guys."

McCann remains impressed by Jefferies' and Brown's decision to take an uncharacteristically cautious approach in the 1998 final. "We'd been cavalier all season, just going for teams hell for leather, but they came up with a plan that meant we were going to play totally different and use our speed on the counter attack," says the winger. "To change a team in the last game of the season, for one game only, when all you've been doing all season is playing this swashbuckling football, tactically it was an outstanding move. It was so clever."

That carefully-plotted 2-1 victory over Rangers earned Jefferies and Brown the defining moment of their long-running partnership as they barged down the barriers of history to land the silverware that had eluded all of their predecessors at Hearts since Tommy Walker oversaw League Cup glory in 1962. "As soon as the full-time whistle went in that final, Jim and Billy instantly became legends," says Houston. "They'll always be held in high esteem as the guys who brought the Scottish Cup back to Hearts."

The sentimental aspect of two childhood friends from East Lothian achieving this feat together isn't lost on either of them. "It means a lot that I achieved so much with a guy I've known since we were schoolkids," says Jefferies. The pair remain close to this day, even if Brown is more likely to be found at the horseracing and Jefferies on the golf course in their spare time. "We still speak a lot and, of course, we reminisce a lot about what we did at Hearts and we talk about what's going on at the club now," says Brown. "We'd both love to see the club doing well all the time."

Jefferies and Brown oversaw four top-four finishes and three cup final appearances in their five full seasons in charge before leaving Hearts in November 2000 amid a cash crisis at the club and increased tension with chief executive Robinson. They continued their managerial partnership at Bradford City and Kilmarnock, and then returned to Hearts in 2010 for another 19-month stint in which they finished third in their only full campaign in charge and put together the guts of the team that went on to win the Scottish Cup under Paulo Sergio in 2012. That proved to be their last job as a double act, with their exit at the hands of madcap owner Vladimir Romanov in August 2011 effectively bringing an end to a hugely fruitful 23-year alliance in professional football. "We were partners for a long time," says Brown. "When we started off I never really thought about where we were going in the game. At the time, it was just a job at Berwick and then we ended up winning the Scottish Cup with Hearts and getting ourselves into the English Premiership with Bradford. It was great, and it was something that we didn't know was going to happen."

Upon listening to his former players wax lyrical about his footballing expertise, it is easy to understand why Hearts owner Ann Budge felt compelled to invite a 69-year-old Jefferies to take on an advisory role with the club in summer 2020. As a genuine giant of Hearts' history, Jefferies is one of the few people who could justify having a statue built in his honour at Tynecastle. Not that any of the 1998 cup-winning squad require a physical reminder of the impact Jefferies and Brown had on their respective careers. "The last time I saw Jim and Billy I thanked them again for giving me the chance to come to Hearts," says Adam, the cup final goal hero. "I owe them so much and I will never forget what they did for me. Jim was a passionate manager; very passionate. He gave everything for the cause. He was tough but fair and he was somebody you trusted; a great guy. I loved Jim, and Billy was the same. They built up the team that brought success back to Tynecastle and they also had the talent to pick the right tactics for the final in 1998. They are two fantastic guys."

Gilles Rousset

*"I stayed in the Caledonian Hotel at
first – I had the Presidential Suite"*

When breaking away from his day job as Lyon's No.1 goalkeeper to spend the
early part of summer 1992 at the European Championships in Sweden alongside
luminaries such as Eric Cantona, Jean-Pierre Papin, Laurent Blanc and Didier
Deschamps in a France squad managed by the legendary Michel Platini, Gilles
Rousset would have been forgiven for thinking his career had peaked in terms of
fulfilment. Particularly so as he was approaching his 29th birthday at that point.
The best was very much still to come, however; and, remarkably, it came at a time
when Rousset's status in his homeland had become diminished, to the extent that
his last notable move in French football involved him grabbing Rennes general
manager Gerard Lefillatre by the throat in protest at what he felt was an unjust
decision to transfer-list him late in the summer of 1995.

Little did the usually mild-mannered Rousset know at that point that the sense
of anger and frustration he felt was merely a precursor to a bold move that would
re-energise him in his mid-30s. Aged 32, he left France for the first time in his
career to sign for Hearts, a club he previously knew nothing about, and ended up
enjoying a magical six-year stint in Edinburgh, largely defined by his prominent
involvement in the team's journey to Scottish Cup glory in 1998. "It was great; it
was basically a brand new challenge, a brand new life for me," says Rousset, reflecting on his move to Hearts. "I didn't think about it too much; I just jumped at
the chance to change everything. At that time, there weren't a lot of French players
playing abroad. There was Cantona and (David) Ginola in England, Deschamps
and (Marcel) Desailly in Italy, but there weren't many, so it was great to get that
chance to go abroad at that stage in my career. I was excited to restart my career,
I was excited to discover the game in a new country, to play at new stadiums and
to play against big clubs like Celtic and Rangers. I was excited to discover

Edinburgh and to improve my English. There were a lot of things I was excited about."

Rousset's enthusiasm proved justified. Indeed, no player's personal story reflected Hearts' travails in Jim Jefferies' first three years in charge moreso than that of the 6ft 5ins Frenchman. Like the Tynecastle club, he was in something of a rut in summer 1995; then in late October, he and Hearts joined forces to help each other off the canvas. "Gilles was one of the main reasons it all started to turn round for Hearts," says Neil Pointon, who arrived at Tynecastle a fortnight before Rousset and whose Lancashire-based agent, Mike Morris, played a part in bringing the keeper to Edinburgh. "My first season at Hearts was really, really good, apart from the cup final!" laughs Rousset. That, of course, was a disastrous day for Hearts, and particularly for the goalkeeper, whose calamitous error effectively paved the way for Rangers to run out convincing 5-1 winners. More on that later. Rousset is able to smile about the 1996 Scottish Cup final now because he knows how the story ends: with him and his team learning from what went wrong, regrouping, improving and coming back stronger to ensure a totally contrasting outcome in the 1998 final, with the goalkeeper the man of the match in an historic 2-1 victory for Hearts against the same opponents who had humiliated them two years previously. "Big Gilles was well loved by all the boys so we were all absolutely delighted for him," says Stephen Fulton, the Hearts captain on their day of glory and another man who joined the club a fortnight before Rousset. "If anybody ever came out saying 'what about your keeper's mistake in the final?', we were able to turn round and say 'well, he got fucking man of the match in the next one'. That says a lot about his character."

Rousset's spirit was nurtured in the affluent west Paris suburb of Boulogne-Billancourt, where he grew up in close vicinity to two of the most prestigious sporting venues in Europe: Parc des Princes and Roland Garros. Inspired by a competitive, athletic family – his mother Lydie played table tennis to a high level in France while his father Gilbert played pétanque (French bowls) and also enjoyed football – young Rousset always felt destined to be a sportsman. "Paris is obviously a big city and it's a great place to grow up playing football because there are a lot of kids playing football and the competitions are very tough," says Rousset, who was born in 1963 in the south of France, near Toulon, before his family moved north to the outskirts of the capital city when he was two years old. "When I was a kid I always had the goal to be a professional footballer because that is what I loved. I played many sports as a kid and I was good at all of them. I grew up in a very sporty family: my parents played sport, my uncles from my dad's side played football and my grandad played rugby in Toulon, so sport was very important in my family. I played basketball, rugby, football, table tennis, tennis and I did swimming. I needed to do a lot of sports to calm myself down because I was a very active and energetic boy. But football was always my favourite.

"I started as striker, I became a midfielder, then a defender and then I ended up being a goalkeeper. I was a decent player outfield but I remember one day my PE teacher at school told my mum he thought I had all the qualities with my hands to be a good goalkeeper and that I should try playing in that position. This guy saw some special qualities in me as a goalkeeper when I was really young. Then one day when I was about nine or ten I was training in a boys' club and the goalkeeper was missing so, because I was very tall, they asked me to go in goals. I had a great game and I kept that position afterwards."

Rousset soon started to thrive in his new position, relishing the unique demands of being a goalkeeper. "When I was about ten or 11, I really started to focus on being a goalkeeper and that was where I played ever since then," he says. "I loved it because it's a position with a lot of responsibilities. I really loved diving about and making saves. I was a crazy boy, very brave as well so I liked to dive about and make saves. I also liked to kick people sometimes! It was a position I really loved."

In his teenage years, while playing for Athletique Club of Boulogne-Billancourt, a highly-regarded boys' club, Rousset began emerging as one of his country's top young keepers. "It started to get serious for me about 14 when I was selected to represent Paris in a big tournament between all the regions in France," he recalls. "All the regions select the best kids of that age-group and I was picked for Paris. Most of the professional clubs pick boys from these selections to go to their academies so it started to get serious for me when I did that. I was selected at under-14, under-15 and under-16 level so I started to make a wee name for myself in Paris."

Rousset's big break came in 1979 when he was recruited by Sochaux, based in the east of France and 300 miles away from his home. "I was spied by a few clubs and when I was 15 and a half I had a trial with Sochaux and they decided to sign me for their academy," he explains. "So when I was about to turn 16 I had to leave my family to live my dream. My mum and dad were very good because they allowed me to move away to become a professional. It was great. It was a brand new life for me. I went from three training sessions a week to two sessions a day. I loved it. It was my dream to become a professional and I grabbed it."

Acknowledging he was "very thin and fragile" in his early years at Sochaux, Rousset had to work hard to add "weight and muscles" in order to be ready to compete at senior level. He played with "aggression" and modelled parts of his game on Harald Schumacher, the West Germany goalkeeper who gained infamy at the 1982 World Cup when he collided with French defender Patrick Battiston and left him in a coma. "When I was at Sochaux, near the Swiss and German border, Schumacher was the goalkeeper I really liked," says Rousset. "He was not very popular in France because of what happened with Battiston but I liked his toughness because I was similar. I was always willing to kick somebody to win a game. I was quite a confident goalkeeper and I was very crazy and aggressive in my game, especially when I was young. All my coaches had to calm me down and make sure I didn't get sent off for doing something crazy. I was much calmer later in my career because I grew up and learned from my mistakes."

Rousset's robust style of goalkeeping in his early years was epitomised by the fact that, in only his second first-team game for Sochaux, he injured Brest striker Milan Radovic in a challenge and prematurely ended the Yugoslav's season. That was a week after Rousset made his debut, aged 19, in a 1-1 draw at home to Lens in November 1982, after long-serving No.1 Albert Rust missed out through injury. "You're always going to be a bit nervous when it comes to making your professional debut because it's a big day," he says. "November 1982; almost 40 years ago, that's crazy. Sochaux were struggling at that time near the bottom of Ligue 1 and Lens were high in the league and we drew 1-1 at home. I had a very good game and Gerard Houllier, who was the Lens manager, came up to me at the end and said I had done well and wished me all the best. My second game was in Brest, in Brittany, and I broke the leg of the opposition striker with a tackle."

Sochaux provided the perfect platform for Rousset to launch his career, although it wasn't until they were relegated to Ligue 2 in 1987 that he got the chance, aged 24, to take over from French internationalist Rust as the club's regular No.1. "Sochaux had a very good reputation for bringing kids from the academy to the professional team so most of the players at the club had come through the youth system," says Rousset. "They would have no hesitation in bringing a young player through so that was great for all of us. It was a great place to start my career."

In Rousset's first season as the club's main goalkeeper (1987/88), Sochaux won the Ligue 2 title and finished runners-up in the French Cup after losing in the final to Metz on penalties at Parc des Princes following a 1-1 draw. Scotsman Eric Black got Metz's goal in regulation time while Rousset scored a kick in the shootout. His team-mates Stephane Paille and Franck Sauzee – both of whom would follow him to Edinburgh in the late 1990s – also netted in the shootout. "We had a fantastic season," he says. "In that team I played with Franck, the fucking Hibee! And Stephane Paille, who came to Hearts. I was friendly with both of them. Stephane was my best friend at the club and unfortunately he died a few years ago (in 2017). I was also very close to Franck. We are great friends as well and when he played for Hibs we went out for dinner a few times but we don't see each other so much now because we have different lives. A great guy though. I played with a few other boys who became internationalists: Franck Silvestre for France and two Yugoslavians, Faruk Hadzibegic and Mehmed Bazdarevic, who were very good. We had a very good team."

While helping Sochaux to back-to-back fourth-place finishes in their first two seasons back in Ligue 1, Rousset earned himself a first call-up to the French national team for a friendly in Sweden in August 1989. He didn't get on the pitch that night but made his debut as a starter in a 1-0 friendly win away to Kuwait in January 1990. Rousset's team-mates for the game in the Middle East included Sauzee, Cantona and Basile Boli, a future colleague of his at Marseille who then went on to spend the 1994/95 season with Rangers. In the summer of 1990, Rousset – who was establishing himself as France's second-choice goalkeeper behind Auxerre's Bruno Martini – landed a move to Lyon and was immediately installed as their No.1 by manager Raymond Domenech, who would go on to take charge of France. "I moved to Lyon because Sochaux were great but every year the best players would be sold and it was frustrating," says Rousset. "I decided to move to Lyon because they had big ambitions. The chairman was young and wanted to create a big club. They signed me on a free transfer because I was out of contract. It was a big move for me because I'd spent 11 years at Sochaux. I felt comfortable very quickly at Lyon."

In February 1992, Rousset made his second – and what would prove to be his final – appearance for France in a 2-0 friendly defeat by England at Wembley in which Alan Shearer and Gary Lineker scored the goals. The goalkeeper made the squad for Euro 92 in Sweden four months later and was an unused substitute as France suffered a humiliating group-stage exit after failing to win a game. Despite being capped only twice, Rousset was proud to be a regular member of the squad for three years under a man of Platini's stature. "I had played all levels for the national team: under-18, under-21, the B team and then the big team," says Rousset. "It was great to get picked by a legend like Platini; he was the manager all the way through my time in the national team. To be honest, he didn't really know about goalkeepers. He trusted the goalkeeper coach. Me and Bruno Martini were friends and I was happy to be No.2 because Bruno was doing so well and there was no reason to change it. I knew my role in the squad and I was happy to do that because it was a tremendous honour for me to be picked by Platini and to be No.2 of my country for about 30 games. That's a big honour. Even though I only played twice, I was very proud to be part of the team, part of the squad and part of the journey. Platini knew I would not cause any problems being No.2, which can sometimes be a problem with a substitute. He took me to Euro 92 and I was on the bench for the three games. There were big names in our Euro 92 squad. We did very well in our qualification group but we didn't do well at the tournament itself. We drew against Sweden and England and lost to Denmark. We got a lot of criticism after that tournament and Platini left. Houllier took over and he decided to pick Bernard Lama instead of me."

After the Euros, Rousset had one more year as Lyon's No.1. Despite his team finishing a disappointing 14th in Ligue 1, he was headhunted by freshly-crowned European and French champions Marseille in the summer of 1993. "I signed pretty much the day before all the problems erupted," says Rousset, referring to a match-fixing scandal which resulted in Marseille being stripped of the 1992/93 French title, chairman Bernard Tapie being jailed and the club encountering financial difficulties before enforced relegation in 1994. "They had won the Champions League and they wanted to strengthen their squad when they signed me. Fabien Barthez was the No.1 but he was young and a wee bit crazy so they said they needed someone beside him to make sure everything was okay. It was a new challenge and I was excited to go back to my native region because Marseille is about 40 miles from where I was born. It was very important to get this chance but unfortunately they discovered the scandal and we had a funny year. We couldn't play in Europe and we had no money. I still got to work with great players like Rudi Völler, Deschamps and Desailly but I didn't play a single game because Barthez was really good and when I was due to play I was injured. It was not a great season for me but it was great to live in Marseille and feel the passion of the fans because they are absolutely mad about their team. Marseille finished second but they got relegated because of the scandal. There was no money left at the club so I moved to Rennes who had just got promoted to Ligue 1."

Rennes proved to be the last French club of Rousset's career after a difficult 1994/95 season with the Brittany club. "I signed a two-year contract but I only played one year there because I never felt comfortable," he says. "The other goalkeeper at the club, Pascal Rousseau, was a fucking bastard. He had won promotion with the club the previous year and he did everything he could to turn the fans and the board against me and make me feel uncomfortable. He was the worst guy I've ever come across in football. After one game against PSG in January I got injured and was out for a month and the club kept him in goals for the rest of the season. I wasn't happy about that because I was better than him but it was political because he was close to the sponsors, the fans and things like that. He left at the end of the season and I stayed on through the summer. I was very angry about what had happened in the first season and I worked really hard during my holidays because I wanted to come back and prove to them in my second season that I was the best keeper at the club. I was in really good form in pre-season and felt ready for the challenge, but they said they were bringing in a new keeper as No.1. They didn't want me to leave before they signed a new keeper though so they kept me all through pre-season until the last day of the French transfer window when they signed a Yugoslavian keeper (Goran Pandurovic) to be No.1 and then they said to me I could leave. I was thinking 'what, the transfer window is closed!' I went into the general manager's office, I took him by the neck and put him in the air. His feet were not touching the ground. I said 'I'm going to make hell in your club for the next year if I stay here'. He was quite unhappy and the club decided to sack me but they still gave me some money. I had no club, no contract, but at least I had got some money from them so I was quite happy about that because it meant I could take some time to decide what to do next. After that I left but I had no club."

Rennes' loss would, after three months of limbo, prove to be Hearts' gain. "I wasn't happy in Rennes so I decided to move back to Sochaux with my family," says Rousset, reflecting on the first period of his distinguished career in which he was without a club. "Sochaux were in Ligue 2 at that time so I asked if I could train with them to keep myself fit. I trained with the academy team at first which was fine because I just wanted a team to work with until I could find a new challenge. After two weeks with the academy team I started training with the first team. It meant I was able to train with a professional team every day without having the pressure of a game at the weekend. It was tough not having a club but it was also good to train and feel free for a while. I stayed almost three months in this situation waiting for an offer to come. I had contact from Galatasaray but I was slightly worried that it might be too dangerous to go there, because I was aware they were having a bit of trouble in Istanbul. They said 'don't worry, there will be bodyguards', but I said 'no, no, no, I don't want to go to a place where I need bodyguards'. It didn't get to the stage where they offered me a contract because as soon as they mentioned bodyguards, I was like 'that's not for me'."

Late in October 1995, Rousset's interest was piqued when his agent, Frederic Dobraje, presented him with an opportunity to move to the United Kingdom. "I remember my agent phoned me on the Tuesday and Sochaux were playing a League Cup game that night (at home to Louhans-Cuiseaux) so he said 'I've got an English club for you, come to the game tonight and we will speak about it'," explains Rousset. "I said 'oh great'. I was very impatient to find out which club it was so I went to the game, met him and I was like 'what club is it?'. He said it's a Scottish club called Heart of Midlothian. I said 'but you told me it was an English club?'. I was a wee bit disappointed because I'd always had an interest in English football. I was a fan of Leeds United because I remembered them playing the European Cup final in Paris (in 1975) and they had a fantastic team with Peter Lorimer, Joe Jordan, Billy Bremner, Johnny Giles and all those guys. I knew of Hearts by name but I didn't know anything about them or where they were from. My agent asked if I was interested in going to Edinburgh on trial and I said 'yes, of course'. He said 'tomorrow, you can fly over and someone will pick you up at the airport and take you to the hotel in Edinburgh'. Another agent called Mike Morris picked me up at Glasgow Airport and as soon as I touched down it was raining cats and dogs. The day after, I went for my first training session with Hearts. There were about seven goalkeepers at the club and apart from H (Henry Smith), they were all young. I trained with them and I was wondering why they had brought me because there were already so many goalkeepers. After training with them on the Thursday, Jim Jefferies organised a practice game in the garden of Murrayfield (Roseburn). I played a practice game and at the end of the day they asked if I would be ready to play for the first team against Falkirk as a trialist the next day. I said 'okay, no problem'. So I played, we lost, we went to the bottom of the table but I had a good game. After that, Hearts offered me a contract before I flew back to France. I didn't agree the contract straight away because I also had an offer from Charleroi and I had promised that I would go to Belgium to speak to them. But sometimes, for whatever reason, you don't feel comfortable in certain places. I didn't feel as comfortable with Charleroi as I had done in my few days with Hearts. That week, I decided to sign for Hearts on an eight-month contract until the end of the season, so that was the start of the story."

The 32-year-old Frenchman was comfortable with the prospect of uprooting his wife and two children to Scotland. "It was a big move as it was the first time I had played outside France but it was not a problem for me," explains Rousset. "I'd always been open to a new challenge, especially in the UK because I could speak a bit of English. But, trust me, the first time I went in the dressing-room I couldn't understand a fucking word! Lockey (Gary Locke) started to speak with me and, oh my goodness, I was like 'what the fuck is he saying to me? I cannae understand him'. The boys were absolutely fantastic with me; honestly, I felt comfortable with them from the first day. Thankfully I had some good games from the start which helped me feel happy and everybody at Hearts did everything to make sure my family and myself were comfortable. I stayed in the Caledonian Hotel at first. I had the Presidential Suite which was absolutely tremendous! I stayed there for a month until I found a flat. I really wanted to stay in the West End, close to Princes Street, and we found a flat in Alva Street, just near Bar Roma."

Despite not having played for more than nine months prior to his debut at Brockville, Rousset instantly brought quality and assurance to a position that had become problematic for Jefferies, with Henry Smith coming to the end of his career and Craig Nelson and Gary O'Connor unable to convince the manager they were worthy of an extended run. Indeed, just a few months after arriving at Hearts, Rousset's impressive form led to him becoming the subject of a bid from Sunderland, who were top of the English First Division at the time and on course for the top flight under Peter Reid, a close friend of agent Morris. "I was very lucky to have some great games and right from the start the team was playing much better; we started to climb the table very quickly," says Rousset, reflecting on a period when his arrival coincided with Hearts moving from last place up towards the top four. "When Sunderland came in for me, Jim told me about it and asked me what I would like to do. I told him 'I am a Hearts player – what would you like to do with me?'. He wanted me to stay so I told him 'okay, my contract is up at the end of the season, so if you want me to stay make me an offer'. I knew Sunderland were willing to offer me a good contract, about five times what I was earning at Hearts. They couldn't afford to offer me what Sunderland were offering but they doubled my wages and offered me a four-year contract so I said 'yeah, okay, I will stay with Hearts'. I was very happy to sign the new contract with Hearts because they were really good with me. They had come to me to save my career so I was delighted to get the chance to give them something back and also to have a long contract which would allow me to settle in a good place. My family loved the city and the club, and I loved playing for Jim and Billy – they were absolutely fantastic to me – so it was a great situation for me."

Rousset endeared himself to everyone at Tynecastle with the way he went about his business on and off the park. "He was a very vocal goalkeeper, a bit like Peter Schmeichel (Manchester United's No.1 at the time), but off the park, he was a quiet person," says Pointon. Gary Mackay, Hearts' record appearance holder, played with Rousset for 18 months. "Big Gilles was the nicest guy I met in football," says Mackay. "He remains a friend to this day."

Rousset's sense of contentment as he neared the end of his first season in Edinburgh was heightened when Hearts reached the Scottish Cup final for the first time in a decade after beating Aberdeen 2-1 in the semi-final in April. They would face Rangers, a side they had defeated – 3-0 at Ibrox and 2-0 at Tynecastle – in each of their two previous meetings on their way to securing a fourth-place finish in the league. "Jim explained Hearts' situation to me when I first came in on trial," says Rousset. "He said that he wanted to change a few things and that he wanted to put some young players in to refresh the squad and the team. He explained the plans for the future and I trusted him, and that's what he did. Very quickly we had fresh legs and a different mentality, and you could tell the way we finished the season was a lot more like what the fans expected. We were all very excited to go to the final. We were playing against a very good Rangers side. Even though we'd beaten them in the previous two league games, we knew they had many quality players who could make the difference. We felt we had a chance but we knew it would be really tough."

In the seconds before referee Hugh Dallas blew the whistle to get the 1996 Scottish Cup final under way, "Rousset, there's only one Rousset" was the most pre-eminent chant coming from the packed stands of Hampden. The popular goalkeeper would need all the support he could get by full-time. Trailing 1-0 to a 37th-minute opener from Brian Laudrup and having lost captain Gary Locke to a knee injury early in the match, Hearts knew at half-time that they needed to score the next goal if they were to have any chance. Their hopes were dashed in galling fashion just five minutes after the break, however, when Rousset – wearing a bright yellow top, full-length black leggings and white ankle socks – let a tame and seemingly harmless inswinging left-footed Laudrup cross from the right squirm through his arms and legs. As the ball skidded under him and into the net, Rousset, kneeling on the ground, glanced over his right shoulder in horror, looked up to-wards shellshocked team-mate Paul Ritchie, who was standing on the edge of the six-yard box, and then pressed both hands against his face in utter despair. "I can still remember the moment," he says, ruefully. "I saw the cross from Laudrup: it was a normal cross, it wasn't dangerous. But on my right I saw a Rangers player moving. Instead of keeping my eyes on the ball and staying concentrated only on the ball, I just lost the ball for a fraction of a second to look to my right to see where the attacker was. It was just at the moment when I was due to catch the ball. I shouldn't have looked away at that moment. It was just a fraction of a second that I lost the ball from my eyes and it squirmed through my legs. I knew straight away what had happened and how big a moment it was. It was horrible, like receiving a big knockdown from (heavyweight boxer) Tyson Fury. I was thinking 'oh, my goodness'. I wasn't just thinking about myself, though; I felt for the team, for the fans, for the club. I felt like I'd let everybody down with my mistake. It was a cup final, everybody had been waiting for it for ages, I had been waiting for it for ages, and I felt like I'd let my team-mates and my family down. It was a terrible feeling; the worst moment of my career."

As if to exacerbate the situation, Rousset had to remain in the eye of the storm for another 40 minutes, stewing over the ramifications of his error, conceding another three goals, and enduring the humiliation of jubilant Rangers fans mockingly cheering whenever he caught the ball. "When we were 1-0 down with half the game to go, we still had a chance but as soon as it went 2-0 against that brilliant Rangers team, we had a mountain to climb," he says. "I tried to concentrate on the rest of the game. You have to try to forget the mistake and stay concentrated on the game. I think I made a few saves later in the game but we lost 5-1. It was a bad de-feat. I remember (Rangers goalkeeper) Andy Goram came to me at the end of the game and he said he was sorry for me. He asked me a few times if I was okay, and I said 'yes Andy, I'm fine'. Andy's a nice guy and I think he was genuinely sorry for me. I remember in the dressing-room afterwards I couldn't look my team-mates in the eye because I felt responsible for the defeat. I was crying in the dressing-room and everybody was saying 'don't worry about it, it's not a problem' and things like that. But I was thinking 'yes, it is a problem'."

The Hearts players – all of whom had underperformed on the day – were in no mood for hanging their despondent goalkeeper out to dry. "I can still remember turning away after Laudrup put the ball in thinking 'great, we'll get a breather here' and then suddenly there's a big massive roar from the Rangers fans and I turn round and see Gilles on the floor and the ball in the net," says Pointon. "I couldn't quite understand what had happened. The game was gone at that point. Gilles was down after the game. We said 'Gilles, don't worry, there'll be other times. Some-thing special's happening here, this won't be the last time you're in a cup final'."

A serious test of character beckoned for Rousset in the following days and weeks;

he had to draw on the support of those closest to him as well as all the qualities that had helped him grow into one of the top French goalkeepers of his generation. As a sure-footed, confident and driven individual with more than a decade of top-level experience under his belt, Rousset swiftly turned his focus to getting his head together and proving that his cup final howler was not a sign of a goalkeeper in decline. "When we went back to the George Hotel for a reception on the Saturday night after the game, there were some Hearts fans there and I stupidly said 'I promise you a trophy before I leave'," he explains. "After that I was thinking 'oh fuck, why did I say that?' because it's very hard to win a trophy in Scotland with Rangers and Celtic so dominant. I didn't really have time to think about my mistake over the summer because a few days after the final I went back to France for the holidays and nobody in France spoke to me about what had happened. I spoke to my wife and she said 'don't worry, we still love you, you will get another chance'. If I had stayed in Scotland, it might have been more difficult to get out of my head because everybody would have wanted to talk to me about my mistake. I think it helped that I went straight to France because by the time I came back for pre-season I was ready for the fresh challenge of the new season. It didn't really affect my confidence the following season because I remember the first competitive game back was the Cup Winners' Cup game away to Red Star Belgrade and I had a very good game (in a 0-0 draw). What happened in that final really made me more hungry for success. I wanted to show everyone that it was a mistake and nothing more so I was just focused on having another good season. I could still feel the trust and love of the fans. There were no problems there. Mistakes happen to everyone but unfortunately it happened to me at a very, very bad time. It could have happened in a league game against Motherwell or Partick Thistle, or when we were 3-0 up, and nobody would have talked about it, but it happened at a crucial stage of a cup final."

Rousset, who retained his status as Jefferies' No.1 in the early months of 1996/97, had a chance to try and exorcise some demons just six months after the 1996 Scottish Cup final when Hearts and Rangers were reunited in the Coca-Cola Cup final. Although the Frenchman conceded four goals in a 4-3 defeat at Celtic Park, he wasn't at fault for any of them and he and his team generally performed better than in their previous final. "We lost two early goals but after we went back to 2-2, only the genius of Gazza (Paul Gascoigne) made the difference," says Rousset. "He was really quiet in that game but in a few minutes he took the ball twice and made the difference. We kept fighting and we got back to 4-3. We had the feeling after that game that we were getting closer and we were much more competitive than in the previous final."

The sense that Hearts were on an upward trajectory continued in Rousset's third season at the club when they mounted a stirring challenge for the Premier Division title. "The young players like Ritch and Lockey had more experience, we had good experience in the team and we had legs, with boys like Stephane Adam, Colin Cameron and Neil McCann who could run," says the goalkeeper, outlining the reasons Hearts became such a strong team in 1997/98. "We had a very well-balanced team. The squad was full of experience and full of desire to win something.

Jim and Billy managed the group very well; they were very good at keeping the enthusiasm but also keeping our feet on the ground."

By the time of the 1998 Scottish Cup final against Rangers, Rousset insists he had long since banished any negativity associated with the events of Hampden two years previously and was full of positive energy as a result of Hearts' remarkable season. "1996 was not really in my head going into the 98 final," he says. "Honestly, it was behind me. It was two years before; what has been done has been done. You cannae change the past but you can build your future. I had learned from it and I had dealt with it. For me, it was finished. I think other people were thinking much more about that situation than I was. I was just focused on what would happen on that day and obviously making sure there was no repeat of what happened in 96."

Rousset was named man of the match by sponsors Tennent's as Hearts pulled off their famous 2-1 triumph in the Celtic Park sunshine. "I think I was just one part of the success," he says, reflecting on his own performance. "It was a real team effort. Everybody was fighting for the jersey, everybody was fighting for the cause. The team was man of the match. I was picked as man of the match, but, honestly, I didn't have to make a lot of saves. I made a few but I was not fantastic. I played my game, I was not bad, but I played many better games in a Hearts jersey than this one. Maybe it was because of 96 that they gave me this tremendous honour of being man of the match, but I don't really feel I deserved it. I've still got the massive bottle of champagne at home. I was happy to take it on behalf of the team, but it could have been anyone in the team who got man of the match that day because everybody fought so hard. Everybody deserved man of the match."

While Rousset played down his own part in the narrative, the significance of him going from sinner in 96 to winner in 98 wasn't lost on others. "One of the things that pleased me most about winning the cup was that Gilles was fantastic that day," says Jefferies. "He was coming for crosses and made great saves from (Lorenzo) Amoruso and (Ally) McCoist. He was commanding and never looked panicked. After he had lost that freak goal in his first final two years earlier, I was so pleased for him that he got man of the match when we won it. Everybody was man of the match in my eyes but he got that accolade from the sponsors on the day. I was so pleased for him after what he'd gone through. It couldn't have happened to a greater guy. He was a magnificent signing for us and he was different class for us that day."

Mackay, watching as a supporter from the stand after departing the club 14 months previously, was thrilled for his former team-mate. "I was delighted for everybody in the team, but I was delighted for some more than others, Gilles in particular," says Mackay. "None of the players or management ever blamed Gilles for what happened in 1996 but it was just great for him as a person, because he was such a gem, that he was able to turn it round full circle and be part of the cup-winning team. You could see how much it meant to him and it was just wonderful."

For Rousset, just three months shy of his 35th birthday, it was the first major honour of his career. "I didn't think about 1996 at all when the full-time whistle went," says Rousset. "I just knew at that moment that I had done something special. Andy Goram came up to me again and said 'well done, you deserved that'. On the way back to Edinburgh after the game, we all had many beers. I remember sitting with Jim Stewart, the goalie coach, at the back of the bus and I was crying. It was an emotional moment; it meant so much to me. It is the top moment for me, the best moment of my career. It is important because it was the only trophy I won and also because it was with Hearts and it meant so much to the Jambo people. The fact it meant so much for them made it also mean so much for me. The club was desperate for a trophy so to be part of the team that brought a trophy back to Tynecastle means so much to me. I've actually lost my medal. I found the two losing medals but I don't know where the winning one is. Honestly, that doesn't matter, I've got the memories, I've got everything. The medal doesn't matter."

Rousset remained Hearts' No.1 for another 18 months before Finnish internationalist Antti Niemi was signed from Rangers to take over from the 36-year-old Frenchman. "To be honest, I had problems accepting it at first," says Rousset of Jefferies' decision to replace him. "When Jim told me he was signing Antti, I wasn't happy. He explained to me that he had the opportunity to sign a younger keeper but that I was a big part of the squad and he still trusted me. He gave me an extra year on my contract, which was very important. I eventually accepted my role and I was very close to Antti and Roddy McKenzie (the third-choice goalkeeper, and previously Rousset's deputy), so there was no problem. I was still part of the team and would play whenever Antti was not fit."

Rousset's last appearance for Hearts proved to be in a goalless draw away to Dundee in April 2000, as he was ravaged by a virus for most of the 2000/01 campaign and forced to retire as a result. "The problem was that in October 2000, I caught a virus in my chest and lungs," Rousset explains. "It was like the coronavirus but I can't remember the name of it. I couldn't breathe. I don't know where it came from but I was out for eight months with it. I saw some specialists in Scotland and France and they said it was a virus that would come and go by itself and they couldn't treat it. I just had to wait and unfortunately it took eight months to leave me. I tried to restart every month by doing some jogging or training but I couldn't breathe; I was absolutely knackered. When you stop for eight months at 36, 37, it's nearly impossible to come back. I wish I could have stayed longer at Tynecastle but, unfortunately, I had to call it a day."

Rousset's job was done though. Over the course of 164 appearances and almost six years in Gorgie, he helped Hearts make history, achieved the crowning moment of his career and entwined himself into the fabric of the club. "It was a fantastic time for me," he says. "When you play for a foreign team you have to adapt to everything: a new life, new language, new lifestyle, new style of play. It's a big thing to do and you have to prove to yourself that you can do it. I did it with a lot of enthusiasm and the club was absolutely different class to myself and my family. It was absolutely wonderful. There was a very friendly atmosphere at the club and it was perfect. The team were struggling when I signed but from the start, I did well and the team improved. It was an absolutely magnificent experience for me and I'm still a big Hearts fan now even though I can't get over as much as I would like because of my coaching work. I follow the news about Hearts practically every day online. The internet gives you all the news you need, so it's great. There will always be a love affair between myself and Heart of Midlothian Football Club."

Spirit And Substance

*"We formed a brotherhood, and it's a
big part of why we were so successful"*

"That team was three years in the making," stresses assistant manager Billy
Brown, as if to enforce the point that Hearts' Scottish Cup triumph in 1998 was no
overnight success story.

In a sustained period of shrewd squad-building by Jim Jefferies and Brown from
August 1995 onwards, homegrown young players were promoted from within the
club and meshed with a smattering of carefully-selected foreign players and burgeoning Scots recruited from the dark blue ranks of Dundee, Raith Rovers and
Falkirk. It resulted in one of the finest Hearts sides since the 1950s – a team loaded
with quality, adventure and spirit – coming to fruition and making its indelible
mark. "Jim and Billy built a side that was good to watch and heralded throughout
the county," says winger Neil McCann, a key man in a squad put together on a
shoestring when compared to Rangers and Celtic, and even some Hearts sides of
more recent times. "We had serious players in that team; it absolutely was a team
of substance."

At the point of winning the Scottish Cup, four members of the starting XI had
played at full international level: Gilles Rousset (France), Thomas Flögel (Austria),
David Weir and Dave McPherson (both Scotland). Within two years and one month
of that glory day in May 1998, another four – McCann, Colin Cameron, Paul Ritchie
and Gary Naysmith – had won their first caps for Scotland. Stephen Fulton was
also called up four months after the cup final for a Euro 2000 qualifier in Lithuania
but didn't make it on to the pitch. When the dust settled on their respective
careers, six of them – Weir (69 caps), Naysmith (46), Flögel (37), Cameron (28),
McPherson (27), and McCann (26) – had represented their country more than 25
times. "I'm not surprised Hearts won the cup with all those guys in the team,"
says Craig Brown, the manager who gave Scotland debuts to Weir, Cameron,

McCann, Ritchie and Naysmith. "That was an outstanding Hearts team. When you go through that team man for man, if they were in the Scottish Premiership just now they would be right up there competing for the league. Celtic have been running away with the league in recent years but they certainly wouldn't have run away from that Hearts team. The guys in that team were not only very accomplished footballers, they're all great guys as well."

Those in the Hearts team who were – or would soon become – full internationalists were augmented by high-calibre operators such as Stefano Salvatori, who had been part of a European Cup-winning AC Milan squad in 1990, and Stephane Adam, who arrived from a Metz side who had just finished in the top five of France's Ligue 1 two years running. Captain Gary Locke, who missed the final through injury, was widely deemed to be destined for full Scotland caps if not for his knee problems, while others who had drifted to the periphery by May 1998, such as Neil Pointon (part of Everton's title-winning squad in 1987) and John Robertson (capped 16 times by Scotland and Hearts' record league goal-scorer) brought further pedigree and experience to the squad. "For me, the biggest reason we did so well that season was simply that we had lots of fantastic players," says Locke. "People go on about tactics and things like that, which obviously help, but you'll be a good manager if you've got good players in your team. The gaffer knew he could trust everyone in that team and, as a player myself, I could trust everyone. You look through that team now and the majority were full internationalists at some point. Although we had some brilliant players, we didn't have any superstars – we obviously didn't have a Paul Gascoigne or a Brian Laudrup – but we had a real togetherness. I think we had our success because of our collective quality."

While several other Scottish sides outwith Rangers and Celtic have finished in the top three or won a trophy, few have achieved these feats in the same season or with the level of panache and promise displayed by Hearts in 1997/98. "They were an absolute joy to watch," says Martin Dempster, the Edinburgh Evening News' Hearts correspondent in the late 1990s. "They conceded goals but you always knew they were capable of scoring two or three in a game. It was the one team I always say to people I would have happily paid money to watch, just because of the brand of football. They were so entertaining."

The fact they plundered an impressive 70 goals in 36 league games, were considered genuine title contenders until mid-April, finished within seven points of both members of the Old Firm and then defeated one of them in a cup final, all in the one campaign, sets Jefferies' swashbuckling Hearts team apart from most – if not all – other sides who have attempted to break the Rangers/Celtic stranglehold on Scottish football since the mid-1980s. "I know it's something a lot of ex-players can be guilty of saying, but I think our team would have handled most Scottish teams since then quite easily," says Fulton. "You could go right through that team and I don't think any of us would struggle to get in a Hearts team right now."

Although they were unable to emulate the Hearts side of 1985/86 or Aberdeen in 1990/91 by maintaining their title fight to the very last day of the season, Jefferies' team were taken seriously for most of the campaign until they started to waver in

the last six games. "I don't think there's any doubt that Hearts were getting progressively better under Jim and Billy," says Archie Knox, Rangers' assistant manager at the time. "Even when Rangers were having their good spell, Hearts were
always in contention for trophies and in 1998 they proved to be title contenders.
They kept themselves up there for most of the season and got their reward in the
cup final. They had a great group of players."

In contrast to the modern game, in which player rotation has become such
a regular feature, Hearts were driven towards glory in 1998 by a core group of
key men. Of the eleven that started the cup final, eight had started 28 or more of
the 36 league games: goalkeeper Rousset; defenders Weir and Ritchie; midfielders Salvatori, Fulton and Cameron; and attackers Adam and McCann. Naysmith
didn't fall into this category although the teenage left-back was well on his way to
establishing himself as a regular by the end of the season after taking the place
of Pointon from January onwards. Captain Locke, who missed the final through
injury, generally started at right-back when fit and top scorer Jim Hamilton, who
was effectively a victim of the change of tactics in the final, was a regular in attack
throughout the campaign. McPherson and Flögel were the two players not considered guaranteed starters in the lead-up to the match, although neither could ever
be considered a fringe man. McPherson had played more than 300 matches for
the club by that point while Flögel, although restricted to 13 league starts in his
maiden season in Edinburgh, had started each of the four cup ties in the run to the
final and would go on to become one of the club's longest-serving foreign players.
"I think the best teams are the ones where you could reel off most of the team and
you knew week to week pretty much what the team was going to be," says sports
journalist and Hearts supporter Ewan Murray. "In that Hearts team, the majority
of them started most weeks; it was pretty much only the right-back position that
changed quite often."

The continuity of selection in 1997/98 was a sure sign that Jefferies and Brown
had established a well-functioning team. "There was a real backbone right through
the team, with good youth and good experience," says Peter Houston, who assisted
Jefferies and Brown as a coach. "Ritchie and Weir were solid with a quality goalkeeper behind them in Rousset. They had real quality in the middle of the park,
with Fulton, who could pass the ball, and the energy of Cameron. Back then central midfielders getting in the box and getting on the end of things wasn't a massive thing, but Cameron had the legs to do that and contributed a lot of goals and
assists. Up front, Adam would chase things down and work defenders. Most importantly for me, they had legs and pace, and they were really hungry. A few of
them hadn't had much success up to that point but they went on to have good success afterwards. There was a real good energy about that team. It was a young, enthusiastic group destined to go all the way; a great Hearts team. They thoroughly
deserved to win the cup after the season they had."

With an experienced international goalkeeper, a balanced defence, a midfield
of steel, creativity and energy, and an attack which possessed power, pace and
potency, Jefferies and Brown had conjured a perfect blend. "We knew we could
destroy teams with what we had," says Hamilton. "We had defenders that could

defend, we had drive from midfield and we had so many options in attack. It was a breath of fresh air to play in that team."

The back four on cup final day contained the two most recent Hearts players to appear at World Cups: McPherson, who started all three games at Italia 90, and Weir, who featured in two matches at France 98 a month after defeating Rangers at Celtic Park. "What Scotland would give to have Weir and McPherson playing in defence for them now," says Craig Brown. "These guys were quality international players for Scotland."

While the full-backs changed over the course of the season, the centre-backs – Ritchie and Weir – missed only three league games between them and were deemed key to the team's success. "The two of them were just outstanding all season," says Jefferies.

Although every member of Hearts' back five (Rousset plus the defence) would end their careers as full internationalists, arguably the most impressive department of the team was the three-man central-midfield unit of Salvatori, Fulton and Cameron. "I would be hard-pressed to think of another Hearts team that had midfielders who complemented one another as well as those three did," says Mike Aitken, a Hearts supporter and former sports journalist at The Scotsman. "Salvatori, Fulton and Cameron were all terrific; together, they were the absolute fulcrum of the team. Looking back to the 1998 final, it would be a complete misrepresentation to say Hearts dominated the game because Rangers, by and large, had more of the ball. But if you looked at Rangers' midfield three – Stuart McCall, Ian Ferguson and Rino Gattuso – they were basically all the same type of player in terms of being strong-tackling midfielders. They certainly weren't without ability, but Hearts seemed to have a much better balance in terms of personnel. They had Salvatori, who was the sitting midfield player; Fulton, who was the great passer of the ball; and Cameron, who would be a No.10 today and had huge energy. His job was to get forward, support the strikers, come into the box late and get goals. When you put those three together, it was terrific."

Jefferies takes pride from the midfield he pieced together. "When you're balancing up a team and you've got three midfielders in the team, you want one who's doing the legwork and winning the ball most of the time, and that was Salvatori," explains the manager. "He could then give it to Stevie Fulton and when that happened Mickey (Cameron) would be on his bike knowing Fulton would find him."

The impact of this magnificent midfield triumvirate was enhanced by the fact they were operating in support of a Hearts attack loaded with dangermen; the fact they netted six league goals more than eventual champions Celtic highlighted just how lethal they were. Indeed, the 1997/98 Hearts team are one of only three non-Old Firm sides to have scored 70 or more league goals in a season since the last staging of a 44-game campaign in 1993/94. Hearts – under George Burley, Graham Rix and Valdas Ivanauskas – hit 71 in 2005/06, and Derek McInnes's Aberdeen netted 74 in 2016/17, although both those teams achieved the feat in a 38-game campaign whereas Jefferies' side did it in 36 matches, averaging almost two goals per game. Eight different players chipped in with at least five goals in all competitions. In fact, of the cup final starting XI, goalkeeper Rousset was the only player who didn't score, with every outfield player finding the net across the campaign. "Flögel, myself, Stephane, Hammy, Robbo, wee Jose (Quitongo), Mickey and Fulters coming from the middle of the pitch," says McCann, listing the threats. "We had seven or eight players who could score and that's before you add in the boys coming up from the back like Slim (McPherson), Ritch or big Davie, who were all a threat from set-pieces. When you're trying to build a side, you try to have more than one avenue of attack and spread goals throughout the team. Once you can do that, you become a very dangerous animal, and that's certainly what we became."

The players loved being involved in such a free-flowing, attack-minded side. "It was an unbelievable team to be part of; so many great players," says Quitongo. "I didn't start many games that season but I remember doing an interview at the time and saying I was just so happy to be part of that squad. I swear, that team was great; one of the best Hearts teams you'll see."

For most of the campaign, Hearts played without inhibitions. All they seemed to be missing in the final reckoning was the title-winning experience required to make their quality count when the championship race entered its most critical phase, with McPherson and Flögel the only players in the team who had previously achieved the feat, at Rangers and Austria Vienna respectively. "Rangers and Celtic had knowledge of winning trophies and we didn't have that at that time," says Weir. "Sometimes you have to learn how to do that; maybe it's the case that you've got to win a cup first before you can win a league. We were the new kids on the block; we were just young and enthusiastic and doing it all on hope rather than experience. There was no pressure on us for a lot of the season but actually winning a title was all new to us."

The exuberance evident in their play for most of the season was one of the most endearing characteristics of this Hearts team as a group of hungry, upwardly-mobile Scots and a quartet of relatively high-pedigree Europeans took the Premier Division by storm. The balance in the Hearts squad between home-based and foreign players was noted at the time by Rangers winger Laudrup, one of the finest overseas players ever to grace the Scottish game and a direct title and Scottish Cup rival to Hearts in 1997/98. "Scottish teams should never lose the Scottish mentality," said the Dane in late March 1998, at a time when Hearts were two points off the top of the table with six games to play. "Every Premier Division team should have five or six Scots. Hearts, without the financial backing of Rangers or Celtic, are right in the race for the title, and that is a tribute to what I've spoken about; it's that elusive mix, the continental influence and the great young players Scottish football does still produce. No-one can argue that players like Stefano Salvatori and Stephane Adam haven't been a huge help for Hearts but so have the likes of Gary Naysmith and Paul Ritchie. And surely Scottish football should salute what one of its own, Jim Jefferies, has done."

The Hearts team that started the final featured seven Scots and four foreign players, while Angolan Quitongo and English pair Pointon and Lee Makel were the other non-Scots in the mix. Whether from Lille or Loanhead, Peterhead or Port Glasgow, Vienna or Kirkcaldy, the Hearts players were all on the same page and pulling in the same direction. "We were lucky that the European boys we had in the team, Gilles, Stephane, Thomas and Stefano – and Pasquale Bruno before that – were all good boys," says Fulton. "They were quite shocked at some of our antics when we had a night out but they all got on brilliantly with the Scottish boys and integrated really well. They were brand new."

Camaraderie was key at late-90s Hearts. "We had a togetherness that was partly down to the social side of things," says Ritchie. "We had nights out, we had trips away and the bond we had was incredible. We formed a brotherhood, and it was a big part of why we were so successful. The foreign boys blended with the Scottish boys in their own way. They were maybe a bit more reserved than some of us but they understood that for us to be successful we had to bond as a team. They came on the trips with us and got involved with everything. I wouldn't say, necessarily, they were more professional than us but they had come from different cultures, so they probably frowned upon the way we did things at times, but there was a mutual respect between us all. We enjoyed our lives back then; going out and partying was part of British football culture at that time. But when Jim and Billy cracked the whip and it came to the hard work, we were all right at it, and as a group we all had each other's backs on matchday."

The foreign contingent were keen to embrace Scottish dressing-room culture. "It was sometimes hard to understand what some of them were saying, particularly when I first arrived, because they didn't always give you time to understand what they were saying," laughs Flögel. "That's probably why I was more with the other foreign boys like Stephane, Gilles and Stefano at the start. But with so many Scottish players, we had to adapt. We had to learn about the Scottish mentality, what the Scots are like and how we could be part of it; we basically spent our time at Hearts learning to live like a Scot! I was more of a wine-drinking boy but some of the boys obviously preferred a beer. It was always funny when we went out. We had great nights out in Edinburgh, at places like Bar Roma, and sometimes we went away to England. It was easy for us to get involved because all the guys were so friendly."

Bar Roma, the iconic and authentic Italian restaurant on Queensferry Street, was a regular meeting point for Hearts' continental players in the late 1990s, and the homely vibe encouraged by the owners helped the likes of Salvatori, Rousset, Flögel and Adam settle in the city. Bar Roma was opened by Mario and Beatrice Cugini, a couple originally from Rome, in 1981 and the family soon became Hearts supporters and forged links with the Tynecastle club. Hearts players of the late 80s and early 90s regularly visited the lively and popular west end eatery, but the late 90s is regarded as a particularly special period by the Cugini family because of the bond they developed with Jefferies' imports and their families. "Bar Roma basically became their kitchen," says Nadia Di Giorgio (previously Cugini), a waitress in the late 1990s and daughter to owners Mario and Beatrice. "At the time, my parents had Bar Italia and Bar Roma, both within walking distance of the Caledonian Hotel. The players liked that we did a proper Italian pizza, good coffee and also Peroni, which wasn't easy to come by at that time. They would come to us for breakfast, even though we weren't actually open, and then they would go to training and come back to us, invariably with their families, for lunch in the afternoon. We knew all their kids and what everyone liked to eat. Our families all became very close and I would often babysit their kids if they wanted to go out. It was like one big Jambo family. The guys would just walk in and get a coffee whenever they wanted. It was basically a meeting point for them, a place for them to hang out. I think they liked the atmosphere we created and we were certainly privileged that they felt so relaxed that they came to us all the time.

"They would frequent the bars around the West End and were happy to chat to people. They were just great guys, gentlemen. In the restaurant trade, you see a lot of people who have an inflated ego, but none of those guys – and I mean none of them – were like that. I think that's what made that group so special. They all got on really well, they liked each other very much and they respected each other. We closed Bar Roma in 2013 but when we look back on it as a family or with any of the other waiters who worked there, that particular period in the late 1990s was definitely the best. We saw a lot of players from Rangers, Celtic, Liverpool and other clubs, but that particular group from Hearts were just really good people who were very grateful to be in Edinburgh and happy to be at Hearts. The success Hearts were having at that time helped it become a special moment in time. The team was doing well and these guys had brought their families over from different countries and it was just a lovely time for everyone involved."

Adam, Flögel and Rousset all spent at least five seasons with Hearts, while Salvatori was there for almost three years but continued to be closely associated with the club in his post-playing days. Everyone involved in that magical 1997/98 season became part of the fabric of the club by virtue of length of service and the success they enjoyed in maroon. It is notable that there were no "one-season wonders" or stop-gap signings who came in to land their slice of the glory on cup final day, with the Hearts career of every player involved spanning at last three seasons. Of the 12 men to appear in the final, nine – McPherson (364 over two spells), Fulton (239), Cameron (189), Flögel (164), Rousset (164), Ritchie (162), Adam (130), Naysmith (120) and Weir (117) – made more than 100 appearances for the Tynecastle club. For context, several notable players from more recent Scottish Cup-winning Hearts sides, such as Takis Fyssas, Roman Bednar, Bruno Aguiar, Ryan McGowan, Danny Grainger and Stephen Elliott, made less than 75 appearances for the club. McCann (96), Hamilton (94) and Salvatori (73) were the only three to appear in the 1998 final who didn't make at least 100 appearances for Hearts in that period, although nobody could doubt the contribution any of this trio made to the cause. Indeed, McCann formed such a strong bond with the club in his initial two-and-a-half years at Tynecastle that he returned in 2006 for a second spell and was able to take himself over the 100-appearance landmark to 127. "That 97/98 season at Hearts was one of the happiest times of my career," says McCann. "We bonded so well as a group, we were so tight. We didn't overly socialise but we just enjoyed each other's company. Training was ferocious, absolutely ferocious. We would go at it hammer and tongs and I don't know how many times we came together as a group, having punch-ups and grabs at each other, and booting each other. It was so competitive and that was a big part of why we were so good; we built up such a rapport. The team was so strong and steady that there was a good consistency of selection, but the guys that came in and played bits and bobs, like Grant Murray and Davie Murie, all played their part. The beauty of that squad was that even guys who were around the squad but weren't starting or weren't even getting chosen were still totally with us. They felt part of it because they were included in everything we did. That's really hard to do in a team, to make sure everyone feels a part of it. When we eventually won the cup, everybody enjoyed it as if they were part of it, and they certainly were."

The inclusive aspect of Hearts' squad remains a source of satisfaction for Locke. "I felt it was important that even when players weren't involved in the matchday squad, they still always went to the games," says Locke. "That was something I prided myself on as the captain. I wanted to keep everyone together and involved. The spirit we had right throughout the club was great. We had a great management team – including guys like Peter Houston, Alan Rae and Bert Logan, who were all brilliant – and there wasn't one bad egg in the place. It was a really close-knit group and I feel that togetherness played a huge part in the success we had."

Leadership was another key trait in the Hearts dressing-room. Of those prominently involved in the 1997/98 squad, Weir, Naysmith, Cameron, McCann, Locke, Robertson, Murray and Flögel all went on to become managers, while Fulton, McPherson, Pointon and Ritchie (at Dundee United) all wore the captain's armband at some point in their careers. This collective strength of character manifested itself in a resilient, strong-willed group, able to step up and challenge the Old Firm. "There were different types of characters in the dressing-room and I think that was another reason we were successful," says Locke. "We had a lot of loud characters and a lot of quieter characters but everybody had a say. It was just a collective team effort. Colin Cameron used to just fucking moan about everything, but he was good in the dressing-room. Neil McCann was a fiery wee character who wasn't shy in voicing his opinion. Davie Weir was a different type because he was calm and relaxed but he would always speak up if he needed to say something. Dave McPherson and Gilles were quite quiet but even they had their moments. Robbo was a character anyway just because of what he'd done for the club. He was brilliant in the dressing-room; when he spoke everybody listened. Neil Pointon was a character and a half as well. The older guys were great with the younger lads. They didn't look at us as stupid wee boys and I think that was why we got on so well. They saw us as good team-mates and good players."

This was epitomised by the fact Murie recalls rooming with McPherson, who was almost 13 years his senior. No matter their age, background or nationality, everyone was in it together. "One of the most important things in that Hearts team was that no player acted like they were better than any of the other guys at the club," says Cameron. "We were all there to try and take the club forward and that showed in the team spirit we had."

McPherson was the oldest outfield player in the cup-winning squad and the 34-year-old felt the balance between youth and experience, Scots and foreigners was just right. "I played in some good Hearts squads but there was a really good blend in that 98 team," he says. "It was a very close-knit team and it always helps make a successful team when you get on well off the pitch as well as on it. We had a lot of good times together."

On the pitch and off it, Hearts were united. "The main thing was that we worked as a unit," says Flögel. "We had lots of fantastic individuals but the most important thing was that they were all team players. It was all about the team, never about any individual. There was a unity I never had before. It was like a family group who were pulling together. That was really strong the year we won the cup and that's what you saw in the final when we all ran our socks off and fought for each other. There were so many good players but the strength of that team was in the collective. I couldn't pick one standout player in that team. For me, all those players were tremendous. They were also great guys who I enjoyed being with away from the football. It was a proper team; a proper unit."

The scorer of their most treasured goal has the final word on what made Hearts' 1997/98 squad so special. "Jim and Billy built up a team of guys who were not at Hearts to show off," says Adam. "They built a team of hard workers, strong characters and passionate people; this is something you have to speak about. There was a lot of quality in the team, but the success we had was because there were only great people in this squad, all working hard together to win something. This was the key to the success: it was a team effort."

Legacy

*"The hardest thing for a club is
to keep a good team together"*

In the heady days and weeks following the 1998 Scottish Cup triumph, everything seemed possible for Hearts. As is generally the way when a team has success, attention – particularly in the media – turned to what the Tynecastle club could achieve next. "There's more to come" and "You ain't seen nothing yet" were among the headlines accompanying chairman Leslie Deans' quotes on the back pages of newspapers the Monday after the landmark victory over Rangers at Celtic Park. "There is no danger of us resting on our laurels," said Deans. "The next step is to take the club up another gear. Saturday's win will act as a springboard – I am sure of it."

On the same day, the headline on pundit Charlie Nicholas's column in the Daily Record was "Jefferies can be the new Fergie", with the former Celtic and Scotland striker suggesting that Hearts manager Jim Jefferies could go on and emulate the type of success the great Alex Ferguson had achieved in charge of Aberdeen more than a decade previously when winning three league titles, four Scottish Cups and a League Cup, as well as the 1983 European Cup Winners' Cup and the European Super Cup. "I see Hearts as potential champions next season because Rangers are in transition, while Celtic will have to bring in a new coach after their mishandling of the Wim Jansen affair," said Nicholas, referring to the fact Jansen had quit as Celtic manager almost immediately after winning the 1997/98 title. The Dutchman would be replaced for the 1998/99 campaign by Slovakian Jozef Venglos. There was a general feeling throughout Scottish football, and particularly within Tynecastle, that a real opportunity beckoned for Hearts – with all of their key players retained and highly-regarded defenders Steven Pressley and Rab McKinnon being added to the mix – to step up and join the Old Firm as the country's leading lights on a consistent basis. In the June 1998 edition of The Jambo magazine – an official

Hearts publication – chief executive Chris Robinson signed off his column, which reflected on the club's progress under he and Deans to that point, with the words: "That's the story so far. There is, I'm sure, much more to come."

Unfortunately, there wasn't. "It was a shame we couldn't grow a bit further as a team," says winger Neil McCann. "I absolutely believed we had more to do as a team. I wanted to go and win the league with Hearts. When we came back for the new season, we played Rangers, who had just spent a fortune under Dick Advocaat, and we beat them at Tynecastle. I think everyone thought 'my God, Hearts are serious'. We did that night as well. We thought we could go on and win the league."

Having beaten Advocaat's side 2-1 in the opening match of the 1998/99 campaign with a team featuring nine of the eleven that started the final less than three months previously – Gary Locke and Jim Hamilton replaced injured pair Dave McPherson and Colin Cameron – Hearts went on to rack up seven points from their opening three matches and sat top of the league following a 2-0 home win over Aberdeen in which Stephen Fulton and new defender Pressley both scored within the opening 11 minutes. "On the back of the cup win, there was obviously high expectations," says Pressley, who joined from Dundee United, aged 24, just a matter of weeks after the Scottish Cup triumph. "There was a real positive feeling around the club. They were drawing big crowds home and away, and the group had played together for a couple of years and had forged really strong relationships. When I arrived, you could see why the club was on an upward curve at that time."

Things swiftly took a turn for the worse for Jefferies' Hearts, however. "We certainly felt that with the team we had, progress was going to happen, but the following season I hardly played and players started moving on because of the success we had," says midfielder Cameron, summarising why things went awry for Hearts after the cup success. "That's the problem, there's always bigger fish out there looking to recruit the best players."

Cameron, who was still plagued by the pelvic problem that afflicted him in the closing months of the 1997/98 campaign, didn't kick a single competitive ball until 20th February 1999. By that point, incredibly, Hearts were second-bottom of the league, had been thrashed 3-0 by St Johnstone in the League Cup semi-final and had put up a meek defence of the Scottish Cup as they lost 3-1 at Motherwell in the third round. "The team that won the cup started to disintegrate a wee bit," says assistant manager Billy Brown. In addition to being without Cameron for the majority of the season, McCann, who had broken his leg in the away leg of the Cup Winners' Cup tie against Real Mallorca at the start of October, was sold to Rangers in December 1998 after just one game back in action following his injury. With Jefferies' two main attacking sparks effectively snuffed out in the first half of the season, the remainder of the team struggled badly to pick up the slack. The sale of David Weir to Everton in February did little to ease the situation, while midfield stabiliser Stefano Salvatori had lost his form and fallen from prominence. Younger players like Locke, Paul Ritchie and Gary Naysmith suddenly didn't look as assured while it didn't help that new recruits such as Pressley, McKinnon, Juanjo, Gary McSwegan and Leigh Jenkinson failed, initially at least, to have the desired impact. "I actually couldn't put my finger on why Hearts struggled that season," says Pressley, who went on to captain Hearts to Scottish Cup glory in 2006. "I can only talk about myself and, in those opening months of the season when we struggled, I struggled myself. I played at right-back and my performances weren't of a high enough level. I was a new player into the squad and I wasn't performing well enough, so that may have been a factor but beyond that, it would be difficult for me to give a specific reason for why the team struggled. I certainly didn't sense any obvious issue in the dressing room, unless there were perhaps certain players who in their own minds were looking to moving on to pastures new. It certainly wasn't something I detected though. All I picked up in my early months at Hearts was that it was a tight group with good quality, and I could see why they had enjoyed success previously. I actually don't know why we struggled."

After slipping to the bottom of the league in March 1999, Hearts eventually rallied to get themselves safe and up to sixth place in the ten-team Premier Division, with fit-again Cameron and McSwegan, who scored eight goals in the last nine games, leading the charge. By the end of the season, McCann, Weir, Hamilton and Dave McPherson had departed the club, while Salvatori was out of the picture and heading for the exit door. Jefferies' side regained their poise in 1999/2000 to finish third once more but the sense of buoyancy and hope generated in 1998 had evaporated, and it felt like the club was veering off course. An ill-advised deal struck by chief executive Robinson with Scottish Media Group late in 1999 – against the wishes of Deans, who stepped down as chairman as a matter of principle – prompted Hearts to push the boat out for relatively high-profile players such as Fitzroy Simpson, Gordan Petric, Robert Tomaschek and Antti Niemi midway through the 1999/2000 campaign but, ultimately, this splurge led the club into a position whereby they were living way above their means. As Hearts drifted into financial difficulty and friction developed between Jefferies and Robinson, the manager resigned in November 2000, proud of his accomplishments in charge of the club of his heart but also lamenting a missed opportunity. "Without a doubt, there's a big regret that we didn't really build on the success we had in 97/98," he says. "It all sort of went a bit flat for us after the cup win. A lot was made about me being the first Hearts manager to win a trophy in 36 years and I said at the time I also wanted to be the next manager who won a trophy after that. We ran Celtic and Rangers close in the league in 98 and we hoped we could kick on from there. I think initially everybody hoped we could all stay together and improve the squad again, but when the likes of Neil and David moved on, I think it had an unsettling effect on other players who maybe started thinking about moving on themselves. When you're missing Cameron through injury and you lose players of the quality of McCann and Weir from your team, and another mainstay like Salvatori loses his way, it's always going to become difficult. It was a big problem for us that year. A lot of them lost their way a wee bit and I think some of them who got new, improved contracts maybe subconsciously got a wee bit complacent, which is always a worry. It was a mixture of a few things, but it was a big regret that we couldn't go on and back up what we did in 1998. There was a lot in the press after the cup final about how we could go on and do great things, and if we'd have kept that squad together, there's no doubt we'd have done that. But you're always going to be a target for other clubs when you've got good players. It's part and parcel of building a successful team when you're not one of the biggest clubs."

On 12th May 2002, almost four years on from the 1998 glory day, the last of the cup-winning heroes departed Hearts as Stephane Adam, Stephen Fulton and Thomas Flögel all made their final appearances for the club in a 3-2 home defeat by Livingston. While this trio were all proud of their own lengthy stints at Tynecastle, there lingers a sense of disappointment at what might have been. "I was hoping there was going to be more days like the 98 cup win to come but obviously that was as good as it got for that team," laments Fulton. "We were quite a young team and I felt we could have had a lot of good years ahead of us as a group. But once Neil McCann, Davie Weir, Gary Naysmith, Paul Ritchie and wee Mickey had all moved on within a couple of years of the final, that was five guaranteed starters we'd lost who all went on to play for Scotland. You always hear people talking about how Hibs would have won the league if they'd kept hold of Scott Brown and all those boys (from Tony Mowbray's team in the mid-Noughties). Well, I think if we'd have kept our team together we wouldn't have been far away."

Flögel is philosophical about the break-up of such an impressive Hearts side. "The hardest thing for a club is to keep a good team together," says the Austrian. "I have found that out as a coach. As soon as players are playing well, there will be other bigger clubs watching them. The time is gone when you can keep a team together for several years. With Hearts, it just wasn't possible because there were so many good young players who were of interest to other clubs in Scotland and England. Some players started to find new clubs to write new chapters in their story but that happens when teams are successful; that's just the way it goes. Players want to climb up to play at a higher level and earn more money. I did it myself when I moved from Austria Vienna to Hearts."

Broadcaster and Hearts supporter Mark Donaldson believes Hearts perhaps lacked the know-how to capitalise on the strong position they had got themselves into in the summer of 1998. "It was a step into the unknown for Hearts to win something," he says. "It was something they always hoped for, but I'm not sure Hearts actually knew what to do in terms of how to build on the success they had. They didn't really seem to know how to kick on. I think they got caught out a little bit. They had such a good side but rather than attracting new players, maybe they could have done more to keep what they had. Having said that, when the Old Firm or teams from England come calling, it's very hard for any player to turn that down. You take Mickey Cameron, Neil McCann and David Weir out of the team, that's the heartbeat of the team. Ultimately, certain circumstances combined to split that team up, which can happen in football."

While it is reasonable to analyse why Hearts didn't hit the heights they had hoped in the aftermath of the 1998 triumph, the positive aspects of the journey they embarked on under Jefferies will always override any notion that things could have been even better. Winning the Scottish Cup was particularly significant on three levels: the historic importance of banishing 36 years without a trophy and laying to rest the demons of the league title capitulation in 1986; the fact it served as the first of three Scottish Cup wins in the space of 14 years; and also simply the exhilarating effect it had on so many people. "I'm lucky because I'm a bit younger but I have a lot of friends who support Hearts and are a lot older and lived through 1986 and all the other disappointments and hadn't seen them win anything," says sports journalist and Hearts supporter Ewan Murray. "I thought it was brilliant for them that the hoodoo was gone; my generation's been quite lucky because we've seen them win three Scottish Cups and a team that, despite the odd bump in the road, has been relatively successful in the context of Hearts' history. It's always hard to place these things in context but 1998 felt far more significant than the 2006 Scottish Cup win (when Second Division Gretna were defeated on penalties in the final). Was it more significant than 2012 (when Hearts beat Hibs 5-1 in the final)? It was in a lot of ways because I think the reality was most people expected Hearts to win that final whereas in 1998 – given the history – you had no right to expect Hearts to win anything. The fact they'd had such a great season and were such an entertaining team, I thought it was massively significant."

Captain Locke believes the 1998 Scottish Cup victory banished the burden of history and helped pave the way for the team's subsequent triumphs in the competition in 2006 and 2012. "We had a fanzine called Always The Bridesmaid because we never won anything, so it was great to be the first Hearts team to win a trophy in such a long time and get the monkey off the club's back," he says. "I think it was the catalyst for the club to go on and win the cup again in 2006 and 2012. Us winning it in 98 probably meant there was less pressure on the lads in 2006. I don't think we necessarily felt the pressure so much in 98 because we felt after the previous two finals that we were getting closer to winning it, but once we eventually won it I think it just lifted the cloud that used to hang over the club, especially after 1986. I think Hearts fans were able to think 'it doesn't matter what happens from now on, I've seen them lift a cup'. That's certainly how I felt. It was incredible. The manager used to sell the club to players by telling them that if they could help the club win a trophy they'd become a hero and that these fans would never forget it, and that's certainly been the case. Look at the reunion we had in 2018; 20-odd years on the boys still get treated like Gods – they can't believe it."

The triumphant team of 98 marked the 20th anniversary of their success alongside more than 800 supporters at a bumper event at Edinburgh International Conference Centre in May 2018. The vibe that night confirmed that the sense of brotherhood created at Tynecastle in the mid-to-late 1990s remains very much intact more than two decades on. "Whenever we meet up for reunions and things like that, we all still have a bond," says defender McPherson. "That's the beauty of being part of a successful football team; even if you've not seen each other for years, when you get back together, it takes just two seconds for everyone to click again. I'd actually like to meet up more with those guys again; I'd like us to keep in touch more often. At a time like this (during the coronavirus pandemic of 2020) I think you appreciate how important it is to have occasions like reunions, rather than just forgetting about things. I keep saying to Gary Locke that I'd like the club to do something, perhaps organise a golf day once a year or something like that, to get everyone together. It's difficult because some of the boys are abroad but I feel it's important to keep the memories alive. I think the supporters would appreciate that as well."

The overriding legacy of Hearts' 1998 Scottish Cup triumph is the sheer joy it gave so many people, leaving memories that will last a lifetime for all involved. "When I go to a Hearts game, so many people still come up to me and want to talk about 98, whether it's when I'm arriving at the stadium, at half-time, or in the hospitality at full-time," says Jefferies. "So many people have told me we gave them the greatest day of their life. A lot of them have seen Hearts win the cup three times but to beat Rangers in Glasgow, in a cup final, was just the greatest day of many of their lives. When you look at the Scottish Cups Hearts have won and see that they've beaten Hibs 5-1 in a final, you would automatically think that would be the best one for most people because it's the city rivals and all that. But so many people say 98 was better because of the years without the cup, the feeling of winning in Glasgow against a top, top side in such a tight, tense match. Let's re-member that Hibs team in 2012 had struggled to avoid relegation and hadn't won the cup for about 200 years. Billy was on their coaching staff (as assistant to Pat Fenlon) at the time and even he would admit it was the poorest Hibs side to get to a final for a long time."

Donaldson is certainly in no doubt about where the 1998 triumph stands in the pecking order of Hearts' Scottish Cup wins. "I can't speak for other Hearts fans, but if a 5-1 win over Hibs in a Scottish Cup final – which was wonderful – doesn't eclipse what happened in 1998, there is nothing that can happen for Hearts that will eclipse 1998 for me before I leave this planet," says the Hearts-supporting broadcaster from Penicuik. "For me personally, it was the best weekend ever."

Memories of arguably Hearts' most celebrated victory of all time so often serve as a source of comfort for those who experienced the joy of events at Celtic Park on 16th May 1998. "When I feel down, it always gives me a boost to think about what happened with Hearts," says Flögel. "It makes me happy. Whenever we meet up, there is always good commitment from the boys and they are all happy and friendly when we meet up. It is fantastic to be a part of this unit and to be part of the history of Hearts."

The day the Scottish Cup returned to Gorgie for the first time in 42 years will be cherished forever by every Hearts-minded person present. "I said to Jim Jefferies at the time, take this in and savour it all because there'll come a time when you're an old man and you'll be sitting with a coffee thinking back to the pleasure you gave hundreds of thousands of people in the city," says Deans. "And sure enough, that is what we are doing now as we reflect on what became."

Stefano Salvatori

*"At AC Milan we referred to him as
'Guerrero Indio' – the Indian Warrior"*

On the evening of Sunday 20th May 2018, 20 years and four days on from the greatest day of Stefano Salvatori's football career, his bereaved wife stepped up to deliver the most courageous performance of her life at the Edinburgh International Conference Centre on Morrison Street. "When I got up to do that speech, the sensation in the room was unreal," says Gillian Salvatori, recalling the moving moments when she brought tears to the eyes of her husband's former team-mates and more than 800 Hearts supporters who had gathered to celebrate the 20th anniversary of the 1998 Scottish Cup triumph, of which the Italian midfielder had played a significant part. "I couldn't finish a sentence without there being a chant of 'Salvatori'. I got interrupted at the end of every sentence with applause and people singing his name. A few of his team-mates had come up to me earlier in the night and said 'I heard you're doing a speech, do you want me to stand up there with you?' because they didn't want me doing it on my own. I said 'no, it's fine, I can do it'. I'd given speeches before and I'd spoken at Stef's funeral, which was incredibly difficult. I was actually holding it together pretty well because I was absolutely determined to get my message across and explain to everyone how much Hearts and Scotland had meant to Stef and thank everyone on his behalf for making him feel so welcome in Edinburgh over the years. About half-way through, Gary Locke came up and put his arm around me but that didn't help because he was sobbing more than I was. It was such a kind and unexpected gesture; it was very moving."

Given the tragic circumstances, Mrs Salvatori could easily have been forgiven had she politely declined the invite from Hearts to attend this landmark reunion and instead chosen to remain at home in Brisbane, Australia, with her two young children, Remo and Lucia, who had lost their beloved father less than seven months previously. Stefano Salvatori passed away, aged just 49, on 1st November

2017 at the end of a torturous – and largely private – three-year battle with cancer, which was metastatic by the time it was detected in August 2014. This was some 17 months after his last appearance in Scotland, when he was the Hearts legend chosen to parade the League Cup trophy on the Hampden pitch prior to the final against St Mirren in March 2013. For context, John Robertson – the club's record league goal-scorer – was the man who performed this role before Hearts' Scottish Cup final victory over Hibs ten months previously. Only players of substance tend to get the gig.

Gillian had learned through the course of the six-and-a-half special years she spent with Stefano that – in addition to being a loving partner and doting father – he was a proud Scottish Cup-winning former Hearts player who was fondly regarded in Edinburgh, the city in which they had met after the Italian started flirting with her in a George Street nightspot in May 2011. Stefano had been back living in Scotland for a short time at that point, working as an agent and exploring the possibility of landing himself a technical director role within Scottish football, while Gillian had completed her specialist training at Edinburgh's Sick Kids Hospital and was working as a paediatrician. When given the opportunity to return to the Scottish capital just a matter of months after her husband's death, Gillian was in no doubt that – as difficult as it would be, emotionally and logistically – she simply had to make the pilgrimage to represent and honour him. It proved a cathartic experience amid her ongoing grief. "I'll never be able to describe what it was like that night," says Gillian, of an evening in which she had everyone present watching on in thrall and sheer admiration. "I knew I wanted to make a speech and I knew that I'd meet his team-mates. I'd only previously met Gary Locke and Jim Jefferies from when we were living in Scotland. I hadn't met any of the other guys or their wives because I wasn't on the scene when Stef played for Hearts. I was just blown away by how kind and caring all his team-mates and coaches were towards me. They were just such gentlemen, really genuine with their sentiments. Almost all of them made time to come up to me individually and chat to me and give me their anecdotes about Stef. There were so many stories I hadn't heard before, so I was really touched by that. It was really amazing to be able to have contact with the Hearts players because I feel I've got a duty to my kids to preserve those relationships so that when Remo and Lucia are old enough they can go and meet all of those guys themselves and hear all the stories directly. Nothing is ever going to make it okay that Stef isn't here and won't see the kids grow up, but moments like that night certainly help. I felt love and support from everyone in the room."

Just six months later, in November 2018, Gillian was back in Edinburgh once again as the entire 1998 Scottish Cup-winning squad was inducted to Hearts' Hall of Fame; proof – not that it was needed – that her beloved husband's place in the Tynecastle club's folklore will be secure forever. "Being back in Edinburgh is always somewhat comforting because that's where we met and we had a wonderful life there together before we moved out to Australia (in 2012)," she says. "I know Edinburgh was a special place for Stef. On the night we first met, he was quite coy about his occupation but he mentioned that he used to play for Hearts and at that stage, even though I'd been living in Edinburgh for over a year, I didn't know who or what Hearts were. I'm embarrassed to say that because I very much know who Hearts are now, and I certainly understand what they mean to him after I went to Edinburgh for those two events."

Although he was the player in the cup final squad who made the fewest appearances – 73 in a spell at Hearts that lasted almost three years – Salvatori's contribution cannot be downplayed. After adapting to Scottish football in his first season at the club following his arrival in September 1996, the long-haired Italian was an unheralded but hugely effective performer throughout Hearts' 1997/98 campaign; he was particularly impressive in the cup final, on a day when Jefferies needed his destructive players to come to the fore. "There are loads of players who like the limelight and are not so happy to do the dirty work – just sitting in, tackling and giving the ball to a better football player than them – but Salvatori never minded that," says assistant manager Billy Brown. "He was happy to be a sitter and let Colin Cameron and Steve Fulton go and express themselves. He fitted into our team really well; he was a team player. I couldn't think any more highly of him, I have to say. The likes of Cameron, Stephane Adam and Neil McCann got all the praise but Salvatori was as good and as big an influence in that team as any of them. In the final, he was as good as any player on the pitch, as good as any player."

Salvatori was 30 at the time of the cup final triumph and much of his afternoon's work involved attempting to subdue his fellow Italian Rino Gattuso, a Rangers midfielder ten years his junior. The Hearts player performed this task impressively, getting the better of a young man who would go on to spend a decade at the base of AC Milan's midfield; this was something Salvatori had genuine aspirations of accomplishing himself when he embarked on his own professional career in the mid-to-late 1980s following a humbling childhood in Rome. Salvatori was born at the end of 1967 and raised by his working-class parents, Remo and Lucia, as the eldest of three children in Albuccione, a deprived suburb to the north-east of Italy's capital city. "I got to know Stefano's family and they are very much like my family," says Marco Simone, a close friend and former AC Milan team-mate of Salvatori's. "We didn't come from rich families and our parents worked hard so this made him very down to earth." Salvatori last visited his childhood home in Albuccione with his wife in 2013. "People in the area who knew him were proud of what he went on to achieve as a footballer," says Gillian. "When we went back to visit his mum, people were hanging out the window waving at him even though they hadn't seen him for years. Stef was proud of where he came from but also sad about it because the area had deteriorated a lot since he was a kid growing up there and he knew life didn't have to be like that."

Salvatori started playing football on the streets of Albuccione and it soon became clear he had a talent. He impressed with San Basilio Lazio, a club in his local area, in his early teens and got the chance, in 1983, to join the academy of AS Lodigiani, who were a lower-league club in eastern Rome renowned for nurturing and promoting young players. Andrea Silenzi, Francesco Totti and Luigi Apolloni were among the most famous names to emerge from Lodigiani, and Salvatori benefitted from its reputation as a fertile breeding ground for quality footballers when he was spotted by a visiting scout from AC Milan in 1985 and given the chance to sign for the Italian giants. Aged 17, Salvatori left his family behind and headed north, moving into the club's on-site guest house at their prestigious Milanello training base, 30 miles north-west of Milan. He spent two years in Milan's academy, the second of which was spent under the guidance of Fabio Capello, a youth-team coach at the time. In the 1987/88 season, he went on loan to Bergamo-based Serie C side Virescit Boccaleone, where he first met an 18-year-old Simone, who was on loan from Serie A side Como. "Stefano and I had two different journeys through our junior careers, but we both went on loan to Virescit Boccaleone and that's where we met," says Simone. "We didn't know each other before, but we quickly forged a friendship where we were more like brothers so we decided to live together in the same apartment. We grew together, we started our professional careers together. What I can say about Stefano is only positive. His generosity was incredible. I met many people in the soccer world and Stefano is the person and player who demonstrated the most kindness as a man."

Salvatori and Simone returned to their respective parent clubs in the summer of 1988, but their separation would be only temporary. Salvatori spent a short period of the 1988/89 campaign on loan at Serie B side Parma before moving to Fiorentina, where manager Sven-Goran Eriksson gave him his Serie A debut, aged 20, as an 82nd-minute substitute in a 3-2 home win over Pescara in December 1988. Team-mates that day included fellow Milan loanee Stefano Borgonovo, 25-year-old Brazil internationalist Dunga and a 21-year-old Roberto Baggio. Salvatori was sent off for two bookable offences in his first Fiorentina start – a 2-1 defeat at Hellas Verona on the last day of 1988 – but the Italian soon became a regular in Eriksson's midfield, starting 22 games in total as La Viola finished seventh in Serie A and qualified for the UEFA Cup. His impressive campaign in Florence meant he got the chance to stake a claim for a place in Arrigo Sacchi's Milan side when he returned to his parent club for the start of the 1989/90 season. At this point, he was reunited with attacker Simone, who joined Milan in summer 1989 following Como's relegation from Serie A. Aged 21, Salvatori made his Milan debut as an extra-time substitute in a Coppa Italia match away to Parma in August 1989; his first Serie A appearance for Rossoneri came two weeks later when he went on as an 82nd-minute replacement for, ironically, Simone in a 1-0 win away to Atalanta. Team-mates that Wednesday evening in Bergamo included Paolo Maldini, Franco Baresi and Carlo Ancelotti, who scored the game's only goal. Other players at Milan that season included Demetrio Albertini, Alessandro Costacurta, Roberto Donadoni and the Dutch trio of Marco Van Basten, Frank Rijkaard and Ruud Gullit. Young Salvatori held his own in esteemed company. "I was at Milan for a lot longer than Stefano, but he spent a good amount of time there," says Simone, who made 259 appearances across his two spells with the Rossoneri. "To be in that historic group of Milan players demonstrated that he had great qualities. When you were chosen to play for the first team in Milan at that time, it meant you were a great player because it wasn't a given that you would be chosen for the first team just because you started your career with them. Competing alongside players like Ancelotti and Rijkaard, he was among world leaders in that midfielder position."

In what would prove to be Salvatori's only full season in Milan's first team, the

Rossoneri finished runners-up to Diego Maradona-inspired Napoli in Serie A, won the European Cup, and also claimed the European Super Cup. In addition to featuring regularly for Italy Under-21s – he won 13 caps at that level in total – Salvatori made 19 competitive appearances, including 12 starts, for Milan in the 1989/90 campaign. He played the full 90 minutes in the first leg of the Super Cup away to Barcelona and appeared in one match on the European Cup run: as a substitute in the first leg of the quarter-final away to Belgian club Mechelen. "On the field, he was the exact copy of what he was in his life: he was generous athletically," says Simone. "At AC Milan and even after he left, we used to refer to him as 'Guerrero Indio' (the Indian Warrior) because, with his Mohican hairstyle and aquiline nose, he looked like an Apache Indian and he was a warrior on the field. He was like a previous version of Gattuso because he played with that same grit and determination and that need to snatch the ball off the opponent. He had a very intelligent strategy in his game and his technique was great. He was a great player who even in today's world of quick and technically strong soccer, would have played with ease. Outside of the field, he was a joker. We were practically together 24/7 when we were team-mates and he always joked around. He loved to go shopping, he was very much into his fashion and paid a lot of attention not only to his hair but to following the latest fashion trends. He was also very attentive to his skin regime, using various creams like women do. He was very particular about his look."

Unlike Simone, who was an unused substitute, Salvatori didn't make the squad for the 1990 European Cup final in Vienna but the midfielder, with short hair at the time and sporting a sharp black club suit, enjoyed the celebrations on the pitch and in the dressing-room after Rijkaard's goal secured a 1-0 win over Benfica. Indeed, there is a now-poignant photo of Salvatori and Borgonovo sitting together on the plane home from Austria proudly posing with the European Cup. Tragically, both men – who played together for Milan and Fiorentina – lost their lives at the age of 49, with Borgonovo succumbing to amyotrophic lateral sclerosis, a form of motor neurone disease, in June 2013. Salvatori played in his stricken friend's charity match between Fiorentina and Milan at Stadio Artemio Franchi in October 2008 and was photographed tenderly kissing Borgonovo on the head as Baggio pushed him past all his former team-mates in a wheelchair. "The love and kindness on Stef's face at that moment was so beautiful," says Gillian. "Stef was very close to him and visited him when he was really sick; I know that affected Stef a lot."

Salvatori appeared in four Coppa Italia games at the start of the 1990/91 campaign before his Milan career came to an end and he followed Borgonovo back to Fiorentina on a permanent transfer in December 1990. "Milan were possibly the best team in the world when Stefano was there," says Pasquale Bruno, who played against the Rossoneri for Juventus at the time and would later become a team-mate and friend of Salvatori's at Hearts. "He was in a midfield with big players like Gullit, Rijkaard and Albertini so it was tough for him but he still managed to get some games."

Regular match action was easier to come by in Florence where Salvatori made 50 appearances – 48 as a starter – in an 18-month stint with La Viola, who added Argentine striker Gabriel Batistuta to their ranks in this period. He dropped out of the top flight in the summer of 1992, aged 24, to sign for Ferrara-based Serie B side SPAL, where he suffered relegation at the end of his first season. After spending the 1993/94 campaign in Italy's third tier – where SPAL made the play-offs but failed to win promotion – Salvatori was back in Serie B the following campaign when Atalanta signed him in 1994. In his first season, he helped the Bergamo club up into Serie A as they finished fourth in the second tier. His first campaign back in the top-flight following a three-year absence proved to be his last, however. Salvatori made 27 appearances in all competitions – 11 as a starter – as his team finished two places above the relegation zone. His spell with Atalanta ended after he appeared as a second-half substitute in both legs of a 3-0 aggregate defeat by former club Fiorentina in the Coppa Italia final in May 1996. Two years down the line, Salvatori and one of La Viola's cup final goal heroes, Lorenzo Amoruso, would find themselves locking horns in another national cup final. In Scotland.

After leaving Atalanta, aged 28 and with his run at the top level of Italian football having lost momentum, Salvatori – who by this point had welcomed two daughters, Fabiola and Linda, into the world with his first wife, Monica – was open to a fresh challenge as he sought career reinvigoration. He would find it in Edinburgh. Bruno, whom Salvatori didn't previously know on a personal level, already had his feet under the Bar Roma table after joining Hearts the previous November. Salvatori's agent, Moreno Roggi, was aware that Bruno – the first of a mini-wave of Italians to arrive in Scottish football in the mid-to-late 1990s – was enjoying a new lease of life in Edinburgh and contacted the former Juventus and Torino defender to ask if he would recommend the free-agent midfield enforcer to Jefferies. "I spoke to Jim and said 'listen boss, there is a good midfielder available who played for AC Milan, Fiorentina and Atalanta and he is a tough lad'," recalls Bruno. Salvatori was invited to Edinburgh for a trial at the end of August 1996, and the Hearts manager immediately liked what he saw and offered him a short-term contract. "I was very impressed with Stefano from day one and knew he could do a good job for us," says Jefferies. "He was a powerful player."

Barely able to speak a word of English at this point, Salvatori had something of a baptism of fire in his first few weeks at Hearts. After making his debut as a late substitute in a 2-1 midweek defeat away to Dunfermline Athletic in early September, the combative midfielder's first start came in the infamous 3-0 defeat away to Rangers when four Hearts players were sent off. Salvatori was yellow-carded after just 21 minutes of that match but, unlike team-mates Bruno, David Weir, Neil Pointon and Paul Ritchie, he managed to avoid a red. For a few days, at least. The Coca-Cola Cup quarter-final at home to Celtic three days after the Ibrox debacle represented Salvatori's Tynecastle debut; he was sent off after an hour when he received a second yellow card for tripping his countryman, Paolo Di Canio, before Hearts went on to win the tie 1-0 after extra-time. Salvatori certainly wasn't a hatchet-man – he had too much quality on the ball to be considered in this way – but the demands of the position he played meant he had to be willing to put the boot in. His robustness on the field, allied to his natural Italian passion and will to win, meant there were moments when others would feel his force. Indeed, his own team-mates weren't immune. "He trained the way he played," smiles Brown.

"He was aggressive and he never liked to get beat. He wanted to train hard and there were one or two wee flare-ups, I've got to say, but nothing that couldn't be handled."

Fulton recalls being on the receiving end. "In what must have been his first week in training, Salvatori hurt me with a tackle, and it was bang out of order," the midfielder laughs. "I spent the next few weeks in training trying to get him back, but I wasn't as good at kicking people as he was." Cameron has a similar tale. "I remember in one of his first training sessions, we were training round at Roseburn and me and him went for a ball," says the Fifer. "It was relatively low, I put my head down and he put his foot up and he burst my eye open. I've got blood pissing everywhere and I'm going mental, saying 'what are you doing, it's only training!', as you do in those situations, and Stefano's like 'sorry, sorry Colin'. I was going mental and I looked at Jim and Billy and the two of them were pissing themselves laughing. To make matters worse, they made me walk back to bloody Tynecastle on my own. That was one of my first recollections of meeting Stefano. After that we became very good team-mates. He was a good guy. You could take the piss out of him and he never took it the wrong way. He was a quality player who improved us as a team. His best attribute was breaking things up. We didn't have anybody better than him for that. It was all down to his knowledge and ability to read the game."

These qualities first became clear to Hearts fans in his fourth appearance, which brought a convincing 3-1 win away to Hibs on the last weekend of September 1996. The Tynecastle side were 3-0 up within 40 minutes after a Cameron double and a John Robertson goal, and Salvatori cruised through his first Edinburgh derby. By full-time his name was being chanted for the first – and certainly not the last – time by an appreciative travelling support. A few days later the Italian was rewarded with a three-year contract. "Stefano was always there to receive the ball off you," says left-back Pointon. "He had a great sense of positioning. Some people say players look good when they have time on the ball but good players create time on the ball and Stefano could do that; he was never flustered. He had that Italian style about him but when he did have to be aggressive, he certainly knew how to do it."

Three weeks later, Salvatori was Hearts' best performer despite going off injured in the 64th minute as they drew 2-2 at home to Celtic following a stoppage-time equaliser from Dave McPherson. "Stefano was a great player for Hearts," says McPherson. "He had a great engine on him and he was technically very good. He kept things simple. He'd harry players and win the ball for us. He was a great all-round player and a great guy. You could see why he'd been at a club like AC Milan."

Off the field, Salvatori spent his early days staying in Edinburgh's prestigious Caledonian Hotel – where Bruno and his family were living – as the midfielder waited for the right time to bring his own family over from Milan. Salvatori relied heavily on Bruno for guidance in his early weeks and months in Edinburgh as he – like most of the foreign players who arrived at Hearts in this period – adapted to his first professional venture away from his homeland. "I didn't speak English either so it was good for me to have someone from my nation at Hearts," says Bruno. "We were together in the Caledonian with our families and we spent a lot of time together. We talked all the time and had a lot of laughs together. He was a really nice boy who smiled all the time. Sometimes you find footballers who think they are God but Stefano was a very simple boy: nice, calm and friendly. Like me, he had a good relationship with everybody at Hearts. We liked a beer: Bar Roma and Indigo Yard. All the time we were in those places; we enjoyed it."

Bar Roma became like a home from home for Salvatori, who continued to visit the popular Italian restaurant in Edinburgh's west end on his regular returns to the city after he finished playing for Hearts. "When Stefano and Pasquale were in the team, Bar Roma just became like a Little Italy in the west end because they would bring their friends and families along," says Nadia Di Giorgio, a waitress at Bar Roma in the late 1990s and daughter to owners Mario and Beatrice Cugini. "Stefano became like a big brother to me. I remember at the time of my 21st (June 1997), I was dating a guy and Stefano turned up at my birthday party at Giuliano's restaurant in Leith and he was like 'what are you doing with this guy, my little sister should be doing a lot better than that'. He was like 'get rid of him'. Him and Pasquale were ripping me. That was the type of relationship we had. Pasquale was the louder one of the two; Stefano was actually quite shy at times. I'll be honest, there were a million women who wanted Stefano, and I remember feeling so embarrassed for him sometimes. He would always have the table next to the cash desk. That was the Hearts players' table, the one we called our VIP table. If he'd been out to Indigo Yard or wherever, he would come in and finish the night with us and you'd often get girls walking by, knocking on the windows. He'd smile and wave at them and I remember thinking how annoying it must be for him. He had this aura about him. When he came in, all the girls turned round. Bless him, I used to get a bit protective of him, and tell them to leave him alone. He was always a gentleman though."

Following the Celtic game in October 1996, Salvatori spent three-and-a-half months on the sidelines as he underwent hernia surgery. This meant he missed the Coca-Cola Cup final against Rangers. Following a frantic introduction to Scottish football in which he'd faced Celtic twice, Rangers and Hibs in his first five starts for the club, the break allowed him a chance to take stock and continue adapting to life in a new country. "Stefano tried hard to learn English," says McPherson. "He found it tough initially but his English got better. You could imagine him coming into a Scottish dressing-room with boys like Gary Locke, Gary Naysmith and John Robertson; not being able to understand the accents, he must have been mesmerised with the banter. Everybody appreciated Stefano. I spent many nights out with him in Italian restaurants in Edinburgh after matches. I always got on great with him, he was a great guy."

Salvatori's struggle with the local language was a source of amusement to friends and colleagues. "His English was dire, bless his heart," recalls Mrs Di Giorgio. "The odd word he'd come out with in broad Scots would have us creasing with laughter. We ended up teaching him bits of English, and how to say certain sentences correctly."

Salvatori always took the dressing-room ribbing in the good spirit it was intended. "He used to make us all laugh without actually knowing he was funny," says Fulton.

"Some of the stuff he came out with had us in stitches because he'd sometimes get his words mixed up. Even though he was probably the one that struggled with the language the most, he didn't keep himself to himself at all. He was always in amongst the boys."

Over time, Salvatori developed "a Scottish twang", according to his wife. "He had a very thick accent when he spoke English," smiles Gillian. "He didn't actually have any lessons until he came to Australia later in his life. He learned English on a football pitch, which is a real credit to him when you think about it."

As well as dealing with the language barrier, Salvatori also had to acclimatise to winter in Scotland. McCann recalls the Italian struggling with the freezing temperature in Aberdeen on a Monday night shortly after his return from injury in February 1997. "I remember at Pittodrie, we were wearing our yellow and black away kit and, this is not a word of a lie, Stefano had a t-shirt, a top and a waterproof jacket under his strip," laughs the winger. "You could see the collar of the jacket sticking out of the top of his strip. He was so cold and I was just thinking 'what a culture shock this is for him'. Another thing I remember about Stefano is the hairdryer. I think he was the only guy I ever played with who dried his hair after training. Most guys are straight out the shower and away home, but every day Stefano would dry his hair with the hairdryer. What a guy he was. I used to pick his brains and get him to tell me stories about his time at AC Milan. Some of his stories were so good. I know he was only a younger player at AC Milan but I just wanted to find out what it was like to play with Franco Baresi and guys like that. He was really calm about the place but he was also charismatic. He was an absolute winner: he would demand from us, and I loved that about him."

By the end of his first season in Scotland, Salvatori had settled nicely into the Hearts dressing-room. "He had real enthusiasm and passion about him and he was really well liked in the group," says defender Weir. "He was a lovely guy and a really good player as well. When we worked, we worked hard, but there was also a good element of fun in that dressing-room and Stefano was part of that. There was him and Bruno – the two Italians – and they were a bit different; they added their experience and their culture to the Scottishness of the team."

Humility was one of Salvatori's defining qualities throughout his life. "He was very quiet off the pitch," says Pointon. "He did his stuff on the pitch and in training but was usually straight home afterwards. I got to know him well and went to his flat a few times. He wasn't one for the trappings of the footballer lifestyle. He wasn't one for throwing himself into nights out with the lads and partying, he just loved his football and he loved life in Edinburgh."

Indeed, he enjoyed it so much that he started buying property in Scotland's capital city. "Stefano loved Edinburgh," stresses Mrs Di Giorgio. "He bought a few apartments here. He had one in Frederick Street that he lived in and one in the west end. When he was buying them he took me along to see what I thought of them and I helped him with the process of buying them."

Salvatori made an impression on everyone he crossed paths with, particularly star-struck Hearts fans. Kevin Daley, a boyhood Jambo in his early 20s at the time, worked in the Pizza Hut restaurant located beneath the Italian's flat on Frederick

Street. "He would pop in maybe once a week, sometimes with his family," recalls Daley, originally from Corstorphine. "Being a Hearts fan all my life, I would always rush to serve him at the counter and we would have a wee chat about the football. I remember one day I walked into Sainsbury's in Craigleith and I had my daughter with me who was about the same age as Stefano's daughter. Stefano recognised me from Pizza Hut, waved at me, said 'hi Kev, how you doing?' and walked over to me for a chat. For a Hearts player who had played at the level he had to walk over with his daughter and coo over my young daughter and talk to me, I just thought 'wow'; for me, that was superb. He was just a really nice, humble guy with no airs or graces."

With Salvatori's first season – as promising as it was – having been significantly disrupted by injury, it was in his second campaign at Hearts that he truly started to flourish in maroon. Throughout 1997/98, the Italian was a mainstay of the team, a bedrock at the base of a three-man midfield which also included the attack-minded Cameron and the cultured pass-master, Fulton. "As a player, it probably took a wee while for us to appreciate exactly what he was bringing to the team," says Fulton. "That often happens with a defensive midfielder because they don't always get the credit that the attacking players get. But he was the perfect foil for me and Mickey (Cameron), and he also protected the back four. He was very, very good at what he did and very good to play with." Cameron certainly felt the benefit of Salvatori's presence. "He was a great player, very intelligent," says the midfielder. "He could sniff out trouble a mile away. With him and Stevie Fulton, I was given a licence to go and try to be productive so the two of them played a big part in how I performed."

In a team loaded with attacking threats, Salvatori brought assurance, steel and protection. "He was a very important player in our team because he did all the dirty stuff," says Austrian team-mate Thomas Flögel. "He was so strong in tackling and he brought a different style of play to our team. He made our team stronger. With a player like him, you know you can always go forward to the goal." Gilles Rousset sums up Salvatori's role in the most simple terms. "He was the one who allowed the cavalry to go forward," says the French goalkeeper. "He was very important for keeping the balance of the team."

Jefferies certainly valued the nous he added to the side, with the manager selecting Salvatori in the vast majority of matches for which he was available in 1997/98. He started 29 of the 36 league games and came off the bench in three others as Hearts mounted a strong title bid before finishing third in the Premier Division. "When Cameron or Fulton went forward, Salvatori had the intelligence to hold the game up until they got back into position," says Jefferies. "If it was two against one he wouldn't dive in, he would just hold his ground. That was down to experience and cleverness. He kept himself so fit: he was a really good athlete, physically strong and difficult to get the ball off."

Salvatori's only goal of the season – and of his whole Hearts career – came when he fired a long-distance strike past Ian Westwater in a 3-2 win at Dunfermline Athletic just after Christmas. As much as he enjoyed this moment – running ecstatically towards the Hearts dugout to celebrate – Salvatori was generally content keeping a low profile. "He was a bit of an unsung hero," says captain Locke. "He just went about his business. He didn't bother about the limelight and getting the headlines but he was a massive part of the success we had that year."

Given the consistency of his performances throughout the campaign, Salvatori's starting place for the Scottish Cup final was never in doubt. "Stefano was huge for us, not only in winning the trophy but throughout that season," says McCann. "What a superb player he was. He didn't do anything fancy; he just broke things up. He didn't care about doing anything that was going to catch the eye but he allowed Mickey the freedom just to snap his anchor and go. He was really good about the dressing-room and very professional in terms of how he trained. He was a huge influence on our team."

The Italian had started three of the four earlier rounds – missing only the fourth-round tie against Albion Rovers, when he was rested – but the final was the one in which he truly excelled, casting himself as one of Hearts' best players on the day as they knocked Rangers out of their stride. "If you look at replays of the cup final, it's amazing the number of times he broke up moves, won the ball and kept it simple," says Jefferies. "He was outstanding."

Salvatori – whose parents had made a rare trip from Rome to Scotland to attend the final – loved every moment of the celebrations. He was one of the first on the scene to congratulate Adam after his goal; he delivered a memorable, impassioned television interview on the pitch afterwards with a Hearts scarf tied round his head; and then he retreated to the dressing-room, where he danced jubilantly in only his pants to the tune of Carnaval de Paris by Dario G. After the party at Tynecastle, he and some team-mates were joined by family and close friends as they brought the night to an end with wine, beer and pizza at Bar Roma. Despite being in the thick of the celebrations when the mighty AC Milan savoured European Cup glory eight years previously, this was the crowning moment of Salvatori's career: the first time he had played in a cup final victory and the first time he had experienced such unbridled joy after a match. Towards the end of a weekend of euphoria, Salvatori, who had gained revenge on Amoruso for his 1996 Coppa Italia final defeat, told newspaper journalists: "Saturday was the best day of my football life. I have also never tasted an atmosphere as good as that which has been in the streets of Edinburgh since we got back to Tynecastle with the cup. I'd really like to thank all the supporters personally for their fabulous backing and can promise them that we will be working even harder in the summer to try to give them more success as quickly as possible. After playing a part in such a triumph, I definitely want to stay at Hearts and will be telling Jim Jefferies that when we sit down in the near future. I still have one-and-a-half years to run on my contract, but I'd love to stay a further two years after that."

Unfortunately, this scenario failed to materialise. Like most Hearts players, Salvatori was unable to maintain his excellent form into the 1998/99 season and the Italian's Tynecastle career effectively shuddered to a halt a little over five months after the cup triumph when he was angered at being substituted at half-time of the Coca-Cola Cup semi-final against St Johnstone at Easter Road with the Perth side leading 2-0. "I remember we were going back to Tynecastle and I was at the back of the bus as usual," says Rousset, in a fit of giggles as he recounts the tale about his dear friend from the aftermath of a chastening 3-0 defeat in October 1998. "Stefano was sitting with me and he said 'I'm not happy because Jim subbed me, I'm going to see him to ask for an explanation'. This was right after the game. I said 'Stefano, no, don't go, I know the gaffer and this is not the right time to ask him the question'. He was adamant he was going and he went to the front of the bus. Ten seconds later, he was back and he said 'Gilles, he just told me to fuck off. He didn't speak to me, he just told me to fuck off'. I said 'Stefano, I told you'. He couldn't believe it. He was funny, he was just a really nice guy."

Salvatori didn't play again for three months and featured in only three more competitive matches – the last of which was a 2-0 home defeat by Aberdeen in February 1999 – before eventually leaving Hearts in September 1999 after friction developed between he and Jefferies. "Jim is one type of character, Stefano is absolutely a different type of character," says Mrs Di Giorgio, who knew both men well from their regular ventures to Bar Roma. "But even though they had their differences in that period, Stefano always had total respect for Jim." Reflecting on how things unravelled for Salvatori in his last full season at Hearts, Jefferies feels the Italian had simply run his course at the club and was starting to look elsewhere. "If you look at Stefano's career, he had quite a few clubs and he tended to only stay in one place for two or three years before he moved on," says the manager. "I remember Stefano told me he had the chance to go to China for big money. I didn't want him to go but it was getting towards the end of his contract and he was showing signs of wanting away. Even at training, you could see it was on his mind; he wasn't the same guy. I told him to go to China and suss it out. The funny thing was Stefano absolutely hated flying. He went to China and decided it wasn't for him but you could tell he was thinking about moving on. That would have been around the time of the semi-final against St Johnstone. He had a poor first half that night. It wouldn't have been intentional from Stefano – he was always committed – but I think he realised there was maybe something else out there for him and it probably subconsciously preyed on his mind. I could tell his mind was starting to go. That semi-final was typical of the way he had been playing pretty much since the cup final. He was no good to us in that frame of mind so we had to do something. It would have been nice to get another year or two out of him but he'd just won the cup and he was clearly thinking about trying something new. These things can happen in football. He was a terrific boy who did a fantastic job for us."

Salvatori left Hearts, aged 31, with 73 appearances to his name and having made a firm impression on those he played alongside. "To have played at the level he played at and with the type of person he was, it was a privilege to play with him," says defender Ritchie. "He was one of the main men in the engine room of that team; he was the one that held it all together. He also gave us a lot of laughs here and there. He was a wonderful human being."

Salvatori returned to Italy to sign for Serie B side Alzano Virescit, the third time in his career he had joined a club from Bergamo. It was there that he became close friends with Ross Aloisi, an Australian/Italian midfielder whom he had first got to know when Aloisi had a two-week trial at Hearts midway through the 1998/99 season. "When I left Grazer AK in Austria, I was supposed to be signing for Treviso, but then an agent contacted me and said Alzano wanted to sign me so I decided to go there because I knew Stefano from my trial at Hearts," says Aloisi. "He was basically the guy who drove me from my hotel to training during my time in Edinburgh and we got to know each other quite well even in that short time. We enjoyed each other's company. I spent most of my time at Alzano hanging out with Stefano. He had his family home in Milan and he also had an apartment in Bergamo where he would stay for part of the week. In Italy we would train at the time we played so we'd train at 2.30pm and then me and Stefano would go for an aperitif, usually non-alcoholic but because I'm Australian and beer is in our culture and Stefano had got used to drinking beer in Scotland we'd occasionally go for beers. Monday was always our day off so we'd meet up and go round a few restaurants and bars in Bergamo's old town, the Citta Alta. Stefano was well known in Bergamo from his time at Atalanta and I met quite a few people through him. He was massively into his fashion. I remember he asked me to bring him a pair of RM Williams boots back from Australia for him; he loved RM Williams (a leather-boot brand from Australia). He was basically the enforcer in our team. He could run and tackle and break things down; he was a beast. We played in midfield together. He was a no-nonsense footballer: he trained hard and played hard. In the end he had a fall-out with the coach, but a lot of players fell out with that coach. All he wanted was respect. Once he had a fallout and the respect wasn't there, he had to move on; he wasn't a person to mess about. Off the pitch and away from football, though, he was an absolute gentleman and loved by everyone. He really was a top guy."

Salvatori played out his career with Serie C sides AlbinoLeffe and Legnano before retiring in 2002, aged 34. He immediately took on a coaching role at Legnano, a club based to the north-west of Milan, and spent three years learning his trade there. During this period he managed to persuade a 36-year-old Simone to come out of retirement and sign for Legnano, although he only made one appearance. "After Milan, we both ended up overseas – Stefano went to Scotland and I went to France – but there was always that bond between us," says Simone. "At the end of our careers, he convinced me to collaborate on a project in Legnano. Our relationship was always very strong even while we were in Europe."

Salvatori then had a two-year stint as technical director at Voghera Calcio, a Serie D side based just south of Milan, between 2005 and 2007. Despite being back in his homeland, he always maintained links with Edinburgh. "He came back a lot to check on his properties and things like that," says Mrs Di Giorgio. "He would always come to Bar Roma, that was his focal point, his meeting place. He would regularly come back from Italy for a few days. In fact, he was the one who tended to come back more often than the other foreign players. He was obviously checking on his properties, but he had a genuine love for Edinburgh. He always said part of his heart was in Edinburgh and that he'd become a bit Scottish. He loved Edinburgh and he loved the Jambos. He would get very emotional talking about Hearts. He wasn't a big drinker – one Peroni was enough for him – so it was never the alcohol making him emotional, it was genuine love for Hearts."

Salvatori started to return to Edinburgh on an even more regular basis when he entered the football agency business in 2007, helping move players between Europe and the UK. One of the most notable transfers he was involved in came in the summer of 2008 when he recommended his countryman, Manuel Pascali, to Jefferies, who was Kilmarnock manager at the time. Pascali, who played the same holding-midfield role as Salvatori, went on to become a modern-day Killie legend over the course of his seven years at Rugby Park. Other players he helped bring to Scotland included Farid El Alagui (to Steven Pressley's Falkirk in 2011) and Jesus Garcia Tena (to Livingston in 2012). "I remember when I used to take Kilmarnock and Hearts (in his second spell as manager) to the training camp at Il Ciocco (in Tuscany), Stefano would come down from Milan and let us see players he recommended," says Jefferies. "He was the man who brought us Pascali and he stayed with us at Il Ciocco for a few days. Once we signed Pascali he came over to see him play a few times and I would have dinner with him. I actually remember I got a shock one day when Stefano said he had someone he wanted me to meet and he turned up at Kilmarnock with Ruud Gullit. The three of us were sitting in the Park Hotel at Kilmarnock having a coffee and a bite to eat and we had a good chat about football. I think Stefano was trying to get Gullit involved in some football venture he was looking into at the time. He also brought a couple of players to me that I signed for Dunfermline later on. For as long as I was in the game, I spoke to Stefano regularly. We communicated regularly and stayed friends."

At the end of 2010, Salvatori, whose flowing black locks had long since given way to short silver flecks, decided to move back to Edinburgh on a permanent basis as he sought the opportunity to land a sporting director role in Scotland. "I met Stefano many times afterwards when he was doing his agency stuff and he hadn't changed at all as a person," says McCann. "It was only his hair that had changed. He was still the same guy I had known as a player."

When he visited the capital, Salvatori would often stay at the Aaron Lodge Guest House on Old Dalkeith Road, owned by his friend, Teddy Baigan. Barry Anderson, the Edinburgh Evening News' Hearts correspondent since 2005, had a link to Baigan and as a result ended up being the last football journalist to interview Salvatori. "The first time I ever spoke to Stefano was in 2008 at Tynecastle when he was in doing a press event ahead of Robbie Neilson's testimonial (Hearts' 2007/08 team against a 1998/2006 Scottish Cup winners' select) and he was really friendly, a really grounded guy," says Anderson. "I didn't speak to him for another few years after that but then Teddy, who was the grandad of a boy in my son's youth team, put us in contact in 2011 because Stefano was keen to do an interview as he had moved back to Edinburgh and was looking to put himself forward for a sporting director role. We met for a bite to eat and he was again very personable. I remember him speaking about Gary Locke because he was his main link to Hearts at that time as he was back at the club as a coach. He spoke about Hearts and how much he loved the fans. He was clearly still right into Hearts. Around the time I met him, I actually remember Teddy saying Stefano was the nicest guy you could ever meet. Apparently, in the guest house he would just get up and serve people at the bar if there was nobody around. He just seemed like a really nice, down-to-earth man."

Kindness came naturally to Salvatori. "He was an extremely respectful man," says Mrs Di Giorgio. "When I gave birth to my daughter in 2012, my husband Ivan went to a restaurant not far from the hospital and Stefano was there with some friends. Ivan told him we'd just had a little girl called Lucia, and Stefano said 'that's beautiful – that's my Mamma's name'. Ivan got up to pay for his meal when he was finished and Stefano had already paid for it; he also sent me flowers. Kindness is one of the first things I think about with Stefano. He didn't look to gain anything out of it; it was just the way he was. He was an extremely kind person and a true friend. He will always remain in my heart."

Although Salvatori's wish to get a job in Scottish football didn't come to fruition, the stylish Italian did find the love of his life shortly after relocating to Edinburgh. "I was out for dinner in Tigerlily with a friend of mine, another paediatrician," says Gillian, who was born in Aberdeen to Australian parents. "Stef was sitting opposite, just a few metres away, and he was just staring at me. He was obviously the most handsome guy I'd ever seen in my life. We eventually got talking and when he heard my accent, he said 'you're Australian, aren't you? You must know my friend Ross Aloisi?'. I didn't know much about football and, needless to say, I didn't know Ross Aloisi, but it's very ironic because Ross and his wife Lisa are now a huge support to me and a really special link to Stef because of the time Ross spent with him in his football career and also the time we all spent together back in Brisbane in Stef's later life."

A little over a year after they met, and despite being from, in Gillian's words, "totally different worlds", Salvatori moved to Australia to start a new adventure with his fiancee in September 2012, four months after he had attended Hearts' 5-1 Scottish Cup final triumph over Hibs at Hampden. When he returned to Edinburgh in March 2013 to collect the last of his belongings and tie up some loose ends, he got the chance to go to Hearts' League Cup final showdown with St Mirren at Hampden, and was invited to parade the cup before it, along with St Mirren legend Tony Fitzpatrick. As well as being Locke's first official game as manager of the club, the 3-2 defeat by the Paisley side would prove to be the last Hearts game Salvatori ever attended. "Stefano was a great guy and he ended up being a great mate of mine," says Locke. "We kept in touch a lot when he left the club."

Upon settling in Brisbane, Salvatori spent much of his time coaching young footballers. The move Down Under also allowed him the chance to visit Aloisi in Adelaide before his good friend, eventually and coincidentally, landed a coaching job in Brisbane in 2015, bringing him closer to Salvatori. Tragically, by that point, the Italian was at the mercy of the cancer which had been found in his body in August 2014, just three months before the arrival of little Remo, who is named after Stefano's father. The outlook was bleak from the moment of diagnosis. Indeed, it was initially feared that Salvatori may not survive to see the birth of his son before he surprised specialists by responding positively to treatment. "We told the doctors not to give us any timeline, but we knew how bad it was," says Gillian. "We made a decision early on to simply give everything we possibly could to fight the diagnosis and make the best of whatever time we had left."

Stefano and Gillian got married in May 2015 and welcomed another child into the world when Lucia – named after Stefano's mother – was born in April 2016.

"Stef wanted to keep his dignity and pride to the end," says Gillian. "He was a private person and was very resolute in not wanting anyone to know except those in our inner circle. Even some of his family in Italy didn't know. He was trying to protect everyone from the awful situation we were in. It was a very deliberate decision on his part and I had to honour it, so we basically circled the wagons. We had two babies through all of that so we had a lot going on. It was exhausting, but Stef never complained; he was so incredibly brave."

Entrenched in a dire fight for life, Salvatori steeled himself and put on a brave face as much as he could for the benefit of those who cared for him. "We only spoke a few times in those last two years and I regret that, but I know he wanted to isolate himself somewhat," says Simone. "I tried to insist that we speak more often but in true Stefano style, even though there was a problem, he assured me everything was okay and that he was okay. I think I spoke to him one or two months before he passed and even then he told me everything was okay, which was exactly how Stefano was. Something I always saw in Stefano was that he loved children. He would spend a lot of time with friends' children or those that would want his autograph. He had a total love for children so I can only imagine what a fantastic dad he was. I'm sure he left his children with lessons that they will carry with them for all their lives."

Aloisi backs this up. "He coached at one of the clubs (Brisbane Olympic) where my son plays and the players he coached absolutely loved him," he says. "Everyone at the club said he was such a gentleman. He loved coaching kids; he just loved to teach and pass on his knowledge. When I asked the players what he was like, they said he was all about encouragement. They said he never got upset or angry, but I obviously saw a different side of him on the pitch. He was never confrontational in every-day life but obviously football is slightly different; on the pitch, he was a beast."

Sadly, the physical and mental strength which took him to such remarkable heights in the prime of his football career was never going to be enough to win his biggest battle. "It was horrible," says an emotional Aloisi. "I was one of the few people outwith the family who knew what was going on. Once he got really sick, we caught up quite a bit. Before then, we didn't know how sick he was because Stefano kept it quiet as he didn't want to be an inconvenience to people; that was him. It affected me really bad, especially seeing the way he was towards the end. The funeral was horrible, I broke down badly. I lost a close friend. It's such a sad story."

When Salvatori eventually succumbed, less than two months before his 50th birthday, it prompted an outpouring of emotion from those whose lives he touched. Baresi – one of the greatest centre-backs ever to play the game – tweeted: "What bad news! I remember you with affection. Bye Stefano, RIP." Simone, meanwhile, posted the aforementioned picture of Salvatori and Borgonovo with the European Cup to his Instagram stream accompanied by the caption "TWO ANGELS" and the prayer emoji. Given his age and the fitness levels he had maintained throughout his career, confirmation of his passing was difficult to comprehend. "It is shocking when someone like Stefano leaves us," says Flögel. "He was one of a kind; a great friend and a great footballer. The foreign players at Hearts would spend a lot of time together. Sometimes we'd be in Stefano's flat on Frederick Street watching the fireworks at Edinburgh Castle, other times we'd be in Bar Roma, his favourite Italian restaurant. He was a very positive guy who made you feel good; an outstanding guy. I didn't look up to him because of the level he had played at; I looked up to him because he was a genuine guy."

The Hearts fraternity were rocked by the news. "I was really devastated when I heard he had passed away," says Pointon. "He was a tremendous person and a great player for Hearts."

The Edinburgh club were the one with which he had the strongest links and they made sure he was given a fitting tribute when they played Kilmarnock at Murrayfield – Tynecastle's main stand was in the process of being redeveloped at the time – on Sunday 5th November 2017, four days after his death and three days before his funeral in Queensland. A poor performance and a 2-1 defeat for Craig Levein's Hearts side meant the match was memorable – from the hosts' perspective – only for the fact it was the day when more than 15,000 Jambos got to show their appreciation for their much-loved Scottish Cup-winning hero. A video package featuring Salvatori's highlights at Hearts was played over the big screen, while there was a minute's applause in the fifth minute because the Italian wore the No.5 jersey. Hearts almost scored during the period of applause when Esmael Goncalves saw an effort touched on to the post by former Tynecastle goalkeeper Jamie Macdonald. The advertising boards running around the edge of the pitch displayed the message "Stefano Salvatori – Hearts Legend – 1967-2017" as "Salvatori, Salvatori, ole, ole, ole..." rang out amid the tears from those in the stands. Jefferies, Brown and Locke, watching together from the main stand, were struggling to contain their emotions. "Stefano will always be held in high esteem at Hearts," says Jefferies. Exactly a month on from his passing, on 1st December 2017, a plaque in honour of Salvatori – funded by members of the Jambos Kickback online fans' forum – was unveiled in the club's memorial garden at Tynecastle. It reads: "In honoured memory of a gifted footballer. HMFC player 1996-1999. Scottish Cup winner 1998. Forever in our Hearts."

Salvatori's status as a Hearts legend was further highlighted when the reunion designed to mark the 20th anniversary of the 1998 triumph became as much about the loss of the Italian as the celebration of his team's accomplishments two decades previously. "It's just tragic what happened to Stefano," says Jim Hamilton, who joined Hearts a few months after Salvatori. "I remember the anniversary event we had a couple of years ago and the tribute the club put on was fitting for an absolute legend of a guy. I couldn't say one bad word against him because he was a total gentleman to me. He's missed by everybody in our team."

For a group of Hearts players who thrived on their togetherness in the glorious 1997/98 campaign, it cut deep among each of them that one of their number wasn't present to share in what was a landmark and eagerly-anticipated anniversary. "At the reunion in 2018, I got a nice plate from the fans for being voted player of the Scottish Cup run, which was lovely, but there was one thing missing that night, and it was Stefano," says McCann. "A real, real shame. His wife came over and it was lovely to meet her but it was really sad to be there with all my team and not have Stefano with us. He's such a sad loss."

Oli Derwin, a 13-year-old Australian boy who Salvatori coached for a spell after moving to Brisbane, wrote a short testimonial for the Italian's football academy website which perfectly encapsulated the way the strong, selfless and spirited former Hearts player conducted himself on and off the football pitch throughout his cruelly-stunted life. It read: "It was awesome how he motivated our team from 11th place to win the grand final. Stefano taught me to be strong on the ball and not be scared of anyone or anything. Most importantly, he taught me that anyone can win. Thank you Stefano for giving me an excellent foundation."

Young Oli's words also give an inadvertent nod to the stirring story of guts and glory at Hearts in the late 1990s, of which the dearly-cherished Salvatori played such a prominent part. "I miss him very much," says Adam, whose goal gave the Italian his greatest day in football. "We were close to each other, we were good friends. Even after our careers finished, we used to meet up. He was a fantastic guy, a gentleman, a very friendly guy who had time for everyone. He was also a fantastic footballer. He should be very proud of himself."

Reminiscing with Legends is dedicated to Stefano Salvatori

Acknowledgements

As a boyhood Hearts supporter who followed the team home and away in the magical 1997/98 season, it was a privilege to be able to bring this story together. When the Scottish Cup was won on 16th May 1998, I was 15 years old. I could never have imagined at that point that I'd get the opportunity to write a book which involved getting the chance to speak to the management team and the players who had just given me the best day of my football-following life.

Thank you, therefore, to Jim Jefferies, Billy Brown, Gilles Rousset, Dave McPherson, Gary Locke, Gary Naysmith, Paul Ritchie, David Weir, Stephen Fulton, Colin Cameron, Neil McCann, Thomas Flögel, Stephane Adam, Jim Hamilton, Neil Pointon and Jose Quitongo for embracing this venture with such enthusiasm and allowing me to embark on what has been the epitome of a labour of love. Without the commitment of all of these guys and their willingness to speak so openly and honestly about their football careers, and specifically their time at Hearts, Reminiscing with Legends would never have come to fruition. They were all a pleasure to deal with throughout.

Thank you to Leslie Deans, Peter Houston, Allan McManus, David Murie, Sandy Clark, Pasquale Bruno, Gary Mackay, Iain Mercer, Robbie Neilson and Steven Pressley for enhancing my knowledge and understanding of Hearts in the 1990s and to everyone else quoted in the book – including several passionate supporters – who helped add extra meat to the bone. John Robertson politely declined an invite to contribute, preferring instead to allow those who played in the 1998 final to lead the way in recounting the story of the team's journey to glory.

Thank you to Gillian Salvatori for her co-operation in the chapter on the life of her beloved husband Stefano, who became a hero of mine in his time at Hearts. Getting the tone and content of Stefano's chapter right was obviously one of the most challenging aspects of writing the book, but Gillian's assistance was invaluable and hugely appreciated. Thank you also to Marco Simone, Ross Aloisi and Nadia Di Giorgio for their heartfelt words and anecdotes about Stefano.

Thank you to Scott Coull, a long-time friend and colleague who devoted so much time and effort to designing and editing the book. Scott – a quality operator – performed the Salvatori role, ruthlessly fending off the threat of rogue commas and doing all the selfless, unseen work in the background that allowed everything to come together. Scott is an Aberdeen fan and obviously had to relive several heavy defeats for the Dandies at the hands of Hearts in the 1997/98 season but he seemed to enjoy it all, nonetheless.

Thank you to The Scotsman and Edinburgh Evening News for allowing me access to their newspaper archives and picture libraries. A mention also for London Hearts, a well-maintained website and excellent source of Hearts-related information. Thank you to Andrew Baguley for pointing me in the right direction regarding the publishing process, and to Paul Greaves for his advice on producing the book.

Thank you to James Morgan and Alan Pattullo for their pep talks and words of wisdom, which were a big help in overcoming the various challenges encountered in the journey. I found Alan's line about there being "no rules for writing a book" particularly reassuring and invigorating, while James' input helped shape my thinking in terms of how to approach parts of the narrative. Thank you to my good friend Cameron Bourhill for helping keep me focused in those difficult early months when the finish line seemed so far away, and to my Auntie Audrey for her advice as well as her help with proof-reading and the transcribing of interviews.

Massive thanks to everyone who has helped me along the way in my career, particularly Donald Walker, Graham Bean, Colin Leslie, Graham Lindsay, Ramsay Laing and Mark Atkinson – the sports editors at The Scotsman and Edinburgh Evening News, respectively – who have given me a platform from which to find my way as a football writer. Thank you to my colleagues in the media such as Barry Anderson, Graham Spiers, Ewan Murray, Martin Dempster, Mike Aitken and Mark Donaldson for their insightful reflections.

Thank you to everyone who has shown interest in the progress of the book and to all who have helped promote it via social media, podcasts or word of mouth. Thanks to all friends and family members for their support. Thanks to my mum and dad for being there, and for encouraging me to embark on a career that has given me the opportunity to bring this book together and fulfil a lifelong ambition. A source of inspiration throughout has been my dearly-missed wee sister Sarah, a Hearts supporter who got her photo taken with the Scottish Cup as an 11-year-old in 1998 and who lost her life on the evening of 28th October 2017, just four nights after attending the 1-0 defeat by Hibs at Easter Road and a week after taking my wee boy to the 1-0 home win against St Johnstone at Murrayfield. I hope this book gives Sarah something to enjoy wherever she may be.

Thanks to my magnificent wife Michelle and children Robbie and Orla for being there every day through all the ups and downs of the journey. Writing a book during the coronavirus lockdown obviously had several advantages, particularly in terms of freeing up extra time for everyone involved to devote to the book, but it also meant Michelle had to spend a lot of time entertaining the kids while I cocooned myself away to transcribe and write. She was tolerant and patient when I had difficulty switching off from the all-consuming nature of a project like this and inspired and reassured me in the moments where I felt like I was losing momentum. Robbie, eight years old at the time of writing, learned about the Hearts team of 98 as we watched re-runs of the Scottish Cup final together and he now knows full well who Jim Jefferies is. He kept cajoling me along in the final weeks by asking "are you not finished this blooming book yet?". It's finished now, wee man.

Anthony Brown
October 2020